Contemporary
American Theologies II

WITHDRAWN

Contemporary American Theologies II

A Book of Readings

Edited by
Deane William Ferm

LIBRARY
BRYAN COLLEGE
DAYTON, TENN. 37321

THE SEABURY PRESS / NEW YORK

77489

1982
The Seabury Press
815 Second Avenue
New York, N.Y. 10017

Copyright © 1982 by Deane William Ferm
All rights reserved. No part of this book may be reproduced, stored
in a retrieval system, or transmitted, in any form or by any means,
electronic, mechanical, photocopying, recording, or otherwise,
without the written permission of The Seabury Press.
Printed in the United States of America

Library of Congress Cataloging in Publication Data

Main entry under title:

Contemporary American theologies II.

1. Theology—Addresses, essays, lectures. I. Ferm,
Deane William, 1927-   II. Title: Contemporary
American theologies 2.
BT80.C66   230'.0973   82-5744
ISBN 0-8164-2407-1   AACR2

*Grateful acknowledgment is made to the following publishers
for permission to use the materials listed:*

Abingdon Press for excerpts from *Black Awareness: A Theology of Hope* by Major Jones, copyright © 1971 by Abingdon Press; *The Evangelicals: What They Believe, Who They Are, Where They Are Changing,* edited by David F. Wells and John D. Woodbridge, copyright © 1975 by Abingdon Press.

Beacon Press for excerpts from *Beyond God the Father: Toward A Philosophy of Women's Liberation* by Mary Daly, copyright © 1973 by Mary Daly; *Gyn/Ecology: The Metaphysics of Radical Feminism* by Mary Daly, copyright © 1978 by Mary Daly.

Bobbs-Merrill Educational Publishing for excerpt from *Naming the Whirlwind* by Langdon Gilkey, copyright © 1969 by Langdon Gilkey.

Dr. James H. Cone for article "Black Theology and the Black Church: Where Do We Go From Here?" published in *Crosscurrents,* vol. 27, no. 2, Summer 1977.

Geoffrey Chapman Publishers for excerpts from *The Emergent Gospel* edited by S. Torres and V. Fabella, 1976.

Christianity and Crisis, Inc. for excerpt from September 20, 1976 issue of *Christianity and Crisis,* copyright © 1976 by Christianity and Crisis, Inc.

The Christian Century Foundation for Article #13 in "The Churches: Where From Here?" Series: "The Roman Catholic Church: Can It Transcend the Crisis?" by Richard P. McBrien, copyright ©1979 by Christian Century Foundation, reprinted from the January 17, 1979 issue of *The Christian Century;* for Article #2 in "How My Mind Has Changed" Series: "American Evangelicals in a Turning Time" by Carl F. H. Henry, copyright © 1980 by Christian Century Foundation, reprinted from the November 5, 1980 issue of *The Christian Century;* for article: "Goddesses and Witches: Liberation and Counterculture Feminism" by Rosemary Radford Ruether, copyright © 1980 by Christian Century Foundation, reprinted from the September 10-17, 1980 issue of *The Christian Century.*

Crossroad Publishing Company for the article "American Evangelicals in a Turning Time" by Carl F. H. Henry from *Theologians in Transition,* edited by James Wall, copyright © 1980 by The Christian Century Foundation.

Leslie Dewart for excerpts from *The Future of Belief.*

Doubleday & Company, Inc. for "The Evaluation of Models" from *Models of the Church* by Avery Dulles, copyright © 1974 by Avery Dulles.

Wm. B. Eerdmans Publishing Co. for excerpt from *Latin American Theology: Radical or Evangelical?* by Peter Wagner, copyright © 1970 by William B. Eerdmans Publishing Co.

Fortress Press for excerpt from *Doing Theology in a Revolutionary Situation* by José Miguez Bonino.

Gill and Macmillan Ltd. for excerpt from *Models of the Church* by Avery Dulles.

Harper & Row, Publishers, Inc. for excerpts from the following: *Essentials of Evangelical Theology,* vol. 2, by Donald Bloesch, copyright © 1979 by Donald Bloesch; *Why Conservative Churches Are Growing* by Dean M. Kelley, copyright © 1972 by Dean M. Kelley; *The Spiral Dance* by Starhawk, copyright © 1979 by Miriam Simos; *Becoming Woman* by Penelope Washbourn, copyright © 1977 by Penelope Washbourn.

Judson Press for *A Different Heaven and Earth* by Sheila Collins, copyright © 1976 by Judson Press.

Macmillan Publishing Co., Inc. for excerpts from the following: *Letters and Papers from Prison* by Dietrich Bonhoeffer; *The Secular City* by Harvey Cox.

A. R. Mowbray for excerpt from *Farewell to Innocence* by Allen Boesak.

Orbis Books for excerpts from the following: *The Emergent Gospel,* edited by S. Torres and V. Fabella, 1976; *Farewell to Innocence* by Allen Boesak; *Christology at the Crossroads* by Jon Sobrino; *Catholic Faith in a Process Perspective* by Norman Pittenger.

Paulist Press for excerpts from: *Liberation Theology* by Rosemary Ruether and *The Intra-Religious Dialogue* by Raimundo Panikkar.

Penguin Books Ltd. for excerpt from *A Rumor of Angels* by Peter L. Berger, copyright © 1969 by Peter L. Berger.

Mr. Richard Quebedeaux for excerpt from *The New Charismatics.*

The Seabury Press for excerpts from the following: *Black Theology and Black Power* by James H. Cone, copyright © 1969 by The Seabury Press, Inc.; *Blessed Rage for Order* by David Tracy, copyright © 1975 by The Seabury Press, Inc.; *Man Becoming* by Gregory Baum, copyright © 1970 by Herder and Herder, Inc.

SCM Press Ltd. for substantial extracts from: *Letters and Papers from Prison* by Dietrich Bonhoeffer; *Christology at the Crossroads* by Jon Sobrino; *Honest to God* by John A. T. Robinson; *The Secular City* by Harvey Cox.

Theology Today for excerpts from article "Thursday's Child" by William Hamilton, published in January 1964.

The University of Chicago Press for excerpt from *The Protestant Era* by Paul Tillich.

Dr. Joseph Washington for excerpt from *Black Religion* published in 1964.

The Westminster Press for excerpts from the following: *Honest to God* by John A. T. Robinson, copyright © 1963 by SCM Press Ltd.; *Liberation and Reconciliation: A Black Theology* by J. Deotis Roberts, copyright © 1971 by The Westminster Press; *Human Liberation in a Feminist Perspective—A Theology* by Letty M. Russell, copyright © 1974 by Letty M. Russell.

Dr. Gayraud Wilmore for excerpt from *Black Religion and Black Radicalism.*

Word Books for excerpts from "The Current Tensions: Is There a Way Out?" by David Hubbard in *Biblical Authority,* edited by Jack Rogers, copyright © 1977.

Contents

Introduction

This book of readings is intended as a companion to my book *Contemporary American Theologies: A Critical Survey* (Seabury, 1981). The purpose of the earlier book was to summarize the major trends in contemporary American Christian theology and to refer to some of the significant literature representative of these developments. This new book contains selections from some of this literature and permits the theologians to express their convictions in their own words.

None of the readings corresponds to the first chapter of my earlier book, which summarizes Protestant theological developments from 1900 to 1960. This historical period has already been amply covered in other surveys. Nor does this collection provide readings on the future of American theology to supplement the final chapter of my earlier work.

Rather, the selections are based on chapters two through seven, in which I focused attention on six theological trends prominent since the early 1960s: secular, black, South American liberation, feminist, evangelical, and Roman Catholic theologies. Although edited works containing readings on some of these trends—taken individually—do exist, I believe that my book is the first attempt to encompass them all in a single volume.

Naturally, one cannot include every important theologian of this period and keep a book down to moderate size and price. Nevertheless, this book does provide a representative sampling of the fascinating field of contemporary theology. I hope that this collection will encourage readers to dig even deeper into this exciting subject which continues to grow by leaps and bounds.

Deane William Ferm
Allston, Massachusetts
February, 1982

CHAPTER ONE

The Secularism
of the 1960s

Paul Tillich

Paul Tillich was one of the first theologians to anticipate the transition in religious thinking which culminated in the secular sixties. This selection is taken from his The Protestant Era. *Chicago: The University of Chicago Press, 1963, pp. 192–93, 202–5.*

The man of today, with whom this discussion is concerned, is not simply the man who happens to be a member of our generation but rather the man whose whole outlook is molded by the present cultural situation and who, in turn, determines, preserves, or transforms it. If we wish to characterize him in a very general way, we may describe him as the man who, on a Christian background that has been qualified by Protestantism, has built an autonomous culture and lives in it, influencing it and being influenced by it. He is the man who consciously carries within himself humanism and the Renaissance, idealism and romanticism, realism and expressionism, as elements of his own intellectual character. This man is, even if he may by actual count be in the minority, the decisive spiritual type of our day. The tensions of his life represent a creative energy that is active in all the spheres of life.

If we look closer to determine his particular characteristics, we must say: *He is the autonomous man who has become insecure in his autonomy.* A symptom of this insecurity is that the man of today no longer possesses a world view in the sense of a body of assured convictions about God, the world, and himself. The feeling of security in a system of theoretical and practical ideas about the meaning of his life and of life in general has gone. Even as recently as two decades ago, our literature was full of discussions concerning the modern world view or dealing with the conflicts between the various tendencies within it. Nothing more of this is to be seen. Only the pieces of former world views are to be found now. Idealism, for instance, concentrates on questions concerning education and has become embodied in movements like neohumanism. But none of the neohumanists has developed a philosophy which, in comparison with German classical idealism, could be called an integrated world view or even a convincing interpretation of human life. Neohumanism has remained a quest without fulfillment. While neither Marx himself nor the main representatives of Marxism accepted metaphysical materialism (Marx attacked it in his *Theses against Feuerbach* as a bourgeois ideology), popular Marxism has largely confused the so-called historical materialism with a materialistic world view. But nobody who would deserve to be called a "man of today" accepts such a metaphysics.

It would be inadequate to call certain other attempts to penetrate into the riddle of existence "world views." I refer to the so-called philosophy of life, whose most brilliant representative was Nietzsche and which has a large group of adherents in Germany and France; or to the philosophy of the unconscious, initiated by Freud, whose influence is growing daily; or to the philosophical and theological movements determined by the rediscovery of Kierkegaard. They all contribute to the destruction of the old world views more than to the building of a new one. They are powerful just because they are not world views. Modern man is without a world view, and just because of this he has the feeling of having come closer to reality and of having confronted the problematic aspects of his experience more profoundly than is possible for the man who conceals these problematic aspects of life by means of a world view.

Obviously, the man of today takes the same attitude toward the message of the churches as he takes toward the autonomous philosophies. He opposes it, though not as the representative of one world view attempting to overcome another one; he sees in it problems and solutions that are in part outmoded but in part significant even for our day. He treats the religious doctrines neither worse nor better than he does the interpretations of the world and life from which he takes his spiritual descent and which he has left behind him—perhaps rather better than worse, for he finds in them more recognition of the mystery of life than he does in much autonomous philosophy. But he is not yet ready to abandon autonomy. He still stands in the autonomous tradition of recent centuries. But his situation is different from that of former generations in that he no longer possesses an autonomy in which he is self-assured and creative; rather, he possesses one that leaves him disturbed, frustrated, and often in despair. . . .

Now it can be said what the Protestant message for the man of today must be and what it cannot be.

The Protestant message cannot be a direct proclamation of religious truths as they are given in the Bible and in tradition, for the situation of the modern man of today is precisely one of doubt about all this and about the Protestant church itself. The Christian doctrines, even the most central ones—God and Christ, church and revelation—are radically questioned and offer occasion for a continuous fight among theologians as well as among nontheologians. They cannot in this form be the message of the church to our time. So long as the genuine representatives of the Protestant message do not understand this, their work is entirely hopeless in the widest circles and especially among the proletarian masses. It cannot be required of the man of today that he first accept theological truths, even though they should be God and Christ. Wherever the church in its message makes this a primary demand, it does not take seriously the situation of the man of today and has no effective defense against the challenge of many thoughtful men of our day who reject the message of the church as of no concern for them. The modern man might well say to the church, using her own language: "God does not demand that man, in order to experience the unconditional judgment, the 'No' and the 'Yes' from above himself, shall first accept a religious tenet about God or shall overcome all doubt concerning him." This sort of legalism lays upon man no less heavy a burden than legalism in morals. The one, like the other, is broken through by the radically conceived doctrine of justification. The profoundest aspect of justification, in our situation and for the man of today, is that we can discern God at the very moment when all known assertions about "God" have lost their power.

The message of the Protestant church must take a threefold form. First, it must insist upon the radical experience of the boundary-situation; it must destroy the secret reservations harbored by the modern man which prevent him from accepting resolutely the limits of his human existence. Among these reservations are the residues of the shattered world views, idealistic and materialistic. The recognition of our situation as indicated by the word *ideology* should alone be a sufficient warning against these doubtful securities. We have learned that philosophical systems often represent the working of subconscious powers, psychological or sociological, which drive in a direction quite different from their conscious meaning. This judgment applies also to the unbroken belief in scientific method as the certain way to truth, which is usually not the attitude of the great scientists but of their half-philosophical popularizers. (Science itself is quite conscious of the crisis of its foundations, in mathematics as well as in physics, in biology as well as in psychology.) This judgment applies also to the pedagogical claim to transform society and to shape personalities. It has become abundantly clear that education as a method presupposes a content, a spiritual substance, to which it must introduce people but which it cannot itself create. The judgment applies to the political creeds, whether they glorify a past tradition or a coming utopia, whether they believe in revolution or reaction or progress. The old traditions have disintegrated; the process has been replaced by horrible relapses; and the utopias have created continuous mass disappointments. The judgment applies to the nationalistic ideologies whose demonic implications have become more and more visible, and it applies to the cosmopolitan superstructure which is envisaged either by pacifistic idealism or by imperialistic will to power. It applies to the recent attempts of all forms of therapeutic psychology to form secure personalities by technical methods which, in spite of their profundity and revolutionary power, are unable to give a spiritual center and ultimate meaning to life. It applies to the widespread activistic flight into job, profession, economic competition, humanitarian activity, as means of escaping the threat of the boundary-situation. The judgment applies to the neoreligious movements offering spiritual security, such as the new forms of mysticism and occultism, will-therapy, etc., which, whatever their merits may be, tend to hide the seriousness of the boundary-situation and to create fanaticism and arrogance. And, finally, the Protestant message should unveil the last, most refined, and most intellectual security of the modern man when he aesthetically dramatizes his shattered state; when, Narcissus-like, he contemplates himself in this situation as in a mirror, sometimes tragically; when he, thus, artfully but self-destructively protects himself from the experience of the boundary-situation. Against all this stands the Protestant message; this is its first function.

Second, the Protestant church must pronounce the "Yes" that comes to man in the boundary-situation when he takes it upon himself in its ultimate seriousness. Protestantism must proclaim the judgment that brings assurance by depriving us of all security; the judgment that declares us whole in the disintegration and cleavage of soul and community; the judgment that affirms our having truth in the very absence of truth (even of religious truth); the judgment that reveals the meaning of our life in the situation in which all the meaning of life has disappeared. This is the pith and essence of the Protestant message, and it must be guarded as such; it ought not to be changed into a new doctrine or devotional method or become a scheme that is used in every sermon; it should not be made into a new form of security—a form that would be an especially disastrous one. It must remain the depth and background of all our pronouncements; it must be the quality that gives to the message its truth and power.

Third, Protestantism must witness to the "New Being" through which alone it is able to say its word in power, and it must do this without making this witness again the basis of a wrong security. The New Being, which for Christian faith is manifest in Jesus as the Christ, is effective in the life of the individual personality as well as in the life of the community, and it is not even excluded from nature, as is indicated by the sacraments. To live out of the power of this New Being is the richness of Protantism which is the correlate to its poverty; for, just because the Protestant principle, the message of the boundary-situation, breaks down all absolute boundaries before the judgment to which everything is subject, Protestantism can be open for everything, religious and secular, past and future, individual and social. All these differences are transcended through the power of the New Being, which works in all of them, breaking through their exclusiveness and separation.

Culture is not subjected to religion, nor is religion dissolved in culture. Protestantism neither devaluates nor idealizes culture. It tries to understand its religious substance, its spiritual foundation, its "theonomous" nature. And Protestantism neither idealizes nor devaluates religion. It tries to interpret religion as the direct, intentional expression of the spiritual substance which in the cultural forms is presented indirectly and unintentionally. In this way, the Protestant principle denies to the church a holy sphere as its separate possession, and it denies to culture a secular sphere that can escape the judgment of the boundary-situation.

This attitude of Protestantism toward church and culture implies the answer to the questions: Where is Protestantism to be found? Who proclaims the Protestant principle? The answer is: Protestantism lives wherever, in the power of the New Being, the boundary-situation is preached, its "No" and "Yes" are proclaimed. It is there and nowhere else. Protestantism may live in the organized Protestant churches. But it is not bound to them. Perhaps more men of today have experienced the boundary-situation outside than inside the churches. The Protestant principle may be proclaimed by movements that are neither ecclesiastical nor secular but belong to both spheres, by groups and individuals who, with or without Christian and Protestant symbols, express the true human situation in face of the ultimate and unconditional. If they do it better and with more authority than the official churches, then they and not the churches represent Protestantism for the man of today.

Dietrich Bonhoeffer

Dietrich Bonhoeffer's writings stimulated a whole new breed of religious thinkers who were seeking a theological understanding that would not be dependent on the religious trappings of the past. This selection is taken from his Letters and Papers from Prison. *New York: Macmillan, 1971, pp. 279–82, 360–61.*

What is bothering me incessantly is the question what Christianity really is, or indeed who Christ really is, for us today. The time when people could be told everything by means of words, whether theological or pious, is over, and so is the time of inwardness and conscience—and that means the time of religion in general. We are moving towards a completely religionless time; people as they are now simply cannot be religious anymore. Even those who honestly describe themselves as "religious" do not in the least act up to it, and so they presumably mean something quite different by "religious."

Our whole nineteen-hundred-year-old Christian preaching and theology rest on the "religious *a priori*" of mankind. "Christianity" has always been a form—perhaps the true form—of "religion." But if one day it becomes clear that this *a priori* does not exist at all, but was a historically conditioned and transient form of human self-expression, and if therefore man becomes radically religion-less—and I think that that is already more or less the case (else how is it, for example, that this war, in contrast to all previous ones, is not calling forth any "religious" reaction?)—what does that mean for "Christianity"? It means that the foundation is taken away from the whole of what has up to now been our "Christianity," and that there remain only a few "last survivors of the age of chivalry," or a few intellectually dishonest people, on whom we can descend as "religious." Are they to be the chosen few? Is it on this dubious group of people that we are to pounce in fervor, pique, or indignation, in order to sell them our goods? Are we to fall upon a few unfortunate people in their hour of need and exercise a sort of religious compulsion on them? If we don't want to do all that, if our final judgment must be that the Western form of Christianity, too, was only a preliminary stage to a complete absence of religion, what kind of situation emerges for us, for the church? How can Christ become the Lord of the religionless as well? Are there religionless Christians? If religion is only a garment of Christianity—and even this garment has looked very different at different times—then what is a religionless Christianity?

Barth, who is the only one to have started along this line of thought, did not carry it to completion but arrived at a positivism of revelation which in the last analysis is essentially a restoration.

For the religionless working man (or any other man), nothing decisive is gained here. The questions to be answered would surely be: What do a church, a community, a sermon, a liturgy, a Christian life mean in a religionless world? How do we speak of God—without religion, i.e., without the temporally conditioned presuppositions of metaphysics, inwardness, and so on? How do we speak (or perhaps we cannot now even "speak" as we used to) in a "secular" way about "God"? In what way are we "religionless-secular" Christians, in what way are we the ἐκ-κλησία, those who are called forth, not regarding ourselves from a religious point of view as specially favored but rather as belonging wholly to the world? In that case, Christ is no longer an object of religion but something quite different, really the Lord of the world. But what does that mean? What is the place of worship and prayer in a religionless situation? Does the secret discipline or, alternatively, the difference (which I have suggested to you before) between penultimate and ultimate, take on a new importance here? . . .

I find, after all, that I can write a little more. The Pauline question whether περιτομή (circumcision) is a condition of justification seems to me in present-day terms to be whether religion is a condition of salvation. Freedom from περιτομή is also freedom from religion. I often ask myself why a "Christian instinct" often draws me more to the religionless people than to the religious, by which I don't in the least mean with any evangelizing intention, but, I might almost say, "in brotherhood." While I'm often reluctant to mention God by name to religious people—because that name somehow seems to me here not to ring true, and I feel myself to be slightly dishonest (it's particularly bad when others start to talk in religious jargon; I then dry up almost completely and feel awkward and uncomfortable)—to people with no religion, I can on occasion mention him by name quite calmly and as a matter of course. Religious people speak of God when human knowledge (perhaps simply because they are too lazy to think) has come to an end, or when human resources fail—in fact, it is always the *deus ex machina* that they bring on to the scene, either for the apparent solution of insoluble problems, or as strength in human failure—always, that is to say, exploiting human weakness or human boundaries. Of necessity, that can go on only till people can by their own strength push these boundaries somewhat further out, so that God becomes superfluous as a *deus ex machina*. I've come to be doubtful of talking about any human boundaries (is even death, which people now hardly fear, and is sin, which they now hardly understand, still a genuine boundary today?). It always seems to me that we are trying anxiously in this way to reserve some space for God; I should like to speak of God not on the boundaries but at the center, not in weaknesses but in strength; and therefore not in death and guilt but in man's life and goodness. As to the boundaries, it seems to me better to be silent and leave the insoluble unsolved. Belief in the resurrection is *not* the "solution" of the problem of death. God's "beyond" is not the beyond of our cognitive faculties. The transcendence of epistemological theory has nothing to do with the transcendence of God. God is beyond in the midst of our life. The church stands, not at the boundaries where human powers give out, but in the middle of the village. That is how it is in the Old Testament, and in this sense we still read the New Testament far too little in the light of the Old. How this religionless Christianity looks, what form it takes, is something that I'm thinking about a great deal, and I shall be writing to you again about it soon. It may be that on us in particular, midway between East and West, there will fall a heavy responsibility. . . .

God as a working hypothesis in morals, politics, or science, has been surmounted and abolished; and the same thing has happened in philosophy and religion (Feuerbach!). For the sake of intellectual honesty, that working hypothesis should be dropped, or as far as possible eliminated. A scientist or physician who sets out to edify is a hybrid.

Anxious souls will ask what room there is left for God now; and as they know of no answer to the question, they condemn the whole development that has brought them to such straits. I wrote to you before about the various emergency exits that have been contrived; and we ought to add to them the *salto mortale* (deathleap) back into the Middle Ages. But the principle of the Middle Ages is heteronomy in the form of clericalism; a return to that can be a counsel of despair, and it would be at the cost of intellectual honesty. It's a dream that reminds one of the song *O wüsst' ich doch den Weg zurück, den weiten Weg ins Kinderland.* There is no such way—at any rate, not if it means deliberately abandoning our mental integrity; the only way is that of Mt. 18:3, i.e., through repentance, through *ultimate* honesty.

And we cannot be honest unless we recognize that we have to live in the world *etsi deus non daretur*. And this is just what we do recognize—before God! God himself compels us to recognize it. So our coming of age leads us to a true recognition of our situation before God. God would have us know that we must live as men who manage our lives without him. The God who is with us is the God who forsakes us (Mk. 15:34). The God who lets us live in the world without the working hypothesis of God is the God before whom we stand continually. Before God and with God we live without God. God lets himself be pushed out of the world on to the cross. He is weak and powerless in the world, and that is precisely the way, the only way, in which he is with us and helps us. Matthew 8:17 makes it quite clear that Christ helps us, not by virtue of his omnipotence, but by virtue of his weakness and suffering.

Here is the decisive difference between Christianity and all religions. Man's religiosity makes him look in his distress to the power of God in the world: God is the *deus ex machina*. The Bible directs man to God's powerlessness and suffering; only the suffering God can help. To that extent, we may say that the development towards the world's coming of age outlined above, which has done away with a false conception of God, opens up a way of seeing the God of the Bible, who wins power and space in the world by his weakness. This will probably be the starting point for our "secular interpretation." ...

He must therefore really live in the godless world, without attempting to gloss over or explain its ungodliness in some religious way or other. He must live a "secular" life, and thereby share in God's sufferings. He *may* live a "secular" life (as one who has been freed from false religious obligations and inhibitions). To be a Christian does not mean to be religious in a particular way, to make something of oneself (a sinner, a penitent, or a saint) on the basis of some method or other, but to be a man—not a type of man, but the man that Christ creates in us. It is not the religious act that makes the Christian, but participation in the sufferings of God in the secular life.

John Robinson

John Robinson created a sensation in 1963 with his affirmation of unorthodox theological views which he believed were consistent with the developing secular spirit. This selection is taken from his Honest to God. *Philadelphia: Westminster Press, 1963, pp., 45, 48–50, 53, 55, 67, 76–77.*

The break with traditional thinking to which I believe we are now summoned is considerably more radical than that which enabled Christian theology to detach itself from a literal belief in a localized heaven. The translation from the God "up there" to the God "out there," though of liberating psychological significance, represented, as I have said, no more than a change of direction in spatial symbolism. Both conceptions presuppose fundamentally the same relationship between "God" on the one hand and "the world" on the other: God is a Being existing in his own right to whom the world is related in the sort of way the earth is to the sun. Whether the sun is "above" a flat earth or "beyond" a round one does not fundamentally affect the picture. But suppose there is no Being out there at all? Suppose, to use our analogy, the skies are empty? . . .

The way of thinking we are seeking to expound is not concerned to posit, nor, like the antitheists, to depose, such a Being at all. In fact, it would not naturally use the phrase "*a* personal God"; for this in itself belongs to an understanding of theology and of what theological statements are about which is alien to it. For this way of thinking, to say that "God is personal" is to say that "reality at its very deepest level is personal," that personality is of *ultimate* significance in the constitution of the universe, that in personal relationships we touch the final meaning of existence as nowhere else. "To predicate personality of God," says Feuerbach, "is nothing else than to declare personality as the absolute essence." To believe in God as love means to believe that in pure personal relationship we encounter, not merely what ought to be, but what is, the deepest, veriest truth about the structure of reality. This, in face of all the evidence, is a tremendous act of faith. But it is not the feat of persuading oneself of the existence of a superbeing beyond this world endowed with personal qualities. Belief in God is the trust, the well-nigh incredible trust, that to give ourselves to the uttermost in love is not to be confounded but to be "accepted," that love is the ground of our being, to which ultimately we "come home."

If this is true, then theological statements are not a description of "the highest Being" but an analysis of the depths of personal relationships—or, rather, an analysis of the depths of *all* experience "interpreted by love." Theology, as Tillich insists, is about "that which concerns us ultimately." A statement is "theological" not because it relates to a particular Being called "God," but because it asks *ultimate* questions about the meaning of existence: it asks what, at the level of *theos,* at the level of its deepest mystery, is the reality and significance of our life. A view of the world which affirms this reality and significance in personal categories is *ipso facto* making an affirmation about the *ultimacy* of personal relationships: it is saying that *God,* the final truth and reality "deep down things," *is* love. And the specifically Christian view of the world is asserting that the final definition of this reality, from which "nothing can separate us," since it is the very ground of our being, is "the love of God in Christ Jesus our Lord." . . .

To assert that "*God* is love" is to believe that in love one comes into touch with the most fundamental reality in the universe, that Being itself ultimately has this character. It is to say, with Buber, that "Every particular *Thou* is a glimpse through to the eternal *Thou,* that it is "between man and man" that we meet God, not, with Feuerbach, that "man with man—the unity of *I* and *Thou*— is God." Nevertheless, as Bonhoeffer insists, "God is the 'beyond' *in the midst,*" "The transcendent is not infinitely remote but close at hand." For the eternal *Thou* is met only *in, with, and under* the finite *Thou,* whether in the encounter with other persons or in the response to the natural order. . . .

There are depths of revelation, intimations of eternity, judgments of the holy and the sacred, awareness of the unconditional, the numinous, and the ecstatic which cannot be explained in purely naturalistic categories without being reduced to something else.

There is the "Thus saith the Lord" heard by prophet, apostle, and martyr for which naturalism cannot account. But neither can it discount it merely by pointing to the fact that "the Lord" is portrayed in the Bible in highly mythological terms, as one who "inhabits eternity" or "walks in the garden in the cool of the evening." The question of God is the question *whether this depth of being is a reality or an illusion,* not whether *a* Being exists beyond the bright blue sky, or anywhere else. Belief in God is a matter of "what you take seriously without any reservation," of what for you is *ultimate* reality. . . .

Suppose the whole notion of "a God" who "visits" the earth in the person of "his Son" is as mythical as the prince in the fairy story? Suppose there is no realm "out there" from which the "Man from heaven" arrives? Suppose the Christmas myth (the invasion of "this side" "by the other side")—as opposed to the Christmas history (the birth of the man Jesus of Nazareth)—has to go? Are we prepared for that? Or are we to cling here to this last vestige of the mythological or metaphysical world view as the only garb in which to clothe story with power to touch the imagination? Cannot perhaps the supranaturalist scheme survive at least as part of the "magic" of Christmas? . . .

Jesus is "the man for others," the one in whom love has completely taken over, the one who is utterly open to, and united with, the ground of his being. And this "life for others, through participation in the Being of God," *is* transcendence. For at this point, of love "to the uttermost," we encounter *God,* the ultimate "depth" of our being, the unconditional. This is what the New Testament means by saying that "God was in Christ" and that "what God was the Word was." Because Christ was utterly and completely "the man for others," because he *was* love, he was "one with the Father," because "God is love." But for this very reason he was most entirely man, the Son of man, the servant of the Lord. He was indeed "one of us"; and the symbol of the Virgin Birth can only legitimately mean what the Fourth Gospel takes it to mean (if, indeed, its description of Christians reflects that of Christ), namely, that the whole of his life is a life "born not of the will of the flesh, nor of the will of man, but of God." He is indeed not "of this world" but "of love." The source and spring of his whole being is God: His is a life conceived and sustained utterly by the Holy Ghost. But he is for that reason only the more truly "the proper Man." In the man, Christ Jesus stands revealed, exposed at the surface level of "flesh," the depth and ground of all our being as love. The life of God, the ultimate Word of Love in which all things cohere, is bodied forth completely, unconditionally, and without reserve in the life of a man—the man for others and the man for God. He is perfect man and perfect God—not as a mixture of oil and water, of natural and supernatural—but as the embodiment through obedience of "the beyond in our midst," of the transcendence of love.

William Hamilton

William Hamilton was in the 1960s a "death of god" theologian who was by his own admission alienated from God, Bible, and church. This selection is taken from his article "Thursday's Child" in Theology Today, *January 1964.*

Nontheological observers have been saying for some time that America is a place and a people without a past and without a future, or, more exactly, without a sense of having a past and without a sense of being able to count on a stable future. America is the place that has traveled farthest along the road from the cloister to the world that Luther and the Reformation mapped out. We are the most profane, the most banal, the most utterly worldly of places. Western Europe is positively numinous with divine substance compared to us, and even the Communist world has a kind of spiritual substance and vitality that we are said to lack. Both the academic sabbatical leave and the conventional summer vacation bear witness to the American's need to go abroad to look for something he has not found at home.

Hope is the way of declaring one's future to be open and assured, and love is the way of standing before your neighbor in the present moment. Taking faith, hope, and love together, the feeling is that the American theologian can really live in only one of them at a time, perhaps only one in a lifetime. If this is so, and if it is also so that as an American he is fated to be a man without a sense of past or future, then it follows that the theologian today and tomorrow is a man without faith, without hope, with only the present, with only love to guide him.

I propose that we should not only acknowledge, but will this faithlessness. What does it mean to say that the theologian in America is a man without faith? Is he therefore a man without God? It would seem to follow. He has his doctrine of God, several of them no doubt, and all correct. But that is surely not the point. He really doesn't believe in God, or that there is a God, or that God exists. It is not that he is fashionably against idols or opposed to God as a Being or as part of the world. It is God himself he has trouble with. Can one stand before God in unbelief? In what sense is such a man "before God"? Faith, or trusting in God, ought to produce some palpable fruits. The theologian may sometimes see these, but never in himself. Something has happened. At the center of his thoughts and meditations is a void, a disappearance, an absence. It is sometimes said that only a wounded physician can heal.

Other pertinent questions can be raised. Does the theologian go to church? The answer is no. He may, in the past, have concealed this no from himself by escaping into church work, speaking to church groups, preaching at church or college, slaking his thirst for worship and word in more protected communities. But now he is facing up to this banal answer to the banal question, and he wills to say no openly.

It used to be otherwise. In the past, the theologian would distinguish between God, Christendom, Christianity, and church, so that a different balance of yes and no could be uttered to each. Now he finds himself equally alienated from each of the realities represented by the four terms, and he says his no to each.

The quality of the theologian's no to the church differs from the impressive, if verbose, debate now being waged by the church's sociological pundits. In this debate, the issue is drawn between a kind of strident despair and a grim hope. The theologian, however, is neither despairing nor hopeful about the church. He is not interested, and he no longer has the energy or interest to answer ecclesiastical questions about What the Church Must Do to Revitalize Itself. One can choose his own language here: the theologian does not and cannot go to church, he is not interested, he is alienated (for a tenser word), he must live outside. He is not thereby a happier man, nor is he a troubled one. He is neither proud nor guilty. He has just decided that this is how it has to be, and he has decided to say so.

Does our theologian write books in systematic theology? That is, does he sit down and decide that he'd better do a theological book? The answer is a clear no. First, he gets his doctoral dissertation published. If it is any good, he can get quite a few years of professional mileage from it, defending it, clarifying, writing articles on relevant new material. From then on, he speaks and writes as he is asked. Editors, ecclesiastics, institutions, and other scholars assign him subjects they think he would be interested in. In this way, he can get a reputation for being skilled and interested in a field in which he has no interest whatever. As the years pass, the gulf between what he wants to do and what he does grows wider. His books, if any, are either private love letters (or hate letters) to fellow guild members or lecture series that offer an extra $500 for publication. Anything serious he manages will probably appear in articles.

What does the theologian read? Does he read religious books in hardcovers? Less and less, perhaps not at all, except when he has a free copy for a review or a bibliography to prepare. He has been unable to read books of sermons for a long time, and he has recently found that he practically never reads a book of theology for the sheer fun of it. He reads a lot of paperbacks, articles, and reviews. Just as less and less theological writing is being put into books, the theological reader is reading fewer and fewer books. One wonders quite seriously if there is any long-range future for hardcover religious book publishing, apart from church materials, reference works, and perhaps textbooks.

Is the theologian reading the Bible? Of course, he is forced into a kind of affable semiprofessional relationship with Scripture in his daily work. But what has gone is the rigorous systematic confronting of Scripture, expecting the Word of God to be made manifest when one approaches it with faith or at least with a broken and contrite heart. Perhaps because he is without either faith or the truly contrite heart, the Bible is a strange book that does not come alive to him as it is supposed to. There are still some pieces of it that come alive, to be sure, although he is not sure why or how: this psalmist, that prophetic call, a piece or two of Job, perhaps even some words of Jesus.

The theologian is alienated from the Bible, just as he is alienated from God and the church. This alienation may not last. If it doesn't last, fine; if it does last, the theologian will have some piercing questions to ask of himself. But there are wrong ways (Karl Barth) and right ways to overcome this alienation, and for now he has to be honest with himself, with the God before whom he stands in unbelief, and he must wait.

Given this state of affairs, what is this theologian really like? How does he act? Is he consciously or unconsciously dishonest? What is the relation between his public and private persona? The theologian can be exonerated from certain coarse professional faults: he is not overly ambitious for position or even notice; he is not moving in this direction so that he can be seen by men or because of some special delight he has *épater le bourgeoisie*. Like all men, he lives in a public and in a private sphere, and like most men, he works hard to keep the first from overpowering the second. On his public and professional side, he is likely to make use of two different masks. One is modestly devout, earnest, and serious, one which he uses for his teaching and church work. The other is a modestly worldly mask for his nonreligious friends and for the forms of their common life. Sometimes, he deliberately decides to interchange the masks, and wears the worldly mask for a church talk, a lecture, or even a sermon here or there. This leads to some harmless fun, and he is careful to see that everybody enjoys himself. Sometimes, he dons the devout mask for his worldly friends and their parties, and this too is quite harmless, for his friends understand and sometimes even admire his willingness to stand up for his odd beliefs.

But back in the private realm, he is coming more and more to distrust this kind of manipulation. God—this much he knows—is no respecter of persons or personas or masks, and the theologian really knows that he is neither mask. He knows that his rebellion and unbelief is both deeper and uglier than his bland worldly mask suggests, and he knows also (a bit less assuredly?) that his devout mask is too vapid. To be a man of two masks is, he knows, to be less than honest. Thus, he has had to come out into the open about his faithlessness even though he may suspect and hope that beneath it is a passion and a genuine waiting for something that may, one day, get transformed into a kind of faith even better than the one he has willed to lose.

Is this theologian alone, or does he live in a community that needs and nourishes him? He is not alone, but he does not ordinarily live in a true community, though he is aware of the existence of such a community. He rarely gets close enough to anybody to identify him as a member of this community, but he knows that there is no place under the sun where a member of this community may not be found. They may, of course, even be found in the church.

The problem is not, as might be suspected, that he has no doctrine of the church; it is with the doctrine of the church that he does have his problem. Professionally, he finds himself working with three quite different understandings of the church, but only the third makes genuine sense to him and it is far too imprecise to be very helpful.

The first understanding of the church states that it is to be defined by the classical marks of the church—unity, holiness, catholicity, apostolicity. In his ecumenical work or in the emerging Roman Catholic-Protestant dialogue, he is compelled to see the church in this way. The second way reminds him that the church is found where the Word of God is preached and the sacraments rightly administered. This doctrine of the church is most congenial to his own theology and theological vocation. He has always been drawn to a theology of the Word, and he has had moments when he has felt that theology might, after all, be able to minister to the church's proclamation.

But somehow he has had to come to define the church in a third way. The church is present whenever Christ is being formed among men in the world. This is a very vague way of describing his feelings about the community, even though it has no outlines, no preaching, sacraments, or liturgy.

One final question needs to be asked: What is the theologian doing now? The answer comes in two parts, the first related to what we have called his loss of God, of faith, of the church. In the face of all this, he is a passive man, trusting in waiting, silence, and in a kind of prayer for the losses to be returned. He does not do this anxiously, nor does he seem a particularly broken or troubled sort of person. If it is true that he is somehow without hope as well as without faith, he is not in despair about himself. His waiting is more docile and patient and has little existential moodiness in it. There is, of course, no single Christian doctrine which he affirms or grasps with guileless joy, but for all of his acute sense of loss, he has an overwhelmingly positive sense of being in and not out; even in his unbelief he is somehow home and not in a far country. He would say, for example: "As long as the Gethsemane prayer stands there somehow close to the center of things, I can stand there. If it should have to go, I might have to go too."

The theologian today is thus both a waiting man and a praying man. His faith and hope may be badly flawed, but his love is not. It is not necessary to probe the cultural, psychological, or even marital reasons for this, but simply to note it as fact. In Christology, the theologian is sometimes inclined to suspect that Jesus Christ is best understood as neither the object nor the ground of faith, neither as person, event, or community, but simply as a place to be, a standpoint. That place is, of course, alongside the neighbor, being for him. This may be the meaning of Jesus' true humanity and it may even be the meaning of his divinity, and thus of divinity itself. In any case, now—even when he knows so little about what to believe—he does know where to be. Today, for example, he is with the Negro community in its struggle (he will work out his own understanding of what "being with" must mean for him), working and watching, not yet evangelizing. He is also with all sorts of other groups: poets and critics, psychiatrists and physicists and philosophers. He is not in these places primarily to make things happen—a new solution to the science-religion problem or a new theological literary criticism—but just to be himself and to be attentive, as a man and therefore as a theologian. This is what his form of love looks like. It is a love that takes place in the middle of the real world, the ugly, banal, godless, religious world of America today.

He has been drawn, then, to these worldly places by love (not by apologetics or evangelism), and it is his hope that in such places his faithlessness and dishonesty may be broken. His love is not a secure and confident one, and thus it is not condescending. It is not, therefore, what some men call *agape*. It is a broken love, one that is needy and weak. It is thus a little like what men call *eros*. To be sure, his whole project may be swept away in a moment, if it can be shown that the theologian is just fleeing from one kind of religion-as-need-fulfillment to another. Perhaps someone will be able to show him that his weak and needy love has some points of connection with the love of the Cross.

Dietrich Bonhoeffer is, of course, deeply involved in this portrait. Have we discovered this in him, and then in ourselves; or in ourselves, and then rejoiced to find it in him? I think the second is nearer the truth. In any case, as Western Europe turns away from Bonhoeffer as a theological mentor, we in America can welcome his fragmentary help.

> Atonement and redemption, regeneration, the Holy Ghost, the love of our enemies, the cross of resurrection, life in Christ and Christian discipleship—all these things have become so problematic and so remote that we hardly dare any more to speak of them. . . . So our traditional language must perforce become powerless and remain silent, and our Christianity today will be confined to praying for and doing right by our fellow men. Christian thinking, speaking, and organization must be reborn out of this praying and this action.

Harvey Cox

Harvey Cox differed from the "death of god" theologians in discerning the hand of the transcendent God in the secular process. He taught in the mid-1960s that we must learn "to speak in a secular fashion of God." This selection is taken from his The Secular City. *New York: Macmillan, 1965, pp. 255–57, 266–68.*

We speak of God politically whenever we give occasion to our neighbor to become the responsible, adult agent, the fully posttown and posttribal man God expects him to be today. We speak to him of God whenever we cause him to realize consciously the web of interhuman reciprocity in which he is brought into being and sustained in it as a man. We speak to him of God whenever our words cause him to shed some of the blindness and prejudice of immaturity and to accept a larger and freer role in fashioning the instrumentalities of human justice and cultural vision. We do not speak to him of God by trying to make him religious but, on the contrary, by encouraging him to come fully of age, putting away childish things.

The Swiss theologian Gerhard Ebeling, though he does not use the term *political,* means something similar when he talks about the "nonreligious." He insists that secular speaking about God must always be concrete, clear, and active or productive (*wirkendes*). That is, it must not consist of generalities but must meet people at a point where *they* feel addressed. God comes to speech truly only as an event in which man and the world are seen for what they really are. In short, ". . . worldly talk of God is godly talk of the world."

The New Testament writers constantly exhorted their readers not to be anxious about what to *say.* They were repeatedly assured that if they were obedient, if they did what they were supposed to be doing, the right words would be supplied them when the moment came. Speaking about God in a secular fashion requires first of all that we place ourselves at those points where the restoring, reconciling activity of God is occurring, where the proper relationship between man and man is appearing. This means that evangelism, the speaking about God, is political, and Phillippe Maury is right when he says that "politics is the language of evangelism." We cannot know *in advance* what to say in this or that situation, what acts and words will reveal God's Word to men. Obedience and love precede the gift of tongues. The man who is doing what God intends him to do at the place he intends him to be will be supplied with the proper words. Christian evangelism, like Christian ethics, must be unreservedly contextual.

To say that speaking of God must be political means that it must engage people at particular points, not just "in general." It must be a word about their own lives—their children, their job, their hopes or disappointments. It must be a word to the bewildering crises within which our personal troubles arise—a word which builds peace in a nuclear world, which contributes to justice in an age stalked by hunger, which hastens the day of freedom in a society stifled by segregation. If the word is not a word which arises from a concrete involvement of the speaker in these realities, then it is not a Word of God at all but empty twaddle.

We speak of God to secular man by speaking about man, by talking about man as he is seen in the biblical perspective. Secular talk of God occurs only when we are away from the ghetto and out of costume, when we are participants in that political action by which he restores men to each other in mutual concern and responsibility. We speak of God in a secular fashion when we recognize man as his partner, as the one charged with the task of bestowing meaning and order in human history.

Speaking of God in a secular fashion is thus a political issue. It entails our discerning where God is working and then joining his work. Standing in a picket line is a way of speaking. By doing it a Christian speaks of God. He helps alter the word *God* by changing the society in which it has been trivialized, by moving away from the context where "God-talk" usually occurs, and by shedding the stereotyped roles in which God's name is usually intoned. . . .

This may mean that we shall have to stop talking about "God" for a while, take a moratorium on speech until the new name emerges. Maybe the name that does emerge will not be the three-letter word *God,* but this should not dismay us. Since naming is a human activity embedded in a particular sociocultural milieu, there is no holy language as such, and the word *God* is not sacred. All languages are historical. They are born and die. Presumably, God will continue to live, eons after English and all other present languages have been totally forgotten. It is only word magic to believe that there is some integral connection between God and any particular linguistic vocable.

If the naming we must do in the secular city requires our dispensing with the word *God* in order not to confuse the One who reveals himself in Jesus with the gods of mythology or the deity of philosophy, it will not be the first time this has happened in the history of biblical faith. It is common knowledge that the people of Israel went through several stages in naming him, and they may not be through yet. At various times, they used the terms *El Elyon, Elohim, El Shaddai,* and—of course—*Yahweh.* They freely borrowed these designations from neighboring peoples and discarded them with what now seems to us an amazing freedom, especially in view of the enormous power inherent in names in Hebrew culture. A remarkable evidence of this daring willingness to move to new names when the historical situation warranted it is found in Ex. 6:2–3, a part of the so-called P document: "And God [Elohim] said to Moses, 'I am the Lord [Yahweh]. I appeared to Abraham, Isaac and Jacob as God Almighty [El Shaddai], but by my name the Lord [Yahweh] I did not make myself known to them.' " One could write an entire history of Israel, charting its cultural and political relationships to its neighbors, by following the conflict and development in naming, both the naming of God and the naming of children. God reveals his name to man through the abrasive experiences of social change.

After the period of the Exile, the Jews again switched their nomenclature. Disturbed by the debasement of the name *Yahweh,* which was considered too holy for everyday use, they began using the word *Adonai,* which is still used in synagogues.

Perhaps for a while we shall have to do without a name for God. This may seem threatening, but there are biblical precedents for it. Moses apparently felt equally uncomfortable when he was told to go down to Egypt and lead the children of Israel to freedom. He anxiously asked for the name of the One who spoke to him from the burning bush. But the answer given to him was not very comforting. His request was simply refused. He was not given a name at all, but was told rather cryptically that if the captives were curious about who had sent him, he should simply tell them that "I will do what I will do" had sent him (Ex. 3:13–14). At one time, this verse was interpreted ontologically. God was revealing himself as "being itself." But today most Hebrew scholars agree that no metaphysical description is implied. The voice from the bush gives an answer which is intended to be terse and evasive. As Bernhard Anderson says, "Moses had asked for information about the mystery of the divine nature [the name], but this information had been withheld. Instead God made known his demand . . . and assured him that he would know who God is by what he brings to pass. In other words, the question 'Who is God?' would be answered by events that would take place in the future."

The Exodus marked for the Jews a turning point of such elemental power that a new divine name was needed to replace the titles that had grown out of their previous experience. Our transition today from the age of Christendom to the new era of urban secularity will be no less shaking. Rather than clinging stubbornly to antiquated appellations or anxiously synthesizing new ones, perhaps, like Moses, we must simply take up the work of liberating the captives, confident that we will be granted a new name by events of the future.

Peter Berger

Peter Berger, in repudiating the "death of god" theologians for their complete capitulation to the secular, contended in the late 1960s that it is possible to discern within the secular realm what he called "signals of transcendence," signs of a deeper order of reality, i.e., the supernatural. This selection is taken from his A Rumor of Angels. *New York: Doubleday, 1969, pp. 52–54, 57–58, 60, 61–62, 64–65, 69–70, 72; Harmondsworth, UK.: Penguin Books, 1971, pp. 70–72, 76, 78–79, 80, 84, 89–90, 92–93.*

I would suggest that theological thought seek out what might be called *signals of transcendence* within the empirically given human situation. And I would further suggest that there are *prototypical human gestures* that may constitute such signals. What does this mean?

By *signals of transcendence,* I mean phenomena that are to be found within the domain of our "natural" reality but that appear to point beyond that reality. In other words, I am not using *transcendence* here in a technical philosophical sense but literally, as the transcending of the normal, everyday world that I earlier identified with the notion of the "supernatural." By *prototypical human gestures,* I mean certain reiterated acts and experiences that appear to express essential aspects of man's being, of the human animal as such. I do *not* mean what Jung called "archetypes"—potent symbols buried deep in the unconscious mind that are common to all men. The phenomena I am discussing are not "unconscious" and do not have to be excavated from the "depths" of the mind; they belong to ordinary everyday awareness.

One fundamental human trait, which is of crucial importance in understanding man's religious enterprise, is his propensity for order. As the philosopher of history Eric Voegelin points out at the beginning of *Order and History,* his analysis of the various human conceptions of order: "The order of history emerges from the history of order. Every society is burdened with the task, under its concrete conditions, of creating an order that will endow the fact of its existence with meaning in terms of ends divine and human." Any historical society is an order, a protective structure of meaning, erected in the face of chaos. Within this order, the life of the group as well as the life of the individual makes sense. Deprived of such order, both group and individual are threatened with the most fundamental terror, the terror of chaos that Emile Durkheim called *anomie* (literally, a state of being "order-less").

Throughout most of human history, men have believed that the created order of society, in one way or another, corresponds to an underlying order of the universe, a divine order that supports and justifies all human attempts at ordering. Now, clearly, not every such belief in correspondence can be true, and a philosophy of history may, like Voegelin's, be an inquiry into the relationship of true order to the different human attempts at ordering. But there is a more basic element to be considered, over and above the justification of this or that historically produced order. This is the human faith in order as such, a faith closely related to man's fundamental trust in reality. This faith is experienced not only in the history of societies and civilizations, but in the life of each individual—indeed, child psychologists tell us there can be no maturation without the presence of this faith at the outset of the socialization process. Man's propensity for order is grounded in a faith or trust that, ultimately, reality is "in order," "all right," "as it should be." Needless to say, there is no empirical method by which this faith can be tested. To assert it is itself an act of faith. But it is possible to proceed from the faith that is rooted in experience to the act of faith that transcends the empirical sphere, a procedure that could be called the *argument from ordering.*

In this fundamental sense, every ordering gesture is a signal of transcendence. . . .

Closely related to, though still distinct from, the foregoing considerations is what I will call the *argument from play.* Once more, as the Dutch historian Johan Huizinga has shown, we are dealing with a basic experience of man. Ludic, or playful, elements can be found in just about any sector of human culture, to the point where it can be argued that culture as such would be impossible without this dimension. One aspect of play that Huizinga analyzes in some detail is the fact that play sets up a separate universe of discourse, with its own rules, which suspends, "for the duration," the rules and general assumptions of the "serious" world. One of the most important assumptions thus suspended is the time structure of ordinary social life. When one is playing, one is on a different time, no longer measured by the standard units of the larger society, but rather by the peculiar ones of the game in question. In the "serious" world, it may be 11:00 A.M., on such and such a day, month, and year. But in the universe in which one is playing, it may be the third round, the fourth act, the *allegro* movement, or the second kiss. In playing, one steps out of one time into another. . . .

The logic of the argument from play is very similar to that of the argument from order. The experience of joyful play is not something that must be sought on some mystical margin of existence. It can be readily found in the reality of ordinary life. Yet within this experienced reality it constitutes a signal of transcendence, because its intrinsic intention points beyond itself and beyond man's "nature" to a "supernatural" justification. Again, it will be perfectly clear that this justification cannot be empirically proved. Indeed, the experience can be plausibly interpreted as a merciful illusion, a regression to childish magic (along the lines, say, of the Freudian theory of wishful fantasy). The religious justification of the experience can be achieved only in an act of faith. The point, however, is that this faith is inductive—it does not rest on a mysterious revelation, but rather on what we experience in our common, ordinary lives. All men have experienced the deathlessness of childhood and we may assume that, even if only once or twice, all men have experienced transcendent joy in adulthood. Under the aspect of inductive faith, religion is the final vindication of childhood and of joy, and of all gestures that replicate these.

Another essential element of the human situation is hope, and there is an *argument from hope* within the same logic of inductive faith. . . .

Human existence is always oriented toward the future. Man exists by constantly extending his being into the future, both in his consciousness and his activity. Put differently, man realizes himself in projects. An essential dimension of this "futurity" of man is hope. It is through hope that men overcome the difficulties of any given here and now. And it is through hope that men find meaning in the face of extreme suffering. A key ingredient of most (but not all) theodicies is hope. The specific content of such hope varies. In earlier periods of human history, when the concept of the individual and his unique worth was not as yet so sharply defined, this hope was commonly invested in the future of the group. The individual might suffer and die, be defeated in his most important projects, but the group (clan, or tribe, or people) would live on and eventually triumph. Often, of course, theodicies were based on the hope of an individual afterlife, in which the sufferings of this early life would be vindicated and left behind. Through most of human history, both collective and individual theodicies of hope were legitimated in religious terms. Under the impact of secularization, ideologies of this-worldly hope have come to the fore as theodicies (the Marxist one being the most important of late). In any case, human hope has always asserted itself most intensely in the face of experiences that seemed to spell utter defeat, most intensely of all in the face of the final defeat of death. Thus, the profoundest manifestations of hope are to be found in gestures of courage undertaken in defiance of death....

Inductive faith acknowledges the omnipresence of death (and thus of the futility of hope) in "nature," but it also takes into account the intentions within our "natural" experience of hopes that point toward a "supernatural" fulfillment. This reinterpretation of our experience encompasses rather than contradicts the various explanations of empirical reason (be they psychological, sociological, or what-have-you). Religion, in justifying this reinterpretation, is the ultimate vindication of hope and courage, just as it is the ultimate vindication of childhood and joy. By the same token, religion vindicates the gestures in which hope and courage are embodied in human action—including, given certain conditions, the gestures of revolutionary hope and, in the ultimate irony of redemption, the courage of stoic resignation....

Finally, there is an *argument from humor.* ... I agree with Bergson's description: "A situation is unvariably comic when it belongs simultaneously to two altogether independent series of events and is capable of being interpreted in two entirely different meanings at the same time." But I insist upon adding that this comic quality always refers to *human* situations, not to encounters between organisms and the nonorganic. The biological as such is not comic. Animals become comic only when we view them anthropomorphically, that is, when we imbue them with human characteristics. Within the human sphere, just about any discrepancy can strike us as funny. Discrepancy is the stuff of which jokes are made, and frequently it is the punch line that reveals the "entirely different meaning." The little Jew meets the big Negro. The mouse wants to sleep with the elephant. The great philosopher loses his pants. But I would go further than this and suggest that there is one fundamental discrepancy from which all other comic discrepancies are derived—the discrepancy between man and universe. It is *this* discrepancy that makes the comic an essentially human phenomenon and humor an intrinsically human trait. *The comic reflects the imprisonment of the human spirit in the world.* This is why, as has been pointed out over and over since classical antiquity, comedy and tragedy are at root closely related. Both are commentaries on man's finitude—if one wants to put it in existentialist terms, on his condition of "thrown-ness." If this is so, then the comic is an objective dimension of man's reality, not just a subjective or psychological reaction to that reality. . . .

This is by no means an exhaustive or exclusive list of human gestures that may be seen as signals of transcendence. To provide one would entail constructing a philosophical anthropology and, on top of that, a theological system to go with it. I am not prepared to be quite as Quixotic as that! . . . My aim has been to explore theological possibilities that take as their starting point what is generally accessible to all men. I have therefore limited myself to a discussion of phenomena that can be found in everybody's ordinary life. . . .

Langdon Gilkey

Langdon Gilkey, also writing in the late 1960s, insisted that there is a hidden dimension of ultimacy in secular experience, that secular individuals as they live their lives are more religious than they think they are. This selection is taken from his Naming the Whirlwind. The Renewal of God-Language. *New York: Bobbs-Merrill, 1969, pp. 111–12, 148–49, 150, 251–52, 296–97, 465–70.*

The central theme that unites the radical theologians is well expressed in the enigmatic slogan "God is dead." Although each of them means by this phrase something slightly different, its general import for all is that, first, the God who has been the center of faith and theological reflection for the Judeo-Christian tradition is now seen to be nonexistent, unreal, and an illusion; and, secondly, that Christianity (or Judaism) must henceforth understand itself without him. In slightly different ways, therefore, this group accepts as the truth the naturalistic viewpoint characteristic of the secular spirit as we have described it: we live in a cosmos without God, without an ultimate coherence or meaning on which we can depend and to which we should in faith, worship, and obedience relate ourselves. And as a consequence, what meaning we can find in life must come from our own autonomous human powers, and what religion we can affirm must be one structured alone on our own worldly obligations and possibilities. . . .

The central theological problem of the radical theology we are discussing—exemplified best in the thought of Hamilton and van Buren—is the inconsistency or contradiction between the two lordships that are there asserted: that of "the world" or of secularity, on the one hand, and that of Jesus, on the other. On the one hand, it is asserted that man has come of age, that he is now autonomous and so needs no divine problem-solver; he is on his own and can, individually or socially, deal with all his major problems—at least those which can in any manner, human or divine, be resolved. Correspondingly, the secular culture he has created out of his intelligence and will is held to be rightfully expressive of man's best hopes for truth and for goodness, and so with regard to valid propositions and valid goals, secular existence provides us with our normative criteria.

It is, let us note, because radical theology, in this context at least, unequivocally asserts this principle of human autonomy and self-sufficiency that these theologies also assert that God is dead. A deity, say they, is not needed by autonomous man; any such discourse is not meaningful to a secular and autonomous age; and any such relation to transcendence is destructive rather than creative for man, who must live wholly within the secular world. Hence God is dead for our age. So far as the personal experience of the absence of God is assumed to be *more* than a report of a mere personal experience, that is, insofar as it is taken as an indication of what is representative of the universal cultural *Geist,* and *a fortiori* what the real ontological situation is—and all radical theologians so take it—it is the assertion of the autonomy of modern man with regard to issues of truth and value that provides the foundation on which this negative side of radical theology rests. . . .

On the other hand, it is asserted with equal force by radical theology that Jesus is the rightful Lord of man's existence. It is he who gives to us our "stance in life," who provides the model for a really human style of life, who not only communicates to us a picture of authentic existence, but seems as well to communicate to us the power or the possibility of that authentic existence—through the "contagion" of his freedom. Thus is he Lord, God for us, the center of our ethical ultimate concern, he around whom we build our humanity and so our active existence in the world. In the view of this theology, we are, seemingly, and at one and the same time, autonomous, mature men, self-directed by our own norms of life and criteria of knowledge, and so reflecting a radically modern secularity—and thus without God in the world. On the other hand, we are *also* dependent, in some strange fashion, on this dim figure from a different cultural context in the distant past for our self-realization as humans and so for authenticity. My present argument is that these two Lords, the one of secular autonomy and the other of Jesus, cannot be united together consistently in the terms given us by radical theology—and, only by implication here, that they cannot be brought together unless God-language be retained. . . .

Secularism has interpreted our existence within the world as if man's being were to be understood solely in terms of those finite forces with which he obviously interacts: the nature that has produced him, the social environment that shapes his capacities, and the latent powers that reside in him. It has emphasized, therefore, the contingency of man's existence and all that surrounds him, the relativity and transience of all that appears in history and so all that he can accomplish, and his autonomy and freedom in a world without ultimate coherence and so one in which he alone can be the creator of security and of meaning. And it has found intelligible only language referent to that realm of finite factors, and unintelligible all symbolic and mythical language referent to a region of sacrality, ultimacy, unconditionedness, and essential mystery. There are no longer any ultimates in either cosmos or history which support and guide man's life, and for the interpretation of which religious symbols are essential; man seems to be on his own, and to create out of the relativities of his experience of finite creatures whatever forms of discourse and practical guidelines may direct him.

Now, while a very great deal of this self-understanding of modern man—expressed in each of his most typical philosophies—is true, nevertheless this vision contains as well a good deal of error. We say error because this self-understanding does not accurately reflect our actual existence in the world, the way we *are* there as autonomous beings amidst contingency, relativity, and transience. It obscures, therefore, a great many undeniable and significant aspects of our ordinary, secular life, and is proved false by the test of secular existence itself. And what is much more important, it is not easy to live as a human in the world on this purely secular basis. Secular autonomy taken as a total view of ourselves is neither a true answer to our intellectual question—What is man like?—nor a helpful answer to the existential and personal question—How am I to live as a human being, in fullness and creativity? For that is what secularity, and all of us, wish to do; but it fails as an enterprise because it misunderstands us. . . .

It is surely true that, for secular man, no ultimate confronts him either through an object in nature or even through an event or an institution in history; these have been relativized, pluralized, and thoroughly desacralized. Our suggestion is, however, that ultimacy has not thereby vanished—and could not vanish from modern experience. On the contrary, it is present, as it always has been in human life, as a base, ground, and limit of what we are, as a presupposition for ourselves, our thinking, our deciding, and our acting—all of which are, to be sure, relative. The ultimate or unconditioned element in experience is not so much the seen but the basis of seeing; not what is known as an object so much as the basis of knowing; not an object of value, but the ground of valuing; not the thing before us, but the source of things; not the particular meanings that generate our life in the world, but the ultimate context within which these meanings necessarily subsist. This range or region of experience is thus best indicated by four words—*source, ground, horizon,* and *limit*—that which is the presupposition and basis of all we are and do, of our experience of things, persons, and ourselves, and that which appears at the limits of our powers and capacities. Religious language is a way of talking of an area beyond and yet within the visible, sensible creaturely flux, where the ultimate origins and source of what we are is located, where the character of the existence in which we participate is ultimately determined, and so where our own role in existence as a whole is shaped. It points to and seeks symbolically to describe the contours of the ultimate horizon of our common being in the world.

The sacred, the ultimate, and the unconditioned, about which religious language seeks to speak, concern therefore the sources, the origins, the foundations, and the limits of our powers, capacities, and hopes. As we shall go on to suggest, there are in general four "situations" where this dimension of ultimacy appears in ordinary experience and so where this language is appropriately (and inescapably) used: (1) where the foundations of our being, of our meanings and our values, appear to us in the "given" which we do not create or control but which creates us and so represents the ground and limits of our powers; (2) when these foundational structures are threatened by fate and we experience our absolute helplessness; (3) in the mystery of ambiguity as it appears within the midst of our own freedom and therefore quite beyond our own deliberate or rational control; and, finally, (4) this dimension appears in man's confidence and hopes despite these outer and inner threats to the security, meaning, and fulfillment of his life. Thus, inevitably in any culture, secular or religious, religious discourse or myths appear in relation to the mysteries of our origins, our limits, our ambiguity and evil, and our hopes for the future. Correspondingly, these forms shape the basic joys, fears, values, and confidences of that culture, and in the end they dominate its practical decisions, its educational programs, its forms of human relations, and its interpretation of the mysteries of good and evil with which every society must in some manner cope. . . .

All religious talk, we have argued, is talk about the ultimate and the sacred as it appears in ordinary experience, that is, as it appears in and through the finite, in its experience of itself, of its being in the world and its being in time. Religious discourse is thus *symbolic* talk about the finite but with regard to its ground, its limits, its ultimate structures, its resources of healing and renewal, and its bases for hope. It is not, therefore, directly talk about God; we cannot know him as he is in himself, and in any case such talk would have no experienced base or content and so would be meaningless. It is talk about the divine *as* it appears in and to us in our experience of finite things as contingent, relative, temporal, and autonomous beings; it is talk about creatures, others and ourselves, as the sacred appears in them. Thus and only thus is it meaningful language, language about a region that is definite to all of us because it is experienced by us all. It is not talk about heaven, but about earth—with regard to its ultimate and sacred ground and limits. Correspondingly, Christian talk about God is language about this ultimate and sacred dimension: our ground, limit, meaning, judge, and resource, in terms of Christian symbols. And those symbols in turn reflect and express those points where *this* apprehension of the divine was manifested in a particular community's life through *those* finite events, persons, media, and symbols. Again, we are talking about the ultimate and sacred dimension of our contingent, relative, transient, and autonomous being; but, as Christians, we know what that ultimacy and sacrality *is,* and so talk about it, as it has manifested itself in *this* history, and so as it is apprehended, conceived, and responded to in and through *these* media and *these* symbols. Thus we use the "biblical" and "Christian" verbal symbols of creation, providence, covenant, law, judgment, Gospel, forgiveness, and new age—and so on—as means with which to conceive the ultimacy and sacrality that appears in all of existence. "God" is this sacred understood in these symbolic terms; Christian God-language is language descriptive of the ultimate which grounds and limits us, but that ultimate apprehended and understood through these symbols.

Again, however, we should be clear, we are talking symbolically as we have defined and used that term. Our direct referent is *not* the divine as it is in itself, or even "God" as he can be imagined or pictured by means of revealed symbols. Such language "about God" quickly loses its touch with experience and so its meaning for us. Rather is our language multivalent, language *about* the finite with regard to what appears in and to our experience, the ultimate or sacral dimension there, but understood in terms of these symbols. Thus, the symbol of God as creator refers not to some pictured absolute, but only to the ultimate and sacral ground of our contingency as that ground is apprehended by us in and through our contingency. Providence refers to the ultimate and sacral context of our life's and our history's meaning; judgment refers to the ultimate norm embodied in Jesus by which our life is evaluated; forgiveness refers to the ultimate love resident in him as a man and which accepts us in and through him—and so on. These are not doctrines about a being called God, but doctrines about the creaturely as the sacred manifests itself in and through the creaturely. The *way* we understand the divine in each of the above is very much shaped by the unique "meaning" or structure of the symbol; it is a *Christian* apprehension and understanding. But *what* we understand through these unique symbols and so in this unique way is the appearance of the sacred in and through the finite, and not the sacred by itself.

Symbols in religion are, in the first instance, creatures, men, or events through which the sacred acts creatively and manifests itself to men. Correspondingly, the verbal symbols of religion, about which we here speak, are *symbolic* precisely in the sense that they are talk about the finite—creatures, history, men, communities, and so on—with regard to their ultimate ground, limit and hope. And the symbol "God" is the way this community, with its experiences and symbolic forms, has apprehended that sacral ultimacy across the entire range of its existence, but centering its delineation of that apprehension on that final event in which the ultimate that is our origin and destiny has manifested itself—in Jesus who is the Christ. In this sense, the task of systematic theology is that of uniting or joining conceptually the biblical symbols about *God:* as Creator, Ruler, Judge, Father, Redeemer and Reconciler, with our understanding of *ourselves* as "symbols" through which the sacred appears; for example, of understanding *God's* creation in terms of *our* contingency and its ground. To speak *only* of God is empty; to speak *only* of ourselves is pointless. To talk meaningfully of God is to talk of our existence in contingency and freedom in relation to its divine ground, judge, and redeeming resource, understood symbolically in the terms of our community's life. This by no means answers all our questions about intelligible symbolic language; but at least it relates religious discourse to concrete and contemporary experience without sacrificing either Biblical or traditional content, its transcendent reference, or its possibility of intelligible ontological and cultural explication.

Our fundamental thesis here has been that the Christian awareness of God grows out of the wonder and the ambiguity of the ordinary life of man in the world, but that it is an awareness that is finally brought to conscious and definitive form by the central experience of illumination and renewal that comes in the community that witnesses to the Christ. For all of us, this original awareness is *there*, at once elusive and real, absent and present, threatening and reassuring, as the fundamental ground and tone to our ordinary existence—until the knowledge of "faith" illumines and clarifies in part, but only in part, this ever-present mystery. The Christian continues to live, therefore, amidst both the ambiguity and clarity of this situation—for faith clarifies but by no means removes the ambiguities and the threats of our natural existence. Our Christian existence participates in both the worlds we have delineated—that of ambiguity, doubt, and the void, and that of confidence, meaning, and reconciliation. Finally, from this characteristic situation of Christian life in the present, the strange religious symbols of the immanence and the transcendence of God, on the one hand, and of eschatology, on the other, begin to make sense. We can understand the symbol of the *immanence* of God as the source of our being and meaning in terms of the common, universal, and secular experiences of the reality, wonder, and joy of life, of the coherences that experience offers to our inquiries, and of the universally apprehended meaningfulness of life's tasks. Correspondingly, we can understand the symbol of the *transcendence* of God through our continual experience of the elusiveness of that security and meaning, in the experience of the radical relativity of our truth, and in our sense of alienation from forgiveness and from the power to love—of all of which our secular friends, as well as we, are so very much aware. Above all, we can know the divine hiddenness in the void of insecurity, despair, doubt, guilt, and death, which every human faces—even Jesus himself in his cry from the cross. The transcendence of God is initially experienced in the void, which is the first terrible face of the divine that, at least in a secular culture, man knows. But then in the joy and acceptance of our contingent being, of our relative life, and of our death, and in the achievement of relative meaning and truth, of love and of community despite our fragmentariness, the renewed immanent presence of God is also known, and we begin to be aware of who that ultimate reality is—and the promise of an end in which God will be all in all takes on concrete, experienced meaning. The beginning of faith then appears in the awareness of the sacred in the profane, of joy and wonder in the midst of insecurity, of meaning and truth in the midst of the meaningless, and of life in the face of death, and it culminates with our understanding and affirmation of their ultimate unity in God.

This dialectic of immanence and transcendence, of hidden presence to all of life and of absence from it when we look for him is, of course, not all of God that we can know, or that the Christian community has believed itself to know. It is only a beginning. "God" here remains perhaps real, deep, but vague and elusive—the mysterious, sacral power from which life comes and which rules our destiny, and the eternity from which we are now separated. When Christian experience and thought move beyond this point and, in the light of those more personal and moral questions raised by our freedom and by our relations to others in community and in history, begin to know the love and acceptance of God in his long relation to his people and especially in the figure of Jesus, then we can say we begin to know the sacred more directly as it is, we begin to know "God." And that knowledge will reflect back on all that has been experienced of the ultimate on the other levels of our existence, shaping our answers to life's dilemmas and so shaping the theological symbols with which we comprehend ourselves, our destiny, and the sacred itself. Then the mysterious source of our being, the dim ruler of our destiny, and the opaque eternity into which we are finally to move become illumined for us through the law and the love shown in Jesus Christ, and we can begin haltingly, but with some sense of meaning and of certainty, to speak of "God." But that the presence of God is real in secular life, and that our dependence on him makes us search for him even in our most worldly affairs, is true, and thus begins the possibility of knowing the reality of God and of speaking of him in a secular age. Our biblical symbols, the treasured vehicles of our community's life and faith, can be understood as meaningful and asserted as valid as forthrightly in our secular existence as in any other age—but only if we retain, both in our thought and in our existence, a lively sense of their relatedness to our ordinary secular life.

Norman Pittenger

Recalling the weaknesses of the theologies of the 1960s, Norman Pittinger affirms his own preference for process theology. This selection is taken from his Catholic Faith in a Process Perspective. *Maryknoll, N.Y.: Orbis Books, 1981, pp. 12–22.*

The furor of fifteen years ago over the "death of God" theology seems to have died down. William Hamilton, among the first who talked and wrote in this vein, has said lately that the "death of God" emphasis belongs to the past—the recent past, surely—and that today we must go beyond it. Whatever may have been the contribution it made, the contribution *has been* made. What has this movement to say to us today?

I do not myself subscribe to the view that theology works in the fashion which Hamilton's remark suggests—a sort of drunkard's progress, with no real direction and without obvious continuities. But I agree on three points: first, that the "death of God" literature *has* made a contribution to theology, even if it is not the contribution which its representatives might think; secondly, that the movement is just as dead as its leaders said that "God" was dead; and thirdly, that we must go forward to a doing of theology, in the Christian mode, which will take account of what that particular literature had to say. In this chapter I wish to speak of these three points.

The talk about the "death of God" was, I believe, an extraordinarily misleading, even if highly provocative, way of saying something important. What was really involved was the death of certain *concepts* of God, rather than a supposed death of God himself. One realizes that this interpretation was denied by Thomas Altizer and other advocates of the view; they insisted that they were talking about a genuine death of God as an historical occurrence. But even they show that the contrary is the case. Altizer himself demonstrated this when he claimed that he was talking about the absolute immanence or "presence-in-this-world" of the Word or Spirit, in consequence of the radical *kenosis* or self-emptying of the transcendent deity usually denoted by the word "God." That Word or Spirit most certainly is *not* dead; and Altizer's "gospel" was precisely the reality in human experience and in the world-order of the Word or Spirit with whom human beings must reckon whether they wish to do so or not.

I am convinced that what died, that whose death was stridently announced, is a series of models, images, pictures, or concepts of deity which for a very long time have been taken by considerable numbers of people to be the Christian way of understanding God. It is important in this connection to note that each of the three leading advocates of the position was in reaction against a notion of God that represents just such a series of models. Paul van Buren was a disciple of Karl Barth, under whom he wrote his excellent doctoral dissertation on Calvin's teaching about Christ as the true life of human beings. Hamilton was an opponent of natural theology in all its forms, even if he studied at St. Andrews under Donald Baillie; it was the so-called "neo-orthodox" line which had attracted him, theologically. Altizer was a slightly different case. He worked under Paul Tillich and with Mircea Eliade, but his reaction was *against* the aspects of Tillich's thought which stressed "being-itself" in God and *for* those aspects which emphasized the need for radical reconception of Christian thought.

Alfred North Whitehead wrote in *Process and Reality* many years ago that the Christian theological tradition has tended to conceive of God in three ways, each of them mistaken: as "the ruling Caesar, or the ruthless moralist, or the unmoved mover." It has failed to give central place to what he styled "the Galilean vision," in which God is shown as persuasion or love. Hence, in his striking phrase, "the Church gave unto God the attributes which belonged exclusively to Caesar," seeing him "in the image of an imperial ruler," "in the image of a personification of moral energy," or "in the image of an ultimate philosophical principle." With certain qualifications I should say that Whitehead stated the facts here. In various combinations and with differing emphases, the concept of God with which many Christian thinkers have tended to work has been composed of exactly those ingredients: absolute power, stark moral demand, and unconditioned and essentially unrelated (in the sense of a two-way movement) "being-itself" as the ultimate cause of everything-not-God, but not in any way affected by that which was not itself—and the neuter here is highly significant, *ens realissimum.* Great theologians, like Augustine and Aquinas (to name but two), have written in this fashion; but they were also strangely discontented in doing so, since their "working" faith was in the biblical God of unfailing love-in-action, effecting his purpose of love in nature and history, and most profoundly open to and receptive of what went on in the world. Hence the ambiguity which (as I think) one can see running through so many of the great theologies.

But it was the stress on power, on "ruthless moralism," and on transcendence in the sense of nonrelationship, which many took to be demanded when one talked of God. Of course one might also add, almost as a kind of after-thought, "Oh yes, he is also loving." I do not parody here, for I myself have found that when I have tried to present a theological point of view which made the reality of love absolutely central, and put the other so-called divine attributes in a place secondary to that love, I have been met with the response, "Of course God is loving, but to talk of God we must begin with his omnipotence, his transcendence, his aseity (self-containedness and self-existence), his absolute righteousness with its consequent demands on human beings." This procedure seems to me to be entirely wrong, however traditional it may be. What we ought to do is to start with God self-disclosed in human affairs as love-in-action. Then, and only then, can we use (adverbially, as it were) the other so-called attributes. God as love-in-action is more than any particular expression of his love (hence he is transcendent); God as love-in-action is always available (hence he is immanent and omnipresent); God as love-in-action is able to envisage every situation in its deepest and truest reality and accommodate himself to it, so that he can indeed achieve his loving ends (hence he is omniscient); God as love-in-action is unswerving in his love, unfailing in its expression, unyielding in his desire to confront human beings with the just demands of love (hence God is righteous). If we had worked in that way, we should have been saved from some of our supposedly insoluable theological problems, many of which are based on taking the other, and as I think wrong, approach.

However this may be, the fact is that for very many contemporary men and women, not only of a sophisticated sort but also of quite ordinary attainments, the notion of God as absolute power, as unyielding moral dictator, and as metaphysical first cause never himself affected by the world, has gone dead. There are many reasons why this has happened. This chapter is no place to discuss them at length, but among others we may mention scientific understanding, psychological discoveries, awareness of sociological conditions, and all that Bonhoeffer summed up in saying that humankind has "come of age." By this he did *not* mean that the human being is an entirely mature and adult creature who now can take the place of God; he *did* mean that we now know our own responsibility and that God treats us, not like slaves nor like little children, but like sons and daughters to whom he entrusts such responsibility. This "going dead" of the notions I have mentioned was stated plainly for us in the writers who spoke of "the death of God."

So much for my first point. My second is to repeat that the movement called by that name is now itself a matter of the past; it has made its contribution, and that is that. It has taught us something, and by now we ought to have learned what it had to teach us. Of course the learning has not been done simultaneously in all parts of the Christian world or anywhere else. Hence for some of us, it might be said, the situation is still *pre*-"death of God"; and for those who are in this situation, the lesson is still to be learned. But for those who have got an inkling of what this is all about, who have learned the lesson, the situation is *post*-"death of God" and we must now go on to the constructive task.

I shall not spend time in showing how and why we are in that "post" era. I only call in witness the remark of Hamilton which I have already cited. He at least feels that the "calling in question," the denials, the stark affirmation of the "end of sheer transcendence, sheer moralism, sheer power" (as I like to put it), has been accomplished. So the problem for us, as for him, may be phrased in a typically American way: "Where do we go from here?" It is with that question that the remainder of this chapter will concern itself. But the one thing that is quite clear is that we cannot "go back," as if we could return to the older ideas and concepts quite unchanged by what has happened during the past few decades. If we cannot rest content in the denials, the "calling in question," and the like, neither can we retreat into the theologies of the past. This is what I find troublesome in the writing of E. L. Mascall on the subject. He has usually been sound in his criticisms of the "death of God" school and, indeed, of the whole "radical theology" which in one way or another is associated with it. But because of his failure to understand *why* such a theology in its various forms has appeared, he has been unable to see any other solution than a "return."

In going forward with Christian theology *after* "the death of God," we have several options. Let me mention some of them, assuming that we cannot work with Thomism (either "classical" or "revised"); nor with that peculiarly Anglican affair known as "liberal Catholicism," in the style of *Essays Catholic and Critical* or the writings of Charles Gore; nor with "liberalism" in its reductionist form as found in Harnack or Harnack *redivivus;* nor with sheer biblicism in its fundamentalist dress. So I mention the following possibilities, some of them also mentioned in an excellent little book of lectures given in Chicago some year ago, *Philosophical Resources for Christian Thought,* in which various conceptualities were discussed at length: (1) existentialism in some mode; (2) phenomenological (and in that sense nonmetaphysical) enquiry; (3) analytical philosophy and its talk about *bliks* and "language games"; (4) process thought in its several forms. To these four I should add the so-styled "secular theology" often advocated today, with a sideglance at revived and restated "biblical theology." Here are six possibilities.

Of some of them I must speak very briefly. For example, the kind of "biblical theology" sometimes advocated today assumes that we should go forward by taking with utmost seriousness the biblical images or motifs—not the literal, textual stuff of Scripture, which would involve us in a kind of new "fundamentalism," but the main-line series of biblical images. I am very much in sympathy with this approach, so far as it goes. For Christians the biblical images and patterns are of *first* importance, since it is from them that the Christian picture of God takes its rise. But it must be pointed out that these images and patterns are most diverse; further, they belong, in their explicit shape, to ages in which we do not ourselves live. Hence what is required is what Leonard Hodgson so often, and rightly, demanded: we must ask ourselves what the case *really is,* so far as we can grasp it today, if people who thought and wrote *like that* phrased it in the way they did. Otherwise we shall be using the Scriptures in a very wooden and unimaginative fashion, even if we do not succumb to literalism in its obvious sense. Furthermore, if we wish to communicate the deepest meaning of those images and patterns, we cannot rest content with them as they stand. That would be to resemble the Chinese who, when ship-wrecked on a desert island, made their living by taking in each others' laundry! We must translate if we wish to communicate.

In the second place, the use of analytical philosophy will help us enormously in the way in which we use words. It will enable us to clarify our language, to avoid contradiction, to stop talking sheer nonsense, to look for some kind of referent which will give the necessary verification to what we are saying as Christians. All this is of great importance, lest we fall into the temptation to use high-sounding words as an evasion of difficulties. It has been said that whenever some older theologians got to a hard place they simply quoted a few lines of Wordsworth or Tennyson, thinking that ended the matter; or that they made a few biblical citations as if that were the complete answer; or (at worst), that when the attack was most fierce, they used the word "mystery" as a kind of "escape-hatch." Analytical philosophy is a neutral discipline, for which we may be grateful. But it gives us no working conceptuality for the statement of the theological implications of Christian faith with the claims which that faith makes about "how things really go in the world."

Once more, in the third place, the kind of phenomenological method which is often suggested is of a non-metaphysical type. It is interested only in description, in terms of how living religion, as a matter of deepest intuitive observation, effectively operates in human experience in the world where human beings live. This is valuable; a Van der Leeuw, an Eliade, and others like them can help us a great deal. How does faith function, what embodiments does it have, what attitudes does it demand? These are questions which ought to be answered. . . . But I cannot think that their answer will provide the general conceptuality which we require if Christian faith is to be grounded in the stuff of reality and if the case for it is to be made in a manner which speaks meaningfully to the men and women for whom it exists and to whom it is supposed to address itself.

We are left then with three possibilities: "secular theology," existentialist theology, and process theology. I shall say something about each of them—and as my ordering indicates, I shall come down in favor of the last of the three as offering us the best conceptuality available today as we go forward from "the death of God."

The phrase "secular theology" may be taken to mean either one of two things: either a theology *of* the secular or a theology which *confines itself to* the secular realm. Since I have spoken critically of Dr. Mascall earlier in this chapter I am glad to say here that I believe that he has written admirably about this distinction in the last part of his *Theology and the Future.* He has pointed out that a theology which is strictly *confined* to the world of "here and now" cannot take account of the ultimate questions which people must ask; whereas every sound Christian theology is indeed required to speak of that "here and now" and yet to relate it to God as creative principle and to see God at work in the immediacies of human existence in the whole range of what we style "secular existence." In other words, I agree that Christian faith must see God *in the world* but that it cannot remain content with "the world" as if it exhausted all there is of God. Whitehead once said that "God is in this world or he is nowhere"; that is entirely sound. But Whitehead also said that the world and God are not identical; and I should interpret this utterance, along with others by him, to mean that there is in the divine life an inexhaustibility or transcendence which makes possible the wonderful novelty which the created order manifests, disclosing what Gerard Manley Hopkins named "the dearest freshness deep down things."

In any event, if a "secular" approach to theology thinks that it avoids all metaphysical conceptions, it is profoundly mistaken. Of course one can mean what one wants by the word "metaphysical." If one intends to speak of a grandiose construction in terms of supernatural entities, with a schematic ordering of everything according to some superimposed pattern, metaphysics may well be denied. The present-day attack on metaphysics is probably nothing more than an attack on idealistic constructions of this type, after the fashion (say) of Hegel or Bradley. But metaphysics can also mean—and process thinkers would say that it ought to mean—the inevitable human enterprise of generalizations widely applied, on the basis of a particular point or event or experience taken as "important," to the rest of our experience of the world and the world which we surely experience. It can mean, then, the development of those principles which most adequately express what we experience and know, in the full range of our human encounters; and the result is a "vision" which can be tested by reference back to experience and to the world experienced. Metaphysics in this mode is not some highly speculative system imposed on the world. It is an induction from what is known of the world and also a demand that we act in the world, as Marx rightly insisted. Everybody engages in this, usually in a very naive manner; the philosopher is one who in a more sophisticated and critical manner engages in this attempt at making sense of things, including human experience.

The self-styled "secular theologian" is often doing exactly that. One has only to read Gregor Smith, whose untimely death we all lament, to observe this. Both in *The New Man* and in *Secular Christianity* Gregor Smith was actively setting forth *this* kind of metaphysics, taking as his "important" moment or event the historical encounters of men and women, specifically with Jesus, and from these developing a view of the generalized situation of "man-in-the-world" which, in my sense of the word, is inescapably metaphysical, even if he himself rejected the word and thought that he was also rejecting the enterprise. What he was rejecting, it turns out, was only that "supernaturalistic" species of metaphysics which idealistic philosophers set forth in a pretentious claim to encompass in their thought all things in earth and heaven. Thus "secular" theology in itself does nothing more than deny a particular kind of metaphysics and leaves open to us the possibility of interpreting the secular world, and everything else in human experience, in some other and more appropriate manner. So as I see it, the options which now remain are in fact two: either an existentialist approach or a process thought approach.

The existentialist approach in contemporary English-written theology has been associated with two names: one is Paul Tillich, the other John Macquarrie. I cannot mention the name Tillich without reverence, for that great and good man was a dear friend of mine and I respected, honored, and loved him. His theology was an attempt to combine an existentialist analysis of the human situation with a Christian faith interpreted along the lines of German idealistic thought; he himself confessed that Schelling had been his great master. His method of a correlation of question and faith's answer to the question is, I believe, very suggestive and helpful; his masterly analysis of what it is like to be human is almost beyond criticism. But his final "system," as he used to call it, seems to me to be too abstract to convey the Christian gospel, although in his preaching he was anything but abstract. I think that Professor Macquarrie's efforts, especially in *Principles of Christian Theology,* offer a much more "available" approach for most of us. His insistence that every existential analysis presupposes and includes ontological affirmations seems to me right and sound; his way of using Heideggerian thought is instructive. He takes the biblical images with utmost seriousness and employs them effectively as being determinative of the total picture of God-world-humankind in the light of Jesus Christ.

If I were to make any criticisms of this existentialist mode of theologizing it would be to say that it is not sufficiently regardful of nature, in the strict sense of the physical world and the material stuff of things. And I should add that it lacks something of the dynamism which I believe is required of any Christian theology, not only because of the dynamic quality of biblical thought itself but also (and more significantly) because of the evolutionary way of things which people like Teilhard de Chardin have so insistently pressed upon us. But I confess that *if* I did not find process theology more appealing I should opt for Macquarrie's approach. At the same time I must say that if those two criticisms of mine were met sufficiently, there would not be too much to differentiate his way from the one to which I now turn in conclusion.

It is not necessary for me to outline fully my reasons for preferring process thought. I have already indicated these in my book *Process Thought and the Christian Faith* to which I may perhaps refer any who are interested. . . . It will suffice here if I note that process thought regards the world as a dynamic process of interrelated (and hence social) organisms or entities, whose intentional movement is toward shared good in widest and most inclusive expressions; and that it interprets deity along *those* lines. God is no unmoved mover, nor dictatorial Caesar, nor "ruthless moralist"; God is the cosmic Lover, both causative and affected, "first cause and final effect," as Schubert Ogden has so well phrased it. He is always *related,* hence always *relational;* he is eminently *temporal,* sharing in the ongoing which *is* time. His transcendence is in his sheer faithfulness to himself as love, in his inexhaustibility as lover, and in his capacity for endless adaptation to circumstances in which his love may be active. He does not coerce; he lures and attracts and solicits and invites and then waits for free response from the creaturely agent, using such response (which he has incited by his providing "initial aims") to secure the decisions which enable the agent to make actual his own (the agent's) "subjective aim." In the historical realm and in human life he discloses himself, precisely as love-in-action, in the total event which we name Jesus Christ. Since his love-in-operation is his essential nature—he *is* love, which is his "root-attribute," not *aseity,* as the older theology claimed—the other things said about him (transcendence, immanence, omnipotence, omniscience, omnipresence, righteousness, etc.) are to be understood, as I have already urged, as adverbially descriptive of his *mode of being love,* rather than set up as separate or even as distinct attributions.

We live in a "becoming" world, not in a static machine-like world. And God himself is "on the move." Although he is never surpassed by anything in the creation, he can increase in the richness of his own experience and in the relationships which he has with that creation. He is the *living* God; in that sense, we may say (as the title of a book of mine dared to do) that God is "in process." In other words, the basic point of the biblical images of God as the living, active, loving, righteous, personalizing agent is guaranteed.

But above all, since he is no dictator after the model of Caesar, no self-contained being after the model of the worst sort of person we know, no moralist after the model of the puritanical and negative code-maker, he is truly to be worshipped. Worship means "ascribing worth"; and this we can do only to a lovable because loving One. We cringe before power expressed coercively and arbitrarily; we tremble in the presence of rigid moralism, when we do not react against it in wild and desperate efforts to be ourselves; we can only be puzzled by the kind of absolute essence which is without effects from what goes on around and about it.

But we can worship, truly "ascribe worth," to the perfection or excellence which is love in its eminent and supreme form. God is that; hence he is adorable.

What is more, he is imitable. We are to imitate God. Both Aristotle and Plato said so, while Jesus gave it content by saying that we were to be "like our Father in heaven." When God is known as love-in-action, disclosed as that love by the event in which Jesus is central; when we are caught up into life "in love" (which, if 1 John 4 is right, *is* life "in God"), we are enabled to become what God intends us to be, created lovers who seek to do "the works of love." That is why we are here; that is our destiny—or else Christianity is a fraud.

CHAPTER TWO

Black Theology

Joseph Washington

Writing in the early 1960s, Joseph Washington was critical of black religion in America and believed the solution for black Christians was to close their own houses of worship and be accepted as full-fledged members in the white Christian churches. This selection is taken from his Black Religion. *Boston: Beacon Press, 1964, pp. 279–91.*

If the responsibility of the white communions is to take the lead in declaring the full acceptance of the Negro as a person who should be encountered with respect and welcome as a son or daughter, the responsibility of the Negro is to insist upon this. The time has long since passed when the Negro should defer this basic right and be defensive in the sense of denying that marriage with another regardless of race is his full due. Rather than a plea of miscegenation, the Negro needs only to plea for the right to accept or reject, the right of all persons. It is not miscegenation that the Negro must seek, but full participation in a church which is based upon social intimacies that exclude him. Until this central issue is recognized, acknowledged, and accepted by the Negro, he will not be. Whether or not miscegenation takes place is totally irrelevant. That he is no longer denied full participation in the community of faith is the central unfinished business of the Negro. Heretofore, Negroes have been frustrated in the area of religion because their basic assumption has been that they could achieve community in faith independent of the dominant society. In this frustration, Negro organizations have become defenders of the status quo and victims of personalities and their ambitions.

The real task is for Negroes to enter the community of faith in the knowledge that, in the words of Saint Paul, "God has placed everything under the power of Christ and has set him up as Head of everything for the Church. For the Church is his Body, and in that Body lives fully the One Who fills the whole wide universe." But there are no signs of this dscovery, "for they live blindfold in a world of illusion, and are cut off from the life of God through ignorance and insensitiveness. They have stifled their consciences and then surrendered themselves to sensuality, practicing any form of impurity which lust can suggest." Compartmentalization will be the future until their white brethren welcome all Negroes, even if according to class, into their communities, as "no longer outsiders or aliens, but fellow citizens with every other Christian," a message which the Negro will be suspicious of until his white brother acts so as to live the message which has never been delivered in face-to-face relationships within the intimate chambers of Protestantism: "You, my brother, are not a servant any longer; you are a son." Only within the community of faith will white and black brother know that the central message of the Christian church is decidedly not, "Slaves, obey your human masters sincerely with a proper sense of respect and responsibility, as service rendered to Christ himself not with the idea of currying favor with men, but as servants of Christ conscientiously doing what you believe to be the will of God for you. You may be sure that God will reward a man for good work, irrespectively of whether the man be slave or free. It is this very continuance of the superiority and inferiority overtones of an era gone by which expresses itself in sexual fear of the Negro and in hatred by him of the white man. The message of the Christian faith is a love without fear or hate, and this can only finally be realized through intimate community in depth:

> Love contains no fear—indeed fully-developed love expels every particle of fear, for fear always contains some of the torture of feeling guilty. This means that the man who lives in fear has not yet had his love perfected.
>
> Yes, we love Him because He first loved us. If a man says "I love God" and hates his brother he is a liar. For if he does

not love the brother before his eyes, how can he love the One beyond his sight? And, in any case, it is his explicit command that the one who loves God must love his brother too.

The Negro has sufficient evidence that his European blood and culture relative "hates his brother" and that his Christian community reveals him to be "a liar." Excluded from the Christian faith, the Negro will never be convinced of the "explicit command that one who loves God must love his brother too" until the white guardians of the Christian community take this admonition so seriously as to live by it: "Finish, then, with lying and tell your neighbor the truth. For we are not separate units but intimately related to each other in Christ."

But "separate units" there are, and this means that Negro and white Christians are neither "intimately related to each other in Christ" nor a unity in the one spirit of Christ. This lack of intimacy in the Christian tradition grows out of the lack of intimacy in the movement of Protestantism. The lack of intimacy within the spirit of Protestantism has resulted in the underdevlopment of the Negro in areas other than those of faith, for Protestantism is more than a movement within the church—it is also the dynamic perspective which has profoundly influenced the American society.

In every other sphere of life, he actively seeks full integration, but in religion the Negro within independent and segregated communions is not really interested in decompartmentalization. This lack of openness does not only mean the Negro recognizes that such a movement would destroy a solid area of security—it also means that the Negro does not identify the church as an inclusive community, toward which he must work by going out of business as a racial compartment and a spirit which he cannot know apart from renewal within the sources of the tradition. As a society for religious organization, the Negro congregation has a very definite future; as a community of faith, it has neither past nor future. The religious fellowship, even in middle-class Negro society, represents the last refuge from the social exclusions of culture even as the Negro religious society was the first refuge from the politico-economic exclusion of the previous centuries. The difference between these two reasons for seeking out religious societies is that, having begun to receive politico-economic rewards with limited social benefits, Negroes have no desperate need for the religious society.

The future of segregated Negro and dependent congregations is growth, through education and good organization, into large congregations which will attract communicants from every corner of the urban community—but without depth and objectives. Where there is no point, however minute, of sensitivity and allegiance to the tradition above race and clan, there is no possibility for renewal. To spend time, energy, and money in the vain hope of reconstituting these bodies for purposes other than those which they now attend would not only be of meager value—it would actually be a fatal concern with the symptoms rather than the disease.

Compartmentalization is a past-present-future malaise of such severity that the only real mercy is to allow these symptoms in Negro congregations to die a natural or quick death. What the Negro needs is choice, not restriction. What he wants in religion, as in all of life, is the opportunity to develop in the context of the mainstream—this is the wave of the future beyond immediate generations. He will certainly resist this distant future at the same time that he will know it to be his ultimate intent. Any attempt to shore up religious apartheid is sure to be hardly more than an illusion that the clock can be turned back a hundred years. The immediate future means superficial exchanges on the upper echelons of the denominational hierarchies. Those who perpetuate "the Negro's church" in the present will be many, not a few, Negroes—but they will not have the respect of their peers now or in the future. The spurious Christian notion that, through education, members of the Negro religious community can be held in readiness for the day when they will be accepted into mainstream faith and community lends support to apartheid compartmentalization in religion. Such compartmentalization needs no support, since it functions very well irrespective of interest in the mainstream Christian community. The idea results in the wrong thing for the right reason. Neither Negroes nor their white counterparts will admit that it is no less realistic (though far more relevant) to be engaged in the process of disestablishment through spending energy in the failing efforts that will finally prevail than to succeed in religious compartmentalization that will finally fail.

The immediate future, like the present, will have an increasingly segregated and dependent Negro religious society based on conformity, homogeneity, economic integration, and active affability—largely without variance from white exclusive and private religious clubs. The difference is that the Negro imitation is but a reaction to the other without its possibility of renewal, since the culture has cut the Negro off from communication at the source of renewal. Negro religious societies will continue to differ from their white images in their intent to search for security and wholeness in reaction to the rejection of their contemporaries. These realities, which will continue to constitute a religious groping without the possibility of faith, mean the prevention of seriousness of purpose beyond functional activities devoid of meaning and responsibility. There is no available evidence that factors will emerge to curb the warped potential of these congregations in the search for economic gain rather than freedom from the pressures of technological conformity and mass-mindedness. The possibility of seeking meaning, purpose, relevance, fullness, and authentic identity cannot but continue to be an impossibility for a body forced to seek its equilibrium in the conscious kingdom of race.

Only the marginal man, the outsider, whose experience by accident or design engages him in a vision of the church as meaning and purpose (however its particular form falters in the peculiar locale), will be able to join the Christian community. While the case of the white Christian varies little—he, too, often seeks authenticity beyond the bounds of the Christian fellowship—the white Christian knows that the sick church to which he is committed is not beyond the possibility of renewal, because its Lord is not race but Jesus Christ. The white church may exist to exclude Negroes, but this it does in denial of the church and its faith, while the Negro congregation has nothing but cultural guides to commend this separation, encouraged as it is by racial pride and socioeconomic necessity. The white church exists because of faith in a tradition; the Negro congregation exists because of social conditions which take precedence over faith and tradition—the denial in the former may be turned to affirmation, but the affirmation of the latter must finally be denied.

Increases in numbers as well as compartmentalization among middle-class dependent and segregated assemblies is the wave of the future insofar as Negroes find their way in white-collar jobs. This religious style which distinguishes middle-class from lower-class Negroes is little more than a mode of nonawareness of the church as a responsible influence in public affairs. The Negro middle class is concerned with privacy of religion. Successful Negroes have arrived without the aid of religion, which hardens their understanding of religion as a private affair. They are a step ahead of the less successful by virtue of managerial hierarchies, civil service, and other bureaucratic escalators. Advancement in these areas may free Negroes to work through various organizations for the health of the community, but not within the Christian community for its health. The religious societies are sought by private individuals and families for the "rounding out of life." Private and public life have nothing to do with each other, except that the private area of religion gives encouragement to, but is not involved in, the public sphere. Religion is a collection of individual devotions. Sermons and messages are expected to reflect the current situation in race tension, but to the middle-class Negro there is no conception of a faithful existence through socio-politico-economic structures leavened by a people who faithfully respond in the daily activities. At the other extreme, there is no concern for the approach which claims that spiritual purity is the way to change society and that a mission to others is therefore based upon the religious identity of the individual. In this way, middle-class Negro congregations do not differ from their white branches except at one decisive point. Negro congregations have no theological tradition or basis for correction—the theological idea of the church is not a framework they have ignored, for Negro congregations are cultural societies without reasons for existence other than cultural ones. The privacy of Negro congregations excludes any spiritually ameliorative purpose, and, apart from reaction to their cultural activities, their members find no real purpose.

From the point of view of the Christian faith, Negro bodies are in a very precarious situation. There is no theological judgment urging them to work for an open and inclusive Christian community. It is on tactical grounds that Negro congregations are as rigid against the inclusion of white participants as white communicants are opposed to the inclusion of Negroes except where either body finds it tolerable to accept token numbers. Without a theological undergirding, there is no basis for the doctrine of inclusion (more implicit than explicit in the Christian tradition), nor for discovery of the meaning of life and work and other latent depths in the white middle-class congregations. However feeble, the stirrings for inclusion are centered in white and not Negro congregations—partly because there is a theological dimension which serves as a lever outside the culture.

Self-expression, entertainment, recreation, aid in meeting crises, otherworldly orientation, and the hope of salvation are no more crucial to the middle-class Negro congregation than is the search for meaning and relevance. The real function of these economically integrated religious societies is to witness to the fact that ambition and good fortune are worthy values which are then offered in evidence among persons of a select but segregated community. These congregations contribute to the American apartheid system by their reinforcement of a style of life in a segregated religious society.

Style without depth is insufficient to hold those who feel no loyalty to a racial institution which offers nothing unique. The loss of youth to these congregations is not incompatible with an old religious sentiment in the new garb of organizational activities with precious little relevance for the real issues of life. Instead of perpetuating respectability within the confines of religion, the youth find their outlets in authentic fellowships with rather definite objectives. Thus, the importance of religion declines with the rise of Negroes to the middle class: "There are indications that the next twenty or thirty years will see a wakening of the Negro Protestant churches, but since most members of the other major groups are unwilling to establish primary-type relations with Negroes, it seems unlikely that the development will weaken the internal solidarity of the group."

It is the loss of the vitality of youth and their imagination to the Negro congregations which indicates the quality of these religious communities. The loss of youth is not peculiar to Negro congregations, but the tendency for Negro youth to abandon religion is even greater than in white churches. Increasing education and sophistication, along with the separation from white peers in this singular area of life are contributing elements. Moreover, religion viewed as a reservoir to be individually tapped and allowed to surge forth when needed, or when ritualistic rhythms of life demand, means that the religion of the Negro does not speak to its youth. Indeed, Negro religion is of importance chiefly to the older generations, who need activities to vary their monotonous routines—with the number of elder citizens, the continued existence of compartmentalized religion is assured.

The Negro middle-class and dependent congregations are the most secure and least revolutionary religious group. In this religion, which avoids faith and seeks privacy, there are no cross-currents *vis-à-vis* the mainstream. The growing middle class in religion is not antiwhite, just realistically Negro. There is no deep resentment nor movement for change. If the Christian faith is understood, it is seen as the white man's peculiarity, and the repudiation of the Christian community as a theological way of life is not an act of aggression. It is a misunderstanding of religion as the private sphere for control and security. Negroes have historically viewed religion differently from their white peers. Disestablishment of Negro congregations and their decompartmentalization concerns middle-class religionists least of all. Excluding religion, the middle class is the most excited about integration and the least open to entertainment of assimilation of all Negro classes, since its members see segregation as the path for all Negroes in the intimate spheres of life.

Indifference to assimilation and affirmation of integration means that the middle-class independent and segregated Negro religious societies are oblivious to the fact that the Negro minority as a minority cannot participate in the fullness of society without merger with the spirit of the majority, wherein its racial identity is lost. Integration means maintenance of the Negro identity, which takes precedence over the Christian faith and community in favor of compartmentalization. The very fact that the middle-class Negro now settles for integration supported by laws, justice, and respect for human dignity widely accepted in the culture means that this attitude will be carried out in religion. And while the Negro will gain opportunities to advance in economic endeavors, this success will reinforce the illusion that religious integration may be equally successful—when, in reality, without replacing racial identity with the identity of faith in community, there can be neither openness to the Christian tradition, nor renewal.

The responsibility of all Negro congregations which exist because of racial ties is to go out of business. The total revolution in which the Negro is involved has only begun. It will be hampered by educational and economic deprivation, housing restrictions, and social exclusion, yet in all these areas the Negro has access to legal and moral resources. But if he is to be included in the Christian community, he will have to work at it virtually alone.

Thus far the revolution has taken place outside the context of the religious community. It is incumbent upon the Negro now to close his houses of worship and enter the white congregations of his choice en masse. This may be impossible in large areas of the South today; it may be impractical in many urban areas where white Protestants are in flight from the Negro. But it can begin in all the small towns and medium cities of the North and West where Negro congregations are obviously inadequate and lack vital leadership. Such a movement may need to begin with Negro youth, who have the least to lose and the most to gain. It is assumed that the separation of the races in the congregations is not the will of the denominations but the intention of the local congregations. Negroes will need to impress upon these congregations their seriousness by their presence at worship, application for membership, and committee involvement. Wherever he travels, the Negro must make a point of worshiping with his white brethren. In resort towns and suburban communities, the Negro will need to go out of his way to participate in worship.

In this way, both the historical and contemporary functions of religion in Negro meeting houses may be preserved. Historically, the meeting house was the congregation for freedom and justice and equality. Presently, it is the place of community and social identity. Negroes would be free to use these centers openly for social action and community fellowship.

Without some voluntary sacrifice of the unessential areas of its past for the essential life of the future, the Negro congregation will simply wither away, a liability rather than an asset to the spirit and the community.

A religious life which is not rooted in the structure of society is ultimately transitory and ineffective. Moreover, the religious perspective which is rooted in the history of a people provides a creative dimension even when it is rejected. Negroes have yet to learn that the Christian faith is the warp and woof of the Western world, and to be excluded from this sphere is to be preempted of full participation in its ethos. Participation in the Christian community is the *sine qua non* of contributing to that society. Without admission to the Christian community, Negroes may be able to change the external structures of democracy, or help them to be realized, but this does not lead to a sense of responsibility and the imperative of contributing to the social milieu. The religion of the Negro has proved that religion is indispensable, whether relevant or irrelevant.

However, militant direct action for participation in the Christian community does not mean that the Negro has to accept the non-Christian tenor of Christian communities. In fact, not only is it true that unauthentic Christian communities can only be changed from within, but it is also true that the Negro provides the greatest opportunity for narrowing the gap between principle and practice. By his very racial difference, he can be a permanent revolutionary within the church, providing the creative tension necessary to sharpen the teeth of justice in the community of love. Insofar as he is isolated from the white community, the Negro is under no pressure to foster a truly dynamic fellowship, but the very process of demanding acceptance within that community forces both Negroes and whites to come to grips with the mission and message of the Christian church.

By voluntarily giving up their segregated worship life, Negroes would be taking the offensive. This burial of the old forms in order that new ones might be reborn would contribute to the purpose of the Church and America. Were Negroes to be assimilated into the Christian community, they would gain much and add new life.

But if Negroes do not take the offensive and demand assimilation in the Christian community, their gains in material goods will hardly be matched by spiritual growth. Separate and segregated worship centers may well continue as the symbol if impoverishment of a segment of the society in all things essential. The choice between being a part of the whole or attempting to be a whole apart is the decision of the Negro. It is within his power to begin the long process of assimilation into the Christian community and therefore the American society, from strength, declaring not that he wishes to have what the white community has nor his intention to be like white people; rather, his declaration must be that alone and separated; white and black America are antagonists of the American dream and the Christian community.

James Cone

Until 1969, however, there had been no overall coherent theological interpretation of black power. James Cone was the first to articulate a black theology consistent with the claims of black power. This selection is taken from his Black Theology and Black Power. *New York: The Seabury Press, 1969, pp. 1-2, 42-43, 56, 68-69, 83, 117-18, 151-52.*

Black Power is an emotionally charged term which can evoke either angry rejection or passionate acceptance. Some critics reject Black Power because to them it means black hating whites, while others describe it as the doctrine of Booker T. Washington in contemporary form. But the advocates of Black Power hail it as the only viable option for black people. For these persons, Black Power means black people taking the dominant role in determining the black-white relationship in American society.

If, as I believe, Black Power is the most important development in American life in this century, there is a need to begin to analyze it from a theological perspective. In this work, an effort is made to investigate the concept of Black Power, placing primary emphasis on its relationship to Christianity, the church, and contemporary American theology.

I know that some religionists would consider Black Power as the work of the Antichrist. Others would suggest that such a concept should be tolerated as an expression of Christian love to the misguided black brother. It is my thesis, however, that Black Power, even in its most radical expression, is not the antithesis of Christianity, nor is it a heretical idea to be tolerated with painful forbearance. It is, rather, Christ's central message to twentieth-century America. And unless the empirical denominational church makes a determined effort to recapture the man Jesus through a total identification with the suffering poor as expressed in Black Power, that church will become exactly what Christ is not.

That most churches see an irreconcilable conflict between Christianity and Black Power is evidenced not only by the de facto segregated structure of their community, but by their typical response to riots: "I deplore the violence but sympathize with the reasons for the violence." Churchmen, laymen, and ministers alike apparently fail to recognize their contribution to the ghetto condition through permissive silence—except for a few resolutions which they usually pass once a year or immediately following a riot—and through their cotenancy of a dehumanizing social structure whose existence depends on the continued enslavement of black people. If the church is to remain faithful to its Lord, it must make a decisive break with the structure of this society by launching a vehement attack on the evils of racism in all forms. It must become *prophetic,* demanding a radical change in the interlocking structures of this society.

This work, then, is written with a definite attitude, the attitude of an angry black man, disgusted with the oppression of black people in America and with the scholarly demand to be "objective" about it. Too many people have died, and too many are on the edge of death. In fairness to my understanding of the truth, I cannot allow myself to engage in a dispassionate, noncommitted debate on the status of the black-white relations in America by assessing the pro and con of Black Power. . . .

With reference, then, to freedom in Christ, three assertions about Black Power can be made: First, the work of Christ is essentially a liberating work, directed toward and by the oppressed. Black Power embraces that very task. Second, Christ, in liberating the wretched of the earth, also liberates those responsible for the wretchedness. The oppressor is also freed of his peculiar demons. Black Power is shouting yes to black humanness and no to white oppression is exorcizing demons on both sides of the conflict. Third, mature freedom is burdensome and risky, producing anxiety and conflict for free men and for the brittle structures they challenge. The call for Black Power is precisely the call to shoulder the burden of liberty in Christ, risking everything to live not as slaves but as free men. . . .

It seems that the mistake of most whites, religionists included, is their insistence on telling blacks how to respond "as Christians" to racism, insisting that nonviolence is the only appropriate response. But there is an ugly contrast between the sweet, nonviolent language of white Christians and their participation in a violently unjust system. Maybe the oppressor's being is too warped by his own view of himself that every analysis made by him merely reveals his own inflated self-evaluation. Certainly, as long as he can count on blacks remaining nonviolent by turning the other cheek and accepting the conditions of slavery, there will be no real pressure to confront the black man as a person. If he can be sure that blacks will not threaten his wealth, his superiority, his power in the world, there will be no need to give up his control of the black man's destiny.

One cannot help but think that most whites "loved" Martin Luther King, Jr., not because of his attempt to free his people, but because his approach was the least threatening to the white power structure. Thus, churchmen and theologians grasped at the opportunity to identify with him so that they could keep blacks powerless and simultaneously appease their own guilt about white oppression. It was only a few years back that King's name was even more radical than that of Rap Brown or Stokely Carmichael. At that time, the question was being asked whether civil disobedience was consistent with Christianity. What whites really want is for the black man to respond with that method which best preserves white racism. All this suggests that white judgments about Christian love related to Black Power are as suspect as their other judgments relative to black America. . . .

Where is "the opening" that Christ provides? Where does he lead his people? Where indeed, if not in the ghetto. He meets the black where they are and becomes one of them. We see him there with his black face and big black hands lounging on a street corner. "Oh, but surely Christ is above race." But society is not raceless, any more than when God became a despised Jew. White liberal preference for a raceless Christ serves only to make official and orthodox the centuries-old portrayal of Christ as white. The "raceless" American Christ has a light skin, wavy brown hair, and sometimes— wonder of wonders—blue eyes. For whites to find him with big lips and kinky hair is as offensive as it was for the Pharisees to find him partying with tax collectors. But whether whites want to hear it or not, *Christ is black, baby,* with all of the features which are so detestable to white society.

To suggest that Christ has taken on a black skin is not theological emotionalism. If the church is a continuation of the Incarnation, and if the church and Christ are where the oppressed are, then Christ and his church must identify totally with the oppressed to the extent that they too suffer for the same reasons persons are enslaved. In America, blacks are oppressed because of their blackness. It would seem, then, that emancipation could only be realized by Christ and his church becoming black. Thinking of Christ as nonblack in the twentieth century is as theologically impossible as thinking of him as non-Jewish in the first century. . . .

More often, however, theologians simply ignore the problem of color in America. Any theologian involved in professional societies can observe that few have attempted to deal seriously with the problem of racism in America. It is much easier to deal with the textual problems associated with some biblical book or to deal "objectively" with a religious phenomenon than it is to ask about the task of theology in the current disintegration of society. It would seem that it is time for theology to make a radical break with its identity with the world by seeking to bring to the problem of color the revolutionary implications of the Gospel of Christ. It is time for theology to leave its ivory tower and join the real issues, which deal with dehumanization of blacks in America. It is time for theologians to relate their work to life-and-death issues, and in so doing to execute its function of bringing the church to a recognition of its task in the world. . . .

Black theology must take seriously the reality of black people—their life of suffering and humiliation. This must be the point of departure of all God-talk which seeks to be black-talk. When that man is black and lives in a society permeated with white racist power, he can speak of God only from the perspective of the socioeconomic and political conditions unique to black people. Though the Christian doctrine of God must logically precede the doctrine of man, black theology knows that black people can view God only through black eyes that behold the brutalities of white racism. To ask them to assume a "higher" identity by denying their blackness is to require them to accept a false identity and to reject reality as they know it to be.

The task of black theology, them, is *to analyze the black man's*

condition in the light of God's revelation in Jesus Christ with the
purpose of creating a new understanding of black dignity among
black people, and providing the necessary soul in that people, to
destroy white racism. Black theology is primarily a theology *of* and
for black people who share the common belief that racism will be
destroyed only when black people decide to say in word and deed
to the white racist: "We ain't gonna stand any more of this." The
purpose of black theology is to analyze the nature of the Christian
faith in such a way that black people can say yes to blackness and
no to whiteness and mean it.

It is not the purpose of black theology to address white people,
at least not directly. Though whites may read it, understand it, and
even find some meaning in it, black theology is not dependent on
white perception. It assumes that the possibilities of creative response among white people to black humiliation are virtually
nonexistent. What slim possibilities there are belong only to those
whites who are wholly committed to the activity of destroying
racism in the structure of the white community. The goal of Black
Theology is to prepare the minds of blacks for freedom so that they
will be ready to give all for it. Black theology must speak *to* and *for*
black people as they seek to remove the structures of white power
which hover over their being, stripping it of its blackness.

Because black theology has as its starting point the black condition, this does not mean that it denies the absolute revelation of
God in Christ. Rather, it means that black theology firmly believes
that God's relevation in Christ can be made supreme only by
affirming Christ as he is alive in black people today. Black theology
is Christian theology precisely because it has the black predicament
as its point of departure. It calls upon black people to affirm God
because he has affirmed us. His affirmation of black people is made
known not only in his election of oppressed Israel, but more especially in his coming to us and being rejected in Christ for us. The
event of Christ tells us that the oppressed blacks are his people
because, and only because, they represent who he is. . . .

The problem with white society is that it wants to assume that
everything is basically all right. It wants black people to assume
that slavery never existed, and the present brutalities inflicted on
them are the working of isolated individuals and not basically a

part of the system itself. In this sense, reconciliation would mean admitting that white values are the values of God. It means black people accepting the white way of life. It assumes that black people have no values except those which are given by the white masters.

But according to black theology, it is the other way around. Reconciliation does not transcend color, thus making us all white. The problem of values is not that white people need to instill values in the ghetto; but white society itself needs values so that it will no longer need a ghetto. Black values did not create the ghetto; white values did. Therefore, God's Word of reconciliation means that we can only be justified by becoming black. Reconciliation makes us all black. Through this radical change, we become identified totally with the suffering of the black masses. It is this fact that makes all white churches anti-Christian in their essence. To be Christian is to be one of those whom God has chosen. God has chosen black people!

It is to be expected that many white people will ask: "How can I, a *white* man, become black? My skin is white and there is nothing I can do." Being black in America has very little to do with skin color. To be black means that your heart, your soul, your mind, and your body are where the dispossessed are. We all know that a racist structure will reject and threaten a black man in white skin as quickly as a black man in black skin. It accepts and rewards whites in black skins nearly as well as whites in white skins. Therefore, being reconciled to God does not mean that one's skin is physically black. It essentially depends on the color of your heart, soul, and mind. Some may want to argue that persons with skins physically black will have a running start on others; but there seems to be enough evidence that though one's skin is black, the heart may be lily white. The real questions are: Where is your identity? Where is your being? Does it lie with the oppressed blacks or with the white oppressors? Let us hope that there are enough to answer this question correctly so that America will not be compelled to acknowledge a common humanity only by seeing that blood is always one color. . . .

Deotis Roberts

Deotis Roberts believed, however, that a black Christ would be as parochial as a yellow or white Christ. He included reconciliation between blacks and whites as an indispensable dimension of Christian liberation. This selection is taken from his Liberation and Reconciliation: A Black Theology. *Philadelphia: Westminster Press, 1971, pp. 137–40, 151–52, 153–54, 176–78, 189–91.*

The visualization of Christ as black may enable the black man to have a real encounter with himself and God through Christ. The black man has in the black Messiah a savior. He discovers his own dignity and pride in a self-awareness that is rooted in black consciousness. Christ conceived in a black image is one of us and in a real sense he becomes our Lord and our God. Like Thomas, the doubter, the black man may now cry out in pride and joy to the black Messiah, "My Lord and my God!" His experience does not preclude the possibility that others may have the same vital experience in a varied ethnic and cultural setting. The black Messiah is also the universal Word made flesh. I do not support the view that Christ is *actually* black in a literal-historical sense. Therefore, I wish to disassociate myself from Cleage's attempt to establish a literal black Messiah on historical grounds.

The appearance of a black Madonna in Europe is *art*. But the appearance of the same symbol, to blacks in Africa or America in search of a savior, is religion. The interpretation of the former is *aesthetics,* while the understanding of the latter is *theology*. It follows that I do not suggest that white people repent for worshiping a Christ in their own image to worship one in my likeness. The worship of a white Christ has dehumanized black men. The worship of a black Christ, for the same reason, would dehumanize the white man. We would be confronted with a false identity in both instances, and thus to exchange one false identity for another would not be an improvement. To overcome the charge of fostering separatism as an end in itself, I will suggest that this could be done for a *different reason*—for reconciliation between equals. The former (the adoration of a black Messiah by blacks) is for *liberation*—to enable an oppressed people to go free. If white Christians can

overcome color consciousness and the inferiority-superiority syndrome associated with it to the extent that they are able to worship
a black Christ, then perhaps reconciliation is nearer than we first
believed. There is too much pathology in this society, however, for
the theologian to recommend further sickness. If the reason for
suggesting that white people worship a black Christ is because of
what a white Christ has or has not meant to the black man, then
our motive would appear to be revenge or punishment. This is a
negative approach to a black Messiah. This is not a proper motive
for a worthy Christological statement. Only unhealthy whites, characterized by a masochistic enjoyment of being abused and dominated
as a release from the torment of a guilt-ridden spirit, will be impressed by this interpretation. There would, on our part, be an
element of sadism if the intention were merely to "repay whites"
or inflict pain. Reconciliation between equals based upon mutual
respect is the only premise upon which blacks and whites may
transcend the "skin color" of Christ and thereby worship the universal Christ. The experience of reconciliation is not pathological
but "holing" and healing to the reconciled.

A universal Christ will be as "existential" to red, yellow, and
black people as he is to white people. One of the reasons why I
would resist the affirmation of a black Christ to the exclusion of a
white Christ is that this would likewise exclude a yellow Christ and
other skin colors in which the existential Christ may confront men
in a cultural-historical setting. Many oppressed people in the Third
World are not white, but they need the Christ of the oppressed just
as much as we do. In our present excitement over Pan-Africanism,
we should not forget that large numbers of colored oppressed people are not in Africa or North America, but in Asia, Latin America,
and the islands around the globe. If we give our Christology the
right shape, we may be helpful in making Christ the "Desire of all
nations." In one sense, Christ must be said to be universal and
therefore colorless. Only in a symbolic or mythical sense, then,
must we understand the black Messiah in the context of the black
religious experience.

A symbol participates in that which it symbolizes while it also
points beyond itself as mere symbol. Against this assertion, we may
make certain affirmations. The black Christ participates in the
black experience. In some sense, Christ makes contact with what

the black Christian is aware of in his unique history and personal experience. He *encounters* Christ *in* that experience and is *confronted* by the claims of Christ also in his black experience. But at the same time, the *confrontation* of the black Christian with the black Messiah, who is also the *universal* Christ, points him beyond the mere symbolism that is rooted in his experience. In other words, the universal Christ is particularized for the black Christian in the black experience of the black Messiah, but the black Messiah is at the same time universalized in the Christ of the Gospels who meets all men in their situation. The *black Messiah* liberates the black man. The universal Christ *reconciles* the black man with the rest of mankind. . . .

There is a need to discover a black Messiah, a black Christ, according to Bishop Johnson, because the white Christ of the white church is the enemy of the black man. This Christ is the oppressor of the black man. Thus, the black preacher and the black scholar are duty-bound "to discover Christ in his image of blackness." To this end, black scholars must not abandon the Christian faith or the biblical record; they must reread the Bible and they must "detheologize" the faith so that the Christian message will speak to their situation with "a disturbing clarity." He tells us somewhat what detheologizing demands. We must rediscover the humanity of Jesus. He refers to the "Jesus [who] was born in a barn, wrapped in a blanket used for sick cattle, and placed in a stall. He died on a city dump outside Jerusalem."

Jesus is the Liberator. The Theological Commission of the National Committee of Black Churchmen, in its Atlanta document of June, 1969, to which Bishop Johnson and the present writer made a contribution, declared Christ to be "the Liberator" and black theology to be "the theology of black liberation." But the statement says little about reconciliation. It does say, however, that insofar as blacks are liberated, whites will "affirm" their own humanity. Black theology has an awesome task. While we speak *externally* to liberation from white oppression, we must speak *internally* to liberation from white oppression, we must speak *internally* to the need for forgiveness from sin and exploitation within our own group life. Black theology must speak of liberation within from black men and liberation from without from white men. But, at the same time, it must speak of reconciliation that brings black men together and of reconciliation that brings black and white mean together both in a multiracial fellowship of the Body of Christ and within the world where a multiracial society must be built.

This means that Christ the Liberator is also Christ the Reconciler. Christ is the one "who brings us together." We remember the promises of President Nixon as he sought the highest office in the nation. His promise was "to bring us together." Within a few months after his election, we discovered that we had never been so far apart. Perhaps this was only a "political promise," which no one should have taken seriously in the first place. Perhaps it was a promise based upon lack of foresight, lack of resources, and lack of knowledge. All human promises are fallible and finite. But in and through Christ, God promises "to bring us together." This is a promise he *can* and *will* keep. Christ liberates, but he also reconciles men to God and man to man.

His cross is a reconciling cross. Black Christians have borne their cross through the years. They know the meaning of unmerited suffering. They now can carry on a ministry of reconciliation across the generations and between races and nations—and become agents of healing in a broken world. . . .

This leads us to say that when we discover Christ as the black Messiah, as the one who enters into our black experience, the meaning of his cross and our suffering are reconciliation. The reconciliation of man to man, through the reconciliation of man to God, releases the healing power of the cross of Christ into this anxious, broken, and bitter world. Only redeemed men can serve as agents of reconciliation. All who would serve as reconcilers must themselves be men of integrity. On the cross, Christ gives himself to mankind. Black men and women, reconciled to God through the cross of Christ, but who through their suffering, their own cross bearing, share the depth of his suffering, are purified, mellowed, and heightened in sensitivity and compassion. Thus healed and released in their own life, they may now become healers of other men. The God, who through Christ reconciles the world to himself, sends us forth to be agents of reconciliation. To such a witness in a broken world, black men may not only be "called," but, indeed, "chosen."

While other scholars continue upon the quest for the "historical Jesus" and as they continue the "new quest," the black theologian's quest is for the black Messiah, the Liberator of his people, the Reconciler of man to God and man to man. Our search has led us to our situation. Others will find him in theirs. In the end, we long for the universal Christ, who will not only set us free, but bring us together. Albert Schweitzer, who found the Christ, not in intellectual research for his quest of the historical Jesus but in his service as medical missionary in Africa, sums up the nature of our quest of the Jesus of history who is also the Christ of faith:

> He comes to us as One unknown, without a name, as of old, by the lake-side. He came to those men who knew him not. He speaks to us the same word: "Follow thou me!" and sets us to the tasks which He has to fulfill for our time. He commands. And to those who obey Him, whether they be wise or simple, He will reveal Himself in the toils, the conflicts, the sufferings which they shall pass through in His fellowship, and, as an ineffable mystery, they shall learn in their own experience Who He is.

It is important to state presently the goal of black-white relations as I view them against the background of my statement of black theology. It do not advocate integration as a goal. Integration is a goal set by whites and is still based upon the superordination-subordination principle of whites over blacks, even blacks with superior education and experience to whites under whom they must live and serve. In any situation where whites write the agenda for integration, whether in government, business, education, industry—even religion, this is what integration means. The slave-master, servant-boss, inferior-superior mentality underlies all integration schemes in which whites write the agenda. *This is the reason why I am against integration.* Black and white relations should be interracial. This allows for two-way participation in the interaction between the races. It overcomes the self-hate implicit in the belief that all whites are superior to all blacks just because white is inherently better than black. Positively, it enables blacks to appreciate their own heritage to the extent that they consider it a worthy commodity to be shared with others. In this manner, *liberation leads to reconciliation between equals.* This position is productive of the psychological and sociological health of blacks. It is needed for a right perspective for better race relations. It is consistent with an understanding of God as lovingly just, the dignity of all men, the sinfulness of all men, and their reconciliation with God and with one another through Jesus Christ.

I am equally opposed to separatism as an end in itself. Separatism is at best only a temporary solution. Just as rugged individualism is giving way to a more socialized economy and strict nationalism of new nations is melting under the weight of the interdependence of nations in a nuclear age and in the time of world history, even so separatism's days are numbered in race relations. It is frankly more rhetoric than reality and it is rather foolish not to be able to see the difference; for we must live or coexist in a multiracial and culturally pluralistic society until and unless we solve the "land" question. It seems that the interracial view offers a more lasting as well as a just solution to the race problem if it can become operative in a massive way. If every merger of black and white institutions can begin with equity as a basis of their union, then we may avoid a lot of undoing and redoing. Henceforth, mergers must be undertaken in such a way as to overcome the powerlessness of blacks. All mergers must be intercultural and based upon equal dignity of all persons involved. A black cultural nationalism can tie into this interracial stance. . . .

Now, every black man who remembers his past and knows his present understands the anger, frustration, even the violence of blacks in the protest against injustice. All who understand do not advocate violent protest. I happen to believe that violence is pragmatically wrong-headed. Violence usually begets violence, and our foe is infinitely more capable of inflicting pain and destruction than we are. Even gains based on fear of violence are spotty, temporary, and surface. Whites who respond to violence do so *negatively* rather than *constructively.* If they operate by the crisis-response motive, they do just enough to stop the violence and await the next wave of violence. What we need is a constructive, deeply motivated, long-range, massive reorientation in black-white relations. Only "crusaders without violence" can heal as well as disrupt and destroy. Even blacks themselves are not safe in the hands of those who hate sufficiently to destroy whites. Hate is blind whether it comes from black or white men. Violence does not meet even the pragmatic test. Pragmatism holds that "truth is workability." The workability of violence as a means to a better position for blacks is in question. As one who has seen the stark face of racial violence in several major cities and observed close up the tragic aftermath for blacks (even at the hands of their own soul brothers), I have yet to be convinced of the pragmatic test of violence.

Violence, I believe, is inconsistent with the Christian ethic. Here I condemn violence that is *covert* or *overt,* violence of blacks against blacks, and violence of whites against blacks. For this reason, I do not believe that it is all right for blacks to be violent to whites because whites have been violent to blacks. Here, as in all instances, "two wrongs will not make a right"; for between right and wrong there is a difference of *kind* and not merely of *degree.* Those who argue for counterviolence, even self-defense, encourage the hatemongers, black and white. Blacks who speak of counterviolence do not distinguish between covert and overt violence. They, therefore, would justify the most rampant form of overt violence as repayment for the violence of whites against blacks whether overt or covert. There have been and are situations in our world in which violent revolution may be the lesser of two evils and the only path to liberation for millions of humans. The history of such violent upheavals indicates that the masses seldom profit from the wholesale slaughter and injustice merely changes hands. The nonviolent revolution led by Gandhi in India and the several bloodless coups in Pakistan are far more productive. I understand Nat Turner's insurrection and Bonhoeffer's plot to assassinate Hitler as springing from righteous indignation—as the only obvious path open to freedom and justice for millions. The cases of South Africa and some Latin American countries have given rise to "theologies of revolution" in which naked violence is proposed as being divinely ordered.

If violence of this type is ever consistent with Christian ethics, it will need to be *programmed* and *measured.* It should be a means rather than an end. It should be used only after all *better alternatives* have been duly tried and it should be used only because it is the lesser of two evils. As dark as the racial conflict is in this country, I do not believe that we face a situation as bleak as slavery, death camps, or even South Africa. There is still enough goodwill among blacks and whites to seek out more constructive progress in racial understanding and the removal of injustices against blacks. Our understanding of God, man, and the moral life requires us to seek out the very best means to overcome racial strife. The matter is urgent and it is serious. The only thing necessary for evil men to take over is for good men (black and white) to do nothing. A great deal depends upon what whites will do as well as what blacks will not do. Black men can no longer tolerate conditions as they are, having affirmed their dignity. It is not the wise thing for whites to counsel the blacks to be patient, but to move White Power to correct the hurt and the wrongs visited too long upon the black brother. Blacks must be liberated. There is no shortcut to reconciliation that does not pass through liberation. There can be no reconciliation that does not include equity. If reconciliation is a proper Christian goal, and I am convinced it is, then violence that destroys the one who is a party to the reconciliation is not a good means. There can be no reconciliation between the dead—at least, not in this life. Violence begets violence rather than goodwill. The result of violence can only be a bloodbath which will be self-defeating as well as self-destructive for blacks. And even though such "black rage" could seriously disrupt the entire nation, it would not be productive of the ends that are being sought in the struggle.

Major Jones

Major Jones, like Roberts, criticized James Cone's separatism, his contention that God is only on the side of the blacks. He raised the possibility that the extremists among the black theologians were more interested in an ideology of revolution and less concerned with God's involvement in that struggle. This selection is taken from his Black Awareness: A Theology of Hope. *New York: Abingdon Press, 1971, pp. 115–18, 127–31.*

The black awareness search for God has been somewhat rationalistic in approach, and it seems to seek a refinement upon the notion of divinity. In the search to reinterpret the concept of God, or the object of that concept, in black art forms, the very character of God is being altered, so that the idea of God, for the black community, is becoming more and more identical with a personal and yet infinite and eternal Being. God, for the black awareness movement, is now no longer a totally transcendent deity, but a Divinity immanent in the black man's struggle. But then religion, for the black church, has never traditionally been merely theoretical and speculative; it has been practical as well. The God of the black man has had to distill and purify the dark experience of brutal oppression. Thus, the search for God, for the black man, has never been a mere intellectual pastime; rather, it has been the result of an inner struggle, and it has been pursued with great and difficult effort. It is against the background of such a search that the black community is now coming to seek a God who is no longer the God of the white oppressor.

One wonders, however, what this altering of God's color will do for the black man. Will it make him, as a mature religious person, any more responsible with the use of his newly acquired black power than the white man was with his white power? Will the black man, with his black God, be a better man than the white man was with his white God? The deeper question may be, Will black man, as God's chosen, act any better than white man has acted? Indeed, is not the idea of God, no matter what his color, an indispensable prerequisite for man's ethical being? . . . One realizes that in much of the black community the suggestion of such a position may be unacceptable to a large segment of black readers, especially those who are strong adherents of black power.

Those who advocate black awareness, and who would adhere to separatism as a means of achieving a true selfhood and the ultimate realization of authentic black self-identity, often ignore the fact that the humanity of man is much deeper than color. It is true that there is great need for the strengths that can be derived from all that is good in the civil-rights struggle. It is true that there is need for the self-esteem that black awareness teaches. But the ultimate manhood or personhood sought should be, under God, fully human. The deeper question is whether it is possible for God to acquire color without becoming identified with that which is too narrow to be fully representative of the total human family, much less that which is divine. All that we know in man is relative, but that which we conceive in God is normative. This is the inherent danger in representing God in any human conception, either concrete or abstract.

The much greater danger in all the current tendency on the part of advocates of black awareness to recolor God is that in the process of recoloring, those who do so may well alter the very concept of being itself. And in so doing, the God of black awareness may become a mere idol god of a folk religion, a god who is only interested in the welfare of a black people, a god who will deliver a special people from a special oppressor. It must be remembered that folk religion, even without a clearly identified god concept, can foster brotherhood, social solidarity, and many other things that are now being promoted within the black community.

Many adherents of the Christian tradition, especially those who have long since been mature enough not to relate God to any particular color, see the danger of the religion of black awareness becoming a cultural manifestation, with God as true living Reality colored out and replaced by a more narrowly conceived God of group interest. The religion of the black community would then be a cult of black awareness, void of true redemptive mission.

If the traditional Christian Gospel of the black church is to survive within the black community, then it must assume its rightful responsibility in the liberation of the black man. If this unique role is to be assumed, the Gospel of the black church must address itself to the following problems, which are live options at every level of community structure.

First of all, the Gospel must address itself to the problems of changing the connotation of blackness in relation to a black people. Blackness, as a concept, has too long been related to all that is unclean, degraded, and undesirable.

Second, the concept of blackness has also acquired some theological meanings which, when applied to persons, are degrading morally and spiritually. The Bible has been used in the process of dehumanizing people, because it has served as a proof text for inequality. Evil and sin have become so much associated with blackness that it is no wonder black people are associated with uncleanliness or wickedness almost unconsciously within the minds of many white Christians. This means that the Gospel must address itself to the radical task of building a new structure of language symbols for the concept of blackness so as to offset the almost unconscious tendency to apply it, in its degrading sense, to human beings.

Third, the Gospel of black awareness must find a new language of hope for the ghetto, a new language of the people, understood by the people, to the end that it will indeed be the good news of liberation and of radical change. It must be a language that will generate a kind of race pride that will make a difference in all aspects of life, conduct, and attitude. Much of the language of the black-awareness movement is of the people; this is why is has the potential of such a great appeal.

Finally, no Gospel of black awareness should ignore the basic tenets of the Judeo-Christian faith. To do so would be merely to establish a folk religion that would not survive the test of history. The Gospel must seek always to clarify the issues that are in focus in the struggle, while at the same time adhering to the faith tradition. If a new theological language of black awareness is not found which will give meaning and validity to the movement beyond that which is now implied, then the present trends will continue, and the black man will have lost the God who brought him over so many difficult places in the past. . . .

In a very real sense, an adequate hope for the black community must rest upon a God concept that will embrace or catch up in its meaning all the aspirations of the black man for the now and for the not-yet of the future. When a black man or any man seeks a God without hope or a future without God, not only is the foundation of his hope in danger, but the very structure of human existence is being assailed. In an age of collectivism, when the tendency is to translate individual hope into the social process, there is a danger that many who adhere to violence will see the ultimate goals of black aspiration as being worthy of the sacrifice of individual life and concerns. Religion as hope is the human quest for fulfillment beyond the present experiences of alienation and destruction within each individual, and within the collective life. Black religion as hope is also related to the possibility of black man's becoming truly fulfilled beyond the deformities of his past. Such a past, rooted in the black experience, and a present, pregnant with hope, calls him to the future, especially beyond the inevitability of his current despair. Indeed, do not man's hopes, if they are rooted in an adequate concept of God for his time, always burst open his present, driving him beyond existing frontiers to search the horizons for an ever-new reality? If man does not hope or need to hope, then what sense does it make for anyone to speak of God? If the God conceived is not adequate, if there are no needs in man and his world which still cry out to be filled, or if all needs can adequately be filled by man himself, then either God has become obsolete or the day of total human fulfillment has already arrived. If there is no hope in the black community, then the question of God will not even arise. Any God who is invoked as the answer to human needs, no matter what they are, is irrelevant in a world that has grown beyond the point of a sense of needing him.

The goals of the black-awareness movement will fall far short of fulfillment if the movement is not rooted in a God of the future. He must be a God who is strong enough to determine the outcome of the future both within and beyond history. There is no future in a God who, at any point, gives up his creation. For God to be adequate for the now and the not-yet of the black man's future, he must transcend the now and and the not-yet in history. He must be a God who is active on man's behalf; he must be a God who is himself engaged in the cosmic battle with evil. If he is thought to be so related to man, then the problem of evil is put on a totally different plane. In the black community, God's righteousness is his power in relation to men who are not in the right, who do not do what is right, who violate the rights of others in self-righteous aggression, who rob God of his rights, his due, by putting him down in their pride. This is not the way many black men see the white man's God.

The image of God's reality and of his future becomes present only where righteousness reigns on earth. The core of his righteousness is justice infused with love. Where God's love is not able to do its work freely, it employs other means such as protest, instruments of law, threats, and punishments. At many points in history, God puts on the ugly mask of his wrath to pressure people to satisfy the needs of others, even when they do not feel like it. Indeed, it is all too true that men, white or black, often do not freely live for others; they too often live for themselves. The future of God, if properly conceived, rejects as its adversary everything and everybody that refuses to seek the fullness of life for self and others.

In this sense, every person is committed with God to the fulfillment of others. Such a commitment means not only that one will contribute to the growth of others, but that he is obligated to allow others the freedom for such development without obstructions. To do otherwise is to invite God's wrath. But the God whose wrath is provoked is also the God of even those who have, by their very acts of evil, invited God's disfavor. God then is the redeemer of the oppressed as well as of the oppressor; he joins the struggle on both sides, seeking to transform both the oppressed and the oppressor.

God, for the black community, must be at work in a visible sort of way. Especially, he must be seen in the progressive development toward a better social lot for a people oppressed. Therefore, any adequate God concept cannot be conceived in the narrow and restricted sense of any particular that does not also relate to all. He cannot be for the black man only, just as he cannot be for the white man only. He must be a God for all, and his concerns must be equally related to all. It is every black man's Christian calling to fight against all the ills and woes that afflict mankind and against their human causes and provocations. To leave misery unalleviated, to leave social revolution to the angry and the selfish, to stand aloof from the agonies of the new world aborning is to make it all too plain that one is not interested in the compassion of God, but only in our own passive hope of his impossible providence. For the black community, there can be but one answer, joined by all the past heroes of the faith, to the problems of evil. It is disconcertingly simple: Evil is overcome by the intelligent, competent concern and actions of people who are willing to pay the price of the conflict. To be sure, there is no "utopia of the beyond" which does not have a real-life relation to the present conditions of history. In a real sense then, no future of history can be merely quantitatively new, it must also be qualitatively new. Faith in God does not supplant history so that present conditions become an insignificant matter to believers; neither should involvement in history so absorb the black man of faith that he forgets God's place in the current struggle. Because he can hope in the future, he can best, under God, oppose the dehumanizing schemes of this world and the systems of the present to the point of perfecting meaningful change.

The danger of the black man's current religious mood is that it may attempt to exclude God from the struggle, and by so doing exclude the power of the future. The temptations of the black man's current attitude consist not so much in the titanic desire to be like

God, but in his weakness, timidity, and weariness, not wanting to do what God requires of him.

God has exalted man and given him the prospect of a life that is wide and free, but man too often hangs back and lets himself down. God, as the power of the future, promises a new creation of all things in righteousness and peace. But too many men act as if everything was as before, and they remain as before. God honors black man with his promises, but black man too often does not believe himself capable of what God has required of him. This lack of self-confidence is the one sin that most profoundly threatens the black believer. It is not the evil he does, but the good he does not do, not his misdeeds, but his omissions of great deeds, that accuse him most congently. They accuse him of lack of hope. For the sin of the omission of great deeds has its ground in hopelessness and weakness of faith. To hope is to become a new person fit for great deeds. There dawns within the being of black man the making of a new counterpersonhood capable of the needed black and white confrontation. This encounter, and the outcome of it, may well determine the future of the country and the future of black-white relations in the world.

Gayraud Wilmore

Gayraud Wilmore suggested that black theology should be rooted, not in Black Power, but in the black religious experience that includes both African and American dimensions. This selection is taken from his Black Religion and Black Radicalism. *New York: Doubleday, 1972, pp. 295–306. Revised edition forthcoming.*

James Cone, as the leading exponent of black theology, has taken the brunt of the criticism that blackness is an illegitimate basis for a Christian theology. The argument has been that there is nothing unique in the historical experience of black people that justifies the particularity of the claim that the whole of biblical revelation points to what is being called black theology. In his first book, Cone states that "Black Theology is Christian theology precisely *because* it has the black predicament as its point of departure." White

Christians, therefore, must become black in order to be Christians. But in his effort to lay the groundwork for a systematic theology of the black experience which meets the requirement of universality, Cone adds: "Being black in America has very little to do with skin color. To be black means that your heart, your soul, your mind, and your body are where the dispossessed are. . . . Therefore, being reconciled to God does not mean that one's skin is physically black. It essentially depends on the color of your heart, soul and mind."

In *A Black Theology of Liberation,* Cone further develops this position by a reference to Paul Tillich's description of the symbolic nature of all theological speech. He writes: "The focus on blackness does not mean that *only* blacks suffer as victims in a racist society, but that blackness is an ontological symbol and a visible reality which best describes what oppression means in America. . . . Blackness, then, stands for all victims of oppression who realize that their humanity is inseparable from man's liberation from whiteness."

Cone's struggle with the legitimation of a black theology, as such, is commendable and he satisfies the norm of universality, which he sometimes seems to believe is necessary for an acceptable systematic. The question is whether the Black religious experience requires such validation by the norms of white systematic theology, and whether the strain toward universality does not, *ipso facto,* rob black religion of its freedom as *one* approach to the knowledge of God and, thereby, of its existential singularity. As J. V. L. Casserley reminds us:

> The advent of Christianity forced a new problem upon the attention of the ancient world—the problem of the singular. . . . There is a profound distinction between the term "particular" and the term "singular." The "particular" is the individual as seen by the man who is looking for the universal, and who will feel baffled intellectually until he finds it; the "singular," on the other hand, is the individual seen from the point of view of the man who is out to capture and enjoy the full flavor of its individuality.

Is black theology simply the blackenization of the whole spectrum of traditional Christian theology, with particular emphasis upon the liberation of the oppressed, or does it find in the experience of the oppression of black people, as *black,* a singular religiosity, identified not only with Christianity, but with other religions as well? To say that being black in America has little to do with skin color is, at best, only half true. It is possible to argue that in a world dominated by white power that has been inextricable from white Christianity, being black, or identifiably "Negroid," is a unique experience and has produced a unique religion, closely related to, but not exclusively bound by, the Christian tradition. Simply being oppressed or psychologically and politically in sympathy with the dispossessed does not deliver one into the experience of blackness any more than putting on a blindfold delivers one into the experience of being blind.

There is no attempt here to denigrate the sensitivity to divine revelation of other oppressed peoples or even to invalidate the provisional authenticity of white Christianity as a true religion— one of several valid approaches to the One Eternal God. It is simply to affirm that black theology authenticates itself in the unique religious experience of black people in the particular circumstance of white, Western civilization since the beginning of slavery in the New World. That Cone himself also recognizes this difference is seen in his statement that "Black Theology seeks to create a theological norm which is in harmony with the black condition and the biblical revelation. . . . Theology cannot be indifferent to the importance of blackness by making some kind of existential leap beyond blackness to an undefined universalism."

He can even speak of "Jesus as the Black Christ who provides the necessary soul for black liberation." In so doing, he opens up the possibility of a black theology which is neither Protestant nor Catholic, but the way black people *think, feel,* and *act* with the intensity of ultimate concern about their liberation from oppression and racism. Such a theology is rooted in the resistance of the historic black church, but it extends beyond organized religion. It embraces also the attempt of black secular and non-Christian groups to express verbally and to act out the meanings and values of the black experience in America and Africa.

Black theology expresses both affirmation and negation. It affirms the real possibility of freedom and manhood for black people, and it negates every power that seeks to demean and rob black people of the determination of their own destiny. Black theology's contribution to the universal knowledge of God does not lie in its being only the reverse side of traditional Christian theology—white theology in black vesture. In this, Leon E. Wright is correct to say that a judgment and protest against white Christianity is not enough. Rather, in its illumination of the religious meaning of black liberation, black theology breaks with the determinative norms of white theology and unveils the deepest meaning of human freedom for all men.

The informal, unsystematic, and, to a large degree, inarticulated "theology" of the black folk has spoken, and still speaks, to their distinctive, singular needs. That theology, confirmed and nurtured not only in the church, but in every institution of the black community, was oriented toward an indestructible belief in freedom. Although political emancipation was the concrete expression of that freedom, it did not exhaust its meaning. The freedom toward which the Afro-American religious experience and early black theology tended was freedom as existential deliverance, as liberation from every power or force that restrains the full, spontaneous release of body, mind, and spirit from every bondage which does not contribute to the proper development of the whole person in community. Not simply political freedom, but the freedom of the human being as a child of God, to be himself; to realize the deepest and highest potentialities of his psychosomatic nature. In short, the freedom to be a man or a woman, rather than a brain, a muscle, or a subhuman appendage to an IBM computer.

The first source of black theology is in the existing black community, where the tradition of black folk religion is still extant and continues to stand over against the institutional church—merging with it at times in the ministry of such men as Henry M. Turner, Adam Clayton Powell, Jr., and Martin Luther King, Jr. This black folk religion has never ceased providing the resources for radical movements in the black community while the organized church receded into white evangelical pietism. Movements of black nationalism, from the Moorish Science Temple to the Shrine of the Black Madonna, have their roots in a tradition which maintained a tenuous but persistent connection with voodooism and the spirituality of the religions of Africa. It continues to be represented in the sects and cults of the black ghetto and has periodically been enlisted as the base of contemporary movements led by such men as Imamu Amiri Baraka, Maulana Ron Karenga, and Brother Imari of the Republic of New Africa. It is reflected in the National Negro Evangelical Association. It breaks out in black music, black drama, and the writing of the new black "alienation" poets. The black middle class has generally sought to evade these influences, but even they are too deeply rooted in the masses, of whom Langston Hughes wrote:

> But then there are the low-down folks, the so-called common element, and they are the majority—may the Lord be praised! The people who have their nip of gin on Saturday nights and are not too important to themselves or the community, or too well fed, or too learned to watch the lazy world go round. They live on 7th Street in Washington, or State Street in Chicago and they do not particularly care whether they are like white folks or anybody else. Their joy runs, bang! into ecstasy. Their religion soars to a shout. Work maybe a little today, rest a little tomorrow. Play awhile. Sing awhile. O, let's dance! These common people are not afraid of spiritu-als, as for a long time their more intellectual brethren were, and jazz is their child. They furnish a wealth of colorful, distinctive material for any artist because they still hold their own individuality in the face of American standardization.

This spirit is still the soul of black religion and black culture. Black theology must begin to understand and interpret it before it turns to white theologians for the substance of its reflection. The ebb and flow of black folk religion is a constituent factor in every important crisis and development in the black community. When the community is relatively integrated with the white society, it recedes from black institutions to form a hard core of unassimilable black nationalism in an obscure corner of the social sys-tem—bidding its time. When the community is hard-pressed, when hopes fade and the glimmer of light at the end of the tunnel is blocked out by resurgent white racism, then the essential folk ele-ment in black religion exhibits itself again and begins anew to infiltrate the institutions which had neglected it. That is the mean-ing of the religion of Black Power today and the renewal of a radical black theology within the contemporary black church.

The second source of black theology is in the writings and ad-dresses of the black preachers and public men of the past. As white theology has its Augustine, its John Calvin, Martin Luther, Ulrich Zwingli, and John Wesley, black theology has its Nat Turner, its Richard Allen, Martin Delany, Edward Blyden, and W. E. Burghardt Du Bois. Not all black thinkers were ministers, but all of them were greatly influenced by black religion. One cannot understand the genius of black spirituality or the work of charismatic leaders like Martin King, Malcolm X, or James Forman, without understanding how their interpretations of the black experience were conditioned by great black men of the past. Forman and Malcolm X belong as much to this theological tradition as Powell or King. In an important and neglected article written in 1964, Carleton Lee indicated the significance of prophecy in the black community as spiritual vision, as a way of "forth-telling" the transcendent meaning of history revealed to the inspired imagination. To the extent that secular prophets draw upon the history of suffering and struggle in the black community and point to its destiny as the fulfillment of the faith and hope of a stolen and oppressed people, they deal with insights, themes, and motifs of the black religious consciousness and interpret black reality in ways that are either religious or are readily incorporated into a basically religious view of life.

... The writings of the nineteenth-century black philosophers and preachers lift up some of the seminal ideas of a black theology—liberation, self-help, elevation, chosenness, emigration, and unity. These are some of the major themes, charged with religious significance, with which men like Payne, Crummell, Turner, and Grimke were obsessed. The broad vistas of black reality which these concepts encompass need to be prospected for the rich veins of theological insight they contain. Cone has made a beginning of this development of a theology rooted and grounded in the black experience, but even in *A Black Theology of Liberation,* he retains the traditional categories, and in so doing finds it necessary to use the arguments of white theologians to buttress his position. This is certainly not prohibited, but neither is it the only option available to black theologians whose ancestors have not produced a systematic theology.

Black theology's interests lie in another direction. What is needed to think theologically about the corpus of black opinion—both written and oral—a "new consciousness," a new way of perceiving and ordering religious, cultural, and political data from the black community. This, of course, requires a new set of interpretative tools, a new hermeneutic. Henry H. Mitchell recognizes the need for the black theologian to break the interpretative strictures of white theology when he observes: "Just as the new hermeneutic of Ebeling and others has sought to recapture the vital message of Luther and the Reformation Fathers for the benefit of their sons, so must the Black hermeneutic seek to look into the message of the Black past and see what the Black Fathers could be saying to Black people today."

Mitchell has not, however, developed that hermeneutic in his two propositions of communicating in the argot of the uneducated black Baptist preacher, and "Putting the gospel on a tell-it-like-it-is, nitty-gritty basis." The problem is infinitely more difficult than that. It has to do with unpacking the mythology, folklore, and norms of the black community as reflected in its verbal tradition and literature, in order to discover the ways in which black people have acted out and linguistically communicated their provisional and ultimate concerns under an exploitative system. What Franz Fanon has done for the native people of Algeria and the Antilles, must yet be done for the oppressed blacks of the United States.

Although Fanon would not agree with its utility, such a black hermeneutic will deal with the morphology of black language, the meaning of black music, poetry, the dance, and, as Mitchell himself has suggested, not only the content, but the accent and cadences of black preaching. In other words, if the God of justice and liberation has identified himself with the struggle of black humanity and has manifested himself, in special ways, in the black subcommunity of the United States, then theologians need to know much more about the life-style of that community and look at it through the eyes of its formal and informal leaders of the past and present. Only so will they be able to unlock the secrets of understanding and communicating the gospel of freedom in a new and meaningful way.

Black people, as Du Bois continually reminded us, are "a spiritual people." The theology of the black community is developed not in theological seminaries, but on the streets, in the taverns and pool halls, as well as in the churches. The evolution of the first African societies into the African Methodist Church or a group of black youths from a fighting gang to a black nationalist club, reforming ex-convicts and fighting dope pushers, will suggest more about the operative religion and ethics of the black community than a study of the literature of the neighborhood Sunday schools. It is out of this welter of knowledge of the thought, feeling, and action of the black fathers and the contemporary black ghetto that a hermeneutic can be constructed which will make it possible for black theologians to read back to the community an interpretation of its indigenous religion that will clarify its basic commitments and integrate black values and institutions around the core of liberation.

The third source of black theology are the traditional religions of Africa, the way those religions encountered and assimilated, or were assimilated by, Christianity, and the process by which African theologians are seeking to make the Christian faith indigenous and relevant to Africa today. Black people are not only a spiritual people—they are also an African people. The dispute about African survivals in Negro culture and religion will go on, but it is clear that black people did not begin on the auction blocks of Charlestown and New Orleans, nor did their religious consciousness commence with the preaching of Christianity to the slaves. It is still possible to recover some of the major beliefs of the traditional religions of Nigeria, Dahomey, Ghana, and other parts of Africa from which our ancestors came. Their development and alteration may be traced to the islands of the Caribbean and, to a lesser extent, to the mainland. It may be true that the contributions of African religion have all but evaporated from black Christianity in the United States, but we do not know enough about the psychic structure of black people, about what the Jungian psychologists call "the collective unconscious," of black Americans to be able to say with absolute assurance that nothing of African spirituality lies deeply impregnated in "the souls of black folk." In any event, black people who have struggled for their humanity against the suffocating domination of a racist, Anglo-Saxon culture need to examine in much greater detail the religious contributions of their ancient homeland, which arise out of a vastly different cultural matrix than Europe and America. Professor Charles Long of the University of Chicago has written:

> Our colleague Mircea Eliade said long ago that the West was in danger of provincialism through a lack of attention to the

orientations and solutions of non-Western man. It would be difficult, if not impossible, to make the case for the non-Western identity of the black community in America, though several make this claim. The element of truth in this claim is that though we are Westerners, we are not Western in the same way as our compatriots, and thus we afford within America an entree to the *otherness* of America and the otherness of mankind.

Those contributions, among others, are: a deep sense of the pervasive reality of the spirit world, the blotting out of the line between the sacred and the profane, the practical use of religion in all of life; reverence for ancestors and their real or symbolic presence with us, the corporateness of social life, the source of evil in the consequences of an act rather than in the act itself, and the imaginative and creative use of rhythm—singing and dancing—in the celebration of life and the worship of God. All of these aspects of African religions were found in some form, however attenuated, in the black religion of the eighteenth and nineteenth centuries and were absorbed into black Christianity in the Caribbean, South America, and the United States. The feeling, spontaneity, and freedom in black religion and life had much to do with their resistance to complete whitenization, but this is also related to the intrinsic discontinuity between African and European religiosity. Black theology must be concerned about the recovery of those values, particularly the recovery of the achievement of freedom, the freedom to be *Muntu*—a man or a woman—in the most profound meaning of that profound Bantu word.

The theological program of Africal scholars for the Africanization of Christianity in modern Africa has much to say to black theology's "ghettoization" of the Christian faith in the United States. In either case, the purpose is not to impose the sterile thought forms and traditions of Western Christianity upon the black community, but by a new approach to general revelation to discover a new and creative *Theologia Africana* which can unveil the reality of the Eternal Christ in the life and destiny of his black people. Related to this quest are the urgent political issues of liberation in southern Africa and the United States, social justice and development, the relationship of Christianity to the separatist and independent churches on both sides of the Atlantic, and the contribution of Africa and Black America to the great social revolution of the Third World. Only by a sympathetic and intensive dialogue between the new younger theologians of Africa and black theologians in the United States and the Caribbean will it be possible to uncover the harmonies and disharmonies in black religion and forge the theological and ideological links which can bind modern Africa and black America together for the unimaginable possibilities of the future.

What of that future? Perhaps the most that can be said is that the reformation and revivification of the faith that has come down to us from Jesus of Nazareth awaits the unhindered contribution of the nonwhite peoples of the world and that black people of Africa and America will play a crucial role in that development. It will be preceded by the end of divisive sectarianism and the beginning of ecumenism in the institution of black religion in the United States, by increasing communication and emigration between African and black American churchmen, and by the development of an incisively relevant theology—on both continents—which will free itself from the false consciousness and impiety of white Christianity and bind black people together, inside and outside of churches, in the solidarity of a new faith in God and humanity.

It can only be a matter of judgment, based upon the history of the black race, and faith in the grace of a God who does not reward us according to our iniquities, to affirm that the black world will not repeat the inhumanities of the white world. And if this judgment and faith are vindicated, mankind will be the beneficiary and the reconciliation for which the whole Church of Christ prays will become a realized eschatological event.

Until that time, too remote to deflect black people from the revolutionary tasks which lie at hand today, white men must take, with utmost seriousness, the words of the National Committee of Black Churchmen in its *Message to the Churches from Oakland* in 1969—the year of the *Black Manifesto:*

> We black people are a religious people. From the earliest time, we have acknowledged a Supreme Being. With the fullness of our physical bodies and emotions we have unabashedly worshipped Him with shouts of joy and tears of pain and anguish. We neither believe that God is dead, white, nor captive to some rationalistic and dogmatic formulation

of the Christian faith which relates Him exclusively to the canons of the Old and New Testaments, and accommodate Him to the reigning spirits of a socio-technical age. Rather, we affirm that God is Liberator in the man Jesus Christ, that His message is Freedom, and that today He calls all men to be what they are in themselves, and among their own people, in the context of a pluralistic world society of dignity and self-determination for all. We believe that in a special way God's favor rests today upon the poor and oppressed peoples of the world and that He calls them to be the ministering angels of His judgment and grace, as His Kingdom of freedom and peace breaks in from the future upon a world shackled to ancient sins and virtues.

The 1969 *Message to the Churches from Oakland* of the National Committee of Black Churchmen and the *Black Manifesto* of the Black Economic Development Conference are, one must concede, merely words on paper, not ideas that have been actualized nor deeds performed. But they are prophecies of things to come and to be worked for. They belong together, and in the course of events they sought each other out. These two documents represent, each in its own way and together, the basic theme we have explored throughout ..., namely, that black religion and black radicalism are historic and complementary aspects of an essential characteristic of the black experience in America—a pervasive "pragmatic spirituality" which, in a world dominated by the peculiar racism and oppression of Anglo-Saxon or Euro-American civilization, has always expressed itself in terms of a religiopolitical struggle for humanization and liberation. Black nationalism and Pan-Africanism, hard-pressed and poverty-stricken, may surrender to the rising forces of political repression nonwhite people and white radicals are now experiencing in the United States, and the main-line black churches, piously complacent, may yet succumb to the temptation of solemn assemblies and bourgeois captivity. If that happens in our time, it will be a retreat in a long history of retreats, but not a decisive repudiation of the fundamental meaning of our striving. That is to say, we will never give up the right to be what we are. We are a spiritual people. We are an African people. And we are determined, by the power of God, to be free.

Allen Boesak

Allen Boesak, a black theologian in South Africa, criticized American black theologians—especially James Cone—who absolutized the black American experience. He put black theology in the context of a wider liberation theology. This selection is taken from his Farewell to Innocence. *Johannesburg, South Africa: Rava Press, 1977, pp. 112–19.*

A Situational Ethic

Black theology's situation is the situation of blackness. We have warned earlier on that a contextual theology should remain critical and prophetic also with regard to the situational experience, because it is critical reflection under the Word of God. This means that the liberation praxis is finally judged not by the demands of the situation, but by the liberating Gospel of Jesus Christ. The danger for a contextual theology to be overruled by the situational experience and as a result to succumb to absolutistic claims is very real.

We fear that in this respect Cone's theology is particularly vulnerable. Cone claims, so we saw, God *solely* for the black experience. We submit that to make *black* as such *the* symbol of oppression and liberation in the world is to absolutize their own situation. Black theology, says C. Eric Lincoln in a critique on Cone, "is bound to the situation in this sense, that God's confrontation with white racism is but *one* aspect of God's action in a multi-dimensional complex of interaction between man and man, and God and man."

Cone's mistake is that he has taken black theology out of the framework of the theology of liberation, thereby making the own situation (being black in America) and the own movement (liberation from white racism) the ultimate criterion for all theology. By doing this, Cone makes of a contextual theology a regional theology which is not the same thing at all. Cone is certainly right in claiming that the only Christian expression of theology in the United States (and for that matter in South Africa) is black theology; inasmuch as the Gospel is a gospel of liberation and Christian theology, therefore a theology of liberation, in our case black liberation to

begin with. But in making this the ultimate criterion for all liberation theology, is Cone not wide open for an ideological takeover?

Moreover, if black is simply determinative for oppression and
liberation everywhere and under any circumstances, if the only
legitimate expression for liberation has to be black, does Cone not
close the door to other expressions of liberation theology? Can the
Latin American theologian concede that the only way to recognize
God's actions in history is "through the most radical deeds of Black
Power"? Can, for instance, the American Indian liberation theology (God is Red!) share in this absolute claim of blackness?

Indeed, black theology is a theology of liberation in the situation
of blackness. For blacks, it is the only legitimate way of theologizing—*but only within the framework of the theology of liberation.*
Black theology, therefore, finds itself in intention and theological
methodology, and certainly in its passion for liberation, not only
alongside African Theology, but also alongside the expressions of
liberation theology in Latin America and Asia. And it is indeed in
these expressions of Christian theology that Western theology will
ultimately find its salvation.

We have already pointed out that black theology speaks of "total
liberation" in the same way that the African heritage speaks of the
"wholeness of life." It focuses on the dependency of the oppressed
and their liberation from dependency in all its dimensions—
psychological, cultural, political, economical, and theological. It
expresses the belief that because Christ's liberation has come, the
total liberation of man can no longer be denied. It follows that this
ethic is an ethic of liberation. Its character is situational, social, and
eschatological. It does not, however, arise out of the situation, but
in the situation. The situation is never an entity *an sich* which
autonomously determines the ethic of liberation. It has a history,
and the results of the action within a given situation will have some
bearing on its future. A black ethic will arise, therefore, in the black
situation, it will be determined by the black experience in order to
be authentic, but it will not be confined to the black experience;
neither will black situational possibilities and impossibilities have
the last word.

Love, Liberation and Justice

Black theology takes Christian love very seriously. Because love stands at the very center of Yahweh's liberating acts for his people, any interpretation of Christian love that makes of it an ineffective sentimentality must be rejected. We contend with King and Cone that it is impossible to separate love from justice and power. Love is always love in righteousness. In speaking of righteousness, we do not mean the forensic righteousness in the Pauline sense of the word, but the kingly justice whereof Jesus speaks. For when Jesus speaks of the "poor" and the "poor in spirit" and of the righteousness that shall be given them, he speaks of those who represent the socially oppressed, those who suffer from the power of injustice, those who depend upon Yahweh for their liberation. Ridderbos has conclusively shown that Jesus did indeed mean this kingly justice in the Old Testament sense and meaning. He writes:

> The poor ... look forward to God's liberation of his people from the power of oppression and injustice that is continued for the present. *And it is this longing for liberation which is indicated as "hunger and thirst after righteousness" in the Beatitudes in Matthew....* It must not be understood in the Pauline sense of imputed, forensic righteousness, but as the kingly justice which will be brought to light one day for the salvation of the oppressed and the outcasts.... It is *this* justice which the poor and the meek look forward to in the Sermon on the Mount.

Speaking of God's love without his righteousness betrays an oppression-mindedness black theology cannot tolerate. Cone is correct when he asserts that righteousness is that side of God's love which expresses itself through black liberation. We cannot accept, however, Cone's contention that "to love is to make a decision against white people." We would have thought that to be able to love white people would mean precisely to make a decision *for* them! For their humanity, however obscure, against their inhumanity, however blatant. For their liberation, and against their imprisonment of themselves. For their freedom, against their fear; for their human authenticity, against their terrible estrangement.

Reading Cone, one sometimes cannot help feeling that Zulu was right to warn against equating God's love with our human understanding of love and against the simplification of "God being on the side of the oppressed with the oppressed being on the side of God." By the same token, we cannot accept Washington's glib assertion: "The enemy may not love the violent aggressor, but he certainly respects him." In reality, this is not love Washington is speaking about, nor respect, but fear. And fear has very little to do with respect. In taking this stand, Washington makes fear the basis for human relations and he advances the very thing he says that Black Power is not: a balance of terror.

Liberation theology reclaims the Christian heritage and reinterprets the Gospel to place it within its authentic perspective, namely, that of liberation. In so doing, it questions the historical role of the Christian church, the alliances of the church with "the powers that be," and insists on a true church, i.e., a church that proclaims and lives by the liberating Gospel of Jesus Christ. In other words, in this regard Cone is right: one cannot speak of a Christian, segregated church. Liberation theology seeks a church that ministers to the poor not merely with a sense of compassion but with a sense of justice. This means that the church ought to discover that the state of poverty and oppression is ugly, impermissible, and unnecessary; that conditions of poverty and underdevelopment are not metaphysical but structural and historically explicable. In other words, poverty is one side of a coin of which the other side is affluence and exploitation. The church must needs discover that oppressed people are not merely loose individuals but a class.

A theology and an ethic thus engaged accept theology not merely in terms of what it says, but in terms of what it is doing for the oppressed. It presses for active engagement of the church in sociopolitical affairs in its search for the truth which shall make free. We must be clear about this: the quest is for a church that dares to be the *church,* that dares to take upon itself, as did its Lord, to side with the poor and the downtrodden and to liberate the oppressed. The truth thus uncovered and so done within the action of the church is not a description of reality but an involvement in reality, just as faith is active engagement in obedience to God, "the action of love within history," as Assmann says. The ethic of black theology, therefore, is an ethic of liberation. As such, it is an ethic of transformation and not merely of survival.

Challenging the internal as well as the external dependency of black people, the change it calls for is a *qualitative* change. It is our contention that black theologians have not yet taken this aspect seriously. We have found that ultimately, Roberts's goal for blacks is to share in "the good life," by which he means the kind of life American society offers the privileged. Preston Williams wants white Americans to keep their promises so that black Americans may also share in the "American Dream" and so that "lower class blacks" may become "middle class blacks." Major Jones and J. R. Washington, we have seen, want "equality" through "rapid change," "revolution"—violent revolution being the only alternative for Washington. Nowhere, however, have we found a social ethic that satisfies us.

Fundamental to this, it seems, is the reasoning that racism is the only demon blacks have to fight. "Any analysis that fails to deal with racism, that demon embedded in white folks' being, is *ipso facto* inadequate." While absolutely not minimizing racism as a demonic, pseudoreligious ideology, (who, coming from South Africa, can?) we must nonetheless ask: Is racism indeed the only *issue*? It seems to us that there is a far deeper malady in the American and South African societies that manifests itself in the form of racism. The deepest motivation of the Portuguese in southern Africa was not racism. Nor is racism the deepest motivation of the economic colonialism of the United States in Latin America, or of the multinationals all over the Third World.

And even in South Africa there are signs that should circumstances but allow, some whites would be quite willing to replace the insecurity of institutional racism with the false security of the "Black Bourgeoisie." In this, black theologians still fail to see what was seen by Martin Luther King and Malcolm X: the relation between racism and capitalism, evident not only in the oppression of blacks in the United States itself, but also in the political and economic structures supported by the United States (and other rich countries) between rich and poor nations.

Let us for the moment focus on James Cone, who writes: "We will not let whitey cool this one with his pious love-ethic, but will seek to enhance our hostility, bringing it to its full manifestation. Black survival is at stake here, and black people must define and assert the conditions." This may sound fine, so far as it goes. But what does Cone have in mind? It is not enough to speak only of survival, as Cone repeatedly does. In a deep sense, this seems to suggest a certain hopelessness, just "making it," "just getting by." Black theology is a theology of survival, says Cone. We contend that it is more than that. If Black theology should only be understood in terms of the mere survival of black people, black liberation will never become a reality. If, indeed, black people now live beyond the Sorrow Songs, if indeed they are determined to define their own future, then one cannot speak merely of "survival."

Cone knows, more than, for example, Williams, that all is not well in America. Even when blacks have some economic and intellectual power, he still considers them "oppressed." His answer to this situation is "revolution." A radical, revolutionary confrontation. What does Cone mean by "revolution"? "Revolution is everything that rejects the 'holy ordinances' of the past, i.e., which questions the domination of the white oppressor." In black/white terms, Cone's revolution means a refusal to accept white definitions, white values, white limitations—any kind of white domination or black dependency. This refusal may have a violent character. It forms the process of liberation for blacks "by any means necessary." This liberation is, as Cone says, not only liberation *from,* but also liberation *to.* What does Cone have in mind? We get a clue when Cone admits that reconciliation is only possible between "equals." So equality is what Cone is after, but he lacks, it seems to us, a sound social critique, a critique of ideology, and hence he lacks the sensitivity to define precisely and constructively this "equality."

Frederick Herzog puts the cogent question to James Cone: "What is the meaning of 'equality' in this society?" Indeed, that is the question. Reconciliation requires a new image of humanity, which is why reconciliation without liberation is impossible. But the new image of humanity requires new structures in society—new wine in new wineskins! How new, then, is the black person who moves out of his old life of poverty and dejection into the unchanged structures of an oppressive and exploitative system? In other words, the question really is, How do black theologians define liberation?

In defining the black American situation, Cone is doubtlessly brilliant. But if he cannot go beyond that, his analysis will become nothing more than an emotional catharsis for blacks and a spiritual masochistic experience for whites—nothing new in the black/white relationship. Because Cone ultimately leaves the American capitalistic system intact, a further question of Herzorg is to the point. Can Cone guarantee, Herzog asks, that his theology will not become a justification for a black bourgeoisie, indeed, servant to it, and whether Black Theology can really offer America an alternative for the present "way of life."

When Cone tries to answer Herzog, he does not answer him at all. The question still remains: not whether blacks want to be equal to whites, but whether they want to be equals in this particular system this society adheres to. To our mind, that would mean becoming equal partners in exploitation and destruction. Surely one must see that "getting into" the mainstream of American society would not really solve the problem at all. American exploitation and oppression do not begin and end with black people (in the United States) only! And the dependency of black people would not be broken by "joining them." Black theology, as an integral part of the theology of liberation, realizes this and in its ethic seeks the solidarity (true solidarity!) with oppressed people all over the world. In this way, it will become clear that racism is but one incidental dimension of oppression against which the total struggle should be waged.

Cone ends his article in *Evangelische Theologie* with this rather revealing sentence: "We've got to make the best of a bad situation." This may be survival, but it certainly is not liberation, and we fear that here an ethic of survival might just become an Establishment ethic. If this is indeed Cone's last word, then what he offers as an "ethic of revolution" will not be much more than a sort of "revolutionary revivalism."

Black theology, then, must mean a search for a totally new social order, and in this search it will have to drink deep from the well of African tradition, to use what is good and wholesome for contemporary society. Blacks should not be discouraged by those who deem this effort "utopian," for all through black history black people have lived through their strong belief in that "land beyond Jordan," in that reality which is there, beyond the whip and the slavemaster, beyond the poverty and dejection, leaving black children a legacy of hope. Blacks who know of the liberation in Jesus Christ, the black Messiah, no longer walk in darkness—they live beyond the Sorrow Songs. In the words of Rubem Alves: "This 'utopianism' is not a belief in the possibility of a perfect society, but rather a belief in the nonnecessity of this imperfect order. Christian utopianism is based on the vision that all social systems are under God's historical judgment."

In breaking away from the old oppressive structures of our society, seeking new possibilities, creating room for the realization of true humanity, black theology seeks the true purpose of life for blacks as well as whites. Blacks want to share with white people the dreams and hopes for a new future, a future in which it must never again be necessary to make of Christian theology an ideology or part of a particular aggressive cultural imperialism. Black theology, by offering a new way of theologizing, desires to be helpful in discovering the truth about black and white people, about their past and present, about God's will for them in their common world.

Black theology sincerely believes that it is possible to recapture what was sacred in the African community long before white people came—solidarity, respect for life, humanity, and community. It must be possible not only to recapture it, but to enhance it and bring it to full fruition in contemporary society. Genuine community lies beyond much struggle and despair, beyond reconciliation, which will not come without conflict. It will come only through faith and courage. For blacks, this is the courage to be black. But again, this need be no otherworldly dream, it is as real as Africa itself. Indeed, *Motho ke motho ka batho babang.* This age-old African proverb has its equivalent in almost all African languages, and its meaning is still as profound as ever; even more so: One is only human because of others, with others, for others. This is black theology. It is authentic, it is worthwhile. It is, in the most profound sense of the word, Gospel truth.

James Cone

By the late 1970s, James Cone has moved beyond an exclusive connection between black theology and racism to a vision of liberation embracing all of humanity. This selection is taken from his "Black Theology and the Black Church: Where Do We Go from Here?" Cross Currents 27, no. 2 (Summer 1977), pp. 147–56.

Since the appearance of black theology in the late 1960s, much has been written and said about the political involvement of the black church in black people's historical struggle for justice in North America. Black theologians and preachers have rejected the white church's attempt to separate love from justice and religion from politics because we are proud descendents of a black religious tradition that has always interpreted its confession of faith according to the people's commitment to the struggle for earthly freedom. Instead of turning to Reinhold Niebuhr and John Bennett for ethical guidance in those troubled times, we searched our past for insight, strength, and the courage to speak and do the truth in an extreme situation of oppression. Richard Allen, James Varick, Harriet Tubman, Sojourner Truth, Henry McNeal Turner, and Martin Luther King, Jr., became household names as we attempted to create new theological categories that would express our historical fight for justice.

It was in this context that the "Black Power" statement was written in July 1966 by an ad hoc National Committee of Negro Churchmen. The cry of Black Power by Willie Ricks and its political and intellectual development by Stokely Carmichael and others challenged the black church to move beyond the models of love defined in the context of white religion and theology. The black church was thus faced with a theological dilemma: either reject Black Power as a contradiction of Christian love (and thereby join the white church in its condemnation of Black Power advocates as un-American and un-Christian) or accept Black Power as a sociopolitical expression of the truth of the Gospel. These two possibilities were the only genuine alternatives before us, and we had to decide on whose side we would take our stand.

We knew that to define Black Power as the opposite of the Christian faith was to reject the central role that the black church has played in black people's historical struggle for freedom. Rejecting Black Power also meant that the black church would ignore its political responsibility to empower black people in their present struggle to make our children's future more humane than intended by the rulers in this society. Faced with these unavoidable consequences, it was not possible for any self-respecting churchperson to desecrate the memories of our mothers and fathers in the faith by siding with white people who murdered and imprisoned black people simply because of our persistent audacity to assert our freedom. To side with white theologians and preachers who questioned the theological legitimacy of Black Power would have been similar to siding with Saint George Methodist Church against Richard Allen and the Bethelites in their struggle for independence during the late eighteenth and early nineteenth centuries. We knew that we could not do that, and no amount of white theological reasoning would be allowed to blur our vision of the truth.

But to accept the second alternative and thereby locate Black Power in the Christian context was not easy. First, the acceptance of Black Power would appear to separate us from Martin Luther King, Jr., and we did not want to do that. King was our model, having creatively combined religion and politics, and black preachers and theologians respected his courage to concretize the political consequences of his confession of faith. Thus we hesitated to endorse the "Black Power" movement, since it was created in the context of the James Meredith March by Carmichael and others in order to express their dissatisfaction with King's continued emphasis on nonviolence and Christian love. As a result of this sharp confrontation between Carmichael and King, black theologians and preachers felt themselves caught in a terrible predicament of wanting to express their continued respect for and solidarity with King, but disagreeing with this rejection of Black Power.

Secondly, the concept of Black Power presented a problem for black theologians and preachers not only because of our loyalty to Martin Luther King, but also because many of us had been trained in white seminaries and had internalized much of white people's definition of Christianity. While the rise and growth of independent black churches suggested that black people had a different perception of the Gospel than whites, yet there was no formal theological tradition to which we could turn in order to justify our definition of Black Power as an expression of the Christian Gospel. Our intellectual ideas of God, Jesus, and the church were derived from white European theologians and their textbooks. When we speak of Christianity in theological categories, using such terms as *revelation, incarnation,* and *reconciliation,* we naturally turn to people like Barth, Tillich, and Bultmann for guidance and direction. But these Europeans did not shape their ideas in the social context of white racism and thus could not help us out of our dilemma. But if we intended to fight on a theological and intellectual level as a way of empowering our historical and political struggle for justice, we had to create a new theological movement, one that was derived from and thus accountable to our people's fight for justice. To accept Black Power as Christian required that we thrust ourselves into our history in order to search for new ways to think and be black in this world. We felt the need to explain ourselves and to be understood from our own vantage point and not from the perspective and experiences of whites. When white liberals questioned this approach to theology, our response was very similar to the bluesman in Mississippi when told he was not singing his song correctly: "Look-a-heah, man, dis yere *mah song,* en I'll sing it howsoevah I pleases."

Thus we sang our Black Power songs, knowing that the white church establishment would not smile upon our endeavors to define Christianity independently of their own definitions of the Gospel. For the power of definition is a prerogative that oppressors never want to give up. Furthermore, to *say* that love is compatible with Black Power is one thing, but to demonstrate this compatibility in theology and the praxis of life is another. If the reality of a thing was no more than its verbalization in a written document, the black church since 1966 would be a model of the creative integration of theology and life, faith, and the struggle for justice. But we know that the meaning of reality is found *only* in its historical embodiment in people as structured in societal arrangements. Love's meaning is not found in sermons or theological textbooks but rather in the creation of social structures that are not dehumanizing and oppressive. This insight impressed itself on our religious consciousness, and we were deeply troubled by the inadequacy of our historical obedience when measured by our faith claims. From 1966 to the present, black theologians and preachers, both in the church and on the streets, have been searching for new ways to confess and to live our faith in God so that the black church would not make religion the opiate of our people.

The term *black theology* was created in this social and religious context. It was initially understood as the theological arm of Black Power, and it enabled us to express our theological imagination in the struggle of freedom independently of white theologians. It was the one term that white ministers and theologians did not like, because, like Black Power in politics, black theology located the theological starting point in the black experience and not the particularity of the Western theological tradition. We did not feel ourselves accountable to Aquinas, Luther, or Calvin but to David Walker, Daniel Payne, and W. E. B. DuBois. The depth and passion in which we express our solidarity with the black experience over against the Western tradition led some black scholars in religion to reject theology itself as alien to the black culture. Others, while not rejecting theology entirely, contended that black theologians should turn primarily to African religious and philosophy in order to develop a black theology consistent with and accountable to our historical roots. But all of us agreed that we were living at the beginning of a new historical moment, and this required the development of a *black* frame of reference that many called "black theology."

The consequence of our affirmation of a black theology led to the creation of black caucuses in white churches, a permanent ecumenical church body under the title of the National Conference of Black Churchmen, and the endorsement of James Forman's *Black Manifesto.* In June 1969 at the Interdenominational Theological Center in Atlanta and under the aegis of NCBC's Theological Commission, a group of black theologians met to write a policy statement on black theology. This statement, influenced by my book, *Black Theology and Black Power,* which had appeared two months earlier, defined black theology as a "theology of black liberation."

Black theology, then, was not created in a vacuum and neither was it simply the intellectual enterprise of black professional theologians. Like our sermons and songs, black theology was born in the context of the black community as black people were attempting to make sense out of their struggle for freedom. In one sense, black theology is as old as when the first African refused to accept slavery as consistent with religion and as recent as when a black person intuitively recognizes that the confession of the Christian faith receives its meaning only in relation to political justice. Although black theology may be considered to have formally appeared only when the first book was published on it in 1969, informally, the reality that made the book possible was already present in the black experience and was found in our songs, prayers, and sermons.

In these outpourings are expressed the black visions of truth, pre-eminently the certainty that we were created not for slavery but for freedom. Without this dream of freedom, so vividly expressed in the life, teachings, and death of Jesus, Malcolm, and Martin, there would be no black theology, and we would have no reason to be assembled in this place. We have come here today to plan our future and to map out our strategy because we have a dream that has not been realized.

To be sure, we have talked and written about this dream. Indeed, every Sunday morning black people gather in our churches, to find out where we are in relation to the actualization of our dream. The black church community really believes that where there is no vision the people perish. If people have no dreams, they will accept the world as it is and will not seek to change it. To dream is to know what is ain't suppose to be. No one in our time expressed this eschatological note more clearly than Martin Luther King, Jr. In his "March on Washington" address in 1963, he said: "I have a dream that one day my four children will live in a nation where they will not be judged by the color of their skin but by the content of their character." And the night before his death in 1968, he reiterated his eschatological vision: "I may not get there with you, but I want you to know tonight that we as a people will get to the promised land."

What visions do we have for the people in 1977? Do we still believe with Martin King that "we as a people will get to the promised land"? If so, how will we get there? Will we get there simply by preaching sermons and singing songs about it? What is the black church doing in order to actualize the dreams that it talks about? These are hard questions, and they are not intended as a put-down of the black church. I was born in the black church in Bearden, Arkansas, and began my ministry in that church at the early age of sixteen. Everything I am as well as what I know that I ought to be was shaped in the context of the black church. Indeed, it is because I love the church that I am required, as one of its theologians and preachers, to ask: When does the black church's actions deny its faith? What are the activities in our churches that should not only be rejected as un-Christian but also exposed as demonic? What are the evils in our church and community that we should commit ourselves to destroy?" Bishops, pastors, and church executives do not like to disclose the wrongdoings of their respective denominations. They are like doctors, lawyers, and other professionals who seem bound to keep silent, because to speak the truth is to guarantee one's exclusion from the inner dynamics of power in the profession. But I contend that the *faith* of the black church lays a claim upon all church people that transcends the social mores of a given profession. Therefore, to coverup and to minimize the sins of the church is to guarantee its destruction as a community of faith, committed to the liberation of the oppressed. If we want the black church to live beyond our brief histories and thus to serve as the "Old Ship of Zion" that will carry the people home to freedom, then we had better examine the direction in which the ship is going. Who is the Captain of the Ship, and what are his economic and political interests? This question should not only be applied to bishops, but to pastors and theologians, deacons and stewards. Unless we are willing to apply the most severe scientific analysis to our church communities in terms of economics and politics and are willing to confess and repent of our sins in the struggle for liberation, then the black church, as we talk about it, will remain a relic of history and nothing more. God will have to raise up new instruments of freedom so that his faithfulness to liberate the poor and weak can be realized in history. We must not forget that God's Spirit will use us as her instrument only insofar as we remain agents of liberation by using our resources for the empowerment of the poor and weak. But if we, like Israel in the Old Testament, forget about our Exodus experience and the political responsibility it lays upon us to be the historical embodiment of freedom, then, again like Israel, we will become objects of God's judgment. It is very easy for us to expose the demonic and oppressive character of the white church, and I have done my share of that. But such exposures of the sins of the white church, without applying the same criticism to ourselves, is hypocritical and serves as a camouflage of our own shortcomings and sins. Either we mean what we say about liberation or we do not. If we mean it, the time has come for an inventory in terms of the authenticity of our faith as defined by the historical commitment of the black denominational churches toward liberation.

I have lectured and preached about the black church's involvement in our liberation stuggle all over North America. I have told the stories of Richard Allen and James Varick, Adam Clayton Powell and Martin Luther King. I have talked about the double meaning in the spirituals, the passion of the sermon and prayer, the ecstasy of the shout and conversion experience in terms of an eschatological happening in the lives of people, empowering them to fight for earthly freedom. Black theology, I have contended, is a theology of liberation, because it has emerged out of and is accountable to a black church that has always been involved in our historical fight for justice. When black preachers and laypeople hear this message, they respond enthusiastically and with a sense of pride that they belong to a radical and creative tradition. But when I speak to young blacks in colleges and universities, most are surprised that such a radical black church tradition really exists. After hearing about David Walker's "Appeal" in 1829, Henry H. Garnet's "Address to the Slaves" in 1843, and Henry M. Turner's affirmation that "God is a Negro" in 1898, these young blacks are shocked. Invariably they ask, "Whatever happened to the black churches of today?" "Why don't we have the same radical spirit in our preachers and churches?" Young blacks contend that the black churches of today, with very few exceptions, are not involved in liberation but primarily concerned about how much money they raise for a new church building or the preacher's anniversary.

This critique of the black church is not limited to the young college students. Many black people view the church as a hindrance to black liberation, because black preachers and church members appear to be more concerned about their own institutional survival than the freedom of poor people in their communities. "Historically," many radical blacks say, "the black church was involved in the struggle, but today it is not." They often turn the question back upon me, saying: "All right, granted what you say about the historical black church, but *where* is an institutional black church denomination that still embodies the vision that brought it into existence? Are you saying that the present day AME Church or AME Zion Church has the same historical commitment for justice that it had under the leadership of Allen and Payne or Rush and Varick?" Sensing that they have a point difficult to refute, these radicals then say that it is not only impossible to find a black church denomination committed to black liberation but also difficult to find a local congregation that defines its ministry in terms of the needs of the oppressed and their liberation.

Whatever we might think about the unfairness of this severe indictment, we would be foolish to ignore it. For connected with this black critique is our international image. In the African context, not to mention Asia and Latin America, the black church experiences a similar credibility problem. There is little in our theological expressions and church practice that rejects American capitalism or recognizes its oppressive character in Third World countries. The time has come for us to move beyond institutional survival in a capitalistic and racist society and begin to take more seriously our dreams about a new heaven and a new earth. Does this dream include capitalism or is it a radically new way of life more consistent with African socialism as expressed in the *Arusha Declaration* in Tanzania?

Black theologians and church people must now move beyond a mere reaction to white racism in America and begin to extend our vision of a new socially constructed humanity for the whole inhabited world. We must be concerned with the quality of human life not only in the ghettoes of American cities but also in Africa, Asia, and Latin America. Since humanity is one, and cannot be isolated into racial and national groups, there will be no freedom for anyone until there is freedom for all. This means that we must enlarge our vision by connecting it with that of other oppressed peoples so that together all the victims of the world might take charge of their history for the creation of a new humanity. As Frantz Fanon taught us: if we wish to live up to our people's expectations, we must look beyond European and American capitalism. Indeed, "we must invent and we must make discoveries. . . . For Europe, for ourselves, and for humanity, we must turn over a new leaf, we must work out new concepts, and try to set afoot a new [humanity]."

New times require new concepts and methods. To dream is not enough. We must come down from the mountaintop and experience the hurts and pain of the people in the valley. Our dreams need to be socially analyzed, for without scientific analysis they will vanish into the night. Furthermore, social analysis will test the nature of our commitment to the dreams we preach and sing about. This is one of the important principles we learned from Martin King and many black preachers who worked with him. Real substantial change in societal structures requires scientific analysis. King's commitment to social analysis not only characterized his involvement in the civil-rights movement but also led him to take a radical stand against the war in Viet Nam. Through scientific analysis, King saw the connection between the oppression of blacks in the United States of America and America's involvement in Viet Nam. It is to his credit that he never allowed a pietistic faith in the other world to become a substitute for good judgment in this. He not only preached sermons about the promised land but concretized his vision with a political attempt to actualize his hope.

I realize, with Merleau-Ponty, that "one does not become a revolutionary through science but through indignation." Every revolution needs its Rosa Parks. This point has often been overlooked by Marxists and other sociologists who seem to think that all answers are found in scientific analysis. Mao Tse-tung responded to such an attitude with this comment: "There are people who think that Marxism is a kind of magic truth with which one can cure any disease. We should tell them that dogmas are more useless than cow dung. Dung can be used as fertilizer."

But these comments do not disprove the truth of the Marxists' social analysis, which focuses on economics and class and is intended as empowerment for the oppressed to radically change human social arrangements. Such an analysis will help us to understand the relation between economics and oppression not only in North America but throughout the world. Liberation is not a process limited to black-white relations in the United States; it is also something to be applied to the relations between rich and poor nations. If we are an African people, as some of the names of our churches suggest, in what way are we to understand the political meaning of that identity? In what way does the economic investment of our church resources reflect our commitment to Africa and other oppressed people in the world? For if an economic analysis of our material resources does not reveal our commitment to the process of liberation, how can we claim that the black church and its theology are concerned about the freedom of oppressed peoples? As an Argentine peasant poet said:

> They say that God cares for the poor
> Well this may be true or not,
> But I know for a fact
> That he dines with the mine-owner.

Because the Christian church has supported the capitalists, many Marxists contend that "all revolutions have clashed with Christianity because *historically* Christianity has been structurally counterrevolutionary." We may rightly question this assertion and appeal to the revolutionary expressions of Christianity in the black religious tradition, from Nat Turner to Martin Luther King. My concern, however, is not to debate the fine points of what constitutes revolution, but to open up the reality of the black church experience and its revolutionary potential to a world context. This means that we can learn from people in Africa, Asia, and Latin America, and they can learn from us. Learning from others involves listening to creative criticism; to exclude such criticism is to isolate ourselves from world politics, and this exclusion makes our faith nothing but a reflection of our economic interests. If Jesus Christ is more than a religious expression of our economic and sexist interests, then there is no reason to resist the truth of the Marxist and feminist analyses.

I contend that black theology is not afraid of truth from any quarter. We simply reject the attempt of others to tell us what truth is without our participation in its definition. That is why dogmatic Marxists seldom succeed in the black community, especially when the dogma is filtered through a brand of white racism not unlike that of the capitalists. If our long history of struggle has taught us anything, it is that if we are to be free, we black people will have to do it. Freedom is not a gift but is a risk that must be taken. No one can tell us what liberation is and how we ought to struggle for it, as if liberation can be found in words. Liberation is a process to be located and understood only in an oppressed community struggling for freedom. If there are people in and outside our community who want to talk to us about this liberation process in global terms and from Marxist and other perspectives, we should be ready to talk. But *only* if they are prepared to listen to us and we to them will genuine dialogue take place. For I will not listen to anybody who refuses to take racism seriously, especially when they themselves have not been victims of it. And they should listen to us *only* if we are prepared to listen to them in terms of the particularity of oppression in their historical context.

Therefore, I reject dogmatic Marxism that reduces every contradiction to class analysis and thus ignores racism as a legitimate point of departure in the process of liberation. There are racist Marxists as there are racist capitalists, and we must struggle against both. But we must be careful not to reject the Marxist's social analysis simply because we do not like the vessels that the message comes in. If we do that, then it is hard to explain how we can remain Christians in view of the white vessels in which the Gospel was first introduced to black people.

The world is small. Both politically and economically, our freedom is connected with the struggles of oppressed peoples throughout the world. This is the truth of Pan-Africanism as represented in the life and thought of W. E. B. DuBois, George Padmore, and C. L. R. James. Liberation knows no color bar; the very nature of the Gospel is universalism, i.e., a liberation that embraces the whole of humanity.

The need for a global perspective, which takes seriously the struggles of oppressed peoples in other parts of the world, has already been recognized in black theology, and small beginnings have been made with conferences on African and black theologies in Tanzania, New York, and Ghana. Another example of the recognition of this need is reflected in the dialogue between black theology in South Africa and North America. From the very beginning, black theology has been influenced by a world perspective as defined by Henry M. Turner, Marcus Garvey, and the Pan-Africanism inaugurated in the life and work of W. E. B. DuBois. The importance of this Pan-African perspective in black religion and theology has been cogently defended in Gayraud Wilmore's *Black Religion and Black Radicalism.* Our active involvement in the "Theology in the Americas," under whose aegis this conference is held, is an attempt to enlarge our perspective in relation to Africa, Asia, and Latin America as well as to express our solidarity with other oppressed minorities in the United States.

This global perspective in black theology enlarges our vision regarding the process of liberation. What does black theology have to say about the fact that two-thirds of humanity is poor and that this poverty arises from the exploitation of the poor nations by rich nations? The people of the United States of America compose 6 percent of the world's population, but we consume 40 percent of the world resources. What, then, is the implication of the black demand for justice in the United States when related to justice for all the world's victims? Of the dependent status we experience in relation to white people, and the experience of Third World countries in relation to the United States? Thus, in our attempt to liberate ourselves from white America in the United States, it is important to be sensitive to the complexity of the world situation and the oppressive role of the United States in it. African, Latin American, and Asian theologians, sociologists, and political scientists can aid us in the analysis of this complexity. In this analysis, our starting point in terms of racism is not negated but enhanced when connected with imperialism and sexism.

We must create a global vision of human liberation and include in it the distinctive contribution of the black experience. We have been struggling for nearly 400 years! What has that experience taught us that would be useful in the creation of a new historical future for all oppressed peoples? And what can others teach us from their historical experience in the struggle for justice? This is the issue that black theology needs to address. "Theology in the Americas" provides a framework in which to address it. I hope that we will not back off from this important task but face it with courage, knowing that the future of humanity is in the hands of oppressed peoples, because God has said: "Those that hope in me shall not be put to shame" (Is. 49:23).

CHAPTER THREE

South American Liberation Theology

Gustavo Gutiérrez

Gustavo Gutiérrez, perhaps the leading exponent of South American liberation theology, has consistently claimed that people should be categorized not as believers or unbelievers but as oppressors or oppressed. This selection is taken from his "Two Theological Perspectives: Liberation Theology and Progressivist Theology" in Sergio Torres and Virginia Fabella, eds., The Emergent Gospel. Maryknoll, N.Y.: Orbis Books, 1976, pp. 240–51.

The Philosophy of People's Struggle and the Theology of Liberation

When the wretched of the earth awake, their first challenge is not to religion but to the social, economic, and political order oppressing them and to the ideology supporting it.

The Latin American poor seek to eradicate their misery, not ameliorate it; hence they choose social revolution rather than reform, liberation rather than development, and socialism rather than liberalization. These options, which seem to the ruling classes utopian, are utterly rational to the oppressed. Dependence on external powers and domination by internal minorities typify the social structures of Latin America. But this theory as first propounded may not have emphasized adequately that the primary confrontation is not between powerful ("developed") nations or continents and weak ("underdeveloped") ones, but between different social classes. Nationalism and racism are more clearly understood in the context of class inequity; so too the economic and political control of multinational corporations over poor countries.

The challenge of the poor to the prevailing order that oppresses them is actual, not theoretical, and it brings together Marxism, social-scientific analysis, and popular movements within the historical process. Similarly, the challenge of the poor juxtaposes Marxism and the social sciences with liberation theology in the present moment of history. Liberation envisions not only a new society but a new kind of person, one increasingly free of the bonds preventing us from shaping our own lives. This implies defects in the prevailing ideologies that have shaped our societies and ourselves, and since religious elements are present in those ideologies, religion must be criticized insofar as it generates or reinforces oppression. For such criticism to be sound, however, religion must be seen in the context of the social order as a whole: Our thinking and actions as Christians are to a great extent socially conditioned, and in creating a theology of liberation we must be aware of the pervasive connection between ideology and theology.

A new society and a new kind of person can only be fashioned by the oppressed themselves, grounded in their values. An authentic social and cultural revolution can only be created by its subjects, never for them.

Given that fact, liberation theology's first question cannot be the same one that progressivist theology has asked since Bonhoeffer. The question is not how we are to talk about God in a world come of age, but how we are to tell people who are scarcely human that God is love and that God's love makes us one family. The interlocutors of liberation theology are the nonpersons, the humans who are not considered human by the dominant social order—the poor, the exploited classes, the marginalized races, all the despised cultures. Liberation theology categorizes people not as believers or unbelievers but as oppressors or oppressed. And the oppressors include people who "call themselves Christians," in the words of Bartolomé de Las Casas.

Note the contrast between the interlocutors of progressivist and of liberation theology: The interlocutors of progressivist theology question faith; the interlocutors of liberation theology "share" the same faith as their oppressors, but they do not share the same economic, social, or political life. But in light of God's Word, faith cannot be separated from historical reality ("real life"); in order to exist, faith must be lived—though for a long time persons claiming to be Christians have falsely contended otherwise.

We must not forget that the common people have their own, popular religion. It is incomprehensible to the bourgeoisie, despised by them, yet manipulated by them to defend their own privileges. It is also true that popular religion contains elements of the dominant ideology. Nevertheless, the concrete religious experiences of the common people also contain valuable elements of protest, resistance, and liberation.

The differences between traditional or progressivist theology and liberation theology are not merely geographical (the former being European and the latter indigenous in origin) or merely theological; the primary difference is political, grounded in social inequity. Both traditional and progressivist theology persist in Latin America as the theologies of the conservative and liberal sectors, respectively, of the ruling class. The locus of liberation theology is the common people seeking to be agents of their own history and expressing their faith and hope in the poor Christ through their efforts for liberation.

Salvation and Social Justice: Bartolomé de Las Casas and the "Scourged Christs" of the Indies

The conquest and colonization of Latin America quickly became a missionary enterprise. Spain's self-imputed motive was the salvation by conversion of these new-found infidels. This Christian motive might have justified an ideal colonial enterprise, but it rebuked the real one. That discrepancy was the heart of the "controversy over the Indies."

Salvation was Bartolomé de Las Casas's passion and the motive of his missionary work. But in his eyes, salvation was so closely associated with social justice that he inverted the usual hierarchy of missionary principles in two respects. First, Las Casas pointed out, the Spaniards' gratuitous or exploitative cruelty toward the Indians was endangering their own salvation: "It is impossible for someone to be saved if he does not observe justice." Second, with deep prophetic insight Las Casas saw the Indians more as "poor" persons in the Gospel sense than as infidels. He did not hesitate to write to the emperor that the destruction and death of the Indians was too high a price to pay for their conversion.

Many shared Las Casas's opinion, and worked hard and cohesively to defend the Indians. But their opinion had determined enemies. One of the most renowned champions of the Spanish conquest and colonization was Juan Ginés de Sepúlveda, whose central argument was that Indians were by nature inferior to Europeans and hence ought to be their slaves. This distinction between naturally superior and inferior people was based on a famous passage in the writings of Aristotle and on some ambiguous comments by Thomas Aquinas on slavery. Their inferiority justified the Indians' enslavement, and to enslave them—as well as convert them—it was necessary to conquer them.

Sepúlveda's argument is brilliantly expounded and abundantly buttressed with quotations from traditional authority. Naturally, the *encomenderos* applauded this theological defense of their oppression-based privileges. We have had many such Sepúlvedas in Latin America since, all of them advocating or justifying the exploitation or enslavement of the majority in the name of "Western Christian civilization." But only Sepúlveda's more recent disciples have approached the candor with which he justified oppression and murder.

Las Casas's ideas are familiar and need not be recapitulated in toto. I should like to summarize those elements of his theology, however, that prefigure current liberation theology.

In his controversy with Sepúlveda, Las Casas precedes his abundant careful rebuttals based on doctrine with one overwhelming confutation from life: The wars of conquest and the *encomienda* system defended by Sepúlveda have brought about "the perdition of countless people and the depopulation of more than two thousand leagues of land." Las Casas repeatedly emphasizes that the criteria of any theology are its practical consequences, not its theoretical assumptions, and he repeatedly criticizes the Spaniards for their intellectualism, their ignorance of the Indies, and the concrete consequences of their theology. Las Casas himself was a man of action, and his theology served his active defense of the Indians.

Las Casas was less tradition bound and academic than any other theologian of his day. Francisco de Vitoria, also a Dominican and the most famous theologian of his era, author of advanced opinions on the rights of nations and international law, was not nearly as advanced as Las Casas on the question of the Indies. He vigorously rejected Sepúlveda's reasons for conquering and enslaving the Indians but claimed that certain hypothetical motives and situations could justify such wars. His centrist theology represented the most enlightened opinion of the ruling class of his day.

Las Casas respected Vitoria greatly, but his own standpoint was very different. His starting point was not the hypothetical case but the actual Indians, exploited members of a despised race. That is why Las Casas rarely cited Vitoria's work and often criticized his intellectualist views as too far removed from concrete experience. All centrism, political or theological, opens the door to ultraconservatism. Vitoria's centrism would have justified "moderate" warfare against the Indians.

It has been charged that a theology of active witness to faith, of practice, of involvement in liberation struggles, must be intellectually less rigorous, and therefore less valid, than an academic, theoretical theology. But is Las Casas's theology less valid than Vitoria's? I think not. Reasoning from a concrete situation is quite different from (but no less rigorous than) reasoning from *a priori* "first principles"—unfamiliar though the ruling classes and their ideological dependents may have found it. Furthermore, participation in a concrete historical process—such as the lives of the oppressed—enables one to perceive aspects of the Christian message that theorizing fails to reveal. Las Casas's insight into the relationship between salvation and justice proves the point. It derived from seeing the Indians not primarily as infidels to be evangelized, which abstracts them from their humanity, but rather as poor human beings in the Gospel sense of the term. The poor Indian was the "other" who was challenging the truths of Christendom. Las Casas carried this insight further when he realized that Christ was speaking to him and his contemporaries through the Indians. His account of his own conversion tells us this, and he repeated it often: "In the Indies, I left behind Jesus Christ, our God, suffering affliction, scourging, and crucifixion not once but a million times over."

Sepúlveda would have found such an identification of Christ with the Indians inconceivable, but Las Casas and those who followed in his footsteps, though trained in traditional theology, saw that in and through the "scourged Christs of the Indies," Jesus is denouncing exploitation, denying the Christianity of the exploiters, and calling people to understand and heed his Gospel message.

Liberation Theology's Modern Antecedents

Intellectual modernity did not produce an innovative or even characteristic Latin American theology. In the nineteenth and early twentieth centuries, Latin American theology pallidly reflected the European liberal-conservative division. Protestantism was closer to the modern spirit than Catholicism, but being less indigenous it was even less theologically significant.

From about 1930 to Vatican II, Latin American theological liberals were content to follow French theology, enthusiastically if not creatively, for French theology then represented the Catholic avant-garde. Social-doctrine Catholicism was followed by theology based on the distinction of planes. Social-doctrine Christianity was a version of social reformism, acknowledging modern reality and, with reservations, liberal ideology, and seeking an alternative to capitalism and socialism. But its timid social concern could not transcend the search for a political alternative or see Christ in the oppressed. Hence it is not really surprising that in Chile, for example, social-doctrine Christianity ended as the ally of ultraconservatism.

The theology based on the distinction of planes had greater theological breadth and sensitivity to modern values. It advocated democracy and social justice and stressed the church's presence in the world and the possible diversity of Christian political commitments. Even prior to Vatican II, from which it derived great impetus, it had led certain groups into progressivist theology.

After Vatican II, the liberal element of the Latin American church turned briefly to the theology of development, which combined positive evaluation of human progress with increased social concern for poor peoples and nations. Its optimism, and dynamism, however, could not conceal its superficial explanation of the underlying causes of poverty and injustice or its paucity of concrete Christian experience.

The theology of revolution sought to escape bourgeois assumptions and embrace radical political commitments, but its perspective was limited. It tended to consecrate the idea of revolution and broaden it so that it lost all meaning, and it tended to lack theory based on concrete praxis.

Liberation Theology

The years 1965–68 were decisive for the popular movement in Latin America and for the Christian participation in that movement. Liberation theology struck deep roots in those years, and we cannot understand what happened at the Medellín Episcopal Conference without reference to the life of Christian communities at that time.

Medellín expressed the experiences of Christians personally involved in the liberation process. It offered them acceptance and support and it pointed new directions for thought and action. Medellín took on a task assigned to Vatican II but not carried out: the task of proposing solutions to contemporary world poverty. Medellín's stated theme was "Latin America in the light of Vatican II"; its aim was to examine Latin American realities from the conciliar point of view. Concrete contact with those realities, however, reversed the theme, and Medellín considered "Vatican II in the light of Latin American reality." That reversal reflected the maturity of the Christian community in Latin America. More important, it expressed the wretchedness, hope, and commitment of the oppressed and their allies. Advocates of social justice were galvanized by Medellín's reversal of theme, while opponents have tried but failed to expunge that conference from Latin America's memory. Once the Christian community has committed itself to the reality of the poor and their achievement of God's promised justice, it can only move forward.

In Latin America today, human rights and social justice are nearly nonexistent. This has generated nostalgic misrepresentation of the years 1965–68 as halcyon times, and a corresponding false claim that liberation theology was an evanescent product of enthusiasm and euphoria. But though the sociopolitical context was indeed more favorable then, those were years of conflict, struggle, failure; 1968, when liberation theology was first tentatively formulated, was hardly a time of easy optimism, let alone euphoria. Moreover, though the times have worsened, our motives for hope remain unchanged. We must bear in mind that whatever the external situation, the people of Latin America are moving toward liberation. To bear witness to a life of authentic faith and hope in the Lord, we must go with them.

Two intuitions are central to liberation theology. They came first chronologically, and they continue first in importance. One is methodological; the other is its frame of reference.

From the start, liberation theology has maintained that active commitment to liberation comes first and theology develops from it. Theology is critical reflection on and from within historical praxis, and the historical praxis of liberation theology is to accept and live the Word of God through faith. We fashion and alter our faith according to frequently ambiguous historical mediations, but liberation theology does not merely replace the deductive with the inductive method. Rather, liberation theology reflects on and from within the complex and fruitful relationship between theory and practice.

Liberation theology's second central intuition is that God is a liberating God, revealed only in the concrete historical context of liberation of the poor and oppressed. This second point is inseparable from the first: If theology is reflection on and from within concrete praxis, the concrete praxis in question is the liberation praxis of the oppressed. It is not enough to know that praxis must precede reflection; we must also realize that the historical subject of that praxis is the poor—the people who have been excluded from the pages of history. Without the poor as subject, theology degenerates into academic exercise. Theological discourse becomes true— is verified—in and through its engagement in the liberation of the poor.

The inseparability of these two intuitions explains why liberation theology must begin with the hopes of the poor, expressed in their own words from within their own world. Speaking for the poor might hasten, initially, the illusion of progress but could not produce real qualitative change, only the old reality tricked out in new phrases. The poor, who have never been allowed to speak for themselves, must now begin.

This will initiate vast historical changes. If liberation theology, with its admitted deficiencies, contributes to those changes and to a new understanding of the faith, then it will have fulfilled its role in this transitional period. Like all theology, it simply expresses how certain Christians interpret their faith in light of their times. The present generation has scarcely begun to cut its ties, conscious and subconscious, to the prevailing system and has only begun to discover the world of the "other" and the Lord's presence there.

History is the concrete locale of human encounter with the Father of Jesus Christ. In Jesus Christ, we proclaim the Father's love for all human beings, but till now we have interpreted history from the standpoint of the "winners," or rulers, or upper classes. The perspective of the "losers" is very different, and we must reinterpret history in terms of their hopes and struggles. The "winners" have done their best to strip the "losers" of their historical consciousness in order to eradicate their will and thereby lull their rebelliousness. Now the downtrodden are trying to recover their past in order to found on it a fitting present.

The history of Christianity has also been written by white, Western bourgeois hands. We must recover the memory of the "scourged Christs of the Indies," of the victims of this world. That memory lives on in elements of our culture, in popular religion, in resistance to ecclesiastical high-handedness. It is the memory that Christ is present in all who are hungry, thirsty, or humiliated (Mt. 25), and that he has set us free to be free (Gal. 5:1).

Reinterpreting history might be mistaken for purely an intellectual exercise, but it is not. It is a necessary part of the active effort to *remake history.* We cannot reinterpret history without being actively engaged in the liberation struggle. To remake history is to subvert it, to channel its course from the standpoint of those on the bottom. The established order has taught us to attach a pejorative connotation to the word *subversive,* but in subversive history we find a new experience of the faith, a new spirituality, and a new proclamation of the Gospel message.

Throughout history, the "winners" have never wholly suppressed their victims' historical memory and attempts to remake their history. We find traces of them in groping expressions of impatience with "the system," in treatises that were ignored or suppressed, in movements put down in blood. Throughout history, we can also detect a theology born out of the struggles of the poor and suppressed or subverted by those in power. Liberation theology must trace the course of the poor in Christian history in order to maintain its historical continuity. It must analyze the great landmarks: the primitive Christian community; the church fathers; the Franciscan movement and Joachim of Fiore in the twelfth and thirteenth centuries; the Hussite movement in the fifteenth century; the German peasant wars and the figure of Thomas Münzer in the sixteenth century; the defense of the American Indians by Las Casas, Juan del Valle, and others; Juan Santos Atahualpa in seventeenth-century Peru; the peasant uprisings and the course of popular piety in our more recent history.

That stream was forced underground most of the time, surfacing—frequently tinged with mysticism—when the poor adverted to the reality of their liberating God. Welling up periodically in the desert of academic theology, it engendered surprising new lines of thought: the rights of the poor hinted at in scholastic theology's discussion of tyranny and the property of others; the first stirrings of social-doctrine Catholicism in eighteenth-century France; religious socialism in twentieth-century Germany and Switzerland; in the United States certain aspects of the "social gospel" and the writings of Niebuhr.

It is instructive in this context to contrast the theologies of Barth and Bultmann. Barth, the theologian primarily of God's transcendence, seemingly theologically unconcerned with the human hearers of God's word, was pastor in a working-class milieu. His experiences there led him to a well-defined and lifelong socialism. However his politics may have influenced his theology, he remained sensitive to the evil of human exploitation. Bultmann, on the contrary, concerned with the great questions of contemporary life and with modern humanity's incomprehension of the Gospel message, was nevertheless limited by bourgeois ideology: His theology is oblivious to the oppression created by and for the very people who were the objects of his theological concern. So the theologian who started from "heaven" was deeply aware of those who lived in "hell on earth," whereas the theologian who started from "earth" seemed oblivious to human exploitation. There is no real paradox here. An authentic and profound sense of God does not preclude awareness of the poor and the questions they raise. "Spirituality" does not preclude "social conscience." The real incompatibility is between bourgeois individualism and spirituality.

In Bonhoeffer too we find both concerns present. Like Barth,

Bonhoeffer's profound sense of God showed him the importance of interpreting reality from the standpoint of the oppressed: "There remains an experience of incomparable value. We have for once learned to see the great events of world history from below, from the perspective of the outcasts, the suspects, the maltreated, the powerless, the oppressed, the reviled—in short, from the perspective of those who suffer. This never became Bonhoeffer's main theme, but personal experiences had certainly turned his thoughts in this new and potentially fruitful direction.

A new historical situation is gradually taking shape as the exploited classes and peoples of the world recognize their centuries-long oppression. Local historical variations (nature and degree of oppression, composition of oppressed and oppressing groups) naturally produce variations in liberation theology (e.g., the theology of black power, feminist theology). All liberation theology originates among the world's anonymous, whoever may write the books or the declarations articulating it. The subterranean stream of liberation theology is surfacing, fed by the rain of current events and the underground springs of past history. It separates into rivulets according to local topography, but then, gradually, the rivulets flow together again, and the stream gains power.

This, then, is the historical and theological context of Latin American liberation theology. It could not have arisen before the popular movement had attained a certain maturity, but its roots reach far into the past and its significance transcends Latin America. Despite the effect of differing national contexts on Christian life and thought, one fact is becoming universally apparent to the oppressed: The God of the lords and masters is not the same God in whom the poor and exploited believe. Local variations and resulting intramural polemics in liberation theology help clarify our postulates, principles, and methods.

The popular movement, and therefore liberation theology, is still in process. The people's struggle is not yet victorious, not even on the high road to victory. Suffering and bondage still exist; the poor are still in exile. But exodus has begun, and hope and rebelliousness against the powers that be remain alive, despite fascism and increased oppression. Liberation theology has arisen from this ongoing tension between a moribund but tenacious past and a future that must be created.

Of late, new dimensions have been added to captivity and exile, however, and it would be suicidally unrealistic to ignore them. At the same time, we must not overestimate their potency. New and creative efforts are being made despite harsh conditions now prevalent on the continent. They may be less glamorous and less well known than efforts of the recent past. They may have been initiated by people whose names are unfamiliar to "Latin America-watchers," but that does not diminish their reality or their significance for the common people.

More than ever before in our history the exodus must be lived, not preached. Beyond their own willingness to suffer, and the compassion of outsiders, the oppressed need a strong spirit of self-affirmation and self-assertion in the face of a life that denies their very humanity. They need to hold fast the knowledge that Christ came to establish not bondage but liberation from bondage. The core of his message is the Father's saving and liberative love. It must also be the core of our Christian life and our theology.

José Miguez Bonino

José Miguez Bonino has taught that liberation theology is a new way of doing theology and, following Karl Marx, contends that the proper role for theology is to transform rather than understand the world. This selection is taken from his Doing Theology in a Revolutionary Situation. *Philadelphia: Fortress Press, 1975, pp. 68–82.*

We are now able to arrive, finally, to some definite proposals: (1) There is a definite, particular option involved for the church. It has to *decide* in favor of a given system at a given time and to support it. Therefore, the church participates in politics. It may make the wrong choice, to be sure, but it cannot avoid making one. In this light, one must understand the option of the Priests of the Third World for Peronism in Argentina. (2) This political action of the church stops, however, this side of access to political power. The mission of the church is a prophetic one, and its power is therefore the power of the *Word* (it announces, denounces, exhorts, teaches, but "it has not been given the task of exercising political power"). (3) A historical project is always an open-ended task: the church participates in a people's project both assuming its aspirations and pushing them critically toward a fuller realization. (4) This latter function requires that the church will understand and accept the values implicit in the people itself. There is here a place for the appreciation of values implicit in folk Catholicism but, even more significantly, in the very life of the people. The most important concrete value in the life of the people (it is the "poor people," the "marginals" which are here mainly in question) is solidarity, the will to be a community. (5) But this value of solidarity must be permeated with the kerygmatic value of justice, joining both in such a way that the people's consciousness of its destiny may be at the same time consolidated and deepened. This is the concrete situation in which the church is called to support a "socialist" project, not as something already done, as a ready-made system, but as something which is "created along the way." The church does not offer a model which it has itself invented; it does not impose a system from above (as in colonial Christianity), but it accompanies the people, "communicating the liberating contents derived from the kerygma." This is "a liberating evangelization."

The "theology of the people" breathes a certain trust in the "popular consciousness"—perhaps a secularized form of the traditional Roman Catholic doctrine of the *sensus fidelium* as a theological criterium. On the other hand, and correspondingly, there is an emphasis on the national character of the socialism it propounds and a mistrust of foreign ideologies, particularly of Marxism (without ignoring, to be sure, its analytical significance). In contrast to this, we must sketch the work of some theologians, characterized by a greater critical and ideological rigor. They are, properly speaking, the creators of "a theology of liberation." Among the many names which could be mentioned in this respect, we shall refer to the Peruvian priest Gustavo Gutiérrez and the Brazilian Hugo Assmann.

This theology is closely related to the development of sociological thought in Latin America. When sociology assumes the problem of dependence and liberation as a basic structure of analysis, displaces the liberal meaning of *liberty* with the revolutionary meaning of *liberation,* and rearranges its categories and tools according to this new perspective, theology discovers a new direction for its own reflection. To be sure, it is not a merely theoretical discovery: rather, the new sociological categories provided the scientific structure necessary to grasp, analyze, and carry forward a phenomenon for which the theologian had no categories: the revolutionary praxis of a growing number of Christians. Gutiérrez insists that this praxis is the point of departure of a theology of liberation. This does not attempt to buttress or justify such practice but to deepen it and give an account of it. In doing it, it finds that the ground has been explored by sociologists and it avails itself of their work.

Gutiérrez is the man who has more carefully traced both the continuity between traditional theological thought on sociopolitical matters and this new perspective and the discontinuity between them. The very notion of liberation, for instance, has a long theological tradition, but has gained recently a breadth of meaning which is new. The value of a term such as this is that it makes it possible to understand the aspirations of peoples and social classes, to conceive history as a process and to speak of man's relation to God as one and the same reality, although differentiated in three levels of meaning: sociopolitical liberation, humanization as a historical process of man's self-realization, and deliverance from sin (fellowship between man and man and man and God). The originality of this theology is not to have discovered these three levels of meaning but to have started from their *unity* as the fundamental point of departure. It seems to me, in fact, that the clue to this theology is "the elimination of all and every dualism." This is why it criticizes and rejects "the distinction of realms" which characterized the last phase of the "social doctrine" of the Catholic Church. Gutiérrez underlines this unity by referring to "the one vocation to salvation" of all humanity (in terms similar to those we met in Segundo). Thus, "the action of man in history, whether Christian or non-Christian, gains . . . religious significance." The three levels constitute, therefore, a unity assumed by the Christian by virtue of his faith in "the recapitulation of all things in Christ." Sociopolitical struggle, human maturity, reconciliation with God, do not belong to different realms but to a single saving reality. God's grace and man's task are therefore also united. The same basic premise is also expressed in the affirmation that there is "only one history," inaugurated in Creation as the beginning both of "the human enterprise and of Yahweh's saving history." The exodus points to the unity between the sociopolitical and the redemptive dimensions, and this liberation is fulfilled and deepened in Jesus Christ. Every promise has a historical *locus* which points beyond itself, both historically and eschatologically. There are not two histories: one sacred and one profane or secular. The one history in which God acts is the history of men; it is in this history where we find God. There is only one "Christ-fulfilled" history. All the chapters in Gutiérrez's presentation take this fundamental unity to different areas of theological thought. The couples liberation/salvation, love of the neighbor/Christology, politics/eschatology, humanity/Church, human solidarity/sacraments, cover the classical *loci* of theology indissolubly relating them to the search for sociopolitical liberation and the building of a new humanity.

We have already indicated that the thought of these men is characterized by a strict scientific-ideological analysis, avowedly Marxist. This is clearly seen in their way of relating praxis and theory and in their insistence on the rationality, conflict, and radicality of the political realm. It can also be seen in the recognition of class struggle. This assumption of Marxism—which is not tantamount to an uncritical acceptance of all its philosophy—is decisive for the theological task and indicates, as Giulio Girardi has said, "a qualitative leap" from the humanist or spiritualist inspiration of the "social concern" to an engagement mediated through a scientific (Marxist) analysis. How is this relation established? It is quite evident that one cannot expect to extract from the Bible models of political or economic organization applicable to society. Gutiérrez solves the problem by distinguishing two levels: that of political action, which is eminently rational/scientific, and that of faith, which is the liberation from sin and the access to fellowship with God and with all men. But there is also, he adds, a third, intermediate level: *utopia,* in which man projects his quest for a new man in a new society. The utopia stimulates science by putting forward a project which goes beyond the present horizon and demands the creation of new instruments and new hypotheses. Faith, in its turn, inspired by the vision of the final liberation, stirs utopian imagination to the creation of these proleptic and propelling visions. "Faith and political action do not relate to each other except through the project of creation of a new type of man in a different society, through utopia. . . ."

Critics have not taken long in objecting to the fact that this theology, with its insistence on praxis and the sociopolitical context as privileged theological *data,* gives to the historical circumstances a determinative weight in theology. This is, according to Assmann, precisely the significance of this theology. The idealism of the "rich world" believes that it can start from abstract conceptions and objective sources. It deceives itself; it only succeeds in idealizing the existing situation and projecting it afterward—thus the "theology of the death of God" and the "theology of secularization" project the conditions of the technological world. The only possible point of departure is the concrete situation. It is therefore very urgent to unmask the ideologies hidden in the theologies of the past (as we saw in Segundo) and to assume the historical character of theological reflection. We do theology "beginning from concreteness," from "particular realities."

This is the reason why we begin from a praxis. It is not merely that theology is at the service of action, as in a way it was in the old Jesuit order: seeing, judging, acting. Rather, action is itself the truth. Truth is at the level of history, not in the realm of ideas. Reflection on praxis, on human significant action, can only be authentic when it is done from within, in the vicinity of the strategic and tactical plane of human action. Without this, reflection would not be critical and projective conscience; it would not be a revision and projection of praxis as such. Another point mentioned in a different connection also belongs here: a praxis is not simply subjective or arbitrary; it means that a situation has been analyzed and assumed by means of an interpretative synthesis. In this way, the sociopolitical analysis and the ideological option implicit in it, which are included in the praxis adopted, are determinative integrants of theological reflection. In view of this fact, and of the Marxist extraction of these elements, somebody may ask: Is this still *theo*logy? Assmann responds, firstly, that every theology obeys, in fact, an assumed situation, whether consciously or not, by means of some ideological option; and, secondly:

> ... the criteria for a good theology are not any more strictly theological, just as the criteria for an effective love of God belong to the historical and human order of the neighbor, i.e., to the order of the nondivine. In fact, just as the *divine*

dimension in the love of the neighbor is the God-reference in the neighbor, so the *theological* in the reflection on the historical praxis is present in the dimension of faith. If the divine, therefore, can only be found through the human, it is entirely logical that a Christian theology will find its ultimate theological character in the human references of history.

Although it is not possible at this point to enter into greater detail, three consequences of this vision deserve to be mentioned: (1) It makes possible to unmask and denounce the false theologies that cover ideologically enslaving political options (theologies of the rich world, theologies of development, "third positions," etc.). (2) It helps to break the blocking of the Christian mind in dealing with questions such as the conflictive character of history, the problem of violence, and others. (3) It brings to light a series of problems inherent in historical praxis which ideologies—the Marxist one, for instance—have ignored or refused to face because they lack categories to grapple with them: death, fellowship, sacrifice. Theology can make here a valuable contribution. But it will do it only insofar as it places itself within a concrete and real historical engagement. It is essential for this theology not to keep a "residuum" outside commitment, not to suppress all dualism between faith and historical praxis and—as I see it—between theological and ideological reflection.

Among the Protestants in Latin America, theological reflection is a new thing. They used to be satisfied with translations, reproductions, or adaptations of European or North American religious books. Lately, nevertheless, a certain creativity seems to have kindled in some Protestant quarters. We shall choose among these "first fruits" the man who has produced the first systematic exploration of the theme of liberation. Rubem Alves, a Brazilian, has done a significant part of his work in the United States of America. His books are published in English, and therefore available to the reader. There are significant similarities and differences between his thought and that of the Catholic theologians indicated in this chapter. Alves moves much more consistently in the world of North European and American thought. His partners in dialogue and his references are almost exclusively taken from this world. He tends to use the philosophy of language, rather than sociological or political sciences, as the coordinates for his own theological construction. Finally, he gives considerable attention to the question of a biblical hermeneutics. (In this sense, he is closer to Segundo.)

The point of departure is, nevertheless, the same. At the beginning of his first book, he disclaims any attempt to have created "a new idea or hypothesis." "I have simply tried to explore critically the elements and possibilities of a language which some Christian groups have begun to speak." A language, at the same time, is not for Alves a purely superstructural creation. "It is an expression of how a community has programmed a solution to its existential problems." Behind a language, therefore, there is a community engaged in a praxis. Alves intends to study the significance of the language that the new "revolutionary" communities (or "communities of liberation") have begun to use. Historical praxis becomes also for Alves, consequently, the matrix of theological thought. In fact, referring to the Hebrew concept of truth, he advocates a new understanding of *truth,* not as an abstract realm of ideas, but as "efficacious truth," as "action," as "the name given by a historical community to its historical deeds, which were, are, and will be efficacious in the liberation of man."

Where is this community? Alves extends the limits to include, to be sure, the Third World, but also the poor and oppressed in the developed world: i.e., the black in the United States of America and protesting youth groups throughout the world. His critique of oppression is also centered more amply in the technological and repressive society which has emerged from capitalism than in the capitalist relations of production. To put it briefly: Marcuse rather than Marx provides the terms of his analysis. As a consequence, human freedom (the possibility of creativity, man as subject) rather than justice is the dominant element in his view of liberation. This is not to say that he ignores the more "material" dimensions (a Brazilian could hardly do it!). But his work is more clearly located in this area.

Alves begins, therefore, with the existence of groups of Christians who are discovering this liberating vocation, and are starting to read the Bible and the doctrine of the church in a new way, to speak a new language, which is born in a concrete historical experience but which, at the same time, recognizes itself as the language of the same historical community of the Old and New Testaments. The exploration of this language (and of the consciousness of the community which created and creates it) demands, logically, two perspectives: the one defined by the relation of the community to its present historical circumstances and the one defined by its "memory," i.e., the relation of the present community with the fellowship of faith in the past, reaching back to the Bible. Methodologically, Alves chooses two parameters: the language of the human quest for liberation, of the engagement with man's historical freedom, of the openness to the future, *humanist messianism;* and the language of the experience of liberation of the community of faith, the language of the exodus, *messianic humanism.* In the critical convergence of these two foci, we will find the authentic project of liberation, the meaning of the community of faith, and at the same time the meaning of historical existence.

How do these two parameters converge? The answer is in their radically critical character, in their adamant denial of "that which is," in their refusal to be determined by precedent and to be conformed to existing reality: "A new future will not be reached through the logic immanent in the facts given in the present state of things." In the theological realm, the experience of the exodus reflects this critical awareness. God manifests himself as the power of liberation who rejects the objective and subjective impossibility of liberation of the "given" condition of the Israelite tribes. For the Bible, God is not the eternally Present One who renders superfluous the movement of history or the eternal Reason who enables man to understand—and therefore to accept—things as they are, but the freedom which intervenes in history in order to prevent the past from determining the future. He is the freedom that impregnates history for the birth of a discontinuous possibility; he is the subverter of the status quo.

Neither messianic humanism nor humanistic messianism conceives the critical principle in isolation, as an end, but only as a necessary and intrinsic means in the creation of a future of freedom for man. Alves weaves through the whole fabric of the book, as a permanent theme, Paul Lehmann's happy expression: "to make and to keep human life human." Toward this goal, both movements converge—the humanist and the messianic. In one of the sections, Alves points out that liberation is at the service of life. God makes himself solidary with man; his freedom is freedom for the history of man. At this point, taking distance from the future-oriented thought of Moltmann and Bloch, with whom he is closely linked, our author inserts his theology in the present situation of oppression, in man's suffering. Liberation is not simply a history that breaks in from a future totally unconnected with the present: it is a project which springs from the protest born of the suffering of the present; a protest to which God grants a future in which man enters through his action.

Man's action, though, will not occur merely in the subjectivity of the individual—as in existentialism's flight from history—nor in the construction of a welfare society—as in the technological flight from freedom and consequently from what is human—but in *politics,* understood as human action carrying out a humanizing project in a historical future. Alves has polemicized with the fathers of modern Protestant theology for not having seen this. Barth in his transcendentalism, Bultmann in his existentialism, and Moltmann in his "futurism," have submitted to languages which do not take human life and action seriously. Once the political language is adopted, a tension appears between the humanist and the messianic. For humanistic messianism, politics is an exclusively human possibility: man's liberation by man alone. For messianic humanism, there is a politics of God, which is manifested in the exodus: Israel is not merely conscious of having liberated itself, but of having been liberated; a future which was objectively and subjectively closed (because of Egypt's oppressive power and its own "slave consciousness") is broken open by a God who reveals himself as free from history (namely, from the determinisms of history) and for history. In acting in this way, God makes human politics possible, opens room for it, drives a wedge which precedes man's creative action. God as the future of freedom and freedom for the future makes the liberating project possible even in the most oppressive circumstances. Humanism, on the other hand, ends in despair and cynicism because oppression subjects the conscience and obliterates the horizon of freedom. Christian hope, far from taking the place of political action, invites and demands that action in the present, in favor of the oppressed, in the light and direction of the promised future. This is the language of the Gospel. The community which enters this action, acquires this consciousness, and uses this language is God's people, in continuity with the experience of Israel and the New Testament—whether they stay within or more outside the visible ecclesiastical institutions. For an engagement with man's liberation and a pressing for God's future are the true marks of the church.

The reader acquainted with recent European and American theology may have felt somewhat puzzled as he was progressing through this chapter. He may have had the impression that he was treading on familiar ground, but things looked at times curiously different. The echoes of the voices of Barth, Bonhoeffer, Rahner, Moltmann, Metz, even of Lehmann, Shaull, and Cox met him every so often and were unmistakable. But they were pitched differently, modified, until they seemed almost different voices. Is there any way of accounting for this phenomenon? I shall try to begin answering this question by suggesting some clues for the interpretation of this theology.

The first has to do with the way in which theology refers to its subject. If theology—however it may be more precisely defined—has something to do with God and his action, it is evident that it cannot refer directly to its subject. Leaving aside the problem of a mystical experience, one must admit that language about God is necessarily analogical. This, which many of the fathers knew, is today an accepted and rigorously investigated fact. In what realm of human experience and activity shall we find the categories for naming the themes of theology? Religion and metaphysics have traditionally provided the answer. But the world of religion and metaphysics has been growing increasingly dim during the last four centuries. Theology has consequently tried to articulate its knowledge in more decidedly anthropological terms, resorting to psychological or existential analysis. But in the last decades, converging lines of human experience and thought and of biblical research have pointed to the realm of history as the proper quarry for theological building material. Consequently, the sciences dealing with historical life—sociology, politics, the sciences of culture—have more and more provided the categories and articulations for theology. This double shift from the metaphysical to the anthropological and from the inner-personal to the public-historical marks the works of the European and American theologians we have just mentioned. Some of them, like Metz, Moltmann, or Cox, have explicitly argued for the use of this historical language and, more precisely, for a *political* transcription of the Gospel. Here is the undeniable kinship with and indebtedness to these authors that our theologians manifest.

The option for a historical, political language has, nevertheless, been radicalized in Latin America, by bringing it down, not merely to the language and categories of a "general" analysis of historical existence, but to the concrete contents of our own social, cultural, political, and economic experience and to the categories that our own sociopolitical analysts have forged in order to grasp this experience. Thus, theological language has gained a painful concreteness which sounds strangely unfamiliar and perhaps irritating. "Terms which point to this sociopolitical infrastructure come in their own right into the language of the most rigorous theology," writes J. L. Segundo, and he illustrates this with such terms as "conscientization, imperialism, international market, monopolies, social classes, developmentalism." We shall discuss later on the legitimacy or otherwise of such a claim. It is enough, at the present point, to indicate some of its consequences.

The choice of a language is never a purely neutral or formal decision. In the very act, a realm of reality, or better said, a relation to reality is introduced as subject matter of theology. This is particularly so in the political case, when the categories chosen do not merely intend to describe human existence but to shape and transform it. A theology cast in political terms cannot satisfy itself with reformulating in a new way the theological heritage; it has to grapple with the dynamics of the language it uses. It has to concern itself with its relation to power. The words it uses belong to a context of militancy. The categories of analysis in which it casts its reflection are engaged categories, and, as they gain a certain determinant power, the theologian cannot remain any more above the realm of political options. Latitudinarianism is dead: Latin American theology becomes therefore a militant theology—a partisan theology, perhaps.

Such an option will certainly strike most academic theologians as strange. It will seem to lead to a sort of ideological and political captivity. Postponing a more careful analysis of this objection, we must nevertheless venture some answers. The first takes the form of a counterquestion: Where is the theologian who has not made such an option, whether he knows it or not? Assmann, Segundo, Gutiérrez attack the attempt of such theologians as Küng, Metz, or

Moltmann to remain at a nonpartisan level. The Latin Americans are constantly engaged in unmasking the ideologies smuggled in apparently neutral theologies. The words *apparently* or *unconsciously* lead into the second question and answer: What are the criteria for judging a theology's commitment? Today we know enough about language, thanks to structural analysis, to realize that the meaning of a language is determined not simply by the intention of the speaker but through the code or context of meanings which are already present and into which the pronounced word becomes inserted, independently of the speaker's intention. Words, for instance, which Moltmann and Metz use as clues, have their own meanings in terms of the ideological conflicts of the present. Unless they be specified in relation to a concrete world of references (the imperialist question, the class struggle, capitalism, and so forth), they will specify themselves through the cultural and political context in which they function. In Europe, for instance, they immediately are integrated into the developmentalist, technological, liberal ideology adopted by the Common Market and its orbit in relation to the Third World. The question, therefore, is not what is intended with words, but how do they operate. And they always operate in a given direction. There are, from this point of view, no nonpartisan languages.

Another way of posing the same problem is to ask for the verifiability of a language. Once we resign reference to a metaphysical realm, a world of ideas in which theological categories have their referents, the only possibility is to relate a language to forms of conduct, to action, to a praxis. There is no direct access from words and meanings to a theological reality outside time and history. God can only be named through the reference to a concrete community of historical existence, in relation to which words define their meanings. This verifiability . . . makes a Copernican change in theology. . . . Theology, as here conceived, is not an effort to give a correct understanding of God's attributes or actions but an effort to articulate the action of faith, the shape of praxis conceived and realized in obedience. As philosophy in Marx's famous *dictum,* theology has to stop explaining the world and to start transforming it. *Orthopraxis,* rather than orthodoxy, becomes the criterion for theology.

Finally, in such an understanding of the language and function of theology, there is no possibility of invoking or availing oneself of a norm outside praxis itself. This does not involve a rejection of the scriptural text or of tradition, but the recognition of the simple fact that we always read a text which is already incorporated in a praxis, whether our own or somebody else's. There is no possibility of extracting the text and projecting it objectively as a norm. There is only the possibility of criticism from within ourselves or in dialogue with others. This simple fact has somber, wide-ranging, practical consequences for hermeneutics (what are the conditions for this immanent criticism of one's own engaged praxis?) and for ecclesiology (how is this dialogue of antithetically committed "readings" related to the community of faith?). The elimination of a distinction of realms, which we saw in Gutiérrez, or the affirmation of one single history, to which many European theologians would also suscribe, proves to lead to some critical questions. If metaphysical reference is removed, and salvation history absorbed in an undifferentiated human history, how is the normative character of the "original events" of faith to be preserved? We face here a number of crucial problems. The modifications in the language and categories in theology reveal a more basic fact: we are being confronted by a new way of "doing theology." Gutiérrez's way of putting it is worth quoting:

> . . . the theology of liberation offers us not so much a new theme for reflection as a *new way* of making theology. Theology as critical reflection on historical praxis is thus a liberating theology, a theology of the liberating transformation of the history of mankind and, therefore, also of that portion of it—gathered as *ecclesia*—which openly confesses Christ. [It is] a theology which does not limit itself to think the world, but which attempts to place itself as a moment of the process through which the world is transformed: opening itself—in the protest against the trodden dignity of man, in the struggle against the plunder of the immense majority of men, in the love which liberates, in the construction of a new, just and fraternal society—to the gift of God's Kingdom.

Jon Sobrino

Jon Sobrino asserts that Jesus was very much involved in political and social issues and that the historical Jesus is the pathway to liberation. This selection is taken from his Christology at the Crossroads. *Maryknoll, N.Y.: Orbis Books, 1978, pp. xv–xix, 33–37.*

In presenting this book to English-speaking readers, I should like to offer a few observations that may help them to understand its background and its point of view. This particular Christology was written against the backdrop of Latin America. Its direct aim is to give Latin Americans a better understanding of Christ and to point up his historical relevancy for our continent. It is a Christology at the crossroads. Behind it lies a long tradition, part of which it proposes to reject. Before it lies a new and authentically Latin American Christology which does not yet exist, which yet remains to be formulated, and toward which this book points.

Let me begin by pointing out some of the things that we wish to reject. Here in Latin America we can read many of the old, classic treatments of Christology as well as more current ones. When we do, and when we notice their practical repercussions on the life and praxis of Christians, we cannot help but formulate certain suspicions. Basically, those suspicions come down to this: For some reason it has been possible for Christians, in the name of Christ, to ignore or even contradict fundamental principles and values that were preached and acted upon by Jesus of Nazareth.

Thus we are led to analyze how it has been possible for Christological reflection itself to obscure the figure of Jesus and to examine the dire consequences of such Christological reflection. This gives rise to a threefold suspicion. First of all, quite frequently Christ has been reduced to a sublime abstraction. Insofar as he is sublime, he always is seen as something positive. But insofar as he is an abstraction, it is possible to ignore or deny Christ's truth. The bad feature of this abstractness is seen in practice, where a separation is introduced between the total or whole Christ on the one hand and the concrete history of Jesus on the other. This opens the way for the theoretical possibility of an alienating comprehension of Christ. The practical consequences are seen in the existence of all sorts of spiritualism and Pentecostalism that invoke the Spirit of Christ but do not look to the concrete Spirit of Jesus for their real-life verification. Here we find the precious alibi used by many to hide and maintain the stirrings of a bad conscience. They keep appealing to some vague spirit that is not the Spirit that served as the driving force behind the concrete history of Jesus.

We cannot get beyond that abstraction by working with some conception of Christ as Love or Christ as Power; for in that case we simply replace the abstraction with formal categories. Considering Christ as Love, for example, Christians maintain an apparent neutrality vis-à-vis the flagrant inequities in our society. Such neutrality is wholly contrary to the partiality that Jesus displayed in favor of the oppressed. By the same token, the notion of Christ as Power has justified the sacralization of power in the political and economic realms, even giving rise to secularized versions of the same idea. So we have the abstract Christ, the impartial Christ, and the power-wielding Christ. These are the religious symbols that those in power need. These are the symbols that they have used, wittingly or unwittingly, to maintain the Latin American continent in its present state.

Suspicion leads to a second observation. This has to do with the affirmation that Christ is the embodiment of universal reconciliation. The statement is true in itself, but it is not given its dialectical thrust. It is an eschatological truth that some seek to pass off as a historical truth pure and simple. Thus they present a pacifist Jesus who does not engage in prophetic denunciations, a Jesus who pronounces blessings but who does not pronounce maledictions, and a Jesus who loves all human beings but who is not clearly partial toward the poor and the oppressed. Even soteriology, as normally employed, has fostered this particular kind of Christology. It affirms that Jesus died on behalf of all people in order to free them from their sins; it tends to ignore the fact that Jesus died as a direct result of historical sins. That still allows the church to preach something about sin, of course. But in a subtle way it prevents the church from uttering its most profound word about sin and its outright condemnation of it.

Sin is that which brought death to the Son of God. Today too, then, sin is that which brings death to the children of God, to human beings; it may be sudden, violent death, or it may be the slow, unremitting death caused by unjust structures. This leads us to a different view of the insistent emphasis on Christ as the embodiment of universal reconciliation, which is ingenuously preached by some and defended by others out of self-interest. Such an emphasis is nothing else but an attempt to exempt Jesus from the conflict-ridden toils of history, to use Christianity as a support for some sort of ideology espousing peace and order and as a weapon against any kind of conflict of subversion. It is an attempt to keep Christians strangers to the sinfulness and conflictual nature of history. When Christians do get involved in the conflicts of history, they can simply be accused of being subversives and phony Christians.

There is room for suspicion in another area as well. Here it has to do with the tendency to absolutize Christ while, once again, neglecting the dialectical side of the matter. This statement may sound radically new and rather shocking to many Christians. In their consciousness, at least on the superficial level, it may seem quite obvious that Christ *is* absolute for the Christian. But the logical and, even more important, the historical consequences of this belief do render it suspect. If Christ is in fact an absolute from every point of view, then we have the theoretical justification we need for any sort of personalist or individualist reduction of the Christian faith. By that I mean the view which sees contact with the "Thou" of Christ as the ultimate and correct correlative for the "I" of the individual Christian. That view also enables Christian faith to justify everything bad or wrong-headed in various strains of popular religiosity. . . .

Here I should simply like to point out that if Christ is the ultimate or the divine pure and simple, then he is functioning as someone who satisfies and fulfills the needs and wants of the oppressed masses on the ideological level while masking their wants and needs on the level of real life. Total absolutization of Christ also introjects a historical conception into the consciousness of Christians. If Christians already possess the absolute, it is not surprising that their interest in the nonabsolutes of history would diminish. Thus, repeated stress on the importance of history would seem to be a mere matter of words, maintained by a sheer act of will.

In such a context, recalling the essential relationality of Christ is not simply a theoretical question to be debated and settled in dogmatic or exegetical terms. If we recall that in the Gospels Jesus did not preach about himself, that the Kingdom of God was his pole of reference, and that even after the Resurrection the Son is related to the Father who is not yet all in all (1 Cor. 15:28), then we realize that our history has absolute importance and that it is only through history that we can envision and arrive at the absolute. The most obvious practical consequences of this realization are bound up with our essential obligation to seek out, here and now, those historical mediations that most clearly seem to point out the way to what is authentically absolute.

Our situation in Latin America, then, may well be somewhat different from that in the developed world when it comes to applying the "eschatological reservation" to concrete mediations of the kingdom of God. In developed countries the eschatological reservation, grounded on the absoluteness of Christ, may serve to relativize and reduce the importance of any concrete mediation of the Kingdom of God. In Latin America, the eschatological reservation makes sense only insofar as we undertake the task of seeking out concrete mediations of the Kingdom. Of course, we must apply the eschatological reservation to them, insisting that they are not the last word. But at the very least, we must find concrete mediations that are decent enough to allow for the application of that reservation. As it stands now in most Latin American countries, asserting that the fullness of the Kingdom has not yet arrived here is not the problem; that is all too obvious. What we must do now is assert that our situation is the formal *negation* of the fullness of the Kingdom, that we must therefore work to create something that resembles it at least a little.

At bottom, the concern to maintain the absoluteness of Christ is bound up with a concern to maintain the absoluteness of the system that now prevails in our Latin American countries. Those who hold economic and political power do not want to see Christians affirming the essential relationship of Jesus to the Kingdom of God. They would prefer to maintain the seemingly orthodox affirmation of Christ's absoluteness so that the supposed absoluteness of the prevailing capitalist system might not be called into question. They want to see absolute religious symbols that command respect in and of themselves, even though they may be tangential or even contrary to history. Why? Because such symbols will provide a religious justification for such economic and political symbols as the state, democracy, and capitalism. In this way, the latter may share in some of the reputed absoluteness of the former.

These, then, are some of the basic suspicions we have about the traditional way of doing Christology. In theory, at least, the same suspicions might be evoked in other places besides Latin America, and to some extent they have been. To this theoretical side our present situation in Latin America adds the weight of clear-cut evidence and the urgent necessity of engaging in some other sort of Christological reflection. At the very least, it should get beyond some of the dangers pointed out above and suggest the proper road to take. . . .

Latin American Christology

For the most part, Latin Americans have not worked out systematic Christologies and full presentations of Christ. The only outstanding exception in this regard is Leonardo Boff's work on Jesus Christ as Liberator. . . .

The theology of liberation serves as the general frame of reference for Latin American Christology. Unlike European brands of theology, liberation theology does not see itself situated in a broader history of Latin American theology, since the latter is of very recent vintage. So rather than engaging in dialogue with other theologies, philosophies, or cultural movements, liberation theology has faced up to the basic Latin American reality of underdevelopment and oppression: "Liberation is then seen as a setting in motion of a process which will lead to freedom."

This facing up to reality itself rather than to mediating factors engaged in pondering reality has taken place in the midst of real-life commitment to the cause of liberation. Thus liberation theology has not arisen primarily as an effort to *justify* real-life involvement. Instead, it has arisen as a by-product of a concrete faith that is pondered and lived out in terms of the questions raised by involvement in the praxis of liberation. Its aim is to make that involvement "more critical-minded and creative."

Pondering the real-life situation only after it has been experienced in concrete terms, Latin Americans have been prompted to see Christ in very new and different terms. As Boff puts it: "Each generation brings a new *parousia* of Christ because in each age he is given a new image, the result of the difficult synthesis between life and faith. . . . Today, in the experience of faith of many Christians in Latin America, he is seen and loved as the liberator." So the basic locus of Christology is the place where faith and life meet.

It is not the first stage of the Enlightenment that seems to pose the real challenge today. It is not such movements as liberalism, Freemasonry, and theosophy that raise questions for Latin American theology today. It is the whole problem of *reality* and concrete life itself, of the second stage of the Enlightenment, that now holds center stage. The problem of the believing *subject,* who may now find it hard to see the import or truth of faith, has taken a back seat. And the sinfulness of the situation is not something just to be explained; it must be concretely transformed. That is why Latin America is not much interested in clarifying people's understanding of such traditional theological problems as transubstantiation, the hypostatic union in Christ, and the relationship between divine and human knowledge in Christ.

Such problems are ignored, I believe, for two basic reasons that have nothing to do with disdain. First of all, theological clarification of that sort does not seem to have any direct repercussions on the social sphere. Second, and more important, to dally over such questions is to play the game of traditional theology, which is seen to be alienating and totally uninvolved with real issues. We are hiding from real problems and serving the interests of ideology if we focus on the traditional theological problems of transubstantiation and the hypostatic union while such issues as underdevelopment and its implications go unexplored.

So Latin American theology aims to be critical and operative, taking life as a whole rather than the individual Christian as its point of departure. From the horizon of liberation, good theologizing means real service.

The impact of the second stage of the Enlightenment is readily seen in the use which is made of Marx's social, religious, and political analyses, though Latin Americans claim to use them with a critical eye. It is even more evident in the fact that Marx's epistemological revolution plays a great role. We come to know reality really only insofar as we come to realize the necessity of transforming it. The second stage of the Enlightenment also exerts an influence on Christology, however sketchy that Christology still may be. Emphasis is placed on those Christological elements that serve to constitute a paradigm of liberation (e.g., the Resurrection as utopia and the Kingdom of God) or to highlight practical ways of understanding and realizing it (e.g., the sociopolitical activity of Jesus and the obligation to follow in his footsteps).

So hermeneutics becomes a hermeneutics of praxis, and the implications for Christology are clear: "It is not enough simply to read about the figure of Jesus purely in the light of his *ipsissima vox et facta* and within the apocalyptic framework and the sociological background of his time. Exegetes, using more and more sophisticated methods, have done this and their work is very valuable, but it is not a science in itself.... The elements that give permanent validity to this message, above the pressures of history, can only be adequately grasped in a hermeneutic approach. From this, the *ipsissima intentio* of Jesus emerges." And the aim of studying Jesus' intention is to pave the way for "effective collaboration" with him. The course that Jesus took is to be investigated scientifically, not just to aid in the quest for truth but also in the fight for truth that will make people free.

The basic quandary that inspires Latin American theology is summed up in the term *liberation*. It is embodied concretely in the coexistence of two fundamental and contradictory experiences: the felt need for liberation as an absolute necessity on the one hand, and the impossibility of achieving it in history on the other. The resulting situation is experienced as one of bondage or captivity, where hope for liberation goes hand in hand with concrete experience of unjust oppression.

In theological terms, then, we are dealing with a question of theodicy rather than a question of natural theology. We must try to reconcile the Kingdom of God with a situation of bondage. Yet Latin American theodicy has peculiar features of its own insofar as liberation theology arose out of active praxis rather than static contemplation. Faced with a pervasive situation of misery, it does not take the classic tack to be found in the Book of Job, in the work of Dostoyevsky, and more recently in Rabbi Rubinstein's query as to how Jews can believe in God after Auschwitz. It is not concerned with finding some way to contemplate God and captivity in a meaningful relationship. Instead, it is concerned with the practical problem of building up and realizing the Kingdom of God in the face of captivity.

The quandary is very much lived as such because there is no evident way out of the dilemma. But it is inspired and sustained by the conviction that the real problem is not to justify God but rather to turn the justification of human beings into a reality. The question of justifying God seems to be all too theoretical in the face of the real-life need to make people just. It is reality that must be reconciled with the Kingdom of God, and the quandary of theodicy must be resolved in praxis rather than in theory.

What, then, are we to say about the Christological concentration of Latin American theology? It is my firm belief that this is one of the most delicate issues in liberation theology. The basic question is, of course, whether the main interest of liberation theology is Christ or liberation. Needless to say, this alternative is not posed as such, either in theory or in praxis, but it will help us to bring the whole matter of Christological concentration out into the open. Only the future course of liberation theology will provide an answer to the problem, but even now some observations can be made.

First, it is worth realizing that certain things which seem to be real alternatives for the mind can be united in lived experience. An example from Paul's theology might help us here. In theory, we might well ask whether his theology is concentrated on Christology or on justification; in practice, we feel sure that the two were joined together in his own experience. We might begin with his Christological experience on the road to Damascus in order to comprehend his experience of being justified. Or, on the other hand, we might begin with his personal experience of the need to be justified and the impossibility of ever attaining it, and then see how the problem was resolved in his experience of Christ. Something similar seems to be the case with liberation theology. I think that liberation theology as "theology" is profoundly Christological; and insofar as it is concerned with "liberation," its most all-embracing theological concept is "the Kingdom of God."

We can see this tension in the practice of liberation theology itself. On the one hand, the notion of the Kingdom of God polarizes the anthropological and historical presuppositions of theology and becomes a hermeneutic principle for the study of Christology: "The

Kingdom of God expresses man's utopian longing for liberation from everything that alienates him, factors such as anguish, pain, hunger, injustice, and death, and not only man but all creation." On the other hand, the Kingdom of God is not "a mere organic extension of this world, as it is encountered in history. The Kingdom does not evolve, but breaks in." It is here, then, that Christology begins to operate. Not only must we try to understand Jesus in terms of the Kingdom; we must also try to understand the Kingdom in terms of Jesus. Without the kingdom Jesus would be little more than an abstract object of study; without Jesus, however, the Kingdom would be only a partial reality.

Hence the Christological concentration of liberation theology is dialectical in nature. It does not try to deduce everything from Christology, but, on the other hand, this "everything" is not real or truly understood without Christology. Within Christology itself emphasis is placed on the Resurrection of Jesus as a paradigm of liberation; but even more insistent is the stress placed on the historical Jesus as the pathway to liberation. It is the historical Jesus who enlightens us with regard to the basic meaning of the task as well as his personal way of carrying it out. Liberation theology is concentrated in Christology insofar as it reflects on Jesus himself as the way to liberation.

Rosemary Ruether

Rosemary Ruether has contended that liberation theology must go beyond political and economic conditions to include the liberation of both oppressors and oppressed. This selection is taken from her Liberation Theology. *New York: Paulist Press, 1972, pp. 10–16.*

The Oppressor and the Oppressed as a Model
for Liberation Theology

Recent theologies of liberation have stressed the role of the "oppressed community" as the primary locus of the power for repentance and judgment. God's liberation is seen as coming first to the "poor." God liberates the slaves from the oppressive system of power, symbolized by Egypt. God comes to overturn the oppressive reign of imperial power symbolized by Babylon (Rome; Amerika).

It is true that such a dualism of the "children of light" and the "children of darkness" can be extracted from prophetic thinking. However, this dualism, in its polarized form, appears primarily in the literature of apocalypticism. The thinking of the prophets addressed Israel as, simultaneously, the community of Promise and the community which must repent and be judged. Liberation, therefore, cannot be divorced from a sense of self-judgment and an identification with the community which is judged. It cannot be merely a movement of revolt against and judgment of an "alien community" for which one takes no responsibility. The paranoid projection of all evil upon the "nations," whereby Israel is seen simply as the "suffering saints," distorts this prophetic dialectic. Indeed such a total polarization is not found even in the apocalyptic writings, which never fail to address Israel itself as the one which must repent and be judged and return to obedience. Christianity inherited, through apocalyptic sectarian Judaism (further accentuated by the break between the sectarian apocalyptic community and ethnic Israel), the possibility of a one-sided distortion of the prophetic dialectic that would locate one community as the "oppressed saints," and the heirs of the Promise, while projecting upon the oppressors (Rome) and the rejectors (ethnic Israel) all evil and condemnation.

Such a viewpoint which judges "God's people" and "God's enemy" from the standpoint of the oppressed and the oppressors has, nevertheless, a real theological validity to it. Contextually, this historical situation does indeed become the primary place of prophetic discernment. Marxist systems, Black theology and Latin American theologies of liberation, constructed on this apocalyptic sectarian model, can carry a process of judgment and liberation a considerable distance. But, at a certain point, this model for the theology of liberation begins to reveal the limitations and disabilities inherent in its inadequate foundations.

There is a sense in which those who are primarily the victims of an oppressive system are also those who can most readily disaffiliate their identities with it, for they have the least stake in its perpetuation. In their revolt against it, they can thus become the prophetic community, which witnesses against the false empire of the "beast" and points to "God's Kingdom." But, in their very situation as victims, they have also been distorted in their inward being in a way that does not immediately make them realized models of redeemed humanity; i.e., the victims are not "saints." They have a very considerable task of inward liberation to do. They have been victimized by their powerlessness, their fear and their translation of these into an internal appropriation of subservient and menial roles. They have internalized the negative image projected upon them by the dominant society. They cower before the masters, but are also filled with a self-contempt which makes them self-destructive and fratricidal toward their fellows within the oppressed community. Typically the oppressed turn their frustration inward, destroying themselves and each other, not the masters.

Liberation for the oppressed thus is experienced as a veritable resurrection of the self. Liberation is a violent exorcism of the demons of self-hatred and self-destruction which have possessed them and the resurrection of autonomy and self-esteem, as well as the discovery of a new power and possibility of community with their own brothers and sisters in suffering. Anger and pride, two qualities viewed negatively in traditional Christian spirituality, are the vital "virtues" in the salvation of the oppressed community. Through anger and pride the oppressed community receives the power to transcend self-hatred and recover a sense of integral personhood. Anger, here, is felt as the power to revolt against and judge a system of oppression to which one was formerly a powerless and buried victim. Pride is experienced as the recovery of that authentic humanity and good created nature "upon which God looked in the beginning and, behold, it was very good." Anger and pride thus stand initially within the context of a prophetic dialectic of judgment and the renewal of creation.

However, at that point where all evil is merely projected upon an alien community, so that judgment is seen merely as rejection of that "other" group of persons, and salvation simply as self-affirmation, *per se* (without regard to a normative view of humanity), then what is valid in this initial perception is quickly distorted. The leaders of the oppressed community are not incorrect when they recognize that they have, as their primary responsibility, the leading of their own people through a process of self-exorcism and renewed humanity. So there is a sense where it is true that they "do not have the time" to be worried about the humanization of the oppressor. Yet they must also keep somewhere in the back of their minds the idea that the dehumanization of the oppressor is really their primary problem, to which their own dehumanization is related primarily in a relationship of effect to cause. Therefore, to the extent that they are not at all concerned about maintaining an authentic prophetic address to the oppressors; to the extent that they repudiate them as persons as well as the beneficiaries of false power, and conceive of liberation as a mere reversal of this relationship; a rejection of their false situation of power in order to transfer this same kind of power to themselves, they both abort their possibilities as a liberating force for the oppressors, and, ultimately, derail their own power to liberate themselves. Quite simply, what this means is that one cannot dehumanize the oppressors without ultimately dehumanizing oneself, and aborting the possibilities of the liberation movement into an exchange of roles of oppressor and oppressed. By projecting all evil upon the oppressors and regarding their own oppressed condition as a stance of "instant righteousness," they forfeit finally their own capacity for self-criticism. Their revolt, then, if successful, tends to rush forward to murder and self-aggrandizement, and the institution of a new regime where all internal self-criticism is squelched. Seven demons return to occupy the house from which the original demon has been driven, and the last state of that place is worse than the first. Such has been the tendency of modern revolutionary movements patterned on the apocalyptic, sectarian concept.

The oppressor community, of course, has a similar problem in finding who it is and what it should do in relationship to the judgment and revolt of the oppressed. The first tendency of the oppressors is, of course, to respond to the liberation movement simply by projecting upon it the negative side of their own self-righteousness. Since they have already identified their own false power with the "Kingdom of Righteousness," their initial tendency is simply to identify those in revolt against this power as the "evil ones" who are ever at work to undermine the security of "God's Elect." Within this paranoid framework, each side merely sees itself as the "saints," and the others as the "beast," and no authentic communication takes place. This paranoid view, by the way, is not merely true of traditional clerical and sacral societies, such as Christendom of the European *ancien régime.* It is equally true of revolutionary societies, which have likewise been founded upon the appropriation of messianic self-imagery, such as the USSR and the USA. These modern revolutionary societies have virtually re-established the traditional problem of Constantinian societies, although it is the opinion of this author that the USSR has a deeper problem since it passed directly from Byzantine Caesaro-papism to Marxist sectarian apocalypticism, as its political identity, without having assimilated the fruits of liberalism that could provide a theory and an institutional base for on-going self-criticism and self-correction.

Yet there are also elements in the dominant society that *are* ready to respond sympathetically to the revolt of the oppressed and to make this revolt the occasion for their own self-judgment. It is this prophetic element in the dominant society, what is usually seen as the "alienated intelligentsia," that has been, typically, the crucial mediating force for translating the protest of the oppressed into an opportunity for repentance in the dominant society. But this mediating role is also fraught with dangers and possibilities of self-delusion. The vitality of this mediating role becomes aborted when this "alienated intelligentsia" becomes concerned primarily with its own self-purification through disaffiliation with its own class, race or nation; when it seeks primarily a parasitic identification with the oppressed, who are viewed, idealistically, as the "suffering saviors," who can do no wrong or in whom all is to be excused. The prophet in the dominant society, thus becomes involved in an endless movement of self-hatred and a utopian quest for identification with an acceptance by the victims, making it impossible for him to see either side of the social equation as it really is.

Instinctively the victimized community rejects such a person, no matter how vehement his repudiation of his own people, because they sense that, in seeking to identify with them, he is taking over a leadership role which they need to learn to do for themselves. From his very social background he brings to them so much knowledge, in the way of self-confidence, expertise and familiarity with power, that he easily drowns their own feeble attempts to learn these things for themselves. Thus he interferes with their own self-discovery. Moreover, the alienated oppressor can never disaffiliate himself enough from his own society, as long as it continues in power and he automatically remains the beneficiary of that fact, to be seen by the oppressed as anything other than an extension of that fact of power over their lives in a novel form. Their own responses to the alienated oppressor who seeks to "help" them are doubtless very confused. This confusion reflects their own lack of inward liberation that makes it impossible for them to see him as other than a continuing symbol of oppression. This reflects the fact that they have not yet broken the hold of this power over their lives, and so they cannot deal with him as simply a "person" or an "exception to the rule," but react to him as a symbol of that power despite his protestations to the contrary. Yet they also discern, in a confused but valid way, that in merely adopting the echo of their own sectarian paranoia, in merely repudiating his own people and seeking identification with them, the alienated oppressor is also aborting the role of mediatorship to his own community, which is the only role in which he can be useful to them. In other words, they do not need him primarily to join what they are doing, but to play a complementary role in relation to that struggle for self-determination, by helping to get his own community off their backs so they can have a place in which to breathe. In seeking primarily to join their struggle and to move away from contact with his own people, he fails to play this vital mediating role which he alone can do for them and which they cannot do for themselves, short of successful violence.

Only when protest and response remain in dialogue in such a way that the society which is condemned is also addressed as a community which has fallen away from its own authentic promise, can there be a liberation without ultimate violence; a liberation that can end in reconciliation and new brotherhood. This cannot easily be proclaimed as a possibility before the conditions for its realization have begun to appear. It can happen only on the other side of "Black power" and "Black pride" in the black community and repentance and surrender of unjust power on the part of the white community. This hope for a new community is aborted when the black prophet refuses to have any part with liberating the oppressor as a part of his own self-liberation. It is also aborted when the white prophet seeks merely self-exculpating identification with the victims, rather than remaining in repentant and suffering identification with his own people, until he can translate this judgment to them as their own self-judgment. This was the vision of Martin Luther King. King never forgot to address Amerika, the oppressor, as also the land of promise for black man and white man alike. This vision, declared obsolete, when King was murdered, was not so much over and done with as it represented a proleptic reaching for a prophetic wholeness, for which neither black Americans nor white Americans were ready at that time. King's vision pointed to a Black ideology beyond black racism, and beyond white paternalism or white self-exculpation, to the only validly prophetic way of doing an American theology. All theologies of liberation, whether done in a black or a feminist or a Third World perspective, will be abortive of the liberation they seek, unless they finally go beyond the apocalyptic, sectarian model of the oppressor and the oppressed. The oppressed must rise to a perspective that affirms a universal humanity as the ground of their own self-identity, and also to a power for self-criticism. The alienated oppressor must learn what it means to be truly responsible for whom and what he is.

C. Peter Wagner

In 1970, C. Peter Wagner, an evangelical theologian, criticized South American liberation theology for being too closely identified with Marxist ideology. This selection is taken from his Latin American Theology: Radical or Evangelical? *Grand Rapids, Michigan: Eerdmans, 1970, pp. 17–21, 60–62.*

A Respectable Minority in the Wake of Vatican II

When historians evaluate this period a century from now, it may well turn out that Pope John XXIII will have been judged to have had more influence on the Latin American continent than any other man in the twentieth century. Roman Catholicism will never be the same as a result of the council he called and the attitude he infused. Inescapably, Protestantism has also received indelible marks from the turn of events.

For one thing, the polemical approach to preaching and theology is now a thing of the past. Roman Catholics freely admit their mistakes, refer to Protestants as "brethren" (although sometimes still modified by the adjective *separated*), read and preach the Bible, say Mass in Spanish, remove the idols from their temples, and sing Protestant choruses in their "Sunday schools." In this type of situation, there is little room for scolding and scandal-mongering. The Gospel preached must be a positive one. Polemically-oriented literature now gathers dust on the bookstore shelves.

One of the most important effects of this new atmosphere is that it has caused a profound rethinking of the theology of evangelism. While relationships between Protestants and Catholics have perhaps become more comfortable, they have also become more confusing. Perhaps this is the first focal point of the distinction we are attempting to make between the new radical left and the mainstream of Latin American Protestantism. The second-generation Protestants, who had long since left polemics, began calling the Roman Catholics "brethren" in return. But how do you evangelize a "brother"? This is no longer evangelism but "proselytism," and within the New Left an aversion to "proselytism" developed as a result of their aversion to polemics. At the same time, the majority of Latin American Protestants would not admit that Roman Catholicism was a legitimate expression of Christianity. While not discounting the possibility that some Catholics might be saved, they felt that it was improbable that they would constitute more than a tiny minority in a church that was undeniably better than it used to be, but still decidedly sub-Christian.

Since Vatican II, Protestantism has become socially respectable in most parts of Latin America. Now, more than ever before, one can be a Protestant and still be a good Latin American. It is no longer necessarily considered as either apostasy or a gringo religion.

With this foot in the door of status, some Protestants, especially those of what we are calling the radical Left, looked for the opportunity to open it wider. They felt that if Protestantism could gain more status, more Latin Americans might become Protestants. They were convinced that the Protestant church should speak with a louder voice. The increased volume, as we have seen, should no longer be employed in "proselytism," but it could be turned up and beamed toward the issue which at the time was the hottest one on the continent: the social revolution. To develop a theology of social revolution and to involve the church in it seemed to be the most important contribution that Protestantism could make to Latin American society, in the thinking of this group. At just this point, the "new radical Left" became more clearly defined, and deeply committed to revolution at the same time.

A Vociferous Minority Committed to Revolution

No one familiar with the Latin American scene can doubt that the process of rapid social change has become the most urgent problem of the second half of the twentieth century there. Social revolution is no longer a theoretical option; it is a fact of life. The tremendous changes that began taking place in the economic, political, and social spheres could not be ignored by any responsible segment of society, including Protestantism. The Protestant church is no longer considered a cloister of refuge from a persecuting world; it is, for better or worse, a community that must relate to the world which has accepted it and offered it hospitality. On this, all agree.

But when it comes to *how* the church should relate to the current Latin American social scene, differences of opinion enter the picture. One of the most precise classifications of the three major opinions has recently been set forth by William Wipfler, editor of the National Council of Churches' *Latin American News Letter:*

> The first is that of the "establishment." It is interested in development and recognizes stability of structures as precondition of development. Whatever measures necessary are justified to provide the necessary stability. The second position, adopted by evolutionists of the liberal tradition, is eager for change, but insists that it be done by whittling away at the barriers and helping to build better facilities to achieve some social justice. The third position is more militant. It consists of those who think that true development requires a break with the present system and the adoption of new forms of social and political organization. Such a radical break is rightly called revolutionary, with proponents more or less prepared to resort to strategies which involve violence. Nonviolent revolutionary strategies, of the sort developed in the U.S. racial struggle, have not, to date, captured the imagination

of more than a few Latin American leaders. Christians, both Catholic and Protestant, are to be found in each camp.

While it is true these three positions are held by those outside the church as well as those within, our particular interest is their reflection within Protestantism. The new radical Left has generally committed itself to the third alternative and the violent, revolutionary expression of it. . . .

Involvement in this particular segment of Latin American Protestantism usually requires several special qualities which all Protestants obviously do not possess. Most likely, the exponent of this point of view will be a second-generation Protestant; or if first generation, he probably will not have had a radical conversion experience but will have been "educated" into the church through Protestant schools. He will be a member of one of the historical denominations; or if not, his commitment to the radical position probably can be traced to some special incentive such as a scholarship obtained through one of the historical denominations or some travel funds obtained from ecumenical sources. He will have been trained in one of the more liberal Latin American seminaries such as the Facultad de Teología en Buenos Aires, the Evangelical Seminary of Río Piedras, Puerto Rico, the Presbyterian Seminary of Campinas, Brazil (in one of its periods of liberal domination), the Theological Community of Santiago, Chile, or the like. He will probably have taken graduate work in Europe or the United States of America in another liberally-oriented seminary on a grant from the World Council of Churches/National Council of Churches (United States of America). He will play down the persuasive aspects of evangelism, the eschatological elements of final personal judgment, and the heaven-hell alternative as eternal destinies.

The continent-wide structures which have been created as a base for the radical Protestant left are well financed, skillfully led, and extremely vocal. Most important are ISAL (*Iglesia y Sociedad en América Latina* or Church and Society in Latin America) and MEC (*Movimiento Estudiantil Cristiano* or Student Christian Movement). Of lesser importance for this particular study are ULAJE (*Unidad Latinoamericana de Juventudes Evangélicas* or Latin American Union of Evangelical Youth) and CELADEC (*Comisión Evangélica Latinoamericana de Educatión Cristiana* or Latin

American Christian Education Council). The master organization to coordinate them all is UNELAM (*Comisión Provisional proUnidad Evangélica Latinoamericana* or Provisional Commission for the Promotion of Latin American Evangelical Unity).

Reflected in all of these structures is the deep-seated conviction that the Protestant church should be concerned with treating the open wounds in Latin American society. While these leaders consistently tip their hats to the foreign missionaries who brought the Gospel to their lands, they now feel that only Latin Americans themselves can fully understand the dimensions of their own social problems and move to take the necessary action. In this they are unquestionably right. They admit that plunging into the social revolution as Protestants involves a risk. Whether they realize that this involvement may easily lead to serving mammon rather than serving God is another question. If a syncretism of the Christian message is a necessary measure for this type of involvement, an even greater risk is taken. It is the terrible risk of disobedience to God.

No one who reads the writings of the new radical Left, much less one who is personally acquainted with its representatives, can doubt the depth of motivation, sincerity of purpose, dedication to high goals, or skill of intellectual analysis of those who have cast their lot on that side. Their interpretation of the relation of the church to the Latin American social revolution springs first and foremost from religious conviction. They are firmly convinced that they are about their Father's business. They are engaged in an intensive search for what they consider to be God's will for themselves, their church, and their countries.

If their understanding of the biblical world view seems deficient, it is usually not because they fail to acknowledge the authority of the Bible as the Word of God. Although they might not agree with Warfield's view of inspiration, the problem does not lie so much in that area. It lies rather in the extreme degree to which their understanding of the secular world has influenced their understanding of biblical truth. In many instances (but not all), truth is not denied as much as it is distorted. Priorities are often shifted out of biblical focus. At times, one gets the feeling that the starting point of this group has been an *a priori* socioeconomic theory, and that theology has been called in only as an afterthought, not to say rationalization. The Bible seems to be used very often as a source book for proof texts rather than the touchstone of all doctrine. . . .

Marxist ideology in the left wing of the church is a fact of life in Latin America. At its deepest levels, it tends toward a deficient anthropology. Some view man as "the creator of his own history, for good or for bad." Although attempts are made to disguise it, man is frequently conceived of in naturalistic terms, and man's problems described in imminent categories. The precarious relationship of sinful man to a transcendent God is not a frequent theme. Redemption is usually viewed in the horizontal man-to-man or society-to-society dimension rather than in the vertical man-to-God dimension. The problem lies not only in a variation of emphases between the two dimensions, but in the almost total indifference to the vertical.

In an attempt to relate the Marxist view of man to the Christian, Julio Barreiro concludes that the basic conflict lies in the difference between "naturalism and incarnation." He says: "While the Marxist . . . places all his emphasis on human naturalism, the Christian, without negating that, puts all his emphasis on Christ made man."

Since Barreiro only develops the thought on the horizontal level of the Christian's responsibility to carry the consequences of the Incarnation "into the heart of society," one is tempted to suspect that such references to Christ as above are a type of pious smoke screen raised around a subbiblical concept of man. New Testament theology describes man's most basic need in terms of sin, repentance, and regeneration. Until these are adequately dealt with, it is hardly possible to develop a valid Christian anthropology.

The two folk heroes of the Latin American Marxist-oriented sector are martyrs Camilo Torres and Ché Guevara. Torres, a priest who turned into a guerrilla fighter, made a statement when he left the priesthood that has served as an inspiring test to all Christian leftists ever since. He said:

> I have left the privileges and duties of the clergy, but I have not left the priesthood. I believe to have devoted myself to the revolution out of love for my neighbor. I will not say the Mass, but I will realize this love to my neighbor in the temporal, economic and social realms. When my neighbor has nothing against me, when I have realized the revolution, I will then say the Holy Mass again. Thus I believe to obey

> Christ's command, "If you are offering your gift on the altar and remember that your neighbor has something against you, leave your gift before the altar and go; first be reconciled to your neighbor, and then come offer your gift."

Shaull's recent statement is more concise, but seems to reflect the sentiments of Camilo Torres. He declares: "Having spent most of my life working for reform within the established order, I am now obliged to give priority to revolution."

The important issue is not really whether a Christian can hold a Marxist-oriented political ideology or not. The issue is whether Christianity obliges a man set free in Christ to hold to *any predetermined* ideology at all. The Christian world view transcends all social, economic, and political systems. As long as a Christian's goals in his relationship to the world are noble and held with a clean conscience, he should be allowed to choose the political means to reach the goals that he feels are best without his very Christianity being called into question. This applies equally to the capitalist and the socialist, the pacifist and the violent revolutionary. Samuel Escobar sums up the matter well when he says: "The Christian's liberty emerges from the fact that he knows that no economic or political system is 'Christian,' and that the destiny of the church of Christ is not tied in with any particular society or manner of life."

Ecumenical Dialogue of Third World Theologians, Dar es Salaam, Tanzania, August 5–12, 1976

An ecumenical dialogue of Third World theologians, meeting in Dar es Salaam, Tanzania, August 5–12, 1976, stressed an increasing awareness of the wider implications of a theology of liberation that encompasses the entire Third World. This selection is taken from Sergio Torres and Virginia Fabella, eds., The Emergent Gospel. *Maryknoll, N.Y.: Orbis Books, 1976, pp. 259–71.*

We, a group of theologians of the Third World gathered at Dar es Salaam, August 5–12, 1976, having spent a week together in common study of our role in the contemporary world, are convinced that those who bear the name of Christ have a special service to render to the people of the whole world who are now in an agonizing search for a new world order based on justice, fraternity, and freedom.

We have reflected from our life experience as belonging to the oppressed men and women of the human race. We seriously take cognizance of the cultural and religious heritage of the peoples of the continents of Asia, Africa, and Latin America. We have expressed our view of history, our perspective on the churches, and our expectations for the future. We invite all persons doing theology in the churches to consider our presentations and participate with us and with all those who are struggling to build a more just world in order that the believers in Christ may truly be involved in the struggle toward the realization of a new world order and a new humanity.

The Third World Political, Social, Economic, Cultural, Racial, and Religious Background

As we are increasingly aware of the impact of the political, social, economic, cultural, racial, and religious conditions on theology, we wish to analyze the background of our countries as one point of reference for our theological reflection.

The concept of the "Third World" is a recent one, referring to the countries outside the industrialized capitalist countries of Europe, North America, Japan, Australia, and New Zealand, and the socialist countries of Europe, including the USSR.

The economic standard of living of these countries is low. They are technologically less advanced and are mainly agricultural in production. Their terms of trade are unfavorable and deteriorating; capital accumulation is small and external debt is large and growing. The Third World is divided into the free enterprise countries under the Western powers and the socialist countries, which generally cut themselves off or have been cut off by the capitalist powers.

The Third World countries are rich in natural resources as well as in their cultural and religious traditions, which have given a deep meaning to their peoples' lives. These countries have been historically slow and late in technological development, in modernizing education, health, and transportation, and in the general growth of their countries. Traditionally, the masses have been subject to long-term exploitation by their rulers and chiefs or aristocracy. However, prior to colonization by the Western powers, they had a rather self-reliant economy, with a strong sense of communal solidarity. In certain respects, some of these areas were superior to the West in science, technology, agricultural and industrial methods, architecture, and the arts. Religion, profound philosophies of life, and cultures have been the soul of these peoples for many generations.

The principal cause for the modern phenomenon of the underdevelopment of the peoples of the Third World is the systematic exploitation of their peoples and countries by the European peoples. From the end of the fifteenth century, a large-scale and unprecedented expansion of the European peoples brought most of the rest of the world under their military, economic, political, cultural, and religious domination. For them it was a triumph of military technology, adventure, and a zeal to "civilize" and "Christianize the pagans." While they contributed a process of modernization in the colonized countries, they reaped enormous material benefits in the process. They plundered the riches of the Americas, Asia, and Africa. Gold, silver, precious stones, and raw materials were taken to add enormously to their capital accumulation. Their countries grew in wealth and power by the underdevelopment of these conquered and colonized countries.

The Western powers took over all the temperate lands that they could populate with their own peoples. Where the numbers were few and relatively weak militarily, they nearly exterminated the native populations—as in North America, parts of South America, Australia, and New Zealand. This was a simple solution, with only a few people left to remind us of this most heinous genocide of human history.

In other areas, the Europeans settled down alongside the local populations, subjugating the latter to their domination as in southern America, Central America, and southern Africa. In South America, intermarriage has produced a large mestizo population, still dominated by the settlers.

In most of the countries that were thickly populated, imperial power was established following the penetration by traders and sometimes by missionaries. Only a few countries like Thailand and the hinterland of China escaped this process. The Russians, on the other hand, expanded southward and eastward up to Alaska.

In the process, the Western powers allocated to themselves the free or freed land spaces of the earth and established new sovereign states in them to preserve the land base of raw materials and power for themselves. Everywhere they established a pattern of economic exploitation in their favor. They exterminated entire peoples, enslaved millions, colonized others, and marginalized all, thus laying the base of their development and the underdevelopment of the Third World.

The colonizers undermined the economy of the colonies for their advantage. They made their colonies suppliers of raw materials based on cheap labor and markets for their finished goods. They forcibly expropriated fertile lands of the oppressed peoples, set up plantations of sugar, coffee, tea, rubber, etc. They transported millions of peoples from one country to another to serve as slaves or indentured labor. Thus we have the black population in the Americas and Indians in Africa, Malaysia, Sri Lanka and the Pacific and Caribbean islands. Paying a mere subsistence wage to the workers and charging high prices for their exports, the colonial powers were able to add further to their capital stock. They continued the pillage of the raw materials of these countries: oil, tin, bauxite, copper, timber, gold, silver, diamonds.

Hence for centuries the western European peoples had a free hand in Asia, Africa, and South and Central America. North America, having become independent, joined the race for colonial power, along with Germany, Italy, and Japan.

As political independence was gained by these colonies, beginning with the Latin American countries in the last century, a new form of exploitation consolidated itself. In Latin America, Spain and Portugal lost their dominance to be replaced by the United States, Britain, and other western European countries as the economic colonizers.

In Asia and Africa too the gaining of political independence led generally to the transfer of power to the local elite that continued the economic system established by the colonial powers. Since the

1950s, the mode of economic exploitation of Third World countries by the United States, Western Europe, and Japan has been further strengthened by the horizontal and vertical integration of companies. We have thus the growth of giant multinational corporations (MNCs), based generally in the United States, Western Europe, and Japan, that have enormous economic, political, and cultural power of domination over entire lines of production and commerce. The MNCs have made the exploitation of the poor countries such a fine art, with the advantage of the most developed technology, that the gap between the rich and the poor in the world and within the countries has continued to grow.

As we have spoken of imperialistic and political domination, it is also necessary to emphasize racial and sexist domination. The oppression of blacks and other races in different areas has been brutal and constant.

Women have been discriminated against and oppressed on all levels of both society and the church. Their condition has not changed in the new independent countries of the Third World. The different forms of oppression (political, economic, racial, sexist) have their own identity. They are interrelated and interwoven in a complex system of domination.

In this centennial exploitation of the Third World by the Euro-American people, the cultural subjugation of the weak has been an important tool of oppression. The languages, arts, and social life of the peoples of Asia, Africa, and the Americas were cruelly attacked by the colonizers.

Unfortunately, the Christian churches were in a large measure an accomplice in the process. The very sense of spiritual superiority of Christians gave a legitimation for conquest and sometimes even extinction of "pagans." The theology of the colonizers in most cases was thus attuned to the justification of this inhumanity; and is this not substantially what has passed for Christian theology during many centuries in its relationship to the oppressed peoples?

The People's Republic of China has entered a path of self-reliant growth based on socialism and the people's participation in the direction of agriculture and industry. By cutting themselves off from the capitalistic system, they have been able to reverse the trend of continuing underdevelopment that characterized the colonies and the newly independent "free enterprise" countries. North

Korea, North Vietnam, and Cuba took similar lines with appreciable results. In recent months, South Vietnam, Cambodia, and Laos in Asia, and Mozambique, Guinea, Bissau, and Angola in Africa, have opted for self-reliant socialist development. Tanzania is attempting a socialist approach without going the whole way of eliminating free enterprise. Other countries in the Third World have varying degrees of socialist experimentation: e.g., Burma, Algeria, Sri Lanka, Ethiopia.

The Soviet Union and Eastern Europe, considered the Second World, often render assistance to the oppressed peoples of other countries in their struggles for liberation—as in Cuba, Vietnam, and Angola. They are a valuable counterbalance against imperialist domination by the North Atlantic powers, along with China and the nonaligned powers of the Third World.

However, socialism too has its own problems to resolve—especially in relation to the safeguarding of human freedom and the very price of the revolutionary process in terms of human lives. The "aid" given by the socialistic countries, while being generally on better terms than that given by capitalist countries, is also not altogether without strings and disadvantages to the recipients. The foreign policies of the socialist countries tend sometimes to be according to their national self-interest and thereby even to divide the antiimperialist cause. Further, our information concerning socialist countries is rather limited, due to the barriers of communication.

In recent years, the very sharpening of the contradictions of capitalism has increased the tensions in the dependent, free enterprise countries of the Third World. The rising expectations of the peoples have led to much unrest and revolt. The response of beneficiaries of privileges has been generally in collaboration with foreign powers—to set up military dictatorships and to declare martial law or emergency rule as in most countries of Latin America, Asia, and Africa. We witness today a growing repression of people's movements, imprisonment without trial of political dissidents, and a trend toward sophisticated and inhuman torture in these countries. Human freedom is a victim in most parts of the Third World. Conflicts among Third World countries further worsen the condition of the masses of the people. Tribalism, caste, and other forms of religious, racial, and sex discrimination are further lines of exploitation.

In international affairs desperate efforts are being made by the Third World leaders to obtain better prices for their exports, ensure integrated commodity agreements, reschedule external debt, control or eliminate MNCs and military bases, and regulate the transfer of technology as through UNCTAD IV. From within the capitalist framework, the OPEC countries, mainly of the Middle East, have been able to obtain for themselves enormous quantities of petrol dollars by the method of confrontation against the consumers of petrol. This has greatly harmed the development plans of petrol-importing poor countries.

A theology of the Third World has to take into account this historical situation. It has to ask: What role has the church been playing throughout these developments at each stage and in every situation? How did Christians react to this phenomenon of the Western invasion of other peoples? What was the prevailing theology? How does Christian theology relate to today's continued exploitation in the world? What is its contribution to the building of a just world society? What contribution will the church make to the liberation of the oppressed peoples who have long suffered due to sexist, racial, and class domination?

The Presence and Role of the Church in Third World Countries

The Christian churches, while taking their origin from Jesus Christ, the Word of God, and the Scriptures, are institutions composed of human beings and hence are subject to human weakness and conditioned by their sociocultural environment.

Christianity was born in Asia and reached Africa before it spread in Europe. According to reliable tradition, the Oriental churches in India trace their origin to the work of the apostle Thomas, and the church in Egypt was begun by the evangelist Mark at the dawn of the Christian era. Christianity flourished in Ethiopia, North Africa, and parts of Asia in the early centuries after Christ.

However the present-day churches of Asia, Africa, Latin America, and the Caribbean have their source in the missionary zeal of the European and North American churches. The Christianization of Latin America and parts of Asia and Africa was mainly the task of the Spanish and Portuguese missionaries. In a later phase, missionaries from the other European countries spread the Christian faith—both Catholic and Protestant—to the corners of the earth. In Korea, lay Christians from China made the first converts and developed Christian groups for several decades without a clergy or European missionaries.

Missionaries who left their countries to propagate the faith in the continents of Asia, Africa, and Latin America were persons generally dedicated to the spiritual welfare of humanity. They often underwent severe hardships of a physical and psychological nature. Their labors have given birth to the Christian communities of these continents and these are a testimony to their zeal and devotion.

All the same, the missionaries could not avoid the historical ambiguities of their situation. Oftentimes and in most countries they went hand in hand with the colonizers—both traders and soldiers. Hence they could not but be, at least partially, tainted by the designs of the searchers for gold, spices, lands, slaves, and colonies. While they were zealous for souls, they tended to think that the commercial and military expansion of Western peoples was a providential opportunity for the salvation of souls and the spread of the evangelical message. Thus they collaborated in the colonial enterprise, even when their Christian consciences sometimes felt revolted by the atrocities of the brutal colonizing process. Hence it is necessary to distinguish their good will and the substance of the Christian Gospel from the actual impact of the Christian missions in these countries.

The missionaries could think of the spread of Christianity in terms of transplanting the institutions of their Euro-American churches, within, of course, the framework of imperial destination. Thus the new Christians were segregated from their fellow human beings and alienated from the traditional religious and cultural heritage and their community way of life. This process strengthened their hold on the new believers. The liturgy was imported wholesale from the "mother churches"; so were the ecclesiastical structures and theologies. A pietistic and legalistic spirituality common in Europe at the time was introduced in the new churches also. In later times, the Western educational system was instituted in the colonized countries largely through the services of the churches. We have thus the establishment of Christian churches in these continents more or less as carbon copies of European Christianity, adapted, however, to the subject situation of the colonized.

In the early phases of Western expansion, the churches were allies in the colonization process. They spread under the aegis of colonial powers; they benefited from the expansion of empire. In return, they rendered a special service to Western imperialism by legitimizing it and accustoming their new adherents to accept compensatory expectations of an eternal reward for terrestrial misfortunes, including colonial exploitation. The crafty merchants and soldiers of the West were not slow to see and take advantage of the presence of missionaries among their captive peoples. The Gospel was thus used as an agency for a softening of national resistance to the plunder by the foreigners and a domestication of the minds and cultures of the dominated converts. In fact, the foreign powers often gave the Christians a privileged position of confidence within their arrangements for the administration of the countries. In the process, Christian teaching got badly tainted by the search for selfish gain of the peoples who called themselves Christian and exercised power in the name of emperors and spiritual rulers.

The theology of the Christian churches at this time not only suited the colonization process but was also fed by it. The sense of military and commercial superiority of the European peoples was underpinned with the view that Christianity was superior to other religions, which had to be replaced by "the truth." For centuries, theology did not seriously contest the plunder of continents and even the extermination of whole peoples and civilizations. The meaning of the message of Jesus Christ was so blunted as not to be sensitive to the agony of whole races. These are not merely sad historical realities, but the immediate predecessors of contemporary Western theologies. For these latter have not yet learned to contest the successors of the colonizers—viz., the powerful countries of Europe, North America, and Japan. Nor have they evolved a theology to counteract the abuses of the heirs of the colonial merchants, viz., the giant predatory multinational corporations of today.

The Christian churches in the tricontinental colonial situation fostered educational and social sciences that helped improve the conditions of the population of these countries. Unfortunately, their value patterns were such as to fit into capitalistic domination and hence were largely academic and individualistic, with the result that the leadership to whom independence was granted in the colonies (except after a revolutionary struggle) were generally persons schooled in the Western capitalistic tradition. In this way, the churches—perhaps unwittingly—contributed to the formation of the local elites that were to be the subsequent collaborators in the ongoing exploitation of the masses of the people even after political independence. The social services too, while relieving immediate needs, failed to generate a critical social conscience or support the radical movements for social justice. The churches thus generally continued to be a sort of ideological ally of the local middle classes, which joined the power elite and shared economic privileges with the foreign companies that continued even after political independence.

We see in the churches on the three continents the growth of a "liberal" trend in more recent decades, as a successor to the traditional "conservative" position. The liberal trends are in favor of the adaptation of the churches to the indigenous cultures and to the operation of parliamentary democracy within the framework of free enterprise capitalism. Local religious, priests, and bishops have replaced the foreign ones. The theology was thus adapted to suit the postindependence situation. However, there was not yet a fundamental alliance of the churches with the masses struggling for radical social justice.

In more recent years, there are groups of Christians all over the world beginning to understand the situation of the exploited peoples more sensitively and more correctly. The leaderships of the churches, such as the Second Vatican Council and the World Council of Churches, have given an impetus to the commitment of Christians for the building up of a just world and for openness to the other religions and ideologies in the world. Several local churches, regional conferences, and episcopates have supported this trend (e.g., the Bishops' Conference of Medellín, 1968). The movements of liberation of the peoples from foreign domination now receive more support from the churches, as in the World Council of Churches' contribution to combat racism. The church groups are beginning to be more conscious of the injustices in the economic system. Human rights are now being defended by Christian groups, including some church leaders, in many countries of Asia, Africa, and Latin America.

The Orthodox churches have struggled for many centuries against different forms of oppression and have preserved their religious and cultural identity. Orthodox theologians share in the process of renewal as they address themselves to the task undertaken by the early fathers of the church, namely, to find the relevant expression of their faith in struggling against alienating forces and finding renewed meaning for the Christian faith in the present world.

A new vision of a theology committed to the integral liberation of persons and structures is now being developed in the very process of participation in the struggles of the people. This takes different forms in different regions. In Latin America, the "theology of liberation" expresses this analysis and commitment. In Cuba and Vietnam, Angola, Mozambique, and Guinea, Bissau, groups of Christians have been involved in the revolutionary struggles. In southern Africa, some Christians are also in the center of the struggle for liberation. Christian rulers in countries like Tanzania and Zambia search for new ways of realizing the Gospel ideals in the contemporary world. In Asia, Christian groups have been in the forefront of the struggle for human rights, especially in South Korea and the Philippines.

The study of the traditional religions and the promotion of indigenous spirituality are preoccupations of Christian groups in Asia and African countries. In several parts of Africa and Asia, serious efforts are being made toward the development of indigenous theologies and liturgies, especially theology of religions. The constitution of truly authentic local churches is a major preoccupation of many theologians in these countries. Latin America has generated new groups of witnesses to the radical gospel of liberation in almost every country of the continent. Various groups such as women, youth, students, workers, and peasants are now contributing much to the renewal of the churches and of a theology relevant to their situations.

There are thus signs of hope in the presence of the churches in these countries. The search for self-reliance, the participation in the peoples' struggles, the indigenized liturgies, the emerging relevant theologies, the modern ecumenical movement, renewal efforts in many churches, and the relative openness to socialistic changes are harbingers of a more radical Christianity.

However, a deep challenge remains to be faced. The churches are still burdened by the traditions, theologies, and institutions of a colonial past, while the countries want to move rapidly into the modern world and peoples clamor for radical changes in favor of justice and freedom, all-round inculturation, and increased inter-religious dialogue and collaboration.

Toward a Theological Approach in the Third World

We affirm our faith in Christ our Lord, whom we celebrate with joy, and without whose strength and wisdom our theology would be valueless and even destructive. In doing theology, we are trying to make the Gospel relevant to all people, and to rejoice in being his collaborators, unworthy as we are, in fulfilling God's plan for the world.

The theologies from Europe and North America are dominant today in our churches and represent one form of cultural domination. They must be understood to have arisen out of situations related to those countries, and therefore must not be uncritically adopted without our raising the question of their relevance in the context of our countries. Indeed, we must, in order to be faithful to the Gospel and to our peoples, reflect on the realities of our own situations and interpret the Word of God in relation to these realities. We reject as irrelevant an academic type of theology that is divorced from action. We are prepared for a radical break in epistemology which makes commitment the first act of theology and engages in critical reflection on the praxis of the reality of the Third World.

The interdisciplinary approach in theology and the dialectical interrelationship between theology and the social, political, and psychological analyses need to be recognized. While affirming the basic goodness of creation and the continued presence of God's Spirit in our world and history, it is important to bear in mind the complex mystery of evil, which manifests itself in human sinfulness and the socioeconomic structures. The inequities are diverse, and account for many forms of human degradation; they necessitate our making the Gospel the "good news to the poor" that it is.

The church, the body of Christ, needs to become aware of its role in today's reality. Not only should it not remain insensitive to needs and aspirations, but also it must fearlessly announce the

Gospel of Jesus Christ, recognizing that God speaks in and through our human needs and aspirations. Jesus identified himself with the victims of oppression, thus exposing the reality of sin. Liberating them from the power of sin and reconciling them with God and with one another, he restored them to the fullness of their humanity. Therefore the church's mission is for the realization of the wholeness of the human person.

We recognize also as part of the reality of the Third World the influence of religions and cultures and the need for Christianity to enter in humility into a dialogue with them. We believe that these religions and cultures have a place in God's universal plan and the Holy Spirit is actively at work among them.

We call for an active commitment to the promotion of justice and the prevention of exploitation, the accumulation of wealth in the hands of a few, racism, sexism, and all other forms of oppression, discrimination, and dehumanization. Our conviction is that the theologian should have a fuller understanding of living in the Holy Spirit, for this also means being committed to a life-style of solidarity with the poor and the oppressed and involvement in action with them. Theology is not neutral. In a sense, all theology is committed, conditioned notably by the sociocultural context in which it is developed. The Christian theological task in our countries is to be self-critical of the theologians' conditioning by the value system of their environment. It has to be seen in relation to the need to live and work with those who cannot help themselves, and to be with them in their struggle for liberation.

There was a considerable measure of agreement in the area of the need to do theology in context as described above; furthermore, we recognize that our countries have common problems. The analysis of the social, economic, political, cultural, racial, and psychological situations showed clearly that the countries of the Third World have had similar experiences of which account should be taken in the task of theologizing. Nevertheless, obvious differences in situations and consequent variations in theology were also noted. Thus, while the need for economic and political liberation was felt to offer a vital basis for theologizing in some areas of the Third World, theologians from other areas tended to think that the presence of other religions and cultures, racial discrimination and domination, and related situations such as the presence of Christian minorities in predominantly non-Christian societies, reveal other equally challenging dimensions of the theological task. We are enriched by our common sharing and hopefully look forward to the deepening of our commitment as Third World theologians.

As we began, so we must end. Our prayer is that God make us faithful in our work and do his will through us, and that God continually unfold before our eyes the full dimension of the meaning of our commitment to the Gospel of Jesus Christ.

Conclusion

Our encounter has been brief but dynamic. We are, however, conscious of having shared in a historic session. The president of Tanzania, Julius K. Nyerere, added light and warmth to our conference by his presence at several of our sessions. We are convinced that what we have gone through these days is a unique experience of theologizing from, as it were, the other side of the earth and of human history. Rarely, if ever, have theologians of our three continents and solely from among the oppressed peoples of the world met together to reevaluate their thought, their work, and their lives. From it certain creative insights have come forth. As we share them with others, we humbly pledge to continue our work together to try to comprehend better the plan of God in Jesus Christ for the men and women of our time.

We have spoken from the depths of our lived experience. We kindly request all to accept our statement as a sincere expression of our consensus from our knowledge of what our peoples have gone through over centuries. We hope it will be of some service in spreading genuine and frank understanding among the peoples of the world.

CHAPTER FOUR

Feminist Theology

Mary Daly

Mary Daly's views have been steadily radicalized. In the mid-1970s, she was seeking a deeper transformation in the meaning of God that would raise the consciousness of women and give them a new vision of their own authentic natures. This selection is taken from her Beyond God the Father: Toward a Philosophy of Women's Libera- tion. *Boston: Beacon Press, 1973, pp. 33–43. Since publication of* Beyond God the Father *the author's thinking has changed in regard to the terms "God" and "androgyny." For an explanation of her more recent thinking see the Preface to* Gyn/Ecology: The Metaeth- ics of Radical Feminism, *Beacon Press, 1978.*

The Unfolding of God

It has sometimes been argued that anthropomorphic symbols for "God" are important and even necessary because the fundamen- tal powers of the cosmos otherwise are seen as impersonal. One of the insights characteristic of the rising woman consciousness is that this kind of dichotomizing between cosmic power and the personal need not be. That is, it is not necessary to anthropomorphize or to reify transcendence in order to relate to this personally. In fact, the process is demonic in some of its consequences. The dichotomiz- ing-reifying-projecting syndrome has been characteristic of patriarchal consciousness, making "the Other" the repository of the contents of the lost self. Since women are now beginning to recognize in ourselves the victims of such dichotomizing processes, the insight extends to other manifestations of the pathological splitting off of reality into falsely conceived opposites. Why indeed must "God" be a noun? Why not a verb—the most active and dynamic of all? Hasn't the naming of "God" as a noun been an act of murdering that dynamic Verb? And isn't the Verb infinitely more personal than a mere static noun? The anthropomorphic symbols for God may be intended to convey personality, but they fail to convey that God is Be-ing. Women now who are experiencing the shock of nonbeing and the surge of self-affirmation against this are inclined to perceive transcendence as the Verb in which we participate—live, move, and have our being.

This Verb—the Verb of Verbs—is intransitive. It need not be conceived as having an object that limits its dynamism. That which it is over against is nonbeing. Women in the process of liberation are enabled to perceive this because our liberation consists in refusing to be "the Other" and asserting instead "I am"—without making another "the Other." Unlike Sartre's "us versus a third" (the closest approximation to love possible in his world), the new sisterhood is saying "us versus nonbeing." When Sartre wrote that "man [sic] fundamentally is the desire to be God," he was saying that the most radical passion of human life is to be a God who does not and cannot exist. The ontological hope of which I am speaking is neither this self-deification nor the simplistic reified images often lurking behind such terms as Creator, Lord, Judge, that Sartre rightly rejects. It transcends these because its experiential basis is courageous participation in being. This ontological hope also has little in common with the self-enclosed "ontological arguments" of Anselm or Descartes. It enables us to break out of this prison of subjectivity because it implies commitment together.

The idea that breakthrough to awareness of transcendence comes through some sort of commitment is not new, of course. It has not been absent from existential philosophy. Karl Jaspers, for example, writing of the problem of getting beyond the subject-object split (which, of itself, without awareness of the Encompassing, yields nothing but dead husks of words), affirms that this happens when people live in commitment, but it is not too clear what sort of commitment he had in mind—a not uncommon unclarity among existentialist philosophers. The commitment of which I am speaking has a locus. It is a "mysticism of sorority." I hasten to put this phrase in quotes even though it is my own, since it is a rebaptism of Metz's "mysticism of fraternity"—a correction I deem necessary since—as by now is obvious—a basic thesis of this book is that creative eschatology must come by way of the disenfranchised sex.

What I am proposing is that the emergence of the communal vocational self-awareness of women is a *creative political ontophany.* It is a manifestation of the sacred (*hierophany*) precisely because it is an experience of participation in being, and therefore a manifestation of being (*ontophany*). A historian of religions such as Eliade insists that there was a sort of qualitative leap made by the biblical religions in the realm of hierophany. Whether or not this is historically true is not my concern at this point. What I do suggest is that the potential for *ontological* hierophany that is already beginning to be realized in the participatory vocational self-consciousness of women does involve a leap, bridging the apparent gap between being and history. In other words, women conscious of the vocation to raise up this half of humanity to the stature of acting subjects in history constitute an ontological locus of history. In the very process of becoming actual persons, of confronting the nonbeing of our situation, women are bearers of history.

In his analysis of history-bearing groups, Tillich saw vocational consciousness as a decisive element. He did not believe that humanity as a whole can become the bearer of history instead of particular groups. There is a particular *eros* or sense of belonging which provides the identity of a group to the exclusion of others. This much is true of the women's movement as existing essentially in polarity with the predominantly androcentric society and its institutions. However, there is an essential way in which the women's movement does *not* meet Tillich's specifications for a history-bearing group. I am suggesting that this "nonqualification" arises precisely from the fact that our transformation is so deeply rooted in being. Tillich insists that a history-bearing group's ability to act in a centered way requires that the group have a "central, law-giving, administering, and enforcing authority." In contrast to this, our movement is *not* centrally administered—although it includes organizations such as NOW and WEAL—and many (perhaps most) radicalized women resist attempts to bring this about because their outlook is nonhierarchical and multidimensional.

I am suggesting that the women's movement is *more than* a group governed by central authority in conflict with other such hierarchical groups. If it were only this, it would be only one more subgroup within the all-embracing patriarchal "family." What we are about is the human becoming of that half of the human race that has been excluded from humanity by sexual definition. This phenomenon, which is mushrooming "up from under" (to use Nelle Morton's phrase) in women from various "classes," races, and geographical areas, can hardly be described as a group. What is at stake is a real leap in human evolution, initiated by women. The ground of its creative hope is an intuition of being which, as Janice Raymond has suggested, *is* an intuition of human integrity or of androgynous being.

When this kind of sororal community-consciousness is present—this "us versus nonbeing"—there are clues and intimations of the God who is without an over-against—who is Be-ing. The unfolding of the woman-consciousness is an intimation of the endless unfolding of God. The route to be followed by theoreticians of the women's revolution, then, need not be contiguous with that followed by Marxist theoreticians such as Roger Garoudy and Ernst Bloch, even though we share their concern to maintain an absolutely open future, and even though in some sense we must share also in their insistence upon atheism. We agree with their atheism insofar as this means rejection of hypostatized God-projections and the use of these to justify exploitation and oppression. However, there is a difference which I believe arises from the fact that Marxism does not fully confront patriarchy itself. Roger Garoudy wrote: "If we reject the vary name of God, it is because the name implies a presence, a reality, whereas it is only an exigency which we live, a never-satisfied exigency of totality and absoluteness, of omnipotence as to nature and of perfect loving reciprocity of consciousness." In effect, Garoudy distinguishes his position from that of even the most progressive Christian theologians by asserting that the exigency of the Christian for the infinite is experienced and/or expressed as presence, whereas for him it is absence. What I am suggesting is that women who are confronting the nothingness which emerges when one turns one's back upon the pseudoreality offered by patriarchy are by that very act saying "I am," that is, confronting our own depth of *being.* What we are experiencing, therefore, is not *only* the sense of absence of the old Gods—a sense which we fully share with Garoudy and Bloch. Our exclusion from identity within patriarchy has had a totality about it which, when faced, calls forth an ontological self-affirmation. Beyond the absence, therefore, women are in a situation to experience *presence.* This is not the presence of a superreified Something, but of a power of being which both is, and is not yet.

One could hasten to point out that various theories of a developing God have been expounded in modern philosophy. Some women might find it helpful to relate their perception of the spiritual dynamics of feminism to ideas developed by such a thinker as William James, who offers the possibility of seeing the perfecting of God as achieved through our active belief, which can be understood as an enrichment of the divine being itself. Others might find it helpful to correlate this experience with Alfred North Whitehead's functional approach to the problem of God, who is seen as a factor implicated in the world and philosophically relevant. Other helpful insights on the problem of the developing God can be found in the work of such thinkers as Max Scheler, Samuel Alexander, E. S. Brightman, and Charles Hartshorne. In my opinion, it would not be the most fruitful expenditure of energy at this point to attempt to fit our thoughts concerning the spiritual implications of radical feminism into theories that might appear tempting as prefabricated molds. Rather, it seems to me far more important to listen to women's experiences to discover the spiritual dynamics of this revolution and to speak these dynamics in our own lives and words.

I have already said that this does not mean that an entirely new language for God, materially speaking, will emerge, *ex nihilo,* but rather that a new meaning context is coming into being as we re-create our lives in a new experiential context. Because the feminist experience is radically a coming out of nothing into a vocational/communal participation in being, I have suggested that it can be perceived in terms of ontological hope. Paradoxical though it may seem, this being-consciousness may mean that our new self-understanding *toward God* may be in some ways more in affinity with medieval thought than with some modern theological and philosophical language about God. It is fascinating to observe that in beginning to come to grips with the problem of our own self-naming in a world in which women are nameless, feminism is implicitly working out a naming toward God that is comparable to, though different from, the famous three "ways" the medieval theologians employed in speaking of God.

There was first of all the *negative way,* variously described, but meaning essentially that we can show "what God is not" by systematically denying of God the imperfections of creatures. A prominent scholar has suggested that current epistemology, influenced by recent developments in science, holds resources for a comparable "negative way," but with a different slant. That is, science itself, by constantly opening up more and more unpredicted aspects of reality, is making us aware that there *is* an unknown, aspects of which may be transcendent. This doesn't "prove" transcendence, but makes room for it. I am suggesting that a new *via negativa* is coming not just from science but from the experience of liberation. Women are living out this negative way by discovering more and more the androcentrism of God-language and being compelled to reject this, and, beyond this, by discovering the male-centeredness of the entire society which this legitimates. Since women are excluded from the in-group of the male intellectual community, and since in fact we begin actively to *choose* self-exclusion as we become more conscious of the limitations on thought and creativity that the inbreeding of the power-holding group involves (witness the deadness of meetings and journals of the "learned societies"), we may be less trapped in the old delusions—such as word games about God that pass for knowledge among those who play them. This discovery, followed by active choice of "not belonging" on the part of creative women, can lead to our finding previously untapped resources within ourselves, and the process yields clues to further possibilities of becoming. The realization of our exclusion from the world-building process is a *neonegative way,* in that we are discovering our previously unknown being, which points our consciousness outward and inward toward as yet unknown Being, that some would call the hidden God.

Second, there was the traditional *affirmative way,* which presupposed that God prepossesses all the perfections of creatures and that therefore any perfection found in a creature which does not by definition include limitation can be predicated of God. Thus it was considered legitimate to say that God is good, wise, etc. I am suggesting that feminism is giving rise also to the beginnings of a *neoaffirmative way.* This is a *living* "analogy of being" (*analogia entis*), and the particular aspect of our existence from which we are enabled to draw the analogy is the courage that is experienced in the liberation process. The *analogia entis* of Aquinas involved an extremely complex reasoning, based upon certain premises, including the notion that God is the first cause of all finite reality and the idea that there is some kind of resemblance between effects and their causes. By contrast, what I am pointing to by the use of the expression "analogy of being" is an experience of the dynamic content of the intuition of being as experienced in existential courage. Women now have a special opportunity to create an *affirmative way* that is not simply in the arena of speculation, but especially in the realm of active self-affirmation. Since through the existential courage now demanded of us we can have consciousness of *being toward* the image of God, this process can give us intimations of the Be-ing in and toward which we are participating. That is, it can be in some sense a theophany, or manifestation of God.

A third way of naming God, the traditional *way of eminence,* was not totally distinct from the other two "ways" but rather included both. Medieval theologians, including the so-called Denis the Areopagite and Thomas Aquinas, believed that even names said affirmatively of God fall far short of saying *what* God is: "So when we say 'God is good,' the meaning is not, [merely] 'God is the cause of goodness,' or 'God is not evil,' but the meaning is, 'Whatever good we attribute to creatures preexists in God' and in a more excellent and higher way."

I propose that the becoming of women is potentially a new and very different *way of eminence.* The positive and unique element in our speaking toward God has to do with what Buber called "the primary word I-Thou [which] establishes the world of relation." By refusing to be objectified and by affirming being, the feminist revolution is creating new possibilities of I-Thou. Therefore, the new *way of eminence* can be understood as follows:

In modern society, technical controlling knowledge has reached the point of violating the privacy and rights of individuals and destroying the natural environment. In reaction against this, social critics sometimes call for the awakening of interpersonal consciousness, that is, of intersubjectivity. But this cannot happen without communal and creative refusal of victimization by sexual stereotypes. This creative refusal involves conscious and frequently painful efforts to develop new life-styles in which I-Thou becomes the dominant motif, replacing insofar as possible the often blind and semiconscious mechanisms of I-It, which use the Other as object. In the realm of knowledge, this means removing the impediments to that realm of knowing which is subjective, affective, intuitive, or what the Scholastics called "connatural." It means breaking down the barriers between technical knowledge and that deep realm of intuitive knowledge which some theologians call ontological reason.

Objective or technical knowledge is necessary for human survival and progress. It is the capacity for "reasoning." Clarity of thinking and the construction of language require its use. So also does the ability to control nature and society. However, by itself, cut off from the intuitive knowledge of ontological reason, technical knowledge is directionless and ultimately meaningless. When it dominates, life is deprived of an experience of depth, and it tends toward despair.

Technical knowledge of itself is detached. It depends upon a subject-object split between the thinker and that which is perceived. It is calculative, stripping that which is perceived of subjectivity. Technical knowledge, cut off from ontological reason, degrades its object and dehumanizes the knowing subject. Because it reduces both to less than their true reality, at a certain point it even ceases to be knowledge in any authentic sense. When it is thus separated from ontological reason, the psychological and social sciences which it dominates become dogmatic, manipulative, and destructive. Under its dominion, philosophy, theology, and all of religion deteriorate.

Widening of experience so pathologically reduced can come through encounter with another subject, an I who refuses to be an It. If, however, the encounter is simply a struggle over who will be forced into the position of It, this will not be ultimately redemptive. It is only when the subject is brought to a recognition of the other's damaged but never totally destroyed subjectivity as equal to his/her own, having basically the same potential and aspiration to transcendence, that a qualitatively new way of being in the world and toward God can emerge. What is perceived in this new way of being is the Eternal Thou, the creative divine Word that always has *more* to say to us. This is the meaning of the women's movement as the new *way of eminence.*

New Space: New Time

The unfolding of God, then, is an event in which women participate as we participate in our own revolution. The process involves the creation of new space, in which women are free to become who we are, in which there are real and significant alternatives to the prefabricated identities provided within the enclosed spaces of patriarchal institutions. As opposed to the foreclosed identity allotted to us within those spaces, there is a diffused identity—an open road to discovery of the self and of each other. The new space is located always "on the boundary." Its center is on the boundary of patriarchal institutions, such as churches, universities, national and international politics, families. Its center is the lives of women, whose experience of becoming changes the very meaning of center for us by putting it on the boundary of all that has been considered central. In universities and seminaries, for example, the phenomenon of women's studies is becoming widespread, and for many women involved this is the very heart of thought and action. It is perceived as the core of intellectual and personal vitality, often as the only part of the "curriculum" which is not dead. By contrast, many male administrators and faculty view "women's studies" as peripheral, even trivial, perhaps hardly more serious than the "ladies' page" of the daily newspaper. Most "good" administrators do sense that there is something of vitality there, of course, and therefore tolerate or even encourage women's studies—but it remains "on the boundary." So too, the coming together of women on the boundary of "the church" is the center of spiritual community, unrecognized by institutional religion.

The new space, then, has a kind of invisibility to those who have not entered it. It is therefore inviolable. At the same time, it communicates power which, paradoxically, is experienced both as power of presence and power of absence. It is not political power in the usual sense but rather a flow of healing energy which is participation in the power of being. For women who are becoming conscious, that participation is made possible initially by casting off the role of "the Other" which is the nothingness imposed by a sexist world.

The burst of anger and creativity made possible in the presence of one's sisters is an experience of becoming whole, of overcoming the division within the self that makes nothingness block the dynamism of being. Instead of settling for being a warped half of a person, which is equivalent to a self-destructive nonperson, the emerging woman is casting off role definitions and moving toward androgynous being. This is not a mere "becoming equal to men in a man's world"—which would mean settling for footing within the patriarchal space. It is, rather, something like God speaking forth God-self in the new identity of women. While life in the new space may be "dangerous" in that it means living without the securities offered by the patriarchal system for docility to its rules, it offers a deeper security that can absorb the risks that such living demands. This safety is participation in *being,* as opposed to inauthenticity, alienation, nonidentity—in a word, nonbeing.

The power of presence that is experienced by those who have begun to live in the new space radiates outward, attracting others. For those who are fixated upon patriarchal space it apparently is threatening. Indeed, this sense of threat is frequently expressed. For those who are thus threatened, the presence of women to each other is experienced as an absence. Such women are no longer empty receptacles to be used as "the Other," and are no longer internalizing the projections that cut off the flow of being. Men who need such projection screens experience the power of absence of such "objects" and are thrown into the situation of perceiving nothingness. Sometimes the absence of women that elicits this anxiety is in fact physical. For example, when women deliberately stay away from meetings, social gatherings, etc., in order to be free to do what is important to ourselves, there is sometimes an inordinate response of protest. Sometimes the absence is simply noncooperation, refusal to "play the game" of sex roles, refusal to flatter and agree, etc. This too hints at presence of another space that women have gone off to, and the would-be users are left with no one to use. Sometimes, of course, the absence of women takes the form of active resistance. Again, it throws those who would assume the role of exploiters back into their sense of nothingness.

In this way then, women's confrontation with the experience of nothingness invites men to confront it also. Many of course respond with hostility. The hostility may be open or, in some cases, partially disguised both from the men who are exercising it and from the women to whom it is directed. When disguised, it often takes seductive forms, such as invitations to "dialogue" under conditions psychologically loaded against the woman, or invitations to a quick and easy "reconciliation" without taking seriously the problems raised. Other men react with disguised hostility in the form of being "the feminist's friend," not in the sense of really hearing women but as paternalistic supervisors, analysts, or "spokesmen" for the movement. Despite the many avenues of nonauthentic response to the threat of women's power of absence, some men do accept the invitation to confront the experience of nothingness that offers itself when "the Other" ceases to be "the Other" and stands back to say "I am." In so doing, men begin to liberate themselves toward wholeness, toward androgynous being. This new participation in the power of being becomes possible for men when women move into the new space.

Entry into the new space whose center is on the boundary of the institutions of patriarchy also involves entry into new time. To be caught up in these institutions is to be living in time past. This is strikingly evident in the liturgies and rituals that legitimate them. By contrast, when women live on the boundary, we are vividly aware of living in time present/future. Participation in the unfolding of God means also this time breakthrough, which is a continuing (but not ritually "repeated") process. The center of the new time is on the boundary of patriarchal time. What it is, in fact, is women's *own* time. It is our *life-time.* It *is* whenever we are living out of our own sense of reality, refusing to be possessed, conquered, and alienated by the linear, measured-out, quantitative time of the patriarchal system. Women, in becoming who we are, are living in a qualitative, organic time that escapes the measurements of the system. For example, women who sit in institutional committee meetings without surrendering to the purposes and goals set forth by the male-dominated structure are literally working on our own time while perhaps appearing to be working "on company time." The center of our activities is organic, in such a way that events are more significant than clocks. This boundary living is a way of being in and out of "the system." It entails a refusal of false clarity. Essentially, it is being alive now, which in its deepest dimension is participation in the unfolding of God.

It should be apparent, then, that for women entrance into our own space and time is another way of expressing integrity and transformation. To stay in patriarchal space is to remain in time past. The appearance of change is basically only separation and return—cyclic movement. Breaking out of the circle requires anger, the "wrath of God" speaking God-self in an organic surge toward life. Since women are dealing with demonic power relationships, that is, with structured evil, rage is required as a positive creative force, making possible a breakthrough, encountering the blockages of inauthentic structures. It rises as a reaction to the shock of recognizing what has been lost—before it had even been discovered—one's own identity. Out of this shock can come intimations of what human being (as opposed to half being) can be. Anger, then, can trigger and sustain movement from the experience of nothingness to recognition of participation in being. When this happens, the past is changed, that is, its significance for us is changed. Then the past is no longer static: it too is on the boundary. When women take positive steps to move out of patriarchal space and time, there is a surge of new life. I would analyze this as participation in God the Verb who cannot be broken down simply into past, present, and future time, since God is form-destroying, form-creating, transforming power that makes all things new.

Letty Russell

Letty Russell has consistently affirmed that there are common methodologies, perspectives, and themes which are shared by liberation theologies. This selection is taken from her Human Liberation in a Feminist Perspective—a Theology. *Philadelphia: Westminster Press, 1974, pp. 50–62.*

Human Liberation and Theology

Like Third World liberation theology, feminist theology is written out of an experience of oppression. It is an attempt to interpret the search for salvation as a journey toward freedom. There are as many liberation theologies as there are people committed to search for the meaning of human liberation in today's world. Wherever the rising consciousness of groups and individuals leads them to critical awareness of the contradictions in society and to actions toward change, the need arises to interpret their new understanding and actions. This challenge emerges out of particular circumstances and reflects a variety of traditions.

Yet, at the same time, for Christians there is a common motif in liberation theology. The action-reflection (*praxis*) arises out of a commitment to Jesus Christ and a desire to understand the meaning of the Good News in the light of the changing world. The praxis of liberation is carried forward in a continuing dialectic of divine-human action. God's actions on behalf of humankind are the basis of reflection and insight in relation to the actions of communities on behalf of others.

There is always a tension between Christian tradition and the new experience gained by advocates of liberation in a specific situation of oppression. This tension can be the creative force of theology in which actions and experience are constantly viewed in the wider horizon of God's concern for all humankind. Interpretations of the Gospel are tested by the experience of Christian communities working with others in society. The actions of the communities are also tested by the biblical witness to the meaning and purpose of human liberation as part of God's plan for all of the groaning creation.

There is also another tension which comes from the fact that human liberation takes on meaning in particular contexts. Liberation is always experienced concretely, as individuals and groups discover ways in which they have found new "room to breathe" in society. Therefore, the various visions of the meaning of humanization and liberation reflect their own situation. Sometimes that situation clearly places one type of liberation theology at odds with another. For instance, black theology may focus on the black experience of oppression to the exclusion of the oppression of women. Feminist theology may have a focus that is quite the reverse. This tension, however, can also be creative, because it leads each group to clarify its position, and provides a variety of perspectives that can illuminate our understanding of human liberation.

The purpose of this chapter is not to assert that all people writing liberation theology say the same thing, but that the dialogue between those concerned with the praxis of freedom is an important task. In spite of much disagreement, many of the goals are held in common and need to be worked on in mutual respect and solidarity. In addition, whatever these theologies may have to say, they make a contribution to the total theological enterprise of using our minds to reflect on the meaning of God's actions in the world. While recognizing that at every point differences can be identified, it is still a significant task to reflect on *common methodology, common perspectives,* and *common themes* which are shared by many liberation theologies. These motifs can then be explored from the feminist perspective, as we join together in the exciting and challenging search for more truly human community in a Christian context.

Common Methodology

Liberation theologies share certain methodological ingredients of task, approach, and purpose that are important to women and men in their theological reflection. Of course, there is *no one style* of theology. Each person is free to choose the particular style that develops out of tradition, education, and life experience. The styles vary according to the premises, perspectives on reality, and types of philosophy. In spite of these differences, there is a growing consensus among liberation theologians in describing their task. What they are about is doing *theo-logy*: Using their *logos* (their mind) in the perspective of God, as God is known in and through the Word in the world. Thus Gustavo Gutiérrez tells us that "theology is critical reflection—in the light of the Word accepted in faith—on historical praxis and therefore on the presence of Christians in the world."

Genitive Theologies. This task is sometimes rather difficult to establish in liberation theologies because they have a tendency to be what are sometimes called genitive theologies: theologies *of* women, *of* blacks, *of* Latin Americans, etc. When we speak of feminist theology, we sometimes think that it is not only *by* women but also *about* women.

Strictly speaking, feminist theology could be written *by* men. There are many men who are also actively engaged in trying to counter the prevailing oppressive situation in which both men and women are trapped. They too are advocating the equality and partnership of both sexes, and searching for new life-styles and structures in church and society. However, it takes a brace man to advocate such theology in the face of the social scorn of those who would label him as "feminine," and the ideological scorn of those who declare that liberation theology, at least initially, must be written from the point of view of those who have experienced a concrete situation of social oppression.

Again, strictly speaking, feminist theology is *not* about women. It is about God. It is not a form of *"ego-logy"* in which women just think about themselves. When women do it, they speak of feminist theology in order to express the fact that the experience from which they speak and the world out of which they perceive God's words and actions and join in those actions is that of women seeking human equality. Another way of expressing this is to say that the *ecology of their theology* is that of a woman living in a particular time and place.

The importance of women doing theology is the same as that of any other group around the world. They make a contribution to the *unfinished dimension* of theology. Women want to add to the understanding of the Christian faith, not to replace the other insights that have been contributed in the past. This is very important to a Christian church that has been dominated for so long by white, Western, male perspectives on God. Women add their small piece of experience about the way God is known to them to all the other pieces, so that theology becomes more wholistic and comprehensive.

Inductive Approach. In general, women, along with other liberation theologians, stress an inductive rather than a deductive approach. In the past, much theology was done by deducing conclusions from first principles established out of Christian tradition and philosophy. Today many people find it more helpful to do theology by an inductive method—drawing out the material for reflection from their life experience as it relates to the Gospel message. Here stress is placed on the *situation-variable* nature of the Gospel. The Gospel is good news to people only when it speaks concretely to their particular needs of liberation. For instance, it is no help to tell the blind woman that she can walk. Good news for the blind must deal with changing the oppressed situation of blindness.

For this reason, liberation theologies recognize that persons and societies find themselves in different situations of oppression, and they try to address themselves to concrete experiences that can illuminate their own experience and can be shared with others. They try to express the Gospel in the light of the experience of oppression out of which they are written, whether that be racial or sexual, social or economic, psychological or physical. Such a method draws upon the contributions of the many disciplines that help to illuminate the human condition and not just on a particular theological tradition. This point of view is reflected in Rosemary Ruether's *Liberation Theology* when she writes:

> . . . a fuller integration of the sciences necessary for the fullest reflection on the question of human liberation today cannot be done by a single scholar. It waits upon a multi-disciplinary teamwork that can integrate the many sources of data and types of reflection and symbolization around the core of theological reflection. Only with such a multi-disciplinary integration of human sciences can we begin to speak of the basis of a theology of liberation adequate to the present human situation.

This inductive approach is *experimental in nature.* It is a process of seeking out the right questions to ask and trying out different hypotheses that arise. It becomes a theology of constantly revised questions and tentative observations about a changing world, rather than the type of theology described by Thomas Aquinas as a "science of conclusions." In trying to develop new models for thinking about God in a Christian context, women discover a vast quantity of questions addressed to biblical and church tradition and to the concepts of creation, redemption, sin, salvation, and incarnation. The experimental nature of this inductive theology leaves no doctrine unchallenged in the search for a faith that can shape life amid rapid, and sometimes chaotic, change. "These doctrines are no longer taken so much as answers than as ways of formulating the questions."

Such an experimental or inductive approach is very much dependent on the *corporate support* of the community of faith and action out of which it grows. Just as Latin-American liberation theology grows out of the small struggling communities working with others to face up to their revolutionary situation, so black theology grows out of the American black community and black churches. As Rubem Alves, a Brazilian theologian, says, "The seed of the future . . . [is the] community of hope." This approach is also important for the corporate style of the women's movement. Not only is much of the work of women done on a multidisciplinary basis, but also in small communities who experiment together in actions and reflection both in groups and through the constant exchange of materials and ideas.

Theology as Praxis. This communal search is doubly important because liberation theology is intended to be put into practice by those who join in the search. The purpose of this type of theology is *praxis,* action that is concurrent with reflection or analysis and leads to new questions, actions, and reflections. In this format, theology flows out of and into action. It is a tool for doing something that can become a catalyst for change among those who believe in the biblical promises for the oppressed. The direction of thought flows, not only "downward" from the "theological experts" but also upward and outward out of the collective experience of action and ministry.

For this reason, liberation theology is not usually *systematic theology.* The purpose of doing it is not to place all the discoveries or conclusions into one overarching system, but rather to apply the discoveries to a new way of action to bring about change in society. Therefore, when things become difficult in a particular situation, or when there seems to be little immediate hope for change, people have a tendency to say: "Liberation theology is finished. It didn't work." Yet as long as the Bible speaks of God as the Liberator of the oppressed, and as long as the situations of oppression continue to exist, there will be those who seek ways to express their faith and confidence in God through whatever means are open to them.

This form of *practical theology* brings action and reflection together. As Bonhoeffer is reported to have said, "We shall not know what we will not do." Certainly the thinking must be systematic in that it tries to be logical, consistent, and documented, but the purpose of the thinking and its verification is found in praxis (action and reflection), and not in the writing of fat volumes of systematic theology. Ethics and application are not simply the ways of relating thought to social situations, because the thought itself is denied if it does not arise in the context of action. Gutiérrez underlines this point in saying, "All the political theologies, the theologies of hope, of revolution, and of liberation, are not worth one act of genuine solidarity with exploited classes."

Whatever the movement, be it a Third World or Fourth World, if its focus is on human liberation, its inductive methodology will be one of thinking about God in the light of concrete oppressive experiences in order to find ways to express the purpose and plan of God for creation in the building of a more humane society.

Common Perspectives

In addition to a common inductive and experimental methodology, liberation theologies also share at least three common perspectives in reflection on the experience of God in the world.

Biblical Promise. The first perspective is that the biblical promises of liberation are an important part of theological reflection. Two major motifs of the Bible are those of *liberation* and *universality*. God is portrayed in both the Old and New Testaments as the Liberator, the one who sets people free. God is not just the liberator of one small nation or group, but of all of humankind. This theme of liberation is, of course, not the only theme, but it is an important part of the biblical understanding of God's *oikonomia* or action for the world in the history of salvation. Joseph Comblin writes:

> The theologians of liberation theology do not say that the Bible teaches a doctrine of liberation for all men [and women] of every age, of all time, and all nations. But they are convinced that in the world we have today the Bible's precept of charity can be interpreted only through a theology of liberation. Any other interpretation would fall short of the demands of charity as it is presented in the Bible. Those theologians aren't in the slightest claiming that their reading of the Bible is valid for all times. But they say it is the right one for the society we live in today—and that is all that matters.

God's *oikonomia* or plan for the world provides an eschatological perspective concerning the future of humanity. Because Christians see themselves as part of "God's utopia," they participate in the work of liberation. Paul points out in 1 Cor. 9:17 that they are "entrusted with a commission *(oikonomia)*." Participation in God's work is the way in which they express hope and confidence in God's intention of liberation and salvation for the whole inhabited world (*oikoumenē*). No longer are lines drawn between Christian and non-Christian, or between one confession and another. Instead, Christians join with all those involved in the revolution of freedom, justice, and peace. As Moltmann writes, "It is time now for all the different freedom movements to cooperate in a brotherly [and sisterly] way, for the misery of humankind has not become less urgent."

Liberation theology places stress on the fact that the Gospels tell of the good news of liberation. Christ has set the captives free and, therefore, there is future and hope. This hope stems, not just from human actions and strategies that are often weak and misguided, but from God's promise for all humanity. Ernst Käsemann says: "I see the whole of the New Testament as involving the cause of Christian freedom, and I have done my best to show that the cause is developed in much diversity, because it exists only in terms of practical mundane affairs, in relation to Christian selflessness, stupidity, misrepresentation and denial, and changes its spearhead from time to time."

In the women's liberation movement, there has been a lot of rejection of the Bible as the basis for theology because of the patriarchal, cultural attitudes that it reveals. Yet those who would do Christian theology cannot abandon the story of Jesus of Nazareth. They find instead that they must use the best tools of scholarship to wrestle with the texts, and to find how liberation and universality apply to their own experience of longing and groaning for freedom.

World as History. The second perspective is that of the world as history. Most liberation theologies are written from the modern point of view that both humanity and the world are to be understood as historical, as both changing and changeable. The Bible views the world as a series of meaningful events that are moving toward the fulfillment of God's plan and purpose of salvation. In the same way, modern thinkers view the world as events that are subject to human intervention, planning, and change. Each human being is made up of her or his individual history, and society is formed out of collective events or histories.

To view the world as history is to think of it not just as a record of past events but also as a process of change from past, to present, to future. This is a process that takes on meaning through the interpretation of events that shape our future. The future that evolves out of the past *(futurum)* is placed at the disposal of women and men who are aware of their own historical possibility and seek out political, economic, and social ways or planning for tomorrow. For Christians, there is also a vision of a future that comes toward us *(adventus)* and that God places at our disposal. Through *hoping* in the coming of God's future, they find new courage and strength to enter into the difficult process of *planning* and acting on behalf of human liberation.

For Christian women, the planning of the future as *futurum* must be based on the "rewriting of history" to include "herstory" in the total picture of the way history has evolved. Out of the strength gained from past accomplishments and the warnings of past defeats comes a new energy to be put to use in changing the social realities of oppression that they face. At the same time, "the horizon of hope" in God's coming future *(adventus)* prevents discouragement and disillusionment when the struggle for liberation is frustrated by powerful, androcentric social attitudes. They enter into the struggle without any guarantee of success, knowing that not only their sisters and brothers but they themselves will often stand in the way of the development of a humane society of partnership. Women enter the struggle because they hope in God's promise of liberation and because, according to Dorothee Sölle, they are driven by the knowledge that the "Gospel's business is the liberation of human beings. . . . Having faith, we put our wager on the liberation of all people." They continue the struggle because to be human is to take part in this historical process or *historicity* and to have an opportunity of transforming the world and shaping the future.

To view the world as history is to become involved in the development of ideologies or sets of ideas that can be used to change and shape this reality. Christians, along with others, make use of these interpretations of reality and history in order to participate in "the revolutions of freedom." Christian women make use of the ideology of women's liberation. Black liberation theology owes much of its perspective on reality to the ideology of the black-liberation movement. Many Latin Americans look to some socialist ideology to provide helpful conceptual tools for change.

The difficulty of this dangerous but important "mix" between faith and ideology is that all ideologies are only partial and, there-fore, distorted descriptions of social reality. Yet ideologies gain their power to change the actions and thoughts of human beings just because of their intention to change the situation in line with that one set of ideas. For Christians, all ideologies must be subject to constant critique in the light of the Gospel. In fact, they do not know exactly what the future will be like. Neither God nor ideolo-gies provide them with a "blueprint." God's promise leads to a confidence that the future is open, but not to an exact knowledge of how liberation will be accomplished or what it will look like.

Because ideologies are helpful in dealing with and shaping the *futurum,* they play an important part in liberation movements. Yet they are always partial in the light of faith in God's coming *adven-tus* and they present a danger for those who must live with "humble agnosticism" about the future. Women, like other people, are often swept up in the currents of ideology, yet as Christians they remain an undependable part of liberation movements, because they must live by the horizon of the *adventus* and not by a blind commitment to any ideology.

Liberation theologies view the world as history and make use of ideologies because their purpose is to participate with God in chang-ing the world to advocate the right of oppressed people to share in building their own "house of freedom." The impact of this com-mon perspective can be seen clearly in the actions of Christian women both in the church and in society. For instance, the Women's Caucus at the General Assembly of the National Council of Churches which was held at Detroit in 1969 presented a statement to the assembly which reflects this point of view.

> Women's oppression and women's liberation is a basic part of the struggle of blacks, browns, youth, and others. We will not be able to create a new church and a new society until and unless women are full participants. We intend to be full participants. . . .
>
> So women are rising; that is our first point. We are rising, black and white, red and brown, to demand change, to de-mand humanity for ourselves as well as others. . . .
>
> Secondly, we wish to present some facts which illustrate the situation of women. Nowhere is the situation of women better illustrated than in our male-dominated and male-ori-ented churches.

Salvation as a Social Event. The third shared perspective of liberation theologies is that of salvation as a social event. In Christian theology today, there is a new awareness of human beings in their body, mind, and spirit and in their social relationships with others. This has led to a broadening of the understanding of individual salvation in the afterlife to include the beginnings of salvation in the lives of men and women in society. Often the Old Testament concept of salvation as *shalom* or wholeness and total social well-being in community with others is stressed.

Emphasis is placed upon the longed-for eternal life as a quality of existence in the *here and now.* It is expressed through the actions of sharing God's gift of liberation and blessing with all people. In a historical view of the world, salvation is not an escape from fated nature, but rather the power and possibility of transforming the world, restoring creation, and seeking to overcome suffering. This stress is especially clear among those searching for ways of expressing the Gospel message as good news for the oppressed, the hungry, the alienated of our own sorry world. In liberation theology, salvation is understood as good news because it includes concrete social liberation in oppressive situations. James Cone states: "Because God's act for ... [humanity] involves ... [human] liberation from bondage, ... [human] response to God's grace of liberation is an act for ... brothers and sisters who are oppressed. There can be no reconciliation with God unless the hungry are fed, the sick are healed, and justice is given to the poor."

In this perspective, sin also takes on a different meaning. Sin as the opposite of liberation is seen as *oppression,* a situation in which there is no community, no room to live as a whole human being. Dorothee Sölle reminds us that sin cannot be understood only as a private matter. "Sin to us is eminently a political, a social term." It includes the sins of our own people, race, and class in which we participate. Therefore, we are faced with responsibility not only for admitting our collaboration in such social sin, but also for working to change the social structures that bring it about. Ruether describes this responsibility in saying:

> We need to build a new cooperative social order out beyond
> the principles of hierarchy, rule and competitiveness. Start-
> ing in the grass-roots local units of human society where

psycho-social polarization first began, we must create a living pattern of mutuality between men and women, between parents and children, among people in their social, economic and political relationships and, finally, between humankind and the organic harmonies of nature.

There are probably other perspectives shared by many women and other people working out liberation theologies in an experimental way, but at least these three (biblical promises of liberation; world as history; salvation as a social event) are important to their praxis. Feminist theology is not alone in bringing these perspectives to bear in the dialogue between faith and the world, but it has a part to play in contributing to the ongoing development of a more complete theology.

Sheila Collins

Sheila Collins has opted for a new vision of "herstory" which broadens a woman's view of life and makes her reinterpret the ways in which the past has been understood. This selection is taken from her A Different Heaven and Earth. *Valley Forge, Pennsylvania: Judson Press, 1976, pp. 139–47.*

> "History, therefore, is nothing but a compilation
> of the depositions made by assassins
> with respect to their victims and themselves."
> Simone Weil

History, Simone Weil pointed out in *The Need for Roots,* has always been written by the conquerors. To the extent that history represents the world view and value system of those who have "won," it is to that extent a distortion of the totality of reality systems which could be extant at any period of time.

Judeo-Christian history, for the most part, has perpetuated a hierarchical, patriarchal world view characterized, as Mary Daly has pointed out, by "social and psychic models of dominance and submission." By projecting this world view onto the heavens and claiming it as divine revelation from "without," breaking in upon human experience, the Judeo-Christian churches have sought to legitimize their own particular world view and authority systems. In doing so, they rejected and devalued the reality system of the ancient world—a system in which the sacred was found, not above, beyond, or in spite of the carnal, but in and through it—a system in which the organic processes of the natural world were found to be conjoint with human activity and relationships—and a system in which woman's natural functions were not demeaned but were actually understood as paradigms of salvation.

It is indeed ironic that a movement which would eventually destroy this reality system and for the next five thousand years would extend its hierarchical and generally imperialistic world view across the globe should have entered the historical drama with an image of itself as victim. Still more ironic is it that its chief salvific model was seen as a victim. But perhaps there is nothing so unusual in all that. The image of oneself as victim, if it does not debilitate, leads almost inevitably to the need for scapegoats; and there has been no lack of scapegoats to which the Christian church has rallied.

As our herstory indicated, the first scapegoat to fall sway to the drive of patriarchal monotheism for predominance in the ancient world was the organic interrelationship of humanity with nature and, concomitantly, the role and importance of woman. As we have seen, the natural world was demeaned. It was no longer the locus of the numinous, the sacred, but an inferior "order" of creation which man was to dominate and subdue. Later on, it became not only inferior, but also the very seat of evil. Woman, as the human equivalent of the natural world, was likewise demeaned and subjugated. Her natural processes—menstruation, childbirth, lactation, and the beauty and symmetry of her body—which were formerly understood as channels of the divine and as resonant with symbolic, salvific meaning, were now viewed as dirty, unclean, contaminated, and evil.

The gods and goddesses which had symbolized for the ancients the depth of their experience of the mystery of life and death were castigated by the monotheists as "false" or "pagan" gods, and the rites surrounding them as mere idolatry. What was happening in the transition from a polytheistic, matriarchal world view to a monotheistic patriarchal system was a reversal in values, or rather, a supererogation by one side of the human equation of the values of the good and a projection of evil onto the other side.

Women's herstory seeks to open up to purview the vast panorama of human experience, so that reality systems may be seen in their relationship to one another. Just as colors assume differing hues depending on the colors they are surrounded by, so Judeo-Christian history and its authority systems take on a different gestalt when juxtaposed with the world view they sought to extinguish.

The development of herstory involves the ability to see through the cracks of the present reality system or "world construction," to use Peter Berger's term, to distinguish the outlines of another. During the course of his apprenticeship to Don Juan, Carlos Castaneda (in *The Teachings of Don Juan, A Separate Reality*) is asked by the old Indian sorcerer to concentrate on the interstices between the leaves of a tree, rather than on the leaves. When he does this, the spaces themselves assume an objectivity, a reality they hadn't had for him previously. Herstory is somewhat like the space between the leaves; it is the forest which could not be seen by patriarchal historians because they had been concentrating so hard on the trees.

What happens when we begin to crack the prevailing reality system to discover new layers beneath and around it? . . . I believe there are certain affirmations which can be made and certain inferences which can be drawn.

The first affirmation is that the imperialism of the historical event as the authority for faith has been broken. Herstory relativizes history as it points to the fallibility of men and institutions to report accurately and fully on the events in which they are immersed. Herstory focuses light on the hidden assumptions and agreements, the disguised structure of language and emotion, and the cultural biases and accretions which determine the telling of patriarchal history. By the same token, herstory realizes its own agreements and assumptions but declares these at the outset, so that at least it cannot be accused of being devious.

In relativizing history, herstory undermines the authority of biblical revelation to be the exclusive channel of truth. It shows that the rise of monotheism and the development of what has been lauded as the "ethical impulse" in religious history were not won without great sacrifice: namely, the rejection of the body as a vehicle for the sacred, the subjugation of women and like "others" whose experience did not fit the right categories, and the rape of the earth.

The herstorian recognizes and affirms the noble impulse, the thrust of promise and fulfillment which lies behind the biblical epic, but laments some of the ways in which this impulse was translated. She is therefore not likely to find in particular biblical passages, events, or people that completeness of intent that the tradition claims for itself, but looks before, behind, beyond, and even outside the tradition as well as at it for her affirmation.

Thus, the feminist herstorian must reject the biblical literalist viewpoint as being unworthy of the true dimensions of the faith she is seeking. Patriarchalism and fundamentalism go hand in hand. It is no accident that researchers have found strong patterns of sexism in the fundamentalist Jesus communes, nor that the Lutheran Church–Missouri Synod and the newly splintered fundamentalist southern Presbyterian churches have strongly denied women the right to leadership positions in the church.

Once the imperialism of the historical event has been relativized, the feminist herstorian is free to choose from the tradition those points of insight and affirmation which speak most forcefully to her own experience and that of her sisters. She is also freed to explore the rich heritage of myth and symbol—both biblical and extrabiblical—and to allow it to speak to her, rather than accepting an interpretation of it as given by Scripture or authority.

The Christian church professes to believe that God is at work in the world. Yet, by locking God into formulations and symbols which may at one time have had meaning for a particular group of people but which since have become formal and static, it has prevented the numinous from breaking through the practical, rational barriers with which most of us surround ourselves.

As the herstory of women relativizes the imperialism of history as fact, event, or narrative, it also widens the historical lens. That is, it establishes a more inclusive range and depth of meanings which human societies have elaborated and which can have transforming power for us. In order to develop a comprehensive anthropology of *homo religiosus,* we cannot simply begin with the revelation of Yahweh to the Israelites because that "revelation" was predicated on the debasement of woman and of the natural world. As Christian and Jewish women, we have participated in that definition of ourselves at the expense of our *selves*. We have become our own oppressors.

We must begin, then, as far back as artifact, myth, legend, and unconscious memory will take us in order to understand ourselves fully as religious beings; and we must look seriously at those religious impulses which lay outside the boundaries defined by the Judeo-Christian tradition.

Some exciting things begin to happen when we dare to go beyond the stated boundaries in order to discover more of ourselves. First, the exclusivity of the linear view of history dissolves, and other paradigms begin to assume an ontological and existential importance for us: for example, the cyclical view of history becomes once again a possibility. When the historical lens is widened, we realize how fallible the Western linear view of history has been. No longer can history be conceived as a progressively upward movement from savagery and ignorance toward civilization and enlightenment. We see it as a much more complex and convoluted process. Whether or not one assigns one age to a higher rank than another depends upon the particular world view one holds. In questioning the value assumptions undergirding the Western theological/historical tradition, women also question the place assigned to certain events and movements on the scale of historical justice.

Who can say, for example, that the "pagans" were more ignorant or more savage than the Israelites? Yet it is precisely this assumption which forms the silent agreements upon which Christian theology rests. When the role, condition, and freedom of women is weighed in the balance, we would probably have to assign the pagans a more enlightened position than the postexilic Hebrews or the medieval Christian church. Likewise, on what basis do we assign the Old Religion—the witch cults of the peasant masses of medieval times—to a place of ignominy in the pageant of history while exonerating the efforts of the Christian church to stamp out this aberrant movement? Some claim that the attitude toward the natural world which is expressed in Gen. 1 (man is to "subdue" the earth) is "better" than the reverence for life which was expressed in the lamentations of Ishtar or in the Mysteries at Eleusis. Idolatry, then, exists in the eyes of the critical beholder, rather than in the eyes of the worship-

er. Were the images constructed by the Judeo-Christian church—
"God, the Father," the untainted virgin, the all-sacrificing mother,
Jesus, the Logos—any less subject to idolatrous use than the figures
of Astarte, Ishtar, and Demeter through whom the forces of mystery, transcendence, and the organic unity of life were mediated for
the pagans?

Without being fully conscious of it, women today are recovering
or rediscovering the pre-Judeo-Christian understanding of themselves as women. The interest in exploring our own bodies and our
sexuality frankly and openly, the decision by many women to have
children regardless of whether they are married, the fierce insistence on defining ourselves in ourselves and not simply in relation
to men, and the deep empathy for the organic world which I see
among many feminists today all have their echoes in the ancient
matriarchal world view. In addition, there is a self-conscious exploration into ancient myth, symbol, and archetype going on among
feminist artists, writers, psychologists, and theologians. In their
experience, the ancient mother-goddesses are being resurrected and
are demonstrating that their transformative and integrative powers
are equal to that of the Christian Christ.

There is at work among women today a powerful religious force
which cannot be fully explained in Christian terminology. It is
inadequate to say that women want to return to the ancient world
view. Such a desire would be both stupid and impractical. But there
is a sense in which we are beginning to understand and incorporate
the deep psychic meanings which that world view expressed, and
which have been continually suppressed in Western culture, in
order to go on to a new synthesis. Women today are able to incorporate these meanings with a self-consciousness which the ancients
did not possess, immersed as they were in a struggle for survival.

Thus, we are involved in a kind of cyclical return to our origins
and are going beyond them to a new understanding of future possibility. The paradigm which expresses this process is more like that
of a sprung spring than an enclosed circle, for we never simply
return to the beginning as it was. We incorporate that beginning
from the vantage point of greater understanding, which then allows
us to go on to incorporate ever larger meanings. A diagram of the
paradigm might look something like this:

Each intersection of lines is thus the beginning and end of one circle or loop and the beginning of still another. This experiencing of life as a continuing spiral is expressed in the comment of a woman who was in a course given by Mary Daly at Union Theological Seminary. "Since being in the women's movement," she stated excitedly, "I am ten years younger and I have more of a future than I did ten years ago."

My own experience reflects the same paradigmatic schema. The more I allow myself to be open to life in the present, the more I discover myself anew in the past, and the greater my future possibilities. I am, as it were, plunged back into my past only to be catapulted into my future. For example, many of my present concerns and many of the insights I thought I had only recently discovered were present in my thoughts as a teenager, although never fully articulated or understood then. I realized this after rereading a diary and several poems I had written during my teenage years and then forgotten.

In a similar way, as women discover themselves in the present, they also discover the sisterhood of souls in the past, who asked some of the same kinds of questions and began to articulate the same kinds of answers. It was surprising to a group of us at a conference on women exploring theology in the summer of 1973 to discover that what we thought were new questions we were raising about certain biblical figures had been raised three-quarters of a century earlier by the authors of *The Woman's Bible*!

Another paradigm for the historical process, which is made possible by a consideration of herstory, is that of radical discontinuity. This paradigm presents more problems for us in light of the evidence pointing to the efficacy of the cyclic or sprung-spring paradigm, but there is some justification for being open to this possibility. Elizabeth Gould Davis's speculations lead to a consideration of this possibility. Based on the assumptions of Immanuel Velikovsky that somewhere around the tenth millennium B.C. a worldwide shifting of the poles occurred, Ms. Davis speculates that the mythical kingdom of Atlantis, the race of Amazons, the mysterious knowledge of the Druids, the inexplicable existence of stone monoliths around the world, and the early evidence of belief in a mother goddess all point to the preexistence of an advanced technological civilization ruled by women—a civilization which was eventually destroyed by the world cataclysms which myth and recent archaeological discoveries record. There is also a sense in which the technological breakthroughs in the biomedical field which have been made in the last few years present us with the possibility of a truly radical future, as radical as the patriarchal age must have been from the matriarchal. The development of cloning, test-tube babies, genetic manipulation, and the like presages a totally different kind of human animal and community. Radical discontinuity is indeed a possibility.

Since feminist women have least to lose from a break with the old system, we are more open to a radically discontinuous future. The question we must ask ourselves is: Will we allow this future to overtake us, as we allowed the patriarchal revolution, or will we have some voice in its direction?

The herstory of women relativizes the historical event; it widens the historical lens and brings into consideration paradigms other than the linear to explain the historical process. As it does this, it also brings into focus the cellular substructure of the religious enterprise, the life-force which determines the genetic character of the system. It focuses on what Christian theologians and historians have consistently ignored in their analyses of the development and function of religious systems: namely, the part played by sexual fears, myths, fantasies, and necessities in the elaboration of religious convictions.

Christian theologians have sought to define God above and apart from the basic sexual duality of the universe; yet each of their formulations has been based on sexually determined assumptions. Our herstory has revealed that the mystery of life and death was originally understood in explicitly sexual, morphological terms. The mother goddesses were powerfully sensual and sexual. Intercourse was a paradigm for creation and regeneration.

With the rise of monotheism, the explicitly sexual imagery eventually went underground, but it continued to inform the determination of doctrine, even though that doctrine was now spiritualized and abstracted. God the Father was above and beyond the contingency of human sexuality, or so the tradition taught us. Nevertheless, he was a very masculine figure. And while Jesus was the incarnate Logos, the "man for others," the "second person of the Trinity," the scandal of his particularity did not extend to interpreting what he was about in feminine terms.

Circumcision, originally the primitive male's imitation of menstruation, became a mark of the Covenant. In the Christian era, Jesus' blood and body—the wine and bread—took on the symbolic resonances formerly associated with the great goddess, while birth from the womb became rebirth through immersion in the baptismal waters (amniotic fluid). Male priests eventually assumed in a professional capacity the nonprofessional roles naturally assigned to women—nurturance, care, maintenance, education.

A look at herstory reveals the extent to which Jewish and Christian doctrine has been determined by the sexual fears and fantasies of men about women. In denying to themselves the psychic origins of these doctrines, Christian theologians have at best been dishonest and at worst tyrannical. Not only have they denied women a proper role in the practice of religion, but also they have denied all of us the chance to explore the fullest dimensions of the sacred.

One further insight which a look at herstory affords us is a broader understanding of the dimensions of human evil and of the longing for human liberation and fulfillment which are expressed in the doctrine of the Fall and in the experiences of the exodus, the Incarnation, and the Resurrection.

Herstory provides us with several different ways of reinterpreting the notion of the Fall, paradigms which seek to make broader and deeper sense of the alienation which lies at the heart of creation. Herstory also points out that we can no longer limit God's work in history to the deliverance of the Hebrews from bondage nor to the Incarnation in Jesus Christ. That lens is just too narrow. Rather, what we see when we look at woman's role in the history of patriarchal religions is that in various eras there is a pattern of the rising of women toward full personhood and transcendence of their culturally defined roles and a concomitant suppression of this force by the patriarchal authority system.

Such a rising, it would seem, was occurring even as the patriarchal Yahwist cult was struggling for supremacy in ancient Palestine. The Yahwistic tirades against idolaters are really a backhanded compliment to the force of feminine expectations. The earliest Christian church, again, witnessed a rising of women and then a suppression of this movement by the postapostolic church fathers. Similarly, the witches of the Middle Ages, and perhaps those who were persecuted in New England, can be seen as examples of the striving of women toward liberation and humanity. The cruelty with which the Christian church exterminated this movement speaks poignantly of the power which must have been alive among these women. The nineteenth-century women's movement is yet another example of the attempt of one-half of creation to be free. Who is to say that a powerful, numinous force is not at work now in the current women's movement? Perhaps only those who have failed to understand herstory will deny the power of the present reality.

Penelope Washbourn

Penelope Washbourn has suggested that feminist theology should be intimately related to the life stages of a woman's experience, that becoming woman is a continuously changing quest for selfhood. This selection is taken from her Becoming Woman: The Quest for Wholeness in Female Experience. *New York: Harper and Row, 1977, pp. 1–3, 154–55.*

My conviction is that religious questions and reflections about the meaning of what is holy or ultimate arise at times of crisis in the life of the individual and of the community. These crises may be historical or personal events, but because of them we are forced to respond to a new situation. The question of the meaning of our identity and our attitude toward life is challenged. A crisis is a time of change, anxiety, and possibility. Something new happens, and we summon resources from the past, as well as discover new strengths, to deal with the implications of our changed situation.

Psychologists since the time of Sigmund Freud have described human development in terms of *life-crises* or stages of personal growth. From the viewpoint of psychology, one must more or less "successfully" negotiate each stage in order to advance to the next.

Erik Erikson views these crises, particularly those from adolescence onward, as involving questions of a religious nature, for the individual's identity must be renegotiated in terms of a new understanding of the meaning and purpose of the whole.

For a woman, the most significant life-crises are associated with having a female body. Most psychological literature writes of the "stages of man" or "man's search for meaning" and to a large extent ignores the distinctive aspect of the female life-crises. I propose that a woman's search for psychological and spiritual wholeness goes through the particular life-crises of being a female body. These stages are not just psychological phases to be negotiated but turning points that raise fundamentally religious questions. At each juncture, a woman must redefine her self-identity in relation to her perception of the purpose of life and in relation to her understanding of her own identity in relation to that ultimate value.

Traditional religious rituals in many societies are associated with these life-crises. In primitive societies as well as in industrialized cultures, we humans have needed to construct rituals around the significant events in the life of a woman and her relation to the community. The birth of a child, the advent of puberty, growth into adulthood, marriage rites, and funeral rites exemplify our need to signify or make meaning out of the major events that mark our lives. Even in our secular society, we have versions of religious rituals to symbolize our passage through life: graduation from high school, the stag party before the wedding, the retirement dinner, the golden anniversary, and the funeral service. These events are personal and communal. They mark significant changes in the life of the individual and the community. Richard Rubenstein in his book *After Auschwitz* suggested that ritual arises out of the need of the individual in community to give meaning to the questions of personal or social identity. Ritual expresses our search for a new identity in relation to the past and to the future and thus emerges from the life-crises—events that force us to deal with questions of self-identity in relation to ultimate value.

Building upon Erikson's understanding of the life-crises and Rubenstein's view of the necessity for "rites of passage" to mark those events, I propose to explore the life-crises of being a woman and the personal and spiritual questions implicit within those crises. The image of the new woman that is emerging from the contemporary discussion on the role of women in society has yet to deal significantly with the search for personal wholeness that includes the implications of being a female body. Women's new search for self-understanding implies an integration of the unique female body structure into a continuing personal quest. I believe that in and through the life-crises the questions of personal meaning are most radically presented to woman today. They force her to choose what she will become, what type of identity she will have, and how she will interpret her femaleness in relation to the whole. The crisis opens an option for personal growth and also offers the possibility for a most destructive form of self-interpretation of femaleness and its relation to others. I call these options the *graceful* and the *demonic* possibilities. At each stage of life, it is possible for a woman to understand and interpret the dimensions of her identity as graceful or demonic. To perceive female sexuality gracefully involves seeing it within the process of becoming more fully human and with an understanding of the purpose of life. To interpret female sexuality demonically means to find a false sense of identity in the female role—to romanticize it, to manipulate it, or to see it as an end in itself. The ability to perceive the graceful dimensions of female sexuality will depend largely upon a woman's ability to express the questions of meaning raised by her life-crises within a community context. Women *need* "rites of passage" that symbolize the hopes, fears, and questions of ultimate meaning in their search for personal and social identity in contemporary society. . . .

Some of these crises are shared by men but raised in a particular manner, and from an essentially female perspective, the problem of personal identity, the nature of ultimate meaning, and the structure of the relation between the individual and society. . . .

Becoming woman is not a process that is ever finished except, perhaps for oneself at any rate, in the moment of death. The task of finding oneself is never completed, but each stage of life brings its own possibilities for renewal and joy and sorrow. There is no fixed female identity. One element of a false solution to life is to stagnate in one identity, one stage, one self-image of womanhood. Each of us is many women, and each stage of life offers the potential for discovering new freedom, new growth, and new pleasures. There is also a necessary sloughing off of the old woman like layers of skin so that we can become the new woman. The life of a woman is like the life of every living creature; it is a series of transitions involving death and rebirth. In human beings, emotional and spiritual development is, however, not inevitable. We do *choose;* we are free to effect what we become even at the last moment of our life. Sometimes we despair that nothing can be done; we have been determined by our childhood, our society, our culture, our age, and there is no hope. We women often tend to see ourselves determined by forces and structures outside of ourselves, our biology, our personal and social condition, and our self-interpretation. Though change may be much harder the older we become and the suffering we will endure to undergo change will intensify, a woman's life is her own; she *is* free to live gracefully or demonically right to the last.

Becoming woman is a spiritual quest of believing in one's unique self, one's freedom to find the transformation in each stage of life. If a woman can trust life, she will find that the action of existence brings renewal; out of despair, hope, and wonder, and love will emerge. The psychological and spiritual dangers are real, however; becoming woman involves risking. "Hell on earth" will result from relying on false self-images of womanhood. The demonic potential of these choices in their destructive effect on ourselves and others is evident wherever frustrated and unhappy women meet the lives of others.

Becoming woman is a spiritual search. It involves finding a sense of one's personal worth in relation to the whole of life, even beyond death. Believing in ourselves, loving ourselves as women, is our most sacred task in and through the many phases of our sexual and personal development. Finding freedom from fear involves risking and trusting our feelings. As we risk, however, we will be given new hope, new strength, and a new love for ourselves and for others. Acting on this trust will enable us to grow in understanding through all the stages of life.

Mary Daly

By the late 1970s, Mary Daly's thinking had changed with regard to the terms God *and* androgyny. *She was developing new language that spins beyond Christianity, suggesting that women should become "Revolting Hags" who seek to affirm their original birth out of the inner mystery of the Other. This selection is taken from her* Gyn/Ecology: The Metaethics of Radical Feminism. *Boston: Beacon Press, 1978, pp. xi–xvi, 27–29.*

This book voyages beyond *Beyond God the Father.* It is not that I basically disagree with the ideas expressed there. I am still its author, and thus the situation is not comparable to that of *The Church and the Second Sex,* whose (1968) author I regard as a reformist foresister, and whose work I respectfully refute in the New Feminist Postchristian Introduction to the 1975 edition.

Going beyond *Beyond God the Father* involves two things. First, there is the fact that be-ing continues. Be-ing at home on the road means continuing to Journey. This book continues to Spin on, in other directions/dimensions. It focuses beyond christianity in Other ways. Second, there is some old semantic baggage to be discarded so that Journeyers will be unencumbered by malfunctioning (male-functioning) equipment. There are some words which appeared to be adequate in the early seventies, which feminists later discovered to be false words. Three such words in *Beyond God the Father* which I cannot use again are *God, androgyny,* and *homosexuality.* There is no way to remove male/masculine imagery from *God.* Thus, when writing/speaking "anthropomorphically" of ultimate reality, of the divine spark of be-ing, I now choose to write/speak gynomorphically. I do so because *God* represents the necrophilia of patriarchy, whereas *Goddess* affirms the life-loving be-ing of women and nature. The second semantic abomination, *androgyny,* is a confusing term which I sometimes used in attempting to describe integrity of be-ing. The word is misbegotten—conveying something like "John Travolta and Farrah Fawcett-Majors scotch-taped together"—as I have reiterated in public recantations. The third treacherous term, *homosexuality,* reductionistically "includes," that is, excludes, gynocentric be-ing/Lesbianism.

Simply rejecting these terms and replacing them with others is not what this book is about, however. The temptation/trap of mere labeling stops us from Spinning. Thus Goddess images are truthful and encouraging, but reified/objectified images of "The Goddess" can be mere substitutes for "God," failing to convey that Be-ing is a Verb, and that She is many verbs. Again, using a term such as *woman-identified* rather than *androgynous* is an immeasurable qualitative leap, but Spinning Voyagers cannot rest with one word, for it, too, can assume a kind of paralysis if it is not accompanied by sister words/verbs.

The words *gynocentric be-ing* and *Lesbian* imply separation. This *is* what this book is about, but not in a simple way. In *Beyond God the Father* I wrote:

> For those who are . . . threatened, the presence of women to each other is experienced as an absence. Such women are no longer empty receptacles to be used as "the Other," and are no longer internalizing the projections that cut off the flow of being. Men who need such projection screens experience the power of absence of such "objects" and are thrown into the situation of perceiving nothingness. . . .   In this way, then, women's confrontation with the experience of nothingness invites men to confront it also.

The primary intent of women who choose to be present to each other, however, is not an invitation to men. It is an invitation to our Selves. The Spinsters, Lesbians, Hags, Harpies, Crones, Furies who are the Voyagers of *Gyn/Ecology* know that we choose to accept this invitation for our Selves. This, our Self-acceptance, is in no way contingent upon male approval. Nor is it stopped by (realistic) fear of brutal acts of revenge. As Marilyn Frye has written: "Male parasitism means that males *must* have access to women; it is the Patriarchal Imperative. But feminist no-saying is more than a substantial removal (re-direction, re-allocation) of goods and services because access is one of the faces of power. Female denial of male access to females substantially cuts off a flow of benefits, but it has also the form and full portent of assumption of power."

The no-saying to which Frye refers is a consequence of female yes-saying to our Selves. Since women have a variety of strengths and since we have all been damaged in a variety of ways, our yes-saying assumes different forms and *is* in different degrees. In some cases, it is clear and intense; in other instances, it is sporadic, diffused, fragmented. Since Female-identified yes-saying is complex participation in be-ing, since it is a Journey, a process, there is no simple and adequate way to divide the Female World into two camps: those who say yes to women and those who do not.

The Journey of this book, therefore, is (to borrow an expression from the journal *Sinister Wisdom*) "for the Lesbian Imagination in All Women." It is for the Hag/Crone/Spinster in every *living* woman. It is for each individual Journeyer to decide/expand the scope of this imagination within her. It is she, and she alone, who can determine how far, and in what way, she will/can travel. She, and she alone, can dis-cover the mystery of her own history, and find how it is interwoven with the lives of other women.

Yes-saying by the Female Self and her Sisters involves intense work—playful cerebration. The Amazon Voyager can be antiacademic. Only at her greatest peril can she be antiintellectual. Thus this book/Voyage can rightly be called antiacademic because it celebrates cerebral Spinning. If this book/Voyage could be placed neatly in a "field" it would not be this book. I have considered naming its "field" Un-theology or Un-philosophy. Certainly, in the house of mirrors which is the universe/university of reversals, it can be called Un-ethical.

Since Gyn/Ecology is the Un-field/Ourfield/Outfield of Journeyers, rather than a game in an "in" field, the pedantic can be expected to perceive it as "unscholarly." Since it *confronts* old molds/models of question-asking by being itself an Other way of thinking/speaking, it will be invisible to those who fetishize old questions—who drone that it does not "deal with" *their* questions.

Since Gyn/Ecology Spins around, past, and through the established fields, opening the coffers/coffins in which "knowledge" has been stored, re-stored, re-covered, its meaning will be hidden from the Grave Keepers of tradition. Since it seeks out the *threads of connectedness* within artificially separated/segmented reality, striving "to put the severed parts together," specious specialists will decry its "negativity" and "failure to present the whole picture." Since it Spins among fields, leaping over the walls that separate the halls in which academics have incarcerated the "bodies of knowledge," it will be accused of "lumping things together."

In fact, *Gyn/Ecology* does not belong to any of their de-partments. It departs from their de-partments. It is the Depart-ment/Departure of Spinning. Since the Custodians of academic cemeteries are unable to see or hear Spinning, they will attempt either to box it out or to box it in to some preexisting field, such as basket weaving. Cemetery librarians will file and catalogue it under *gynecology* or *female disorders*. None of this matters much, however, for it is of the nature of the Departure of Spinning that it gets around. Moreover, it is of the nature of Women's Movement that we are on the move. Eventually we find each other's messages that have been deposited in the way stations scattered in the wilder-ness.

The cerebral Spinner can criticize patriarchal myth and scholarship because she knows it well. Her criticism has nothing to do with "jumping over" tough discipline of the mind. The A-mazing Ama-zon has no patience with downward mobility of the mind and imagination. She demands great effort of herself and of her sisters.* For she must not only know the works of The Masters; she must go much further. She must see through them and make them trans-parent to other Voyagers as well. To borrow an expression from Virginia Woolf, she must take a "vow of derision": "By derision—a bad word, but once again the English language is much in need of new words—is meant that you must refuse all methods of advertis-ing merit, and hold that ridicule, obscurity and censure are preferable, for psychological reasons, to fame and praise."

Who and where are "the deriders"? The reader/Journeyer of this book will note that it is not addressed only to those who now call themselves members of "the women's community." Many women who so name themselves are Journeyers, but it is also possible that

---

* WARNING: This book contains Big Words, even Bigger than *Beyond God the Father*, for it is written for big, strong women, out of respect for strength. Moreover, I've made some of them up. Therefore, it may be a stumbling block both to those who choose downward mobility of the mind and therefore hate Big Words, and to those who choose upward mobility and therefore hate New/Old Words, that is, Old words that become New when their ancient ("obsolete") gynocentric meanings are unearthed. Hopefully, it will be a useful pathfinder for the *multiply mobile:* the movers, the weavers, the Spinners.

some are not. It seems to me that the change in nomenclature which gradually took place in the early seventies, by which *the women's movement* was transformed into *the women's community,* was a symptom of settling for too little, of settling *down,* of being too comfortable. I must ask, first, just *who* are "the women"? Second, what about *movement?* This entire book is asking the question of movement, of Spinning. It is an invitation to the Wild Witch in all women who long to spin. This book is a declaration that it is time to stop putting answers before the Questions. It is a declaration/Manifesto that in our chronology (Crone-ology) it is time to get moving again. It is a call of the wild to the wild, calling Hags/Spinsters to spin/be beyond the parochial bondings/bindings of any comfortable "community." It is a call to women who have never named themselves Wild before, and a challenge to those who have been in struggle for a long time and who have retreated for awhile.

As Survivors know, the media-created Lie that *the women's movement* "died" has hidden the fact from many of our sisters that Spinners/Spinsters have been spinning works of genesis and demise in our concealed workshops. Feminists have been creating a rich culture, creating new forms of writing, singing, celebrating, cerebrating, searching. We have been developing new strategies and tactics for organizing—for economic, physical, and psychological survival. To do this, we have had to go deep inside our Selves. We have noted with grief that meanwhile another phenomenon has appeared in the foreground of male-controlled society: pseudofeminism has been actively promoted by the patriarchs. The real rebels/renegades have been driven away from positions of patriarchally defined power, replaced by reformist and roboticized tokens.

This book can be heard as a Requiem for *that* "women's movement," which is male-designed, male-orchestrated, male-legitimated, male-assimilated. It is also a call to those who have been unwittingly tokenized, to tear off their mindbindings and join in the Journey. It is, hopefully, an alarm clock for those former Journeyers who have merged with "the human (men's) community," but who can still feel nostalgia for the present/future of their own be-ing.

Naming the Enemy

This will of course be called an "antimale" book. Even the most cautious and circumspect feminist writings are described in this way. The cliché is not only unimaginative but deadeningly, deafeningly, deceptive—making real hearing of what radical feminists are saying difficult, at times even for ourselves. Women and our kind—the earth, the sea, the sky—are the real but unacknowledged objects of attack, victimized as The Enemy of patriarchy—of all its wars, of all its professions. There are feminist works which provide abundant examples of misogynistic statements from authorities in all "fields," in all major societies, throughout the millennia of patriarchy. Feminists have also written at length about the actual rapist behavior of professionals, from soldiers to gynecologists. The "custom" of widow-burning (*suttee*) in India, the Chinese ritual of footbinding, the genital mutilation of young girls in Africa (still practiced in parts of twenty-six countries of Africa), the massacre of women as witches in "Renaissance" Europe, gynocide under the guise of American gynecology and psychotherapy—all are documented facts accessible in the tomes and tombs (libraries) of patriarchal scholarship. The contemporary facts of brutal gang rape, of wife-beating, of overt and subliminal psychic lobotomizing—all are available.

What then can the label *antimale* possibly mean when applied to works that expose these facts and invite women to free our Selves? The fact is that the labelers do not intend to convey a rational meaning, nor to elicit a thinking process, but rather to block thinking. They do intend the label to carry a deep emotive message, triggering implanted fears of all the fathers and sons, freezing our minds. For to write an "antimale" book is to utter the ultimate blasphemy.

Thus women continue to be intimidated by the label *antimale.* Some feel a false need to draw distinctions, for example: "I am antipatriarchal but not antimale." The courage to be logical—the courage to name—would require that we admit to ourselves that males and males only are the originators, planners, controllers, and legitimators of patriarchy. Patriarchy is the homeland of males; it is Father Land; and men are its agents. The primary resistance to consciousness of this reality is precisely described in *Sisterhood Is*

Powerful: "Thinking that our man is the exception, and, therefore, we are the exception among women." It is in the interest of men (as men in patriarchy perceive their interest) and, in a superficial but Self-destructive way, of many women, to hide this fact, especially from themselves.

The use of the label is an indication of intellectual and moral limitations. Despite all the evidence that women are attacked as projections of The Enemy, the accusors ask sardonically: "Do you really think that *men* are the enemy?" This deception/reversal is so deep that women—even feminists—are intimidated into Self-deception, becoming the only Self-described oppressed who are unable to name their oppressor, referring instead to vague "forces," "roles," "stereotypes," "constraints," "attitudes," "influences." This list could go on. The point is that no agent is named—only abstractions.

The fact is that we live in a profoundly antifemale society, a misogynistic "civilization" in which men collectively victimize women, attacking us as personifications of their own paranoid fears, as The Enemy. Within this society, it is men who rape, who sap women's energy, who deny women economic and political power. To allow oneself to know and name these facts is to commit antigynocidal acts. Acting in this way, moving through the mazes of the antifemale society, requires naming and overcoming the obstacles constructed by its male agents and token female instruments. As a creative crystallizing of the movement beyond the State of Patriarchal Paralysis, this book is an act of Dis-possession; and hence, in a sense beyond the limitations of the label *antimale*, it is absolutely Anti-androcrat, A-mazingly Anti-male, Furiously and Finally Female.

Starhawk

"Starhawk" sees in witchcraft a way of eliminating false self-perceptions and achieving harmony with the immanent mother goddess. This selection is taken from her The Spiral Dance. *San Francisco: Harper and Row, 1979, pp. 187–98.*

In thinking about the future of religion and of culture, we need to look at the present through the acrostic eye. That slightly skewed vision reveals those underlying mind-sets I think of as the scabies of consciousness—because they cause us extreme discomfort and yet we can't ordinarily see them. They are embedded in us, under the skin. In this chapter, I want to examine the destructive forces, as well as the creative forces, that are influencing the direction of our evolution as a society. Only when we understand the currents of the present can we clearly envision the future.

If we accept the responsibility of claiming the future for life, then we must engage in the demanding task of re-creating culture. A deep and profound change is needed in our attitude toward the world and the life on it, toward each other, and in our conceptions of what is human. Somehow, we must win clear of the roles we have been taught, of strictures on mind and self that are learned before speech and are buried so deep that they cannot be seen. Today women are creating new myths, singing a new liturgy, painting our own icons, and drawing strength from the new-old symbols of the Goddess, of the "legitimacy and beneficence of female power."

A change in symbols, however, is not enough. We must also change the context in which we respond to symbols and the ways in which they are used. If female images are merely plugged into old structures, they too will function as agents of oppression, and this prospect is doubly frightening because they would then be robbed of the liberating power with which they are imbued today.

Witchcraft is indeed the Old Religion, but it is undergoing so much change and development at present that, in essence, it is being re-created rather than revived. The feminist religion of the future is presently being formed. Those of us who are involved in this reformation must look closely at the cultural context in which our own ideas about religion were formed, and examine the many regressive tendencies present in society today. Otherwise, the new incarnation of the Goddess will be subtly molded on the very forms we are working to transcend.

One regressive tendency is what I call *absolutism,* which stems from an intolerance of ambiguity. Our culture is highly symbol-bound, and we carry the unconscious assumption that symbolic systems *are* the realities they describe. If the description *is* the

210 / Feminist Theology

reality, and descriptions differ, only one can be true. *Either* God created Adam and Eve, *or* they evolved à la Darwin. *Either* unresolved unconscious conflicts are the final cause of our unhappiness, *or* economic and material conditions. We may change ideologies, but we do not examine the underlying idea that there is One Right, True, and Only Way—Ours!—and everybody else is wrong.

Absolutism is divisive. It sets up false conflicts; for example, between politics and spirituality. In an article entitled "Radical Feminism and Women's Spirituality: Look Before You Leap," Marsha Lichtenstein writes, "the contradiction which is the seed of the distance and distrust between spirituality and politics is that each perceives consciousness in *antithetical* [italics mine] ways. . . . An analysis of consciousness growing from spirituality seeks final causes in *a priori* categories of thought, as in the discovery of archetypes, as in the mythology of Eve as the repository of evil . . . processes of change emphasize an inward journey. . . . Radical feminism analyzes the historical material conditions under which women's consciousness has developed . . . the orientation toward social change is outer-directed, directed at transforming those societal conditions which shape our lives."

The key word in this passage is *antithetical.* A feminist spirituality based on the Goddess immanent in the world will see these analyses as complementary, rather than in opposition. They are both true. *Of course, a priori* categories of thought influence consciousness—and, *of course,* material conditions affect our ability to be whole. We need both inner and outer change—either one alone is not enough.

The Judeo-Christian heritage has left us with the view of a universe composed of warring opposites, which are valued as either good or evil. They cannot coexist. A valuable insight of witchcraft, shared by many Eastern religions, is that polarities are in balance, not at war. Energy moves in cycles. At times, it flows outward, pushing us to change the world; at other times, it flows inward, transforming ourselves. It cannot be indefinitely exerted exclusively in one direction; it must always turn and return, push and pull, and so be renewed. If we label either end of the cycle as "wrong" or unnecessary, we cut ourselves off from any possibility for renewal or for the exercise of sustained power. We must win clear of the tendency to associate religion and spirituality with withdrawal from the world and the field of action. The Goddess is ourselves *and* the world—to link with her is to engage actively with the world and all its problems.

Dualism slides over into what I call the "chosen-people syndrome." When there is One Right True and Only Way—Ours!—and everybody else is wrong, then those who are wrong are damned, and the damned are evil. We are excused from recognizing their humanness and from treating them according to the ethics with which we treat each other. Generally, the chosen people set about the task of purifying themselves from any contact with the carriers of evil. When they are in power, they institute inquisitions, witch-hunts, pogroms, executions, censorship, and concentration camps.

Oppressed and powerless groups also tend to see themselves as the chosen people. Since they are not in a position to weed out undesirables from society, they can be "pure" only by removing themselves from the larger community. In the women's movement, this has given birth to separatism.

I distinguish between separation and separatism. Women need women's spaces, especially at this point in history when many of us are recovering from hurts inflicted by men. There is a special intensity in women's mysteries and an unequaled intimacy in women's covens. Women who love other women, or who live virgin, belonging to themselves alone, attain a very special power. But it is not the *only* form of power inherent in feminist spirituality, nor is it the best form for everyone. The Goddess is Mother, Crone, Lover, as well as Virgin; She is bound up with the birth, love, and death of men as well as of women. If she is immanent in women, and in the world, then she is also immanent in men.

A matrifocal culture, based on nature, celebrates diversity, because diversity assures survival and continuing evolution. Nature creates thousands of species, not just one; and each is different, fitted for a different ecological niche. When a species becomes overspecialized, too narrow in its range of adaptations, it is more likely to become extinct. When political and spiritual movements become too narrow, they are also likely to die out. The strength of the women's movement lies in its diversity, as old and young women, gay and straight, welfare mothers and aspiring bank presidents discover common interests, common needs, and common sisterhood. If our culture as a whole is to evolve toward life, we need to foster diversity, to create and maintain a wide range of differences in life-style, theory, and tactics. We need to win clear of the self-righteousness that comes from seeing ourselves as chosen people, and need to create a religion of heretics, who refuse to toe any ideological lines or give their allegiance to any doctrines of exclusivity.

Another spurious conflict created by absolutism is that between religion and science. When God is felt to be separate from the physical world, religion can be split off from science, and limited to the realm of things having to do with God. But the Goddess is manifest in the physical world, and the more we understand its workings, the better we know her. Science and religion are both quests for truth—they differ only in their methodology and the set of symbols they use to describe their findings. The field of inquiry is the same.

"Understanding a thing is to arrive at a metaphor for that thing by substituting something more familiar to us," writes Julian Jaynes (in *The Origin of Consciousness in the Breakdown of the Bicameral Mind*); "We say we understand an aspect of nature when we can say it is similar to some familiar theoretical model." Scientific knowledge, like religious knowledge, is a set of metaphors for a reality that can never be completely described or comprehended. Religion becomes dogmatic when it confuses the metaphor with the thing itself. Metaphors themselves are not contradictory or antithetical; many can be true at once. They point to something beyond themselves; they are separate lights beaming at the same spot.

Scientific metaphors strive to be consistent and testable. They are expected to conform to objective reality. The myths and symbols of nature-oriented religions also began as metaphors for observed reality: for the movement of sun and moon, plant growth and decay, animal behavior and seasonal changes. They resonate on many levels, engaging both our verbal-analytical awareness and our holistic-imagistic awareness. They touch our emotions, determining not only what we know but also how we feel about nature. If we describe the vagina as a flower, we feel differently about it than if we call it "a piece of meat" or a "genital orifice." If we call the ocean "our Mother, the womb of life," we may take more care not to pump her full of poisons than if we see the ocean merely as "a mass of H_2O."

I would like to see the Goddess religion of the future be firmly grounded in science, in what we can observe in the physical world. Observation is meditation, as the builders of Stonehenge—temple, astronomical observatory, calendar, and calculator—knew well. Witchcraft has always been an empirical religion; herbs, spells and practices were constantly tested, and results compared at gatherings of the covens. Today, when we introduce a new ritual, exercise, or invocation, the question is always "does it work?" The tests are more subjective than those of science: Did we feel anything? Were we changed? Did we get the results we expected? Were we excited? Ecstatic? Anxious? Bored? Why?

The old symbols were drawn from observation of recurring patterns in nature. Some have merely been deepened by our expanded knowledge of those patterns. For example, the spiral was the ancient symbol of death and rebirth. We now recognize it as the shape of the DNA molecule, which sets the pattern for an organism's growth, and so it takes on another level of meaning. The galaxy is a spiral; "As above, so below."

Other myths and symbols may change to reflect new knowledge. Many of the old seasonal myths are based on the experiential perception that the sun moves around the earth. Even our language reflects this misconception; we say, "the sun rises," although we know intellectually that it does not and never has; instead, the earth turns. Because our physiology and psychology evolved under the apparently-rising-and-setting sun, the old myths "work" to connect our internal cycles with those of the outer world and cannot just be discarded. Yet perhaps there is an esoteric meaning in the earth's motion too: We do not just await the light; we journey toward it.

In future or contemporary Goddess religion, a photograph of the earth as seen from space might be our mandala. We might meditate on the structure of the atom as well as icons of ancient Goddesses; and see the years Jane Goodall spent observing chimpanzees in the light of a spiritual discipline. Physics, mathematics, ecology, and biochemistry more and more approach the mystical. New myths can take their concepts and make them numinous, so that they infuse our attitudes and actions with wonder at the richness of life.

Spirituality leaps where science cannot yet follow, because science must always test and measure, and much of reality and human experience is immeasurable. Without discarding science, we can recognize its limitations. There are many modes of consciousness that have not been validated by Western scientific rationalism, in particular what I call "starlight awareness," the holistic, intuitive mode of perception of the right hemisphere of our brains. As a culture, we are experiencing a turn toward the intuitive, the psychic, which have been denied for so long. Astrology, Tarot, palmistry—all the ancient forms of divination are undergoing a revival. People seek for expanded consciousness in everything from yoga to drugs to expensive weekend seminars, and they see no value in a religion that is merely a set of doctrines or a dull Sunday morning's entertainment. Any viable religion developing today will inevitably be concerned with some form of magic, defined as "the art of changing consciousness at will."

Magic has always been an element of witchcraft, but in the Craft its techniques were practiced within a context of community and connection. They were means of ecstatic union with the Goddess Self—not ends in themselves. Fascination with the psychic—or the psychological—can be a dangerous sidetrack on any spiritual path. When inner visions become a way of escaping contact with others, we are better off simply watching television. When "expanded consciousness" does not deepen our bonds with people and with life, it is worse than useless: It is spiritual self-destruction.

If Goddess religion is not to become mindless idiocy, we must win clear of the tendency of magic to become superstition. Magic—and among its branches I include psychology as it purports to describe and change consciousness—is an art. Like other arts, its efficacy depends far more on who is practicing it than on what theory they base their practice. Egyptian tomb painting is organized on quite different structural principles than twentieth-century surrealism—yet both schools produced powerful paintings. Balinese music has a different scale and rhythmic structure from Western music, but it is no less beautiful. The concepts of Freud, Jung, Melanie Klein, and Siberian shamanism can all aid healing or perpetuate sickness, depending on how they are applied.

Magical systems are highly elaborate metaphors, not truths. When we say "There are twelve signs in the zodiac," what we really mean is "we will view the infinite variety of human characteristics through this mental screen, because with it we can gain insights"; just as when we say "there are eight notes in the musical scale," we mean that out of all the possible range and variations of sounds, we will focus on those that fall into these particular relationships, because by doing so we can make music. But when we forget that the signs are arbitrary groupings of stars, and start believing that there are large lions, scorpions, and crabs up in the sky, we are in trouble. The value of magical metaphors is that through them we identify ourselves and connect with larger forces; we partake of the elements, the cosmic process, the movements of the stars. But if we use them for glib explanations and cheap categorizations, they narrow the mind instead of expanding it and reduce experience to a set of formulas that separate us from each other and our own power.

The longing for expanded consciousness has taken many of us on a spiritual "journey to the East," and Hindu, Taoist, and Buddhist concepts are infusing Western culture with new understandings. The East-West dialogue has become a major influence on the evolution of a new world view. Eastern religions offer a radically different approach to spirituality than Judeo-Christian traditions. They are experiential rather than intellectual; they offer exercises, practices, and meditations, rather than catechisms. The image of God is not the anthropomorphic, bearded God-Father in the sky—but the abstract, unknowable ground of consciousness itself, the void, the Tao, the flow. Their goal is not to *know* God, but to *be* God. In many ways, their philosophies are very close to that of witchcraft.

As women, however, we need to look very closely at these philosophies and ask ourselves the hard-headed, critical question, "What's in it for *me*? What does this spiritual system do for women?" Of course, the gurus, teachers, and ascended masters will tell us that, even by asking such a question, we are merely continuing in our enslavement to the lords of mind; that it is simply another dodge of the ego as it resists dissolution in the All. The truth is that while men, in our society, are encouraged to have strong egos and to function in competitive, aggressive, intellectualized modes that may indeed cause them pain, for most women the ego is like a fragile African violet, grown in secret from a seed, carefully nursed and fertilized and sheltered from too much sun. Before I toss mine out into the collective garbage heap, I want to be sure I'm getting something in return. I don't feel qualified to discuss the way Eastern religions function within their own cultures. But if we look at women in the West who have embraced these cults, by and large we find them in bondage. An ecstatic bondage, perhaps; but bondage nevertheless.

Eastern religions may help men become more whole, in touch with the intuitive, receptive, gentle feelings they have been conditioned to ignore. But women cannot become whole by being yet more passive, gentle, and submissive than we already are. We become whole through knowing our strength and creativity, our aggression, our sexuality, by affirming the self, not by denying it. We cannot achieve enlightenment through identifying with Buddha's wife or Krishna's gopi groupies. While India has strong Goddess traditions—of tantra, of Kali worship—these are less easily popularized in the West, because they do not fit our cultural expectation that truth is purveyed through male images, by charismatic males. If we look closely at the symbols, the hierarchial structure, the denial of sexuality and emotion purveyed by the gurus who do attract popular cults in the West, we can only conclude that, while they may be using different instruments, they are playing the same old song.

Another dimension of absolutism is our tendency to think that truth is somehow more true if it is expressed in extremes; that a theory to be valid must explain everything. For example, a psychologist discovers that rats can be conditioned to respond to certain stimuli in predictable ways and concludes that all learning is nothing more than conditioned responses. This makes for ringing pronouncements and endless arguments in professional journals—after all, how do we *prove* what we innately feel—that somewhere in the gap between the rat in its maze, and Makarova learning to dance, some other factor enters in? But were the psychologist to say simply "*Some* learning is a matter of conditioning," who would listen? A statement like that is not impressive, it doesn't sound new or original; it furnishes no grounds for starting experimental utopian communities, and leads to no international recognition or lucrative lecture tours. It sounds flat, obvious. Its sole virtue is that it is true, which the fine-sounding generalization is not.

Absolutist statements are often extremely appealing. Something in us wants life to be neatly organized around clear principles, with no loose ends left hanging. We desperately wish all problems in long division would work out to whole numbers, not fractions. But if we are interested in solving problems rather than manipulating pretty patterns, we have to accept that they don't. Only when we are ready to confront the muddiness and unclarity of reality can we hope to transform it.

In the past few years, a spate of secular gurus have traded heavily on our cultural longing for simple organizing principles around which to base our lives. The basis of many of the "growth" movements and human potential movements is the absolutist concept, "I create my own reality." It is in some ways comforting to believe this; in other ways, it is a terrifying thought. It seems to be true that we do create more of our lives, our opportunities, our physical health, than we ordinarily take responsibility for. If I blame my unhappiness on my mother, on the "system," on bad luck, I will continue being unhappy rather than taking action to change my situation. It is up to no one but me to create for myself meaningful work, money to live on, and important relationships, and nothing outside of myself stops me from having them all. I am, of course, like most members of these movements, white and middle class. If my skin were another color, if I were mentally retarded because of early malnutrition, or disabled, I doubt that I would be quite so sublime about my ability to create reality. Does the rape victim create the assault? Did the children of Vietnam create napalm? Obviously, no.

Much of reality—the welfare system, war, the social roles ordained for women and men—are created collectively and can only be changed collectively. One of the clearest insights of feminism is that our struggles are *not* just individual, and our pain is not private pain; it is created by ways in which our culture treats women as a class. Sexism, racism, poverty, and blind accident do shape people's lives, and they are not created by their victims. If spirituality is to be truly life serving, it must stress that we are all responsible for each other. Its focus should not be individual enlightenment, but recognition of our interconnectedness and commitment to each other.

Feminist religion does not make false promises. It does not set people up for the pain and disillusionment that comes when the growth groupie bumps up against a reality that can't be changed. Night will follow day, and there's not a damn thing you or I or Werner can do about it.

The paradox, of course, is that we are the Goddess: We are each a part of the interpenetrating, interconnecting reality that is All. And, while we can't stop the earth from turning, we can choose to experience each revolution so deeply and completely that even the dark becomes luminous. To *will* does not mean that the world will conform to our desires—it means that *we* will: We will make our own choices and act so as to bring them about, even knowing we may fail. Feminist spirituality values the courage to take risks, to make mistakes, to be our own authorities.

We need to win clear of the belief that only a few individuals in history have had a direct line on truth; that Jesus or Buddha or Mohammad or Moses or Freud or Werner Erhard know more about our souls than we do. Certainly, we can learn from teachers, but we cannot afford to give over our power to direct our lives. A feminist religion needs no messiahs, no martyrs, no saints to lead the way. Instead, it must validate us in discovering and sharing our experiences, inner and outer. Its goal should be that impossible task of teaching ourselves—because we have no models and no teachers who can show us the way—to become human, fully alive with all the human passions and desires, faults and limitations, and infinite possibilities.

Many forces today are shaping the genesis of new myths. I have discussed the changes science has brought to religion, and the impact of the East-West dialogue. Our growing awareness of ecology, the impending environmental apocalypse, has forced on us a realization of our interconnectedness with all forms of life, which is the basis of Goddess religion. Our changing cultural attitude toward sexuality is also influencing our spirituality.

Feminists have quite rightly pointed out that the so-called sexual revolution has too often meant the open marketing of women's bodies and the objectification of women. But this is because we are not yet sexually free. Pornography, rape, prostitution, sadomasochism simply bring out into the open the theme that underlies asceticism, celibacy, and Christian chastity—that sex is dirty and evil, and by extension, so are women. Under patriarchy, sexuality provides the rationale for violence against women—the stoning of adultresses, the burning of witches, the snickering probe into the conduct of rape victims.

Goddess religion identifies sexuality as the expression of the creative life-force of the universe. It is not dirty, nor is it merely "normal"; it is sacred, the manifestation of the Goddess. Fortunately, this does not mean you have to be ordained before you can do it. In feminist spirituality, a thing that is sacred can also be affectionate, joyful, pleasurable, passionate, funny, or purely animal. "All acts of love and pleasure are my rituals," says the Goddess. Sexuality is sacred because it is a sharing of energy, in passionate surrender to the power of the Goddess, immanent in our desire. In orgasm, we share in the force that moves the stars.

The strongest mythogenic force at work today, however, is feminism. Women have dared to look through the acrostic eye, and the molds have shattered. The process of cultural change is a long and difficult one. The laws, the language, the economic and social system do not yet reflect our vision. We are discovering and creating myths and symbols and rituals that do. We need images that move us beyond language, law, and custom; that hurl us beyond the boundaries of our lives to that space between the worlds, where we can see clear.

The feminist movement is a magicospiritual movement as well as a political movement. It is spiritual because it is addressed to the liberation of the human spirit, to healing our fragmentation, to becoming whole. It is magical because it changes consciousness, it expands our awareness and gives us a new vision. It is also magic by another definition: "the art of causing change in accordance with will."

If we are to reclaim our culture, we cannot afford narrow definitions.

And when we have won clear, "we must return to the circle." The circle is the ecological circle, the circle of the interdependence of all living organisms. Civilization must return to harmony with nature.

The circle is also the circle of community. The old family structures, the networks of support and caring are breaking down. Religion has always been a prime source of community, and a vital function of feminist spirituality is to create new networks of involvement. Community also implies broader issues of how equitably power, wealth, and opportunities are shared among different groups, and the issues of who cares for children, the aged, the sick, and the disabled. When the divine becomes immanent in the world, these are all areas of spiritual concern.

The circle is also the circle of self. Our view of the self—what it is, how it perceives, in what modes it functions—has changed greatly. Feminist spirituality is also an inner journey, a personal vision quest, a process of self-healing and self-exploration.

To return to the circle does not necessarily mean to embrace witchcraft specifically. I hope the religion of the future will be multifaceted, growing out of many traditions. Perhaps we will see a new cult of the Virgin Mary and a revival of the ancient Hebrew Goddess. Native American traditions and Afro-American traditions may flourish in an atmosphere in which they are given the respect they deserve. Eastern religions will inevitably change as they grow in the West—and part of that change may be in the roles they assign women.

But there are valuable underlying concepts in Witchcraft, on which other feminist traditions can draw. The most important is the understanding of the Goddess, the divine, as immanent in the world, manifest in nature, in human beings, in human community. The All-That-Is-One is not now and never has been separate from this existing physical world. She is here, now, *is* each of us in the eternal changing present; is no one but you, is nowhere but where you are—and yet is everyone. To worship her is to assert, even in the face of suffering and often against all reason, that life is good, a great gift, a constant opportunity for ecstasy. If we see it become a burden of misery for others, we have the responsibility to change it.

Because the Goddess is manifest in human beings, we do not try to escape our humanness, but seek to become fully human. The task of feminist religion is to help us learn those things that seem so simple, yet are far more demanding than the most extreme patriarchal disciplines. It is easier to be celibate than to be fully alive sexually. It is easier to withdraw from the world than to live in it; easier to be a hermit than to raise a child; easier to repress emotions than to feel them and express them; easier to meditate in solitude than to communicate in a group; easier to submit to another's authority than place trust in oneself. It is not easy to be a witch, a bender, a shaper, one of the wise; nor is it safe, comfortable, "laid back," mellow, uplifting, or a guarantee of peace of mind. It requires openness, vulnerability, courage, and work. It gives no answers: only tasks to be done, and questions to consider. In order to truly transform our culture, we need that orientation toward life, toward the body, toward sexuality, ego, will, toward all the muckiness and adventure of being human.

Withcraft offers the model of a religion of poetry, not theology. It presents metaphors, not doctrines, and leaves open the possibility of reconciliation of science and religion, of many ways of knowing. It functions in those deeper ways of knowing which our culture has denied and for which we hunger.

The world view of witchcraft is cyclical, spiral. It dissolves dualities and sees opposites as complements. Diversity is valued; both poles of any duality are always valued because between them flows the on-off pulse of polar energy that sustains life. That cycle is the rhythm of the dance, to which the hunter, the seeker, is always drawn back.

Finally, the Craft provides a structural model: the coven, the circle of friends, in which there is leadership, but no hierarchy, small enough to create community without loss of individuality. The form of ritual is circular: We face each other, not an altar or a podium or a sacred shrine, because it is in each other that the Goddess is found. Every witch is priestess or priest: there are no hierophants, no messiahs, no avatars, no gurus. The Goddess says, "If that which you seek, you find not within yourself, you will never find it without. For I have been with you from the beginning."

Rosemary Ruether

By 1980, Rosemary Ruether had become concerned about some of the excesses of feminist theology—e.g., the advocacy of witchcraft— and was pleading for a feminist spirituality that would put together a new synthesis, utilizing the elements of earlier traditions, but within a new context. This selection is taken from her article "Goddesses and Witches: Liberation and Countercultural Feminism," The Christian Century, *10–17 September 1980, pp. 842–47.*

Western social movements have a tendency to "trifurcate" into three trends: liberal reformist, socialist, and countercultural romanticist. This division was evident in the movements of the 1960s, and it is not surprising to find similar trends in feminism. Liberal reformers are basically concerned to achieve greater democratic participation and access of all persons to the existing system. Socialists doubt that this can be accomplished within the system and project a transformation of the economic-social structure within which persons exist. Countercultural romantics try to adopt an alternative culture and life-style.

Within feminist religion and spirituality, there seem to be similar tendencies. The liberal reformer wants to gain greater access to education, ordination, and employment for women in the church and to carry out some reform of language and exegesis, while maintaining a belief that the dominant religion itself is reformable in the direction of equality between the sexes. Feminists who espouse liberation theology believe that within biblical faith there is a critical tradition which can be the basis for the liberation of women, as well as of other oppressed people. But they see this tradition as being informed by conflict. Just as society is divided by class struggle, so the church and its theology are divided between an ideological use of religion to sanctify the ruling class and a prophetic tradition that denounces this misuse of religion.

Countercultural feminists reject the idea that any critical biblical tradition or any theological tradition has relevance for women. What liberation feminists would call the biblical tradition's patriarchal ideology, countercultural feminists would declare to be its *only* ideology. In their view, Judaism and Christianity exist for one purpose only—to sanctify patriarchy. Consequently, any woman who is concerned to find a feminist spirituality must withdraw from these religious institutions, purge herself of any inherited attachment to their authoritative symbols, and seek an alternative female-centered religion.

Since there are no established female-centered religions around, countercultural feminists have been engaged in trying to rediscover or create them. Following nineteenth-century anthropologists such as Jakob Backofen, countercultural feminist spirituality accepts the idea that human society was originally matriarchal. The original human religion, during the long millennia of Stone Age culture, was the cult of the Mother Goddess and her son, the hunter, which reflected matriarchal society. This religion was subdued by the patriarchal nomadic warriors who conquered the Indian subcontinent and the Mediterranean world in the second millennium B.C. These nomadic warriors replaced the dominant symbol of the Mother Goddess with that of the sky god, and subsumed the goddess into the cult of Zeus Pater in the form of subordinate wives, mistresses, or daughters. From the eighth century B.C. to the seventh century, A.D., the patriarchal reform religions of Judaism, Christianity, and Islam suppressed the goddess altogether and substituted the exclusive reign of the sky father.

The Maternal Ground of Being

However, the cult of the Mother Goddess did not die out altogether. It survived underground as a persecuted religion, named witchcraft or devil worship by its patriarchal enemies. Medieval witchcraft is believed to constitute the continuation of the cult of the Mother Goddess and the horned god (cf. the writings of Dame Margaret Murray). Either in exclusively female or in mixed groups, her followers gathered in secret societies called covens, limited to the mystic number of thirteen. Reportedly, nine million women were sacrificed to the fires of persecution. Nevertheless, a remnant of the true believers survives into the present. Today this "old-time religion" is being revived in the movement known as Wicca (supposedly the Anglo-Saxon word for witches). Followers of the Wicca movement believe that the dominant patriarchal history suppresses the truth about these matters.

Wicca, as delineated by its theoreticians—such as Starhawk (Miriam Simos) in her book *The Spiral Dance* (Harper & Row, 1979)—is a feminist and ecological religion. It operates on the natural rhythms that connect our bodies with the cosmic body around us. It is not without its own ethical code, since to bring the human community truly into harmony with nature is not merely a personal but a social discipline as well. We must not only alter our personal life-style but also struggle against the polluting systems of corporate capitalism that proliferate warfare and waste. Starhawk sees spells and incantations as ways of transforming one's own consciousness, purging oneself (individually or in groups) of depression, anger, and hatred, and putting oneself in right relation to the self, others, and the universe.

Starhawk would also reject female-dominant and separatist interpretations of Wicca, believing that such narrow forms lack the redemptive vision of the Craft and could be destructive to men just as patriarchal religion has been to women. Her version of Wicca would include males and females as equals. Both men and women are able to integrate the intuitive capacities of the right hemisphere of the brain, which has been repressed into unconsciousness by the cerebrally one-sided patriarchal religions.

The mother goddess is fundamentally an immanent deity, the maternal ground of being of the coming-to-be and passing-away of all things, the womb of creation. In relating to her, we relate ourselves to the true divine foundations of reality that do not force us to deny our bodies and our material existence, as does patriarchal transcendence. Matriarchal religion allows us to accept the naturalness and goodness of things as they are. It teaches us to see not only all human beings but also the animals and plants, stars and rocks as our sisters and brothers.

Starhawk presents Wicca in an attractive manner. She is concerned to imbue it with an ethic of social responsibility. Another spokesperson of the movement of feminist witchcraft is Z. (Zsuzsanna) E. Budapest, who outlines the female-dominant or "dianic" form of Wicca in her book *The Holy Book of Women's Mysteries.* Two women professors of religious studies influenced by Budapest are Carol Christ (*Woman Spirit Rising*) and Naomi Goldenburg (*The Changing of the Gods*). The magazine *Woman Spirit,* published in Wolf Creek, Oregon, is a popular organ of the movement of women's spirituality and communalism.

If feminist spirituality claims to be making public statements about truth and liberation and not just idiosyncratic statements concerning personal preference, then those claims need to be tested for the sake of the best interests of such movements themselves, as well as for their possible impact on the rest of us. Several pertinent questions arise, which can be discussed under the following headings: (1) historical truth and self-knowledge; (2) anthropology, maleness and femaleness, good and evil; (3) nature and civilization; (4) the relation of immanence, transcendence, and fallenness; and (5) the methodology for a feminist critique of culture.

Historical Truth

Although feminist scholarship as a whole is developing an impressive record in new historical research, it is characteristic of countercultural spirituality to be quite arbitrary toward historical data, often relying on repeated quotation of outdated nineteenth-century works on matriarchal origins. There is little effort to conduct new research or to consult primary documents. Most of all, there is little interest in dealing with such cultural and historical artifacts in the complexity of their cultural and historical settings. A tendentious use of historical material reduces everything to one drama: the story of original female power and goodness, and the evil male conquest and suppression of the same.

For example, it is true that ancient Near Eastern cultures had female deities—goddesses who were powerful, sexual, warlike, independent, and dominant over their male consorts. It is not true, however, that this picture of female deity can simply be read as an image of women in those societies and their relation to males. Nor is it clear that women created or defined these cults or predominated in their sacerdotal elite (even though women may have been included in them). E.g., in the neo-Babylonian psalms to Ishtar, the devotees who address the goddess are clearly of the ruling class—propertied persons who are concerned with restoration of economic prosperity and with victory over enemies in war and politics. If the devotee might occasionally be a queen rather than a king, the concerns are identical with those of the male ruling class.

The parallelism with Old Testament Psalms is striking. In the cult of the goddess and the king, it is the latter who represents the human community. The goddess represents the encompassing divine-material cosmos on which the king and the human community that depends on him rely for their fortunes. The king is the son of the goddess, much as the Davidic king in the Hebrew Psalms is the son of Yahweh. The Near Eastern goddess has no daughters! Although it is not insignificant that the female image can be used to portray this concept of god, the result is not a feminist religion or one concerned with liberating the oppressed; rather, it is a religion fundamentally interested in keeping Middle Eastern male kings on the thrones of their city-states. One might argue that these historical texts of goddess religion represent the transformation of a still earlier truly female-centered pattern to a patriarchal system. But no one has yet discovered the sources for determining whether that is so.

Let us turn to another example. I have not seen the slightest evidence from medieval records that witchcraft was regarded by either its opponents or its alleged proponents as being centered in a female deity. The Devil, who is regarded by the inquisitors as the center of this cult, is always male. Nor have I seen satisfactory evidence indicating that witches, or those accused of being witches, were organized in any way into cultic groups such as covens. The former idea appears to have originated with Margaret Murray, drawing on nineteenth-century romantic scholarship. The latter idea is a fantasy contrived by the medieval inquisitors in order to make the case that witches constituted a heretical sect.

Although women came to predominate among those accused of witchcraft, they were never the sole targets. Almost a quarter of those who were put to death were male. Responsible scholarship sets the number of those executed at several hundreds of thousands. Given the fact that for every person finally executed, dozens more were interrogated and tortured, the result—in the period roughly from the fourteenth to the eighteenth centuries—was no small attrocity. Nevertheless the figure of "9 million women burned," which is continually cited in feminist literature on the issue, appears to be completely unsubstantiated. So far as I can figure out, the motivation behind the repetition of this fallacy is a desire to "top" the Jewish Holocaust. I personally have trouble with competitions for top atrocity honors. Things have been bad enough without making them worse.

Self-Knowledge

The creation of a feminist goddess-centered religion need not be dependent on whether the worship of Ishtar or the practice of witchcraft was such a religion in the past. It is possible to start something new, using images from the past but transforming their meaning and imbuing them with contemporary experience. Every existing historical religion once did exactly this, and there is no reason why it cannot be done today by women concerned with a spirituality of women's liberation. But to make up a history out of misinterpreted evidence is a dubious procedure. At the very least, it means that one does not really understand either the meaning of appropriated symbols in their original context or their subliminal effects when unleashed into present-day experience.

To take over the goddess-king mythical pattern uncritically, and to misinterpret the goddess as a divine identity for women, may have an effect that is far from liberating or egalitarian. To do so may actually allow women to play the role of imperial dominance and vengefully and contemptuously to seek to reduce the status of males to that of dependent children, sexual toys, or alien devils—in short, to do unto males very much what feminists have accused males of doing to women in patriarchal religion. Dianic Wicca, as described by Z. Budapest, has a strong flavor of this tendency of "reversal of dominance." Revenge may be sweet, but can it be the mark of truly feminist spirituality or ethics?

Dubious historical pedigrees should be challenged not merely in the interest of academic fastidiousness, but because bad history never leads to good self-knowledge. Bad history is a tool of delusion, self-inflation, and negation of others. One of the great contributions of reformed Christianity is that it has established the norm of self-critical knowledge of one's own origins and history as the key to religious self-knowledge. It seems to me that a feminist religion that would be better cannot do less.

Assigning Good and Evil

Anthropologically, separatist spirituality embodies a broad general typology of maleness and femaleness. Females are seen as loving, egalitarian, mutual, holistic, ecological, and spontaneous. Males are seen as oppressive, alienated, dualistic, rapacious, and destructive. In short, women are the authentic human beings, while males are inauthentic and evil subhumans. The origin of these stereotypes lies in the nineteenth-century Victorian cult of femininity. Victorian women, confined to the private, domestic sphere, were idealized as the incarnation of a higher and better humanity; males, split between the private personalized life and the public competitive life, were considered less moral, less spiritual, less altruistic and sensitive, and needing the "feminine touch" to humanize them. Separatist feminism "radicalizes" the Victorian doctrine of complementarity.

Most feminists use some version of this "critique of masculinity." But they view it as a matter of social systems that have socialized males to an extreme that favors power and control, while assigning women the more "humane" qualities but placing them in a powerless and dependent position. Separatist feminists move from identifying this split with socialization to seeing it as constituting inherent male and female "natures." This, of course, is what patriarchal ideologies have traditionally done to women. Mary Daly, in her most recent work, *Gyn/Ecology* (Beacon, 1979), comes close to such identification of goodness with women and evil with men.

One can well ask whether such stereotypes are not unfair and wounding to males. But more important here (since few males are going to expose themselves to being wounded by feminist separatists!) is the question of whether those stereotypes are conducive to valid female self-knowledge and development. If evil is male, then women don't have to take any responsibility for it. They can be the great innocents or victims of history. Their only ethical task is to purge themselves of all traces of male influence; then their naturally good selves will be revealed and will re-create the world. There is no need for women ever to examine themselves to see whether they are capable of oppressiveness and injustice. In such an outlook, evil is always alien to true femaleness.

Oddly enough, such a position does not lead to female bonding or sisterhood, as is claimed, but to increasing paranoia and sectarianism on the part of women in their dealings with each other. Having relegated all males to the subhuman, women eye each other suspiciously. Few are believed to have true "feminist consciousness"; most are dupes of males. One shares sisterhood with fewer and fewer women. One cannot have sisterhood with any women who are married, who have male children, who engage in heterosexual relations, who remain within patriarchal religions. These limitations exclude most women. The circle of the elite becomes smaller and smaller, and less and less relevant to the day-to-day needs of most women.

This sectarianism is rooted in a false anthropology. Women need to acknowledge that they have the same drives and temptations to sin as males have—not just sins of dependency but also the sins of dominance, of which they have been less guilty (not for want of capacity, but for want of opportunity). When women are given more opportunity to play the power games, they do so and can learn to like it.

If we are really to effect change, we must take responsibility for the capacities for both good and evil in all people. We must stop projecting evil onto the "other." And in this way women will be liberated from the self-absolutization and paranoia that have so often created "revolutions," with the result that seven devils return to occupy the place from which one has been driven. We will be able to cultivate a sense of humor, to be sensitive to the ambiguity in all of our efforts to do good, to be inclusive in our sympathies toward all persons. This is a better pattern not only for liberation but also for personal psychic health and equilibrium. To follow it does not mean any lessening of judgment on the evils done in the name of male prerogatives, but rather not to allow the evil to overwhelm and destroy our souls.

Nature and Civilization

The male-female dualism of countercultural spirituality tends to be identified with the dualism of nature and civilization. Nature is seen as an unspoiled realm of spontaneous harmony that is to be found by getting in touch with the world outside of human intervention. In so doing, we rediscover the deep rhythms that connect unspoiled nature and women's bodies. A woman's body becomes a microcosm of the universe, rather than an object of exploitation and contempt. Much of separatist ritual has to do with celebrating those rhythms and connections. Although there is much in this perspective that is an important corrective to the negation of woman, of the body, and of nature in patriarchal religions, one must also be aware of certain dangers in it.

The source of this type of nature-civilization split (and its connection with femaleness and maleness) is again nineteenth-century romanticism. In separatist spirituality, the split is typically identified with ancient "paganism" or goddess religion. But in actuality, the concept of goddess worship as nature religion is a fantasy of European Christianity. Ancient Near Eastern goddesses were not figures of "nature religion" in this sense; rather, they represented wisdom and order that restore the harmony not only of the natural environment but also the humanly managed urban and agricultural worlds, rescuing them as well from threatened disruption by the forces of death and chaos.

The romantic nature-civilization split seems to me to be an essentially escapist notion, rather than the basis for a genuine social ethic. One projects onto the world of human artifacts one's sense of frustrated alienation, then imagines that an escape from this system is by means of a retreat into an unfallen paradise of "nature." This attitude relieves one from ever really having to take responsibility for trying to change the human world. Western males have been playing various versions of this "retreat into nature" for some time; they have stereotyped women, Indians, and South Sea islanders as the "natives" in Eden. It is rather odd to find women identifying themselves with the same labels.

A much more sinister use of the nature-civilization dualism characterizes the type of German romanticism that was exploited by Nazi ideology. Here Germanic blood and soil were identified with the unspoiled realm of organic nature—a realm to which the German *Volk* needed to return in order to be made whole. Urban civilization and technology were viewed as the realm of alienated rationality, which is the destructive virus of modern civilization. Nazi ideology took up this romantic dualism and related it to the racial split between German and Jew. The Jew was seen as the secular urban rationalist who alienated the German soul from its organic spiritual wholeness with nature and the cosmos. If the Jew could be purged from the German body politic, it was argued, this wholeness could be restored.

Some forms of feminist separatism seem close to making the same kind of identification of females with the organic true *Volk* and males with the rationalist, materialist alien. Not surprisingly, such circles seem "fascistic" in some ways. We find abrupt refusals to allow males to speak in assemblies, or to be present at all, and even efforts to purge women of all connections with males by refusing entry to those who engage in heterosexual relations or who have male offspring. One thinks of the Nuremberg laws which tried to ban all interpersonal relations between Germans and Jews. Although obviously such feminist groups lack the power to do to males what Nazis did to Jews, one shudders to think what might happen if they were in power—or, more important, what these women are doing to their own humanity when they reduce the rest of the human race to nonpersons.

Immanence and Transcendence

It is widely assumed in feminist spirituality that the concept of transcendence represents an alien patriarchal ideology that separates God from nature, mind from body, heaven from earth. Feminist theology, therefore, must be a theology of immanent divinity. The goddess represents the immanent harmony of the existing natural ecology found in the turn of the seasons, the tides of the sea, the cycles of the planets. Once one has repudiated the alien world of male civilization, this natural mother is waiting for us, her arms outstretched. The concepts of sin and fallenness are lies which males have imposed on females in order to subject them to an inferior status.

In my opinion, this kind of immanentism is an inadequate base for the feminist theological agenda. Although feminists obviously have to reject certain understandings of sin, fallenness, transcendence, and future hope found in patriarchal theology, these concepts themselves need to be appropriated and reinterpreted in feminist terms. If human history has really been a history of gynecide, rape, and war, then that fact itself bespeaks a formidable reality of sin and fallenness. It means that human nature has the capacity to depart from and destroy its own harmony with the cosmos and, in the process, not only to distort its own nature but also to distort the cosmos itself—in a way that today leaves very little of "nature" unspoiled by human intervention.

The original goodness of humanity and nature is not available simply for the price of a romp on the beach or a chant around the campfire. Original goodness exists as a lost potential that has to be reimagined and reclaimed, not simply by changed consciousness but through an ethical struggle to re-create the world and our own individual and social existence in it. The original harmony of humanity with nature and God exists not as a present reality but as a lost paradise and future hope, which we taste now and again in the midst of our broken existence. It is that future Shalom of God on earth for which we hope and struggle—and which was announced by the prophets of Israel and by Jesus of Nazareth. Far from repudiating this biblical pattern of thought, a feminist denunciation of sexism as a primal expression of human fallenness can reinterpret that pattern with new power and meaning. In so doing, we can also rediscover the union that the Hebrew tradition itself makes between God's Shalom as social justice and as ecological harmony.

A Methodology for a Critique of Culture

Judeo-Christian religion and its stepchild, Western culture, have succeeded in monopolizing public reality, at least in our experience. This means that those who are a part of and yet are alienated from this culture have a difficult time arriving at a genuinely holistic alternative. If they try to negate the culture completely, they find themselves without a genuine tradition with which to work, and they neglect those basic guidelines which the culture itself has developed through long experience in order to avoid the pathological dead ends of human psychology.

This religious and cultural monopolizing of public reality has a formidable shadow side, a suppressed animus forming the underside of its own dominant identity. This animus is commonly identified with all those cultural "enemies" conquered in the past; it is called nature religion, goddess worship, paganism, witchcraft, demonism, and the like. For a long time, Judaism also existed in Christian consciousness as a force in this suppressed animus. The great mistake of any group seeking an alternative is to identify that alternative with the Christian animus. Jews, fortunately, were able to keep alive a genuine alternative religion and culture through centuries of Christian suppression, and so they were always able to differentiate between authentic Jewish identity and the Christian anti-Jewish animus.

But women are not so lucky in this regard. If there ever was an autonomous women's religion, it has not survived as an existing independent tradition. It is doubtful that the goddess worship of antiquity was such a religion. And even if it should hold clues to some alternatives, it has not come down as living tradition. To pretend that it has and to construct an imaginary line of descent for a feminist religion indicates a false understanding of origins. To a large extent, this means that instead of creating a more holistic alternative, such feminist spiritualities succumb to the suppressed animus of patriarchal religious culture.

There is nothing objectionable in the effort to create a feminist spirituality as such. But actually to do so is both more difficult and more dangerous than one might realize, and demands both greater modesty and greater maturity than those still deeply wounded by patriarchal religion have generally been able to muster. The best way to create such a spirituality is not by means of separatism and rejection, but by means of synthesis and transformation. We need to work through, with great breadth and depth, what our actual experience has been, both in the dominant culture shaped by males and in the suppressed experiences of women. Then we can begin to put together a new synthesis that utilizes many of the elements of earlier traditions, but within a new and liberated context.

CHAPTER FIVE

Evangelical Theology

Dean Kelley

Many individuals, unsettled by the chaos of the 1960s, opted for a conservative faith that would give them a sense of meaning and belonging in a world of insecurity. Dean Kelley has been a prime interpreter of this swing to the right. This selection is taken from his Why Conservative Churches Are Growing. *New York: Harper and Row, 1972, pp. 174–79.*

Human beings cannot live without trying to make sense of their experience, to find the meaning in it. When they discover a broad explanation that satisfies them, they are shielded by it from dejection and dread. The same answer will not work for everyone, and some are more satisfying than others. Most such explanations originate with a religious group, since their convincingness and continuity derive from the commitment given to them by a community of devotees. These communities begin as high-demand religious or quasi-religious movements capable of changing the lives of men and the course of history. As the level of demand decreases, they "run down" and decline in social strength and numbers until they reach a state of minimal activity, which may continue for centuries.

This process of decline can be delayed—though probably not reversed—by the exercise of "strictness," which is the consequence and evidence of the seriousness of meaning. Even from declining religious groups many people derive what meaning they have; for some it may be all they need. And from declining groups new movements spring, which may lend vitality to the old or may begin a new evolution or both.

Strictness has led to grievous excesses in the past (such as crusades and inquisitions), which should remind us that the pursuit of meaning is serious business and can become dangerous. Without such seriousness, however, the meaning-quest becomes lax and desultory—which can also be dangerous, since a failure of meaning may have a destructive effect on society as well as on individuals.

We are living in a day when strictness is out of favor, and the qualities which are popularly esteemed in religious groups are those that conduce, not to the strength of the quest for meaning, but to its weakening: relativism, diversity, dialogue—leniency. What are the implications of this situation for the major Protestant denominations? If a religious group—old or new—wants to keep from dying, how should it proceed?

Implications for the Ecumenical Churches

To the person who is concerned about the future of the ecumenical churches, this theory can offer little encouragement. The mainline denominations will continue to exist on a diminishing scale for decades, perhaps for centuries, and will continue to supply some people with a dilute and undemanding form of meaning, which may be all they want. These dwindling denominations may spawn new movements which, if they pursue the hard road of strictness, may have vital effects on human life, such as the declining churches had in their youth but can no longer achieve.

The plans for the amalgamation of the chief ecumenical churches into one body—the "Church of Christ Uniting"—and hopes for a really inclusive National Conference of Churches or a worldwide parliament of all religions, all are symptoms and confirmations of the process of relaxation described in this book. Such ecumenical endeavors may be conducive to brotherhood, peace, justice, freedom, and compassion, but they are not conducive to conserving or increasing the social strength of the religious groups involved or— more important—the efficacy of the ultimate meanings which they bear.

Conserving Strength in an Adverse Era

Suppose a pastor or a layman in one of the ecumenical denominations wanted to strengthen the congregation of which he was a
part. How would he go about it? . . . To begin with, he might try to
put into effect the "Minimal Maxims of Seriousness.". . . It will do
no harm to review them concisely here.

1. Those who are serious about their faith do not confuse it
with other beliefs, loyalties, or practices, or mingle them together
indiscriminately, or pretend they are alike, of equal merit, or
mutually compatible if they are not.
2. Those who are serious about their faith make high demands
of those admitted to the organization that bears the faith, and they
do not include or allow to continue within it those who are not
fully committed to it.
3. Those who are serious about their faith do not consent to,
encourage, or indulge any violations of its standards of belief or
behavior by its professed adherents.
4. Those who are serious about their faith do not keep silent
about it, apologize for it, or let it be treated as though it made no
difference, or should make no difference, in their behavior or their
relationships with others.

The ways in which Anabaptists and Wesleyans tried to put such
seriousness into effect . . . might be generalized as follows:

a. Be in no haste to admit members.
b. Test the readiness and preparation of would-be members.
c. Require continuing faithfulness.
d. Bear one another up in small groups.
e. Do not yield control to outsiders, nor seek to accommodate to
their expectations.

Perhaps the initial and essential step in all this is for the members
of the congregation to determine what ultimate meanings they are
going to embrace and embody. If as a whole they are not ready to
do so, perhaps it will be necessary to begin with a nucleus of those
who are, and organize them into a discipleship group (an *ecclesi-*

ola) to which others in time may be attracted. This will not be easy, and the dangers of elitism will need to be guarded against. Still, there will be in every congregation some who *want* to be called to a really serious discipleship.

This tactic has been used many times in many places; sometimes it results in schism, sometimes in revitalization of the church. Often, the degree of new seriousness is not sufficient to withstand the inertia of the congregation, and the effort soon collapses. Sometimes it is "domesticated" by the congregation, its challenge tamed, contained, and channeled to some limited objective such as visiting the sick or greeting new members. Sometimes it is distracted by or diverted to some too-large objective which does not clearly communicate ultimate meaning, such as a campaign for open housing or world peace. This does not mean that such activities are always inappropriate or may never be the expression of ultimate meaning; their appropriateness has to do with the meaning to be conveyed and their proportion to the group's energies: an aim is overbroad whose sheer logistical demands would devour all the time and effort of the group without producing visible results or effective communication of ultimate significance. The meaning which the *ecclesiola* tries to embody and express may be radical or conservative from the standpoint of the world. There is no reason why the group could not preach and practice radical and voluntary poverty or pacifism if it desires. In fact, the more radical the meaning, the higher the demand upon members who embody it, and the stronger the group will consequently be. But whatever the final meaning to be expressed and embodied, the group must be thoroughly and uncompromisingly committed to it.

The same principles apply in the organization of a new group outside existing traditions. Any commune, for instance, seeking to survive its first winter would be well-advised to determine what it is trying to accomplish, distill its purpose into brief compass, and eliminate everything that distracts or detracts from them. This does not necessarily mean drawing up a creed or a set of rules and regulations; the Anabaptists never had either, but they hammered out—by costly trial and error—a fairly clear stance and attitude, so that it became readily apparent who belonged to the group and who did not.

Both new groups and old must find an effective yet humane way to exercise the only power a voluntary group possesses to preserve its integrity: the power of the gate. They must be willing and ready to exclude those who do not measure up to the group's standards, whatever those may be. Many groups have high and admirable standards, but when it comes to enforcing them against specific offenders, they lack the will—the seriousness—to do so. It is not necessary to be cruel or harsh about such enforcement, nor to condemn the offender as worthless or abhorrent. He has simply failed to meet the qualifications of the group and is therefore no longer a member; it is as simple as that, but must not be blurred or glossed over.

In or *out:* upon this distinction the survival of any serious group depends. If it fails to separate out those who are not in earnest about its purposes, it may go on—for a while—as a group, but its real purposes do not go on. They will deteriorate quickly under such neglect, and so eventually will the group itself.

Groups which preserve their seriousness through strictness will not only mediate effective meaning to their members and others, but as a consequence will thrive and grow. Having avoided many forms of failure as well as having survived scorn, ridicule, and persecution, they will attain the eminence from which decline is certain—that is, success. As in other areas of life, the rewards of successful functioning often undermine the very qualities that produced it.

Strictness is not congenial to the prosperous, and so it ebbs away, and with it social strength.

Yet it should not be necessary for great meaning movements to throw away their strength by capitulating to the expectations of outsiders, by organizational promiscuity, by lowering of membership standards, and by loss of insistence on their seriousness. If this book has cast some light on the critical importance of meaning in human affairs—how it is engendered, propagated, and appropriated, and how organizations can serve the cause of meaning with seriousness or betray it by leniency, indulgence, and inertia—it will have benefited the churches more than if it were devoted simply to their praise or blame.

Richard Quebedeaux

A significant aspect of the evangelical upsurge has been the movement for Charismatic Renewal. This movement has been strong on experience and weak on doctrine. Richard Quebedeaux's selection is taken from his The New Charismatics. *Garden City, New York: Doubleday 1976, pp. 148–59, 195–97.*

Theology: Fundamentalism vs. "Progressive Evangelicalism"

Since 1901, biblical literalism has reinforced dispensational (theological and cultural) fundamentalism as the basic theology of Classical Pentecostalism. This is easily discerned in the doctrinal statements and moral demands of the major Pentecostal denominations. Historically, the fundamentalist label has been attached to those individuals and groups that accept what have become known as the five fundamentals of the faith: the virgin birth of Christ, his substitutionary atonement for human sin, his bodily resurrection from the dead, and his literal and imminent second coming in glory, together with the inspiration and authority of Scripture as the only infallible rule of faith and conduct. But fundamentalism has also become associated with (1) a total rejection of (nontextual) biblical criticism, (2) complete separation from nonfundamentalists (theological liberals, especially) and the wider society more generally, and (3) the moral negativism and cultural taboos of American revivalism.

Charismatic Renewal, however, seems to be moving from rigid fundamentalism ("The Lord appears to be making a lot of Episcopalian Fundamentalists in these end time days!" Jean Stone, 1962) to a "progressive evangelicalism" that affirms the authority of Scripture, the necessity of a personal commitment to Christ as Savior and Lord, and the mandate for evangelism, but rejects and repudiates fundamentalist cultural excesses and theological extremes. Although dispensational expectations are still widespread among Neo-Pentecostals, *some* prominent Charismatic Renewal leaders such as Larry Christenson, Howard Ervin, Josephine Ford, Donald Gelpi, Michael Harper, Edward O'Connor, Kevin and Dorothy Ranaghan, and Rodman Williams are firm in their disavowal of dispensational fundamentalism. Michael Harper summarizes the characteristic Charismatic Renewal stance on this key issue as follows:

> Pentecostalism in some people's minds is equated with a belief in the verbal inspiration of Scripture (usually the King James version only), a kind of proof textualism, whereby chapter and verse answers every question irrespective of context. It seems to require a belief in the pre-millennial view of the Second Coming, and an almost complete distrust in theology....
>
> The present-day charismatic movement, generally speaking, is not ... a movement of unthinking fools floating on a wave of emotional experience.... But the danger is still there. An unthinking old-fashioned fundamentalism will always be a hindrance to the forward surge of the Holy Spirit.

Worship: "Spirit of Confusion" vs. "The Quiet Spirit"

Influenced deeply by the black religious experience, worship in classical Pentecostalism has ordinarily been noted for its radical enthusiasm and spontaneity (which includes the exercise of *charismata*), on the one hand, and its almost total disregard for "liturgical order," on the other (less so in Great Britain than in the United States, however, and increasingly less so with the passage of time and the greater upward mobility in Pentecostal denominations). "A Pentecostal meeting where you know what is going to happen next is backslidden," Donald Gee declares. Typical of a Church of God (Cleveland, Tennessee) service (in many places, still), for instance, might be the following:

> 7:40 P.M.—Our Annual Saturday Evening Testimony and Praise Service, V. R. Sherill in charge. Charles, Harper, Davis and Ted sang, "I shall Ride on the Cloud." Brother Sherill called on the different sections in the balcony to praise the Lord, starting on one side and going all around. This ended in a shout of praise on the platform. The quartet sang, "I see the light house." The congregation stood and clapped hands. A march was started on the platform and continued on the main floor of the building. The blessings of the Lord were upon the people and they danced, shouted and rejoiced in the Lord. One clerk described the outpouring thus: "A march of victory is started on the large platform with leaping, shouting

and praising the Lord. Now they move down and make their way through the shouting congregation. Such unity of the spirit I have never felt. The large congregation is aflame with the fire and power of the Holy Ghost and almost everyone is shouting. The large platform is quaking from the impact of hundreds of feet striking the surface as God continues to shower blessing after blessing upon His people. The people on the main floor testified by sections, one after the other. The praises rang out around the balconies again and then all praised the Lord together. At the close of this praise service, Clayton Sherill, his wife and Louise Sherill sang, 'I'm So Glad He Found Me.' "

Like many other scholars, Walter Hollenweger associates this general pattern of worship with liberation from psychological stress caused by various kinds of deprivation (e.g., economic and social).

Wade Horton, a Church of God (Cleveland, Tennessee) overseer, criticizes Charismatic Renewal for subduing the Classical Pentecostal manner of enthusiastic worship. He speaks against the voice that

accepts the mechanical, quiet, sophisticated tongues speaking, but rejects the emotional, unspeakable joy, spiritually intoxicated, rushing-mighty-wind kind of Pentecostal experience. This group wants to be sure that the multitudes are not confounded and amazed at their actions, and most certainly that they are not accused of being drunk as were the first Pentecostal believers. They want to steer their ship clear of the Pentecostal pattern as recorded in Acts 2. This voice says, "I will accept glossolalia, but, please, not as the Pentecostals do."

Neo-Pentecostals, as we have seen, reject what they sometimes regard as the (non-middle-class) "spirit of confusion" typical of traditional Pentecostal worship (part of classical Pentecostalism's cultural baggage—"adiaphora," not belonging to the center of the Pentecostal experience). They tend, rather, to stress order ("the quiet Spirit," in Kathryn Kuhlman's words) within formal services of worship. Although uplifted hands in prayer (the ancient *orans* posture) and being "slain in the Spirit" (falling backward "under the Spirit's power") are generally permitted in such services, most Charismatic activity is relegated to small prayer groups of *believers* (and others seriously interested in Spirit baptism) so as not to frighten and deter newcomers attending worship. Furthermore, exercise of the spiritual gifts is *always* regulated (e.g., speaking in tongues only with interpretation, and one person at a time). Again, Charismatic Renewal has adopted the *charismata* to a framework of "ordered respectability" suitable for educated, middle-class Christians who are members of the historic denominations. In 1964, Jean Stone suggested the following rules of conduct for glossolalia and related phenomena in a group context. Her words reflect the normative Neo-Pentecostal position today:

> Speaking in tongues is not spooky; it's wholesome, good, clean, beautiful. We use no weird positions, no peculiar gymnastics. Don't add your own little goodies to it. If you make it sound peculiar, you'll scare people pea-green. I remember one pastor's wife moaned, and it scared my husband to death! Don't moan or shriek. Remember, the gift is to edify and shrieking isn't edifying. And beware of personal prophecy, or prophecy about catastrophic happenings. If we seem too strange to outsiders, we're not going to get many outsiders to become insiders. You'll only attract desperate people. Don't develop separatist tendencies. Instead we are trying to save souls and be witness for Christ in what we say and in the way we live. And don't make the Bible a magical thing; be grounded in the Bible, but don't be a Bible thumper.

Ecclesiastical Stance: Sectarianism vs. Ecumenism

With their new experience, the first classical pentecostals were not welcomed in their own "respectable" churches. This fact—together with the typically fundamentalist attitudes most of them shared (e.g., noncooperation with Roman Catholics and with denominations that included theological liberals)—led these Christians to form other churches and denominations according to the characteristic sectarian pattern. But by the early 1940s, some influential Pentecostal leaders began to question the isolationist stance that their movement had taken during the preceding two decades, at least. Thus, in 1943, a number of the major American Pentecostal denominations joined the National Association of Evangelicals; and in 1947, the first triennial Pentecostal World Conference was held in Zurich—both events indicating that Pentecostals were ready to strengthen ties with their own denominations and to extend their fellowship to non-Pentecostal evangelicals. Then, in the early 1960s, two Chilean (and later one Brazilian) Pentecostal denominations took the "ultimate" step by joining the World Council of Churches (an action vigorously denounced by American Pentecostals). And since the advent of Charismatic Renewal in 1960, it has become increasingly difficult for classical Pentecostals as a whole to continue separating themselves altogether from the historic denominations, many of which include large numbers of Neo-Pentecostals within their ranks who share the same experience.

When Dennis Bennett, the Charismatic Renewal pioneer, then rector of Saint Mark's Episcopal Church, Van Nuys, California, was put under pressure to resign from his pastorate in 1960 as a result of his recent Pentecostal experience, he told his parishioners that he was *not* leaving the Episcopal Church—that "no one needs to leave the Episcopal Church [or any other church] in order to have the fullness of the Spirit." Among Pentecostals, that nonsectarian position was at the time revolutionary and still prevails today in Neo-Pentecostalism.

As we have said already, Charismatic Renewal participants understand the Pentecostal experience as transcending denominational and ideological walls while it clarifies and underscores what is authentically Christian in each tradition without demanding structural or even doctrinal changes in any church body. They are usually friendly in their attitude toward the World Council of Churches, its regional counterparts, and other ecumenical structures. Furthermore, the Protestant-Catholic encounter within Charismatic Renewal is so intense and heartfelt that it is probably unparalleled in contemporary ecclesiastical experience. Protestants and Catholics, conservatives and liberals, do not automatically discard their own theological and ecclesiastical differences when they come together in this movement. Nor do the movement's leaders themselves agree on the precise definition of baptism in the Holy Spirit or the exact nature of the *charismata* and their operation as outlined in 1 Cor. 12–14, for instance. But whether one is theologically liberal or conservative, it is felt that he will almost inevitably come to have a more vivid sense of God as a *person,* since by the baptism of the Holy Spirit God has *demonstrated* his reality to him in a personal way. Likewise, it is felt that the Pentecostal experience may well initiate or restore a person's interest in serious Bible study and give him a fresh awareness of the efficacy of prayer. Regardless of his theological outlook, the Neo-Pentecostal *must* develop a genuine openness to other Christians and the church as a whole if he is to continue successfully as a participant in Charismatic Renewal.

The very unconcern in Neo-Pentecostalism about doctrinal formulations is in contrast to most sects—and in some considerable contrast to traditional Christianity, which has been an intensely "intellectual" (in the sense of being concerned about intellectual distinctions) and doctrinally oriented religion. Charismatic Renewal reflects other currents in our times in being reluctant to create boundaries or to establish firm and objective criteria. There is a powerful subjectivist element in it all.

Mind and Spirit: Antiintellectualism vs. Intellectual Motivation

Classical Pentecostalism was born in the Bible school tradition among people with very little formal education. Fundamentalist in character, it has tended to distrust "modernist" (i.e., nonfundamentalist) theology and the academic world in general, discouraging (for the most part) its prospective ministers from university and seminary education. Training at Pentecostal Bible schools has been primarily training in piety—education geared to the study of the English Bible and fundamentalist exposition of the text. But with the increasing middle-class nature of the major Pentecostal denominations, more classical pentecostal young people are being educated—and educated in non-Pentecostal church-related colleges and in purely secular colleges and universities. Also, some of the traditional "Bible institutes" (of the Assemblies of God [United States of America], the Church of God [Cleveland, Tennessee], and the Pentecostal Holiness Church, for example) have gradually been transformed into "respectable" (sometimes fully accredited) liberal arts colleges. (The Assemblies of God and the Church of God [Cleveland, Tennessee] are even considering the establishment of a graduate theological seminary.) Furthermore, in 1971, the Society for Pentecostal Studies was formed. This professional organization (of scholars, chiefly) is open to anyone interested in the study of Pentecostalism—with or without a faith commitment—and its leadership is dominated by classical Pentecostal academics including Russell Spittler (Assemblies of God), Vinson Synan (Pentecostal Holiness Church), and Hollis Gause (Church of God [Cleveland, Tennessee]). Spittler, dean of southern California College (Assemblies of God), Costa Mesa, California, and a Harvard University Ph.D. in New Testament, was president of the society in 1973; while Synan, a prominent historian of Pentecostalism and general secretary of the Pentecostal Holiness Church, succeeded him. Participant speakers at the 1973 meeting included Martin Marty of the University of Chicago and *The Christian Century,* a Lutheran church historian; Basil Meeking of the Vatican's Secretariat for Promoting Christian Unity; Edward O'Connor of Notre Dame University, a Catholic Pentecostal; Timothy Smith of The Johns Hopkins University, a Church of the Nazarene minister and eminent historian; and Thomas Zimmerman, long-time general superintendent of the Assemblies of God (United States of America). The theme for the 1974 Society of Pentecostal Studies gathering was "The Third Force and the Third World." Various black Pentecostal leaders and Walter Hollenweger were featured speakers at this fourth annual meeting.

Despite the lack of formal higher education of a number of Neo-Pentecostal leaders (e.g., Oral Roberts, Kathryn Kuhlman, and Ralph Wilkerson), Charismatic Renewal (unlike classical Pentecostalism as a whole) tends to be intellectually motivated. For example, Neo-Pentecostals always emphasize the academic background and respectability of their educated leaders. Oral Roberts University (its somewhat revivalistic ethos notwithstanding) boasts exceptional facilities and a reputable faculty, and has adopted the novel policy (within Pentecostalism) of "educating the whole person for a whole life—spirit, mind, body" (not the spirit alone, as in the Bible school tradition). Melodyland Christian Center has recently established a Neo-Pentecostal "School of Theology" and "Ecumenical Research Academy." Headed by Rodman Williams (a Columbia University-Union Theological Seminary Ph.D. and former professor of theology at Austin [Texas] Presbyterian Theological Seminary), the School of Theology does not yet *require* a baccalaureate degree for admission, but is clearly developing a standard graduate seminary curriculum for both men and women. Finally, in this connection, Catholic Pentecostalism experienced its initial thrust within the university itself—at Duquesne, Notre Dame, and Michigan State, and at the University of Michigan; and some of the most sophisticated Charismatic Renewal literature to date has been penned by participant Roman Catholics. Michael Harper's assertion that Neo-Pentecostalism is *not,* generally speaking, "a movement of unthinking fools floating on a wave of emotional experience" is, in fact, justified.

Religion and Society: Social Unconcern vs Social Conscience

Classical Pentecostalism has most often been associated with indifference to social conditions and political issues. Kilian McDonnell, as we have seen, attributes this stance (until World War II), in part, to the political and social apathy common to the lower socioeconomic levels. But with the increasingly middle-class character of classical Pentecostalism (after World War II), its continued widespread social unconcern might be linked more properly to the sociopolitical and cultural conservatism inherent in fundamentalism and evangelicalism as a whole since the latter part of the nineteenth century.

Within Charismatic Renewal, however (again, as we have already seen), there are at least a few strong indications of an emerging social conscience and a mandate for social involvement. For instance, the once-dying inner-city Episcopal Church of the Redeemer, Houston, Texas, was transformed and revitalized—through the Pentecostal experience of its former rector, Graham Pulkingham—into a successful experiment in communal living, and a force for social good in its community. Melodyland Christian Center's support of a national toll-free telephone "hot line," and its alcoholic and drug addict rehabilitation programs, have become well known as effective social-action projects; while numerous Catholic Pentecostals (especially) have shown themselves to be deeply involved in political life and social change.

Rodman Williams insists that the Pentecostal experience *ought* to motivate human feelings to "become more sensitive to the moods, the concerns, the hopes of the world and of people; the will finds itself strengthened to execute with more faithfulness and determination those ethical actions to which it gives itself. . . . Here truly is the transcendence of ancient walls of creed and tradition, race and nationality, cultural, economic, and social differentiation by the overarching Spirit of love." Michael Harper is even more specific about the issue: "When we are filled with the Holy Spirit there should be an immediate concern for the world in every area of its life. . . .

Let [Charismatic Renewal] . . . lead Christians in a war against racism, the exploitation of the environment, inflation, property speculation, and other evils of our age."

Thus Neo-Pentecostalism offers evidence that it is beginning to repudiate the sociopolitical apathy characteristic of classical pentecostalism. Only time will tell if and how fast Charismatic Renewal as a whole will move toward a *significant* sense of social and political concern.

Christ and Culture: Culture Rejection vs. Culture Affirmation

Classical Pentecostalism shares with American fundamentalism in general the rejection of participation in the wider culture—"the world." Emphasizing to an almost Gnostic degree the spiritual life over against "the desires of the flesh," classical Pentecostalism enforces the usual taboos against the (even moderate) use of alcohol and tobacco in any form, social dancing, gambling and card playing, attendance at the theater and cinema, (secular) rock music, "immodest dress," and sometimes even "mixed bathing." Legitimate recreation (escape?) is to be provided by the church ("in the Spirit") and, really, nowhere else. But since these taboos are part of the cultural baggage of revivalism, and have been traditionally enforced only within those churches deeply rooted in the revivalistic culture (e.g., Baptist and Methodist churches, and their offshoots, including classical Pentecostal bodies), Neo-Pentecostal Catholics, Eastern Orthodox Christians, Anglicans, Lutherans, Presbyterians, and the like are often quite shocked when such taboos are introduced as binding upon them after their Pentecostal experience. Given the presence within Charismatic Renewal of former classical Pentecostals and others of the fundamentalist-revivalist tradition, together with numerous fellowship contacts between Neo-Pentecostals and classical Pentecostals, the nontransferable baggage of classical Pentecostalism piles up in Charismatic Renewal and is often not easily sent away. It is most difficult for a typical classical Pentecostal (or Baptist Neo-Pentecostal, for instance) to accept as one who shares the same experience a Catholic Pentecostal who drinks, smokes, dances, and gambles—though such acceptance *is,* in fact, becoming increasingly common.

Despite inherent difficulties, however, there is within Neo-Pentecostalism, as we have seen, a noticeable trend in the direction of culture affirmation (as a new or continuing attitude). Holiness is still an important concept; but in Charismatic Renewal circles, classical Pentecostal legalism is officially shunned, and holiness is being spiritualized and socialized as an attitude of the heart, having more to do with healthy relationships with people and "the life of discipleship" and less to do with moral privatism and negativism— more with what you *do* than with what you don't do.

Constituency: Working-Class vs. Middle-Class Standing

Classical Pentecostalism began as a movement of the poor, the uneducated, the minorities, the disenfranchised, and the socially and economically deprived. To a large degree—but not universally—the same basic kinds of people are attracted to it today (hence, its special strength in the American South and Midwest among rural folk, in the West among "migrants" from the South, in black and Latin ghettos in urban centers, among women, and in the Third World, in Latin America especially). Yet, Walter Hollenweger points to the relatively large proportion of Pentecostal pastors in his own survey research with middle-class and historic-denomination backgrounds. Furthermore, like Luther Gerlach and Virginia Hine, Hollenweger insists that attempts to understand the classical Pentecostal subculture as "an inferior culture, as the expression solely of social, intellectual and economic deprivation" are contradicted by the most recent sociological and psychological research.

Charismatic Renewal, however, as we have seen, has always been predominantly middle-class in nature. It first emerged in a "fashionable" suburban Episcopal church in Southern California. (An early sampling of monthly prayer groups that gathered at Jean Stone's home in 1964 showed about equal numbers of men and women, an average age of forty-two years, a median monthly income of $630 [with persons earning in excess of $1,600 also present], a large proportion of men in the "professional and technical" occupational grouping and women in the "housewife" category, and

Republicans outnumbering Democrats seven to one.) Until Neo-Pentecostalism became a force within Roman Catholicism, the movement seemed very much in continuity with the assumptions of white Anglo-Saxon Protestant traditions as they are stereotyped. Even at the present time, Charismatic Renewal appears chiefly among the white, middle-class, suburban populations of the Western world—North America, Great Britain (including present and former Commonwealth countries such as [white] South Africa, New Zealand, and Australia), Germany, and Scandinavia. It is classical Pentecostalism, rather, that is experiencing phenomenal growth in the underdeveloped Third World. . . .

It is apparent that we are living in an era of mesmeric prophets and religious fads that are products of the 1960s and early 1970s. Among these can be numbered Krishna Consciousness, Transcendental Meditation (Maharishi Mahesh Yogi), the Divine Light Mission (Guru Maharaj Ji), Satanism (Anton La Vey), and, in the Christian tradition, the Unification Church (the Reverand Sun Myung Moon), and the many groups and cults of the Jesus movement, including the Children of God (David "Moses" Berg). Related to the emergence and success of all such movements are, again, the contemporary quest for religious experience, the trend toward interiorization, and a rediscovery of the supernatural. Their present popularity is, to some degree at least, the product of the times and the concerns of the wider culture (and counterculture). Some of these movements can easily be understood as mere religious "fads" or "crazes." Those centered on the charisma of a particular "prophet" may well rise and fall with his fortunes. The antiinstitutional church Jesus movement was more closely aligned with the counterculture and its distinctive style and attire—especially the phenomenon of the "hippies"—than with any one leader. Hence, with the decline of a readily visible counterculture (including street people and "longhairs"), the Jesus People also have lost visibility over the course of the same few years. As Ronald Enroth has suggested, many of the Jesus People have already gone back to the churches they once branded as hypocritical and "irrelevant."

The situation with Charismatic Renewal, however, is somewhat different. Although this movement's present popularity may indeed be related to contemporary trends in the wider society, we must also acknowledge the fact that Neo-Pentecostalism has apparently grown without abatement since its emergence in 1960; that classical Pentecostalism has been an important religious force since its inception in 1901; and that Pentecostal phenomena were apparently widespread in the primitive church and in various periods of church history thereafter. To think of Charismatic Renewal as merely a fad, therefore, would probably be a mistake. Furthermore, it is quite reasonable to suppose that, given the strong New Testament justification for the operation of *charismata,* the present "renewal" of those same spiritual gifts in the life of the historic churches may signal their return on an ever-increasing scale to the church as a whole. Charismatic Renewal might well represent a movement "beyond fadism."

A Personal Assessment: Can Charismatic Renewal Really Renew the Church?

Emmanuel Sullivan, a Franciscan friar, proposes at least three ways in which the Pentecostal movement in the historic churches may be regarded as a force for renewal. First, he suggests that there is a real *feeling* that the church, in its teaching and ritual, is not meeting the needs of the human spirit. "A theology of renewal is not renewal." Faith must be *expressed,* he says, emphasizing the fact that perhaps "too much has been claimed in the past by cerebral theologians who have allowed a chasm to develop between the intellect articulating the faith and the emotions expressing it." Pentecostals, of course, stress, above all else, the expression of their faith.

Second, Sullivan views the Pentecostal movement as a "prayer movement," leading Christians to appropriate words of love and service. He points out that where it is allowed to grow, Pentecostalism creates "a zealous clergy and a genuinely involved laity." Furthermore, this prayer movement, in his opinion, leads to a sense of community that is much more than a mere expression of "togetherness," in that it is truly a manifestation of the church as the body of Christ.

Third, Sullivan argues that the church is of its very nature "Charismatic." New Testament teaching, to him, stresses that "God is pouring out in his Spirit the richest variety of gifts to bring us to the close of the age when God will be all in all (1 Cor. 15:28)." Christians must, therefore, *expect* new and different things to happen while living in a Spirit that is "creative, loving, disturbing, and absolutely free."

For Emmanuel Sullivan, spiritual renewal in the church emphasizes the presence of the Holy Spirit and his gifts. Spiritual ecumenism, he goes on to say, stresses spiritual renewal in the church as an inner law of ecumenical growth and development. Sullivan feels that the Pentecostal witness "unites spiritual renewal and spiritual ecumenism by its emphasis on the role of the Holy Spirit, the diversity of sharing his gifts, the call to conversion."

Whatever we may think of the distinctives of Pentecostal faith and practice, it is necessary for us to admit that the Pentecostal experience in its Charismatic Renewal form has brought together clergy and laity of most Protestant, Anglican, Eastern Orthodox, and Catholic denominations in a heartfelt spiritual unity that the institutional ecumenical movement has been unable to match in the course of all its deliberations and pronouncements. Furthermore, it is readily apparent that Charismatic Renewal does indeed produce among its participants "a zealous clergy and a genuinely involved laity." Thus, if renewal of the church is inherently linked both to the realization of Christian unity and to the reemergence of enlivened congregations, then Charismatic Renewal ought to be regarded as a legitimate contemporary force for renewal of the church.

Donald Bloesch

Donald Bloesch continues to dispute the popular view that evangelicalism signifies a particular kind of experience rather than a doctrinal basis. He insists that experience and doctrine are mutually essential. This selection is taken from his Essentials of Evangelical Theology, *Vol. 2, Life, Ministry and Hope. New York: Harper and Row, 1979, pp. 265–78.*

The Outlook for Evangelicalism

That there is a renewed interest in evangelicalism today no competent observer would deny. Whether we are actually entering upon an evangelical renaissance is another question. My position is that the present situation holds much promise for evangelicalism, but at the same time there are accumulating shadows on the horizon that bode ill for genuine biblical revival.

One of the continuing banes of modern evangelicalism is a biblical literalism and obscurantism which effectively nullify the solid gains in biblical-historical research over the past several decades. The first eleven chapters of Genesis, for example, are integrally related to objective history, but most scholars agree that the literary genre of this material reveals that large sections of it are mythopoetic. Though we can say that the event of the Fall happened in objective space and time, many of the details of the story are indubitably symbolic. This does not imply that it is any less inspired than those sections of the Bible that give us exact history, but it does mean that unless we become somewhat more sophisticated in our exegesis, we will be erecting for our contemporaries false stumbling blocks to faith. If we take the genealogies in the Old Testament as literal chronologies, we will have to opt for a recent date for the creation of the world and man (5000–4000 B.C.?), and we will then have to resort to spurious science to support our allegations. This is not to say that current science supplies the norm for settling these issues, for this would make scientific rationality the criterion for truth. It does mean that if we use science, we must do so honestly, and much of contemporary evangelical apologetics in this area is dishonest.

Again, we must be alert to the worldliness within evangelicalism, especially when it comes in the guise of religiosity. Notwithstanding the allurements of the positive-thinking cult, we should not seek to use the Gospel to gain the goods of life or to find self-fulfillment. We must be cognizant of the incontrovertible chasm between the values of the world and the transcendent Word of God. To equate happiness as the world knows it and the blessedness of the Kingdom is inadmissible. We must not lose sight of the tragic dimension of life even though Christianity transcends tragedy. The ineradicable gulf between Christian faith and culture-religion is underlined by Luther: "For that is the highest thing that men want, to have joy and happiness and to be without trouble. Now Christ turns the page and says exactly the opposite; He calls 'blessed' those who sorrow and mourn."

Another pitfall that evangelicals must strive to avoid is parochialism, which can be just as damaging as eclecticism. This refers to the inveterate tendency to interpret God and the world through the lens of one's own cultural and religious background and to reject insights that seem to call into question the particular tradition in which one stands. Parochialism is manifest in those persons who seek to be more Calvinistic than Calvin or more Lutheran than Luther or more Wesleyan than Wesley. It is evident too in conservative Christianity's current fascination with the details of biblical prophecy. "Such activity," one critic aptly observes, "is part of a defensive, separationist mentality that removes itself from modern life culturally (by its blue laws) and temporally (by its prophetic mania)." Parochialism is associated with a hyper-orthodoxy and sectarianism that exclude from Christian fellowship those who do not subscribe to the particular tenets of the party in question. It is well to remember that the luminaries of evangelical history have almost unanimously sought to transcend a narrow parochialism for an ecumenical vision, and this includes Calvin, Zinzendorf, Wesley, Spener, and Edwards.

Experientialism is another temptation to which evangelicals seem particularly vulnerable in our time. The search for extraordinary signs of the gift of the Spirit is one obvious example, but in the less charismatic churches there is also a yearning for transforming experiences, and the objective work of Christ on the cross recedes into the background. One reason why modern evangelicalism has produced so little systematic theology is that experience is valued more highly than theology, and soul-winning is regarded more laudable than intellectual endeavor. Theology must not be rejected in favor of either practical piety or devout mysticism (Gordon Rupp).

Finally, we need again to call into question the bent toward rationalism in current evangelicalism. Carl Henry argues that the truth of revelation can be known prior to commitment to Christ, otherwise people would not be culpable for its rejection. In John Warwick Montgomery's schema, Christianity can be objectively validated by the historical method alone. Norman Geisler, in his *Philosophy of Religion,* seeks to state the case for belief in God without ever once appealing to divine revelation. For him, as for Hegel, the rationally inescapable is the real, and, so it seems, rational verification is the presupposition of faith as well as its necessary preparation. Francis Schaeffer contends that one does not believe until one examines the evidence and is satisfied intellectually that the claims of faith are true.

Many evangelicals are currently attracted to Pannenberg's theology, which gives reason a creative role prior to faith. According to Pannenberg, the Spirit enables one to believe what reason can already know. The meaning of revelation can be comprehended by reason alone, but the commitment to revelation is not possible apart from the work of the Spirit. By contrast, we hold that the Spirit must give to man the divinely-intended meaning of Scripture so that he can make an intelligent commitment.

Our position is that revelation is not at the disposal of reason and is never a conclusion of human thought. The outsider can arrive at a limited understanding of the biblical proposition by examining its literary and historical context. But he invariably misunderstands the divine intent of this proposition. Historical understanding and perception of theological significance are two different things. While reason can grasp the historical side of revelation, only faith can perceive the revelatory side of history (Paul Althaus).

In the tradition emanating from Protestant scholastic orthodoxy and the Princeton School of theology, systematic theology is simply the coordinating and harmonizing of the axioms of Scripture, which are self-evident as well as clear and distinct (cf. Descartes). The method of Gordon Clark and Carl Henry is deductive, deriving conclusions from given rational principles. The method of Charles Hodge is inductive, arriving at general principles by systematizing the historical data in the Bible. In this general tradition, a high confidence is placed in the capacity of reason to judge the truth of revelation.

In our view, the concrete reality from which theological concepts are derived is the irreversible and incomparable act of God in Jesus Christ. Insofar as Scripture participates in this act, Scripture too is a primary and indispensable source for theological work. The task of theology is to ascertain how the text of Scripture is related to the material norm, the revelation of God's love and judgment in Jesus Christ. Our goal is not to think the right thoughts and statements (as in Gordon Clark) but to think realities through thoughts and statements. Because the reality of Jesus Christ is more than rational, we can only approximate this transcendent truth in our conceptualization and verbalization. The judgments and operations of God are "inscrutable" and "mysterious" even to the believer (Rom. 11:33), and therefore our theological systems will forever be imperfect and rudimentary, as Thomas Aquinas also recognized. This does not mean that some theologies are not superior to others, but it does mean that even the most ingenious theological system falls drastically short of the existential system which is in the mind of God. We *intend* the truth in our theological statements, but we do not *possess* the truth, since reason is always the servant and never the master or determiner of revelation.

The knowledge of faith is not an empirical objectifying knowledge but a knowledge in which we are lifted above reason and sense into communion with the living God (Luther). Faith must believe against human thought, feeling, and perception, since reason admits the validity only of that which can be perceived or conceived. We do not discount the salutary role of historical investigation and criticism, but the positiveness of historical knowledge is illusory. Historical research can show the historical probability of certain events happening, but it can give only approximate, not final, certainty. The ground of certainty is not what reason can show or prove but what faith grasps and knows as the human subject is acted upon by the Holy Spirit in conjunction with the reading or hearing of the biblical word. Yet a living faith is not possible apart from hard thinking concerning the promises and claims of Scripture.

In seeking understanding, faith must be on guard against making its cardinal doctrines too clear and distinct (à la Descartes), since this serves to undercut or deny the mystery in revelation. Richard Hooker has aptly remarked: "Heresy is more plain than true whereas right belief is more true than plain." Heresy tries to overcome the tensions and paradoxes in Christian faith by overemphasizing one side of the Gospel or reducing the Gospel to what is logically explicable. Orthodoxy, on the other hand, feels the pull of the opposites, but keeps them from flying apart and thereby keeps them true (G. K. Chesterton).

The Need to Reappraise Biblical Authority

Biblical faith cannot be recovered until we recognize anew the divine authority and inspiration of the Bible. This authority has been eroded both by higher critics who read into Scripture a naturalistic philosophy, which *a priori* rules out the supernatural, and by its uncritical devotees, who absolutize the outmoded world view reflected in the Bible and thereby render the biblical witness incredible.

The crisis in biblical authority has recently come to a head with the concerted attempts of liberal spokesmen in the main-line denominations to reconceive homosexuality as a viable alternative life-style and to approve the ordination of avowed, practicing homosexuals despite the clear witness of Holy Scripture that sexual perversion is morally reprehensible in the sight of God. Proponents of a more relaxed position on this question argue that the biblical strictures against homosexuality are a product of the mores of the culture of that time and cannot be considered binding upon man in the twentieth century. It is also asserted that through the knowledge gained in the social sciences God is speaking a new word in our time that fulfills and even supersedes his revelation to peoples in another era and in a supposedly more primitive culture. This, in effect, denies the divine authority and normativeness of biblical teaching.

As we seek to reaffirm biblical authority, however, there is a need to reinterpret this authority, particularly in light of the present-day impasse in evangelicalism on this question. Rightly understood, infallibility and inerrancy can indeed be posited of the Bible, but wrongly understood, these ideas can create division and confusion. Unfortunately, a great number of inerrancy advocates today want a rationally guaranteed authority, but this makes reason, not revelation, the final criterion. Paul Holmer astutely comments: "Inerrant Scripture gets to be an epistemic crutch, a pseudo-certainty, which while it purports to push doubt away, also inserts a humanly devised conceptual scheme by which to get the Scriptures to disclose the Almighty."

We go astray if we base the authority of Scripture on the inerrancy of the writing and then try to demonstrate this according to the canons of scientific rationality. The authority of the Bible is based on the One whom it attests and the One who speaks through it in every age with the word of regenerating power. We here concur with Calvin: "The highest proof of Scripture derives in general from the fact that God in person speaks in it." This by no means implies that the biblical witness is fallible or untrustworthy. Instead, we hold that this witness does not carry the force of infallible authority apart from the Holy Spirit who acts in and through it. Whenever the Bible functions as the sword of the Spirit in the community of believers, it wields indisputable divine authority in all areas pertaining to faith and practice.

It is possible to discern three basic approaches to Scripture in the history of the church. The first is the sacramental, which sees revelation essentially as God in action and regards Scripture as the primary channel or medium of revelation. Here Scripture is thought to have two sides, the divine and the human, and the human is the instrumentality of the divine. In this category we include Augustine, Calvin, Luther, Spener, Francke, Edwards, Pascal, Forsyth, and such noted representatives of Protestant orthodoxy as Flacius, Voetius, Gerhard, Bavinck, Kuyper, and more recently Geoffrey Bromiley and G. C. Berkouwer. The second position is the scholastic, which understands revelation as the disclosure of a higher truth that nonetheless stands in continuity with rational or natural truth. The Bible becomes a book of revealed propositions which are directly accessible to reason and which contain no errors in any respect. The humanity of the Bible is regarded as an aspect of its divinity. Here we can list Protestant scholastics such as Quenstedt, Wolff, Turretin, and Warfield, as well as contemporaries such as Gordon Clark, Francis Schaeffer, Carl Henry, and John Warwick Montgomery. Finally, in the liberal-modernist approach, revelation is understood as inner enlightenment or self-discovery; in this category are to be placed Schleiermacher, Herrmann, Troeltsch, Harry Emerson Fosdick, Tillich, Gilkey, Bernard Meland, Gregory Baum, J. A. T. Robinson, and Rudolf Bultmann.

Karl Barth succeeded, at least in part, in recovering the sacramental character of the Bible and revelation in his middle period (when he wrote the first several volumes of his *Church Dogmatics*), but he was unable to maintain this position because of certain overriding concerns in his theology. In this middle period, he conceived revelation as the divine content of Scripture, a content that can only be apprehended by the interior witness of the Holy Spirit. Here he stood very close to Calvin and Luther. Yet later, in volume IV, 3 of this *Church Dogmatics,* he began to refer to Jesus Christ alone as the Word of God and to the Bible and the sermon, as well as baptism and the Lord's Supper, as signs and witnesses of this Word. The old Reformed principle that the finite cannot bear the infinite (*finitum non capax infiniti*) was undoubtedly at work, together with the growing concern to safeguard the freedom of God in the face of a theology of repristination and a revival of confessionalism. Barth still referred to the Bible as the primary witness of revelation and the church as a secondary witness. He even allowed for true words about God in the secular world, but neither these words nor the words of the Bible or church could be equated with the Word of God itself, the transcendent Gospel concerning Jesus Christ and his reconciliation. Revelation was now seen as a direct word from God spoken to the soul, and the biblical word as only a human witness and pointer to revelation. Barth could no longer speak of the Bible as the Word of God, nor could he consistently affirm the threefold unity of the revealed Word (Christ), the written word, and the proclaimed word, as he did in his middle period. Arthur Cochrane has astutely observed that, in his last years, Barth returned to his much earlier position enunciated at Barmen that Jesus Christ is the one and only Word of God.

To uphold a sacramental approach to Scripture in no way rules out cognitive revelation. Revelation is truly given in and through the words of Scripture, and this means intelligible content as well as spiritual presence (cf. Rom. 16:25, 26; Col. 1:25–28). The action of God in disclosing his will and purpose to man not only entails revelation *through* Scripture but also revelation *as* Scripture. Yet this is not to say that the words of Scripture are directly revealed (as in the scholastic approach) but that Scripture embodies the truth that God desires us to hear. The unity between the revealed Word, Jesus Christ, and the written word lies both in the inspiration of the Spirit, whereby he guarantees a trustworthy witness to Christ, and in his revelatory action, in which he speaks through this witness to people of every age (cf. 1 Cor. 2:10–13).

Luther recognized the sacramental role of Scripture when he described the Word as the carriage of the Spirit. Ragnar Bring perceptively shows the similarity between Luther's understanding of Scripture and his understanding of the Lord's Supper: "Just as Christ's body and blood are given under the elements even though the bread and wine are not transformed, so also the divine Word is given through the temporally and historically conditioned Scriptures."

Some neofundamentalists object to speaking of culturally conditioned words and concepts in Scripture, but we contend that if justice is to be done to the true humanity of Scripture, we must fully acknowledge the human element. This in no way detracts from its divine authority but instead establishes Scripture as an authentic witness to a real revelation in history. Inscripturation signifies that the Word of God takes on human dress and imagery as it relates itself to humankind. The Holy Spirit accommodated himself to the thought patterns and language of the peoples of biblical times and so entered into their cultural and historical limitations. Yet because inspiration also means that the Spirit guided and directed the writers not only in their ideas but also in their selection of words, we can affirm that the Bible is a divine as well as a human product. Moreover, we must likewise contend that, because of the superintendence of the Spirit, the Bible is a fully reliable and trustworthy witness to the truth revealed in the history that it records. It gives us an accurate reflection of the mind and purpose of God though not an exact duplication of the very thoughts of God. Its message or teaching transcends human culture and history, though it is mediated only through human language and imagery. Because there is one Divine Author within and behind the many human authors, the Bible has an underlying doctrinal and theological unity, despite significant variations in stress and style.

The Bible's authority is functional in that it is a signpost to Jesus Christ. But it is not simply functional. There is an integral and organic relation between Christ's promises and the written word. The word not only points to Christ, but it was brought into being by the Spirit of Christ acting upon the prophets and apostles. It not only conveys the truth of Christ but also embodies this truth. When we say that the Bible is the Word of God we mean two things: that all the words are selected by the Spirit of God through his guidance of the human authors; and that the truth of God is enshrined in and mediated through these words. The Bible is the Word of God in all that it teaches, though this teaching is not immediately self-evident but must be unveiled by the Spirit.

The Bible is neither the direct, unmediated speech of God (as we sometimes find in Warfield) nor simply an indirect historical witness to divine revelation (as in Barth). It is the Word of God in human clothing, the revelation of God transmitted through human concepts and imagery. Yet the human concepts do not capture the full impact and significance of what is given in revelation, as Augustine makes clear in his comments on John the apostle: "Because he was inspired he was able to say something; but because he who was inspired remained a man, he could not present the full reality, but only what a man could say about it." At the same time, we can know this reality when the Spirit of God acts in and through the written witness. "The word of God indeed is sharp as a two-edged sword," says Jonathan Edwards, "but it is so only through the cooperation of that Spirit that gave the word. The word alone, however managed, explained, confirmed and applied, is nothing but a dead letter without the Spirit." A similar sentiment is expressed by Robert Preus, who here presents the view of Lutheran orthodoxy at its best: "The efficacy of the Word of God does not inhere in the letters and syllables and words as they are written. These are merely symbols, the vehicle (*vehiculum*) of the divine content, the *forma,* of the Word, which alone is the Word of God, properly speaking."

In left-wing neoorthodoxy, revelation is dissolved in an existential encounter. In right-wing scholastic orthodoxy, revelation is frozen into a propositional formula. In biblical evangelicalism, revelation refers to the whole movement of God into biblical history, culminating not only in the prophetic and apostolic witness but also in the act of faith and surrender on the part of those who are caught up in this movement. Thus the reader does not possess the truth, which would be the case if it were merely the writing of Scripture, but instead is possessed by the truth, which is the living, dynamic Word of God.

What is infallible and inerrant is the Word within the words, the divine meaning given in and through the human testimony. Our ultimate norm is not simply what the human author intends but what God intends through the witness of the author (cf. 1 Pet. 1:10–12), though there is always a certain congruity between the latter and the former. It follows that not everything reported in Scripture should be accepted at face value. To hear the eternal, living Word means to have to search the Scriptures, to try to see every text in the light of the divine center, Jesus Christ. It means to distinguish the shell and the kernel, form and content. The evangelist Dwight L. Moody referred to the need for "digging out" the divine truth of Scripture, since this truth is not directly available to the "uncircumcised eye." Johann Christian Konrad von Hofmann remarks that to regard statements about world history or the cosmos as infallible simply because they are reported in Scripture is "the evil consequence of a merely rational doctrine of inspiration, and creates many conflicts with the actual world." Bavinck is helpful here in his distinction between the historical and normative authority of Scripture. Only in the second sense can we regard Scripture as absolutely binding and therefore supremely authoritative.

While fundamentalists are prone to stress the infallibility of the original manuscripts and liberals the infallibility of conscience, our emphasis is on the infallibility of Word and Spirit, one of the salient themes of the Reformation. The written word partakes of divine infallibility because it is grounded in the incarnate or revealed Word, Jesus Christ. Moreover, it is an effectual sign of the revealed Word in that it serves to communicate the significance of this revelation through the power of the Spirit. There is a union, but not a fusion, between the written word of Scripture and the divine word of revelation.

The present impasse in evangelical circles concerning the authority of Scripture could be overcome if we would but return to a sacramental understanding of revelation: that Scripture is a divinely-appointed means of grace and not simply an earthly, historical witness or sign of grace; and that Scripture is inseparable from the revelation which produced it and which flows through it but that the words of Scripture in and of themselves are not divine revelation. We should also probably substitute what George Eldon Ladd calls historical-theological criticism for the historical-critical method, which has been too often associated with naturalistic presuppositions. Or perhaps it is better to speak of historical-critical methods than of one single critical method, for criticism varies according to the theological outlook of the critic. We need to be free to examine the Scriptures as human literature; yet we must not stop there but go on to find and hear the Word of God in and through the words of the human authors. Historical and critical studies may help to cleanse the lens of Scripture so that it is not simply an opaque medium of the Word of God. Yet "what really makes Scripture a transparent medium is the divine light that shines through it from the face of Jesus Christ into our hearts."

It is important to recover the dynamic and divine character of revelation without separating it from the earthen vessel of the Scriptural writings. We need to recognize anew the element of mystery in revelation, which was generally acknowledged by the church fathers and Reformers. We need to affirm with Pascal that God hides himself in the measure that he discloses himself. This means that our language about God can be at the most analogical, not univocal, for there can be no direct or exact correspondence between human ideas and the veritable Word of God. It is also imperative for us to reaffirm the mystery of the accommodation of the Holy Spirit to the deficiencies and limitations of human language, an insight fully acknowledged by the great teachers of the church, including Origen, Augustine, John Chrysostom, and Calvin. It must never be forgotten that the Bible is time-bound and time-related even as it is timeless. Finally, we would do well to abandon a rationalistic epistemology (whether of the inductive or deductive type) in determining the truth-content of Scripture and confess anew that God can be known only through God. Scripture is authoritative by virtue of its relation to the living Word, not by virtue of its truthfulness as such. This is because its truth is only understood in relation to Christ by the work of the Holy Spirit, not because of any rational hermeneutic.

The Need to Recover Evangelical Distinctives

Part of the current dilemma of evangelicalism is that the crucial doctrines of the historic faith are being underplayed, while peripheral or sectarian tenets occupy the center of attention. This has been aptly described as majoring in minors. It is sad but true that in many evangelical circles today epistemological and eschatological concerns take precedence over the salient themes of the Reformation, and that various of these themes have become foreign to the modern church (including the conservative branch). A pronounced preoccupation with apologetics, in which rationalistic unbelief is challenged on its own ground, has prevented many evangelicals from seeing that the great problem of the church is not with the hearer, not with modern man, but with the authenticity of the church's own message.

In calling for a rediscovery of evangelical distinctives, we need to be aware of heresies on the right: perfectionism, dispensationalism, religious enthusiasm, and hyperfundamentalism. The great evangelical doctrines of *sola Scriptura, solus Christus,* and *sola gratia* contradict the synergism and anthropocentrism in conservative Christianity as well as in liberalism. Even the doctrine of *sola Scriptura,* understood in the Reformation sense, exists in tension with the current evangelical stress on personal religious experience as well as the fundamentalist appeal to arguments from reason and science in support of total biblical reliability.

This is not the place to enumerate the evangelical distinctives, since this entire work is devoted to their explication, but we would like to give special attention to the doctrine of salvation by grace, for it is the heart and soul of evangelicalism. This tenet lies at the basis of the meaning of the cross as well as of the new birth. In it are involved the themes of predestination, justification, reconciliation, and sanctification. It means basically that man the sinner is elected for salvation without regard to his intrinsic merit or worthiness. We cannot affirm with Schleiermacher that election "is grounded in the faith of the elect, foreseen by God." Election means grace going out to the faithless and thereby creating faith where there had previously been only unbelief. The decision of faith itself is a gift of God, and this truth is too readily lost sight of in current revivalism.

The evangelical distinctive of *sola gratia* has its roots in the tradition of the whole church, not just the Reformation. It was Anselm who declared: "Whatsoever our heart rightly willeth, it is of Thy gift." And in Augustine's words, "Men are not saved by good works, nor by the free determination of their own will, but by the grace of God through faith." Grace moreover is not merely an ontological energy instilled into man, but primarily the personal favor of God toward man. "Grace is the royal and sovereign power of God," said Karl Barth, "the existential presentation of men to God for His disposal, the real freedom of the will of God in men."

Besides being the work of God *for us* in Jesus Christ, grace is also the work of God *in us* through the gift of the Holy Spirit. Yet our trust should not be in our own inner renewal, in the presence of grace in our hearts, but only in Christ's perfect work of redemption, the objective reconciliation effected by him (John T. Mueller).

As we have seen, the emphasis in the later Luther and Barth was decidedly on the work of Christ outside us, the perfect or finished work of redemption on the cross. Luther referred to the "alien righteousness" of Christ, by which we are justified while still in our sins. Barth placed the accent on the accomplished reconciliation realized objectively in God's becoming man in Jesus and subjectively in the obedience of Jesus to God. Sometimes Barth spoke of Jesus believing in our place, but this undercuts the urgency of faith and the call to decision. Evangelicalism is seriously deficient if the interior dimension of salvation is downplayed or denied. Thielicke seeks to correct the objectivism in Lutheranism when he says: "The alien righteousness of Christ is not something that lies in a remote 'outside me.' It is imparted to me. It is also my righteousness. It includes me." Luther himself made a real place for the mystical or inward dimension of faith, even describing his conversion in this way: "Then I suddenly felt that I was born again and entered through open doors into paradise."

As we strive to recover evangelical distinctives, we would do well to qualify and reformulate traditional slogans in the light of Scripture and with an ecumenical sensitivity. The sovereignty of God must not be construed as the unlimited power of an arbitrary God but as the sovereignty of grace, of the God who acts in love. Likewise, total depravity must be redefined to allow a place for the remnant of goodness even in the most hardened sinner. The doctrine of the substitutionary atonement must be rethought so as to meet the valid criticism that it portrays a wrathful God who would not otherwise forgive except for the offering of an innocent victim. Thielicke presents this corrective: "Christ does not simply offer himself to God in the name of man, so that God is the object of atonement (as in Anselm). He also offers himself to man in the name of God and as God's sacrifice."

Certainly every reform in the church must spring out of obedience to the Word of God as given in sacred Scripture. Even reforms pertaining to the external life of the church must emanate from an existential encounter with the Scriptures. John Stott expresses it well: "Evangelicals . . . regard as the only possible road to the reunion of churches the road of biblical reformation. In their view the only solid hope for churches which desire to unite is a common willingness to sit down together under the authority of God's Word, in order to be judged and reformed by it."

In the quest for evangelical renewal and church unity, we must be cautious in our use of slogans and phrases that are unduly polemical. Instead of always speaking of *irrestible grace,* we should probably employ such terms as *effectual* or *efficacious* grace, which are less offensive to our Arminian brethren. Instead of *limited atonement,* one of the hallmarks of Reformed orthodoxy, it would be biblically more appropriate to speak of *particular redemption* or of a redemption that is both universal and particular. It is universal in its scope and intention and particular in its implementation. Instead of *total depravity,* we might more often refer to the *radicality of sin.* We should seek words that have an ecumenical as well as a biblical ring. This does not mean that in academic discourse the older words cannot be used, but they need always to be clarified and redefined.

The call to recover evangelical distinctives is not necessarily an invitation to doctrinal conflict, though it will often entail this, since wherever theology is taken seriously, controversy abounds. Yet doctrinal conflicts may also be a sign of acculturization. Doctrine can be a tool in the struggle for technocratic power, and some observers see this in the recent uproar in the Missouri Synod Lutheran Church. Yet if a particular charge of heresy has little basis, this does not mean that real heresy does not exist. In view of the drift of the main-line churches into unitarianism and universalism, the need to reaffirm evangelical distinctives will indubitably create tensions and perhaps division in the church. But a true church can only exist on the basis of doctrine and biblical truth, and where this truth is diluted or ignored we have a false church.

David Hubbard

*David Hubbard has contended that to revere the Bible is important,
but that should be no substitute for using critical tools to understand
it. This selection is taken from his article "The Current Tensions:
Is There a Way Out?" in Jack Rogers, ed.,* Bibilical Authority.
Waco, Texas: Word Books, 1977, pp. 157–64, 176–81.

How We Got Where We Are—
The Liberal-Fundamentalist Controversy

Standing on this side of the liberal-fundamentalist controversy,
we may find it helpful to weigh its results. The smoke of that
particular battle, which waged hot and heavy for nearly fifty years,
started to thin out after World War II, when the breezes of the
neoorthodox theologies of Barth, Brunner, and Bonhoeffer began
to blow in our shores. The battle itself has abated somewhat—in
the sense that the old optimistic, humanistic liberalism has been
replaced with a deeper understanding of human sin, divine grace,
biblical revelation, and Christian discipleship. But the effects of
that battle are much with us and cry out for clarification.

The defense of the Bible's authority which Hodge, Warfield, and
the Princeton school set up has kept sound *the confidence in the
Scriptures* of literally millions of Christian people. Our debt to
them is substantial.

At the same time, it is only fair to mention that one of the side
results has been a *misunderstanding of the place of biblical scholarship.* It is not that the Princeton school was directly responsible for
this. Indeed, men like Warfield, Robert Dick Wilson, and J. Gres-
cham Machen were models of scholarly ardor and discipline. Yet
often, to the minds of conservative evangelicals, because of the
particular situation in which Hodge and Warfield worked, the scholars became the enemy. After all, it was scholars who had questioned
the accuracy and validity of the Bible in the first place. The label
"higher critic" became a largely negative term to describe the skep-
tically minded professors who picked and probed at the biblical
documents, trying to prove that they were not what the church
through the ages had claimed them to be. And many biblical scholars had justly earned that reputation.

But the task of scholarship remains essential even though it is sometimes done badly or put to destructive purposes. The answer to skeptical, negative study of the Bible is not to ban investigation, but to engage in better investigation. The full meaning of the Bible—despite the basic clarity of the Bible's message of salvation, taught by the Reformers and confirmed in our experience—cannot be discerned apart from sincere, thorough, and devout investigation of (1) the meaning of biblical language, (2) the background—historical, cultural, political—of the biblical events, (3) the types of literature through which God has spoken, (4) the situations in the life of Israel or the church which sparked comment from prophet or apostle, and (5) the process by which the Spirit of God produced the books which he has caused his people to gather in the Bible.

Another legacy of the nineteenth-century evangelical scholars, whose heirs we are, is the *strong system of apologetics* with which they defended the faith. In an era when the church was confronted with many reasons why the historic doctrines should not be believed, evangelicals were offered a solid basis on which to ground their beliefs. The rationalistic attacks on the validity of God's Word and the reality of divine revelation were met by what were considered ironclad arguments that proved the entire Bible to be the Word of God, and, if the Word of God, then inerrant in all its teachings and details. Who knows how many thousands of intelligent Christians were armed to maintain their system of belief by these apologetic tools?

But the legacy—precious though it be—has not been without defects. Where it is proposed that the divine character of Scripture is established by the inerrancy of even the minutest detail and that this in turn must become an essential item of faith, any negative evidence from scholarly investigation—whether scientific, historical, archeological, or literary—has the possibility of placing faith itself in jeopardy. If the strong reasonings of Warfield and his followers have "saved the faith" of some believers, they may also have "cost the faith" of others. Faced with the conflict between a doctrine of "literal" inerrancy and the conclusions of respected biblical scholars that seemed to contradict it, they felt forced either to give up their system of belief or to give up their sense of intellectual integrity. Where literal inerrancy is made the chief defense of the truth of the Gospel, a collapse of belief in that definition of inerrancy may lead to a collapse of trust in the Gospel itself. Does not the statement of a prime reviewer of Harold Lindsell's *The Battle of the Bible* imply this? "[Abandoning inerrancy] raises an unanswerable question regarding the determination of accuracy in the Bible and also effectively undermines its reliability." Articles in a creed tend to stand and fall together. Where inerrancy becomes a creedal issue—which it never did for the Reformers—the other items in that creed may be victims of doubt when inerrancy is called into question.

The worthy, even crucial, *emphasis on the inspiration of all parts* of the Bible has made an invaluable contribution to the health and power of the evangelical movement. It has helped us resist the error, so typical of theological liberalism, of treating some parts of Scripture as divine word while ignoring or even rejecting others. It has caused us to treasure all parts of Scripture and to seek to apply their teachings to our life and thought. It has encouraged devotional reading and Bible study in millions of homes and thousands of churches. Bible schools and Bible conferences have sprung up in every region of the land to give opportunity for a closer acquaintance with God's Word.

Yet even this contribution has been a blessing somewhat mixed. The emphasis on the inspiration of all parts of the Bible has sometimes resulted in *the attempt to apply equally all parts of the Bible to our conduct and doctrine.* Promises given specifically to one person in a special context have been appropriated by believers in ways that have no warrant. Texts from Zophar or Bildad have been claimed as life-verses, without any appreciation of the role in revelation that those "friends" of Job were called to play. The close-your-eyes-and-point-to-a-verse form of determining God's will is only a slight caricature of the way well-meaning people have used the Bible.

In our zeal to seek spiritual truth from even the most minute parts of the Scripture, we have frequently been led to neglect the major theological themes that are its heart—the revelation of God's glory and grace in the face of human sin and the sending of the Christ to reveal God's nature and reconcile us to God's favor. Detailed study of the parts is essential. But it has often kept us so close to God's canvas that we have failed to stand back and let the whole painting speak to us of God's grand design for our salvation.

While we have rightly treasured every book, every verse, every line, every word of the sixty-six sacred documents, we have not always been eager to hear what those words mean. Sometimes it is our very doctrine of literalistic inerrancy that has gotten in our way. If every verse is equally God's Word, then may we not look for a special, even hidden, meaning in every verse? Unhappily, allegorical interpretation which the Reformers wisely left behind them has often been brought back into our biblical exposition as part of our attempt to defend the spirituality of the entire text. One has only to cite the common evangelical interpretations of the wilderness tabernacle or Solomon's Song to make the point.

The wrong definition of inerrancy has often led to the opposite extreme from allegory—a literalism that fails to understand how biblical truth comes to us in literary forms. Modern standards of accuracy have been imposed on books that God was pleased to inspire in ancient Oriental contexts, with their very different standards of accuracy. Claims have been made about the meaning of the text without recourse to the ancient documents of Egypt, Mesopotamia, and Ugarit which provide part of the background for understanding both the Bible's meaning and its uniqueness. This may have been excusable a hundred years ago at the beginnings of archeological and epigraphical research; it certainly is not in the last quarter of our century.

To revere the Word is admirable; it is, however, no substitute for using every possible—every God-given means—for understanding it. Reading literal meanings where they were not intended or spiritual meanings where they are not present or forcing harmonizations where they were not intended is just as dishonoring to the Bible as failing to hear its intended spiritual message.

The human process by which God chose to make his Word known in earthly languages is as crucial to our knowledge of what he is saying in Scripture as is our recognition of Scripture's full inspiration. The God who chose to speak to us through writers who lived in specific historical, social, cultural, and linguistic contexts has, by that method of speaking, determined how his Word is to be studied. Technical biblical scholarship, when it works correctly, is not a method imposed on Scripture from without. It is an approach demanded from within. In Genesis, God revealed the creation story over against a setting alive with belief in pagan deities and flooded by myths that described the beginnings of human life and history. How can we possibly catch the full thrust of those magnificent early chapters of our Bible if we do not see it against the Middle-Eastern social and religious setting which serves as their backdrop? The Genesis accounts of creation are not at all an academic account of our beginnings. They are a powerful sermon (almost a song) that celebrates God's power and glory over all the elements and objects of the universe which Israel's neighbors falsely worshiped.

Large sections of the Old Testament are written in poetry. They are not to be read as prose; that is obvious. What is not so obvious is that they are written in Hebrew poetry, which means that they have to be interpreted accordingly. The parallelism, the creative repetition which is the heart of Hebrew poetry, has to be considered. So does the nature of Hebrew song, which usually arises out of specific use in daily life. Work songs, love songs, battle songs, worship songs, complaint songs, lament songs combine with judgment speeches, salvation speeches, court arguments, and a host of other literary forms to comprise what we call Hebrew poetry (and there are at least a similar number of prose forms). A knowledge of Shakespeare or Tennyson helps only a little in reading this kind of poetry. We do best when, by careful investigation of the parallel passages in the Bible and by judicious comparison of the Hebrew literature with its counterparts in other cultures, we don the sandals of those ancients whom God elected as the bearers of his Word.

At no time did God snatch the biblical authors from their settings; at no time did he transform them into other than what they were—citizens of an ancient time and place. Yet it is the wonder of his providence, the miracle of his power, that what they said and how they said it were precisely what he wanted.

Though the examples used are drawn from the Old Testament, the task of accurately reading the New Testament is just as formidable. Take the Gospels, for instance. They represent a unique literary genre, unparalleled anywhere in antiquity. Though the closest parallel may be a book like Jeremiah that both traces a prophet's life and preserves his teachings, we have nowhere in the biblical period a set of writings comparable in style and character to Matthew, Mark, and Luke. This means that we have no clues from outside the Scripture to help us know how to read them. Patience and humility, therefore, have to be the rule, along with a certain amount of trial and error. What is certain is that we must not be content to read Mark as we do the *Los Angeles Times*. Mark has to be understood on his own terms, not on terms which we sons and daughters of a modern Western era bring with us. Indeed, even the *Los Angeles Times* requires considerable hermeneutical insight: we do not read Ann Landers with the same approach we bring to Peanuts; an Associated Press dispatch is different from a letter to the editor, and both are different from the weather predictions, the crossword puzzle, and the used-car ads.

It is basic to our understanding of truth that the literary form and the subject matter contain the keys to their own interpretation. A valentine cries out to be read one way and a recipe another. To confuse them is both to ruffle the course of true love and to jeopardize the workings of our digestive systems.

Hodge and Warfield were able theologians. Unhappily, their theological heirs have not always been. The positive influence of a concern for Bible study which American evangelicals have exhibited has not always been accompanied by an acquaintance with the great theological affirmations of the first four centuries and the Reformation. We have often gone at Christian truth piecemeal. We see that, for example, in a preoccupation with the detailed interpretations of passages in Daniel or Revelation that speak of end-time events. I grew up with a detailed understanding of the precise sequence of events of the end times yet without really knowing why Christ was to come again, what were the purposes of final judgment, what God was seeking to achieve by the resurrection of the dead. I suspect that I was all too typical of many evangelicals formed in a dispensational mold. Forty years later, are we in danger of breeding a generation of evangelicals who have pat answers to the problem passages of biblical prophecy furnished by highly successful best-selling books but who cannot fit the end-time events into the redemptive and creative programs of the triune God?

Adherence to the truth of Scripture without a knowledge of how the best spirits in the church have understood it through the centuries has left many evangelicals ripe for faddistic attractions from Jehovah's Witnesses to British Israel, from Flat Earth societies to outer space cults, from political right-wingism to revolutionary ideologies. If we cut ourselves off, as we sometimes have, from communion with the brightest of the teaching doctors and the soundest of the creedal formulations of the past, we reside in a theological ghetto susceptible to the lures of any suburb where the grass looks slightly greener.

This is not the place to grapple with the massive questions of hermeneutics and historical theology. It is enough for us to note that, with all its valued contributions, inerrancy as defined by many American evangelicals, who consider themselves followers of Hodge and Warfield, is not an unmixed blessing. It has helped us treasure the biblical revelation without always helping us to hear it; it has encouraged us to study the Bible without always pointing to the right tools; it has taught us to believe the Bible without always giving us the right reasons.

Caution, therefore, is in order as to insisting on the perpetuation of the old Princeton approach to inerrancy, in its modern expression, as the only valid theological option for evangelicals. We can salute it without canonizing it. And we can seek a better approach to leave with our children, perhaps an approach that supports their belief as firmly without contorting it as markedly as the earlier view has done to our generation. . . .

This does not mean that we can glibly accept all the results of biblical scholarship. It does not mean that liberal, unbelieving scholars have vanished. It does mean that we can be open to the use of all tools and resources. And we can be open to them not as a grudging concession to creeping liberalism, but as the valid—indeed the God-ordained—means of determining the God-inspired meaning of the text. Carl F. H. Henry ("Agenda for Evangelical Advance") has called for a renewed vigor in American evangelical scholarship, which has been overdependent on Britain and Europe. I cannot speak for the scholars who specialize in philosophical or systematic theology. But I have a hunch that one explanation accounts for the silence of evangelical *biblical* scholars more than any other: the basic fear that their findings, as they deal with the text of Scripture, will conflict with the popular understanding of what inerrancy entails. Where a rigid system of apologetics becomes the basic definition of orthodoxy, true biblical scholarship becomes difficult if not impossible.

Can we in our evangelical institutions begin to enjoy the freedom to give public expression to the results of our scholarship? No evangelical constituency or administration should value safety more than truth and accuracy in biblical interpretation. Without freedom responsibly used, we will be incapable of leaving to our generation a legacy of biblical learning anything like what the evangelical scholars of the nineteenth century left to us.

It may be well for us to keep in mind that the conclusions to which we come as to the meaning and intent of a book or passage may disagree with the tradition in which we have been raised. This should come as no surprise to us who believe in human sin and human limitations. And it should surprise least of all those of us who are heirs of the Reformation, with its insistence that Scripture has priority over the teachings of the fathers—even, on occasion, our own evangelical fathers.

But our gains can be immense. Devout and cautious use of all the tools and insights possible will be one of the great gifts of providence to Christ's church. With patience, intelligence, and prayer, we will be able to look inside the life and faith of our biblical forebears with an accuracy and a perception that will bring true knowledge to our generation and glory to God's name. The way out of our impasse in understanding is both back and forward.

Living with our differences is a monumental lesson to be learned. By and large our generation of evangelicals has not done badly. In Billy Graham crusades for more than twenty-five years, we have set aside our differences in the definition of evangelism and gotten on with the task of pointing men and women to Christ. In mission gatherings like those at Berlin (1966) and Lausanne (1974), we have prayed and planned together about world evangelization despite conflicts in matters like the relationship between church growth and social action.

And we have a heritage that has surmounted theological controversy to form Bible societies, mission boards, campus ministries, rescue missions, and interdenominational Bible schools, colleges, and seminaries.

Anglicans and Baptists, Methodists and Lutherans have affirmed each other's rights to be called evangelical despite major differences in views of church government and the sacraments. The bitter Reformation debates between Luther's followers and Calvin's concerning the nature of Christ's presence in the communion have long since cooled, as have the sharp disagreements between them on the precise manner in which Christ's humanity and deity relate to each other in the Incarnation.

With so much to gain from cooperation, and with so much to lose in understanding and insight from hostility, the time has long since come for evangelicals to accept their differences in the precise formulation of views of infallibility and inerrancy. The opportunism that finds one evangelical church agency or institution claiming to hold a higher view of Scripture than others is scarcely worthy of Christ's kingdom. The possibility of our motivation to go sour in such rivalry is so great that we ought to lean over backwards to avoid it. To recruit students or rally support or withhold fellowship over a definition of biblical inerrancy or the appropriateness of using the term seems futile, if not wicked.

Surely we need our best minds and spirits working on such questions. That work will have a much better chance of success in the clear air of fellowship than in an atmosphere fouled by competition.

Where evangelical affirmations—the Triune nature of God, the true humanity and deity of the Christ, his virgin birth, vicarious death, bodily resurrection, glorious ascension, and personal coming, the reality of the Spirit's mission in the church, the need for conversion and new life, the call to discipleship and participation in the tasks of world evangelization and social action—are shared, let these be the ground of unity.

The questions, as I hear them, do not turn on whether the Bible is errant or not. Biblical errancy is not an option for most evangelicals. The questions are: (1) Is inerrancy the best word to use to describe the Bible's infallibility and truthfulness? (2) If inerrancy is to be used, how do we define it in a way that accords with the teachings and the data of Scripture? That is an important agenda, but one far too limited for us to divide over.

Evangelical variety seems to be evident even in the ways our doctrines of Scripture are phrased. A thorough examination of the official doctrinal statements of our evangelical agencies and schools would reveal a number of patterns which have been used to express a firm commitment to Scripture's unique character.

Some organizations employ a specific statement about the inerrancy of the original documents: "We believe that the Bible, consisting of the Old and New Testaments only, is verbally inspired by the Holy Spirit, is inerrant in the original manuscripts, and is the infallible and authoritative Word of God" (Interdenominational Foreign Mission Association).

Others specifically apply the concept of inerrancy to the rule or guidance that Scripture gives: "We receive the Bible in its entirety, and the Bible alone, as the Word of God written, and therefore the inerrant rule of faith and practice" (Inter-Varsity Christian Fellowship).

It is worth noting that the National Association of Evangelicals chose the word *infallibility* rather than *inerrancy* for its statement: "... we believe the Bible to be the inspired, the only infallible, authoritative word of God."

Perhaps more surprising is the fact that the center of the doctrinal stance of one of the great Bible schools of our land is on verbal inspiration, with no mention of inerrancy: "The Bible, including both the Old and New Testaments, is a divine revelation, the original autographs of which were verbally inspired by the Holy Spirit" (Moody Bible Institute).

This brief sampling of doctrinal statements suggests that we have lived with variety for some time in the way we express our commitment to Scripture. Perhaps we should continue to enjoy this variety, while we go back to the text to hear afresh what God is saying.

Guidelines for evangelical constancy are a further topic for discussion. Whether or not we accept the "domino theory" that suggests that the drift toward liberalism begins when a view of inerrancy akin to that of Hodge and Warfield is given up, concern for evangelical constancy is something that we all should share.

Creedal affirmations are important. Christian agencies do well to have sufficient consensus on the fundamentals of the faith to make their purposes clear and to keep them stable.

Institutional or churchly discipline also needs to be exercised in the selection and retention of key personnel. Careful screening and periodic review should be part of this discipline. Whatever range of theological expression is present must be tested by the norm of the Scripture and by the organization's statement of faith.

Vital experiences of worship and fellowship are also necessary. Whatever Christian theology may be, it is never purely academic. It is unto nurture and worship. Openness to the renewing Spirit of God is certainly one mark of what it means to be evangelical.

If the Protestant principle of *sola scriptura* is to be honored, statements of faith should be subject to periodic review and occasional change. This is especially true when special, unwritten interpretations have grown up around the statements. Such traditions can become dangerous. If they are not crucial, they should be dropped; if they are, they should be incorporated into the official statement.

Inasmuch as the historic creeds of the church have rarely spelled out a full doctrine of Scripture, and almost never of inerrancy, it is better for us to judge the evangelical orthodoxy of our brothers and sisters by the adherence to the great evangelical doctrines—like those of the *Fundamentals* (1910–11) or the appropriate classical evangelical creeds—than by the use or nonuse of specific phrases or catchwords.

In the long run, what has to be weighed is the impact of a colleague's ministry on those whom his life touches. It is possible for a person to be creedally correct and still have a negative impact because of pride, rigidity, or spiritual shallowness. And it is possible for a person to struggle inadequately with precise doctrinal wording and still make a wholesome impact on those whom he serves through his devotion to the Word and his firm Christian faith.

Maybe all of this is asking too much. Can we understand the mixed impact that the narrow, precise definition of inerrancy has had on evangelical vitality? Can we take the road back to the Reformation to remind ourselves of how far we have moved in our ways of defending and interpreting Scripture? Can we begin discussion afresh on our exegesis of key passages, our openness to the methods of historical research, our tolerance of detailed differences in doctrine, our approaches to assuring our continuity as evangelicals?

None of this is easy. Almost all of it will carry pain. Yet the stakes are high. As evangelicals, hearing the Bible is our highest priority. That is best done not in the clamor of battle but in the quiet of diligent study, firm fellowship, and fervent prayer.

Richard Quebedeaux

Richard Quebedeaux has noted that many evangelical theologians have shifted from right to center in their biblical scholarship and their acceptance of historical criticism. This shift has caused increasing tensions within the evangelical movement. The following selection is taken from his article "The Evangelicals: New Trends and New Tensions" in Christianity and Crisis, *September 20, 1976, pp. 197–202.*

The evangelicals are a talking point everywhere. Their growing churches, highly visible campus and youth ministries, phenomenally successful publishing and other media efforts, and unlikely "twice-born" celebrities such as Charles Colson, Jeb and Gail Magruder, Johnny Cash, Graham Kerr, and Jimmy Carter have caught the eye of main-line Protestants, Roman Catholics, and secular journalists. Meanwhile, the new social and political activism of younger evangelicals has been a great encouragement to burned-out liberal and radical theologians and denominational-ecumenical leaders. Garry Wills suggests that "evangelical chic" is impending.

Most people outside the evangelical community itself, however, are totally unaware of the profound changes that have occurred within evangelicalism during the last several years—in the movement's understanding of the inspiration and authority of Scripture, in its social concerns, cultural attitudes, and ecumenical posture, and in the nature of its emerging leadership. Only a decade ago it would have been well nigh impossible to imagine the degree to which this metamorphosis has now actually taken place.

To be sure, the vanguard of what I have termed a "revolution in orthodoxy" is centered primarily on a small, highly literate, zealous elite, many of whose spokespersons hammered out the Chicago Declaration of Evangelical Social Concern in 1973. But the influence of these "younger evangelicals" is no longer restricted to seminaries, colleges, and campus ministries alone. Increasingly, it is being felt even within the institutional bastions of the evangelical Establishment itself—the National Association of Evangelicals (NAE), the Billy Graham Evangelistic Association (BGEA), the Evangelical Theological Society (ETS)—and in the congregations and ministries of distinctively evangelical denominations, from the Southern Baptist Convention to the Lutheran Church–Missouri Synod, from the Christian Reformed Church to the Assemblies of God.

To begin, evangelical theologians have begun looking at the Bible with a scrutiny reflecting their widespread acceptance of the principles of historical and literary criticism (redaction criticism being the current favorite). Traditionally, the "inerrancy" (or "infallibility") of Scripture, not only in its teaching concerning faith and conduct but also in its assertions about history and the cosmos (including biology and geology), has functioned—explicitly or implicitly—as the watershed of twentieth-century American evangelicalism.

The roots of the inerrancy doctrine can be traced to the Westminster Confession of Faith and, more directly, to the Reformed scholasticism of Charles and Archibald Alexander Hodge, Benjamin B. Warfield and the "Old Princeton" school of theology they represented in the late nineteenth and early twentieth centuries. Gradually, in the course of the modernist-fundamentalist controversy and its aftermath, even pietist, Wesleyan, holiness, and Pentecostal groups that had once been far more concerned about right conduct and spirituality than about correct doctrine per se moved toward the total inerrancy position that stressed an intellectual assent to doctrinal propositions (grounded in the Bible, its proponents believed) over against the "holy living," with its personal and social dimensions, emphasized by their forebears. The inerrancy of Scripture, in the whole and in the part, was for these evangelicals—who were rooted in the earlier fundamentalism—derived logically from its divine inspiration and was the one consistent basis for accepting the Bible as the final and supreme authority for the church.

After "Limited Inerrancy," What?

With the inroads of modern science and biblical criticism into American evangelical theological circles, however, the total-inerrancy position has become increasingly difficult to maintain. Thus a doctrine of "limited inerrancy" began to be promulgated during the 1960s that was finally, in 1972, incorporated into the statement of faith held by Fuller Theological Seminary, evangelicalism's most prestigious graduate school of theology.

This position—affirming that Scripture is inerrant or infallible in its teaching on matters of faith and conduct but not necessarily in all its assertions concerning history and the cosmos—is gradually becoming ascendant among the most highly respected evangelical theologians. They feel strongly that the doctrine of limited inerrancy both preserves the Bible's authority for the church and makes feasible the use of the historical-critical method in studying its contents.

As profound as the shift from total to limited inerrancy has been for the evangelicals, more recent developments indicate further changes in the evangelical attitude toward the inspiration and authority of Scripture. A bombshell hit the evangelical community when Paul K. Jewett of Fuller Seminary published his positive theological treatment of feminism, *Man as Male and Female* (Eerdmans, 1975). In it, Jewett emphasizes the cultural conditioning of the Bible more than any previous evangelical theologian has. He challenges the limited inerrancy position (indirectly, at least) by stating that Saint Paul, in his *teaching* about the subordination of women to men, was influenced both by his male-dominated culture and by rabbinic traditions representing a time-bound authority not applicable to later Christians. In other words, Saint Paul was wrong.

Understandably, Jewett's hermeneutic has rocked the conservative evangelical establishment, many of whose leaders still hold to the doctrine of total inerrancy; those affirming limited inerrancy, though somewhat disturbed, seem less shaken. What is most interesting, however, is the fact that a large number of younger evangelicals scoff altogether at their elders' stress on inerrancy by whatever definition. They insist that a precise doctrine of the inspiration and authority of Scripture is far less important than unconditional obedience to what it demands—pointing out that those Christians *most* committed to inerrancy have tended to be the *least* passionate about the biblical requirements of justice, righteousness, and peace.

Another major diversification has occurred in the movement's social concerns. By and large, twentieth-century white evangelicals have either been outwardly apolitical or have taken the conservative position on almost every social, economic, and political issue. For a long time, there has been a visible alliance between the evangelical establishment and the Republican Party, culminating, perhaps, in the Graham-Nixon friendship and the evangelist's public endorsement of Richard Nixon's candidacy in 1972.

Evangelicals did not so uniformly identify themselves with the status quo in the past. Nineteenth-century leaders—especially those grounded in the Wesleyan, holiness, or New School Presbyterian revivalistic traditions such as Jonathan Blanchard (founder of Wheaton College in Illinois), Charles G. Finney, Phoebe Palmer (Methodist lay evangelist), and William and Catherine Booth— were influential participants in the abolitionist and feminist struggles of their day.

At the triennial missionary convention of the Inter-Varsity Christian Fellowship—"Urbana '70"—it became clear that a new generation of evangelicals who repudiated the modern alliance of theological conservatism with the forces of political and social reaction was emerging. The college students in attendance and their invited speakers surprised the evangelical establishment by denouncing the blatantly racist character of white evangelical churches and U.S. participation in the Vietnam War.

From that major beginning, the discontent among young evangelicals became increasingly visible until about fifty of them, together with a few evangelical elder statesmen like Carl F. H. Henry, founding editor of *Christianity Today,* and Rufus Jones of the Conservative Baptist Home Mission Society, hammered out the much-publicized Chicago Declaration over the Thanksgiving weekend in 1973. (See John Howard Yoder's "Evangelicals at Chicago: a New Openness to Prophetic Social Critique," February 18, 1974 issue.) This statement was a confession of evangelical complicity in the racism, sexism, militarism, and economic injustice of the wider U.S. society. Even *Newsweek* called attention to the leftward trend of contemporary evangelicalism, while *National Review* lamented the fact that evangelicals could no longer be counted on to support en masse the conservative Republican stance.

The Trend Leftward

Much has happened since 1974. The trend leftward among younger evangelicals has continued unabated, but it has begun to move in several different directions. At the far left are the so-called radical evangelicals, influenced heavily by the Catholic left (the Berrigans and Dorothy Day), William Stringfellow, Jacques Ellul, and the nonviolent communitarian Anabaptist tradition represented most notably by John Howard Yoder.

Many of these Christians came out of the New Left and the counterculture of the 1960's (including the Jesus movement), and they all question deeply the possibility of transforming culture-bound political or religious structures by the participation of Christians within them. Christ stands *against* culture. Christian responsibility rests in the formation of alternative communities that model a simple life-style, genuine concern for the poor and outcast, first-priority commitment to one another as sisters and brothers in Christ, and a prophetic critique of the institutional church (conservative *and* liberal) and the capitalist system in general. Radical evangelicals publish a number of widely read magazines including *Sojourners* (formerly the *Post-American*) of the People's Christian Coalition in Washington, D.C.; *The Other Side* (Philadelphia); and *Radix* (formerly *Right On*) of the Berkeley Christian Coalition in California.

Somewhat to the right of the radical evangelicals stand, on the one side, the Wesleyan evangelicals and, on the other side, the Neo-Reformed evangelicals. The Wesleyans are thoroughgoing Arminians who emphasize right practice over orthodox doctrine and stress the "social holiness" of John Wesley. Many are United Methodists or members of the smaller holiness denominations such as the Wesleyan Church, the Free Methodist Church, and the Church of God (Anderson, Indiana).

The Neo-Reformed evangelicals are Calvinists of the first order who have been deeply influenced by Bonhoeffer, Barth, and Reinhold Niebuhr. They tend to be "political realists" and lean in the direction of *Worldview* magazine. Two of their number signed the Hartford Appeal, and many of them write for the *Reformed Journal* (Grand Rapids). Doctrine is more important to the Neo-Reformed evangelicals than it is to the radicals and Wesleyans. Their major spokespersons are members of the Christian Reformed Church.

Both the Wesleyans and Neo-Reformed are more open to the middle-class life-styles than the radicals; they are less critical of the institutional church; and most of them believe that social change is possible through the Democratic or Republican parties (in which some of them are quite active). Not overtly committed to non-violence in the manner of the radicals, they are beginning to look with favor on liberation theology. For the most part, these "liberal" evangelicals believe in the Christ who *transforms* culture.

Unlike their young white counterparts, the "new black evangelicals" do not look with contempt on the recent history of their inherited religious tradition. They point out that, by and large, black evangelicals *and* fundamentalists have never separated evangelism from social concern the way white theological conservatives have. The new black evangelicals focus their efforts on the struggle against racism, strengthening black identity, and building up the larger black community. Mainly Democrats and Baptists (with increasing numbers of Pentecostals among them), they are committed church people who believe in working to transform existing ecclesiastical and political structures. They disagree strongly with the radical evangelicals' emphasis on creating alternative communities rather than working within the system. Like other black Christians, they read James Cone.

Finally we should mention the growing number of (Roman and Anglo-) Catholic evangelicals. Some of them, the charismatics especially, share similarities with the radical evangelicals—simple life-styles, communitarianism, and deep concern for the poor. Others are much more akin to the Neo-Reformed or Wesleyan evangelicals. But all are committed to the institutional church and its historical tradition, emphasizing sacramental celebration and a renewed spirituality.

The women's movement has made substantial gains within all these subgroups. Most young evangelicals accept the use of inclusive language, the ordination of women, egalitarian marriage, and the Equal Rights Amendment (though new black evangelical women feel that the fight against racism must take precedence over the struggle against sexism). The Evangelical Women's Caucus, a fellowship of evangelical (or "biblical") feminists, has a number of chapters across the country and is growing steadily; the new evangelical feminist publication, *Daughters of Sarah* (Chicago), is enjoying increased subscriptions.

Though all evangelical feminists end up in the same place scripturally, the more conservative party (limited inerrancy types) stands on the principle that the Bible does not teach what it has been assumed to teach about the subordinate role of women in church and society; rather the *interpretation* of Scripture has been cultural-ly conditioned. The radical party, however, following Jewett, argues simply that the New Testament conveys liberation for all people and was not intended to oppress modern women by imposing on them a first-century patriarchal family structure. Saint Paul said what we thought he said; when he demands the subordination of women to men, he is wrong.

Questioning Cultural Attitudes

To what extent have the evangelical establishment and the masses of no less than 40 million "mainstream evangelicals" been influenced by the young turks? The answer to this question is still evasive; but young evangelicals have been encouraged by the way their concerns helped shape the 1974 Lausanne Covenant that even Billy Graham, together with a host of other establishment figures, signed. The covenant affirms: "The message of salvation implies also a message of judgment upon every form of alienation, oppres-sion and discrimination, and we should not be afraid to denounce evil and injustice wherever they exist." Graham himself was re-cently forced by pressure to have a woman sit on the board of directors of his association, which appears to have finally estab-lished a framework for evangelical social response. The social-concerns commission of the National Association of Evangelicals—that organization's haven for Democrats, minorities, and pacifists—now chaired by a new black evangelical, has been revitalized.

Most mainstream evangelicals outside the South remain Repub-licans. But the Watergate revelations cast doubt in their minds as to the moral purity of the Republican Party in general, and its head in particular, even if he happens to use religious language and befriends Billy Graham. The present widespread interest in Jimmy Carter would hardly have been possible among evangelicals just a few years ago. Prior to the emergence of the young evangelicals and the fall of Nixon, it would have been unthinkable for mainstream evangelicals to support a Democrat and "liberal" for president—even a "born-again" Christian—rather than a (more) conservative Republican of *whatever* religious stripe.

A third major change in contemporary evangelicalism has occurred in its cultural attitudes. Separated from the wider culture by
a simplistic and individualistic Christian ethic characteristic of
modern revivalism, the righteous life for evangelicals was most
often marked by a platitudinous legalism. Smoking, drinking, dancing, theatergoing, and gambling, for instance, were disallowed.
Reacting against what they consider oppressive legalism, younger
evangelicals have almost universally rejected these taboos as binding; and the use of four-letter words, even, is readily apparent at
times in their conversation and writing (though traditional profani-
ty against the deity, such as *goddamn,* remains generally absent).
It is also clear that, with upward social mobility and cultural accommodation, evangelicalism as a whole—even some of the more
conservative evangelical churches, colleges, seminaries, and campus ministries—no longer spends much time condemning many of
the older distinctive taboos that have now become socially dys-
functional, drinking in particular.

The one major area in which virtually all evangelicals—young
and old—remain "conservative" and distinct from the wider society is in their sexual ethics. Premarital and extramarital intercourse,
and homosexual practice, in all circumstances, are still totally unacceptable (except, for example, in the largely evangelical gay
Metropolitan Community Churches).

Nevertheless, it is not impossible that even this characteristic
evangelical stance will eventually be undercut. If Jewett can render
as not binding the Pauline injunctions regarding the subordination
of women to men—because of cultural conditioning—it is only one
step away to do the same thing with Saint Paul's admonitions
against premarital intercourse and homosexual practice (in selected
situations, at least). If this happens, we may discern the emergence
of a "new morality" for evangelicals in which love becomes the
only absolute ethical norm.

Beyond "One-Way" Ecumenical Cooperation

A fourth highly significant transformation in contemporary
evangelicalism has been in its ecumenical posture. The modernist-
fundamentalist controversy left most evangelicals with their own
distinctive denominations, mission boards, evangelistic associa-

tions, campus and youth ministries, world relief organizations, publishing houses, and periodicals. Those who stayed inside the main-line Protestant denominations tended to keep to themselves, generally avoiding contact with nonevangelicals both within and outside their denominations. When Billy Graham began his "ecumenical evangelism" in the 1950s—seeking the support and participation of main-line church leaders (Protestants and, later, Roman Catholics) for his crusades—the hard-core fundamentalists who once allied themselves with his efforts repudiated him for cooperating with "modernist unbelievers," but the evangelicals remained in his camp, feeling that *this* kind of ecumenical cooperation was itself evangelisitic; liberal pastors and their congregations could be "reached for Christ."

The young evangelicals, however, have gone one step beyond a *one-way* ecumenical cooperation ("getting the liberals saved"). Not having participated in the modernist-fundamentalist dispute, they harbor no bitterness and see no reason not to consider the possibility of relating to main-line Protestants as equals—sisters and brothers in Christ. The young evangelicals' willingness to engage in dialogue, fellowship, and joint action with Christians of other persuasions has been apparent almost from the beginning. They have been courted by the World and National Councils of Churches, main-line Protestant denominations, major ecumenical campus ministry organizations, and theological seminaries.

In addition, the newly rediscovered social conscience of mainstream evangelicals and the fresh interest in prayer, Bible study, spirituality, and evangelism displayed by main-line Protestants have begun to advance ecumenical-evangelical cooperation even among the more conservative evangelicals. What is most significant here is the growing awareness among evangelicals of all stripes that they are not the *only* Christians—a conviction greatly facilitated by the "relational theology" of Faith at Work, Bruce Larson, and Keith Miller (teaching that theology is relational rather than conceptual), and by the charismatic movement's insistence that, biblically, the experience of the Holy Spirit is given to men and women as a uniting factor *before* they are united in doctrinal truth.

A final change in contemporary evangelicalism can be discerned in the nature of its emerging leadership. The influence within the movement of the establishment organizations mentioned previously (NAE, BGEA, and ETS)—dominant just a few years ago—is already on the wane. Other centers of power and conviction will amost inevitably come into being in the next decade. The new generation of evangelicals has its share of celebrities, including Senator Mark Hatfield; black evangelist Tom Skinner; Leighton Ford, Billy Graham's heir apparent; and John R. W. Stott, the English Anglican exegete and Inter-Varsity hero.

Evangelicalism Will Never Be the Same

More important, however, are the young evangelical leaders themselves. Most visible among the radical evangelicals are Ron Sider of Messiah College in Philadelphia; Jim Wallis, author of *Agenda for Biblical People* (Harper & Row, 1976), and Wes Michaelson, both of *Sojourners*; John F. Alexander of *The Other Side*; and Sharon Gallagher of *Radix*. Notable among the Wesleyan evangelicals are Donald W. Dayton of Chicago's North Park Theological Seminary, author of a ground-breaking historical work on the "radical" origins of evangelicalism, *Discovering an Evangelical Heritage* (Harper & Row, 1976); and Howard A. Snyder of Light and Life Men International (Free Methodist), author of *The Problem of Wineskins: Church Structure in a Technological Age* (Inter-Varsity Press, 1975). Prominent Neo-Reformed evangelicals include Paul B. Henry, political scientist at Calvin College in Grand Rapids and author of *Politics for Evangelicals* (Judson Press, 1974); Richard Mouw, philosopher at Calvin College, author of *Political Evangelism* (Eerdmans, 1973) and a signer of the Hartford Appeal; and Marlin J. Van Elderen, managing editor of *The Reformed Journal* and editor in chief of William B. Eerdmans Publishing Company.

Leading representatives of the new black evangelicals include William Pannell of Fuller Seminary, author of *My Friend the Enemy* (Word, 1968); John Perkins of the Voice of Calvary in Mendenhall, Mississippi, a ministry to the rural poor; Ron Potter, contributing editor to *The Other Side*; Wyn Wright Potter, executive secretary of the National Black Evangelical Association; Ruth Lewis Bentley, head of minority affairs at the University of Illinois Medical School; and Clarence Hilliard, head of the NAE's social-concerns commission.

Important Catholic evangelicals include Robert Webber of

Wheaton College's division of biblical studies; Graham Pulkingham, former rector of Houston's Episcopal Church of the Redeemer and author of *Gathered for Power: Charisma, Communalism, Christian Witness* (Morehouse-Barlow, 1972); and Ralph Martin, former editor of *New Covenant* in Ann Arbor, the Catholic charismatic monthly, and author of *Hungry for God* (Doubleday, 1974).

Prominent evangelical feminists include (in addition to Sharon Gallagher) Evon Bachaus, organizing secretary of the Evangelical Women's Caucus; Letha Scanzoni and Nancy Hardesty, coauthors of *All We're Meant to Be: A Biblical Approach to Women's Liberation* (Word, 1974); Lucille Sider Dayton, editor of *Daughters of Sarah*; Judy Brown Hall, cochairperson of Evangelicals for Social Action (the Chicago Declaration people); and Virginia Ramey Mollenkott, author of *Women, Men and the Bible* (Abingdon, 1976).

Of all contemporary evangelical leaders, however, the person to watch is David Allan Hubbard, president of Fuller Seminary. Hubbard, an Old Testament scholar, was inaugurated as president in 1963 when the seminary had 300 students. He was thirty-six at the time. Now Fuller has more than 1,100 regularly enrolled students in three graduate schools—Theology, Psychology, and World Mission.

David Hubbard is an ecclesiastical statesman par excellence. An ordained Conservative Baptist minister, he impresses everyone with his preaching ability, charm, and political savvy. He was a theological adviser to the Fifth General Assembly of the World Council of Churches (Nairobi) and cochairperson of The Danforth Foundation's recent national consultations on "dialogue with evangelicals in campus ministry."

At present, Hubbard serves on the board of directors of the National Institute for Campus Ministries (Protestant, Catholic, and Jewish), and is president of the Association of Theological Schools in the United States and Canada, the accreditation body for all North American theological seminaries. As better relationships between evangelicals and main-line Protestants continue to develop, he is bound to be an increasingly visible enabler of the process.

In a word, all these new trends among the evangelicals are highly significant. They indicate that evangelical theology is becoming more centrist, more open to biblical criticism, and more accepting of science and broad cultural analysis. One might even suggest that the new generation of evangelicals is closer to Bonhoeffer, Barth, and Brunner than to the Hodges and Warfield on the inspiration and authority of Scripture. Their evangelism looks more like the call to social justice and discipleship than the traditional call to conversion. One can even discern among them a subtle shift in the direction of belief in universal salvation. And some of the younger evangelicals, anyway, may be just about ready to celebrate the secular city. (There is scant reference to heaven or hell in their publications.) Only time will tell to what degree all of this will eventually become pervasive. But one thing is certain. Evangelicalism will never be the same.

Martin Marty

Martin Marty has warned that as evangelicals move to the left, they are going to lose part of their distinctiveness and face the same problems of accommodation so troubling for mainstream groups. This selection is taken from his article "Tensions within Contemporary Evangelicalism: A Critical Appraisal" in David F. Wells and John D. Woodbridge, eds., The Evangelicals: What They Believe, Who They Are, Where They Are Changing. *New York: Abingdon Press, 1976, pp. 176–87.*

By the 1970s, evangelicalism had permanently parted company with the shapers of the fundamentalist gestalt. Its leaders could not go the fundamentalist way; their organization, cognition, intention, and behavior now differed so vastly that they would have to desert evangelicalism itself to take the fundamentalist course. Yet evangelicals also had difficulty moving further toward the mainline Protestants, who also had much claim on the nineteenth-century lineage. While many elements of their behavior patterns were increasingly converging, they honestly differed too much on the appropriation of doctrine to be at ease with each other. The younger evangelicals sometimes found pragmatic alliances with main-line church people to be advisable. But Carl F. H. Henry, doughty warrior for the original restatement of modern evangelicalism and a man who made more than most of the intellectual formulation of the movement, demurred. Even in the ethical realm, because of differences in motivation, goals, and ethics, "it would be naïve to argue . . . that liberals and evangelicals need each other for complementary emphases." Alliance could mean that the biblical view of God would be destroyed and the welfare state produced.

Insofar as Henry is representative, it would seem that evangelical leadership is enjoying its evident majority status and, in a way, "going it alone" in its claim on the heritage, however blurred its boundaries may be becoming. If, in effect, it is turning out to be *the* Protestant mainstream, it will increasingly take on the burdens of typicality and of cultural predominance. Indeed, its self-critics are regularly pointing to just such tendencies. Evangelicals are ecumenical under the banner of "cooperation without compromise." By this they mean that none of their churches will compromise their distinctive and separating dogmas. Yet in practice and behaviorally they cooperate with nonevangelicals, including mainstream Protestants and Roman Catholics in some of their most prized ventures, including evangelism—witness the effort called Key '73—and are perceived by the public as creatively compromising cooperators.

Evangelicals' increasing cultural openness leads them to an embrace, albeit a critical one, of intellectual and artistic currents that subtly alter the character of faith's expression.

They also, their internal critics contend, too often uncritically embrace some of the practices of popular culture that their fathers and mothers had shunned. Donald Bloesch is not alone in stating this, and he is certainly mild in his comment:

> This brings us . . . to the carnality and frivolity in much modern-day popular evangelical religion. This can be seen in the glorification of beauty queens and athletes who happen to be Christian. It is also noticeable in the fascination of many evangelicals with public relations and showmanship. In some schools and churches technique and method are valued more highly than right doctrine, and group dynamics is given more attention than prayer and other spiritual disciplines. The popularity of gospel rock groups that appeal to the sensual side of man is yet another indication of accommodation to worldly standards. Culture-religion is also evident in the camaraderie between some evangelical leaders and right-wing politicians.

He quotes A. W. Tozer on this tendency toward culture-religion: evangelicalism is "fascinated by the great, noisy, aggressive world with its big name, its hero worship, its wealth and garish pagentry." Millions of disappointed persons who never found worldly glory could through evangelicalism have a shortcut to their heart's desire in the realm of social acceptance, publicity, success in sports or business or entertainment. "All this on earth and heaven at last. Certainly no insurance company can offer half as much."

If evangelicalism has drifted, perhaps irretrievably, into much affirmation of and some accommodation to culture-as-it-is, its future life will also be complicated by the presence of vital critical groups within it. These are counterparts to the liberals' social gospel and Christian realist voices that in the early 1900s and in the 1930s and 1960s troubled the peace of mainstream Protestantism. Influenced by men like Jacques Ellul, Helmut Thielicke, and William Stringfellow or issuing in numbers of evangelically radical groups like the Christian World Liberation Front and publications like the *Post-American,* these forces are beginning to disrupt evangelicalism's uncritical bond with the social status quo. They will, if they survive, make it possible for a biblically prophetic note to be heard with more consistency—at great expense to evangelicalism's popularity and its sanctioning by the powers that be.

In short, while fundamentalism and evangelicalism both defer to each other and show some respect for the way each retains at least nominal assent to the old nineteenth-century Protestant symbols, their behavior patterns show such divergences that we must be alerted to the possibility of needing to say that their similarities have "died the death of a thousand qualifications." On the levels of social behavior and, presumably, of the ideas that motivate such behavior, evangelicals often show more similarities with and affinities to mainstream Protestants, with whom they disagree more openly on the cognitive level but with whom they have more profound similarities so far as world views are concerned. Brief comments on the evangelical-vs.-fundamentalism polemics in four areas will illustrate particularly the first half of this thesis.

Not necessarily in the matter of the doctrine of the church itself, but rather in that of the *ecclesia-in-praxis,* qualitatively different ideas are finding expression in the patterns of social behavior of evangelicalism as against those of fundamentalism. The evangelicals would seem to have more rightful claim on the nineteenth-century heritage. For all the denominational competition, the fathers of that century were ecumenical in outlook. Europeans complained that Americans were not enthusiastic partners in the Evangelical Alliance (after 1846), not because they were not ecumenical or cooperative but because cooperation came so instinctively and naturally to them that they did not need the international organization. Yet these evangelicals who were cooperating were by no means wholly agreed cognitively or substantively with each other.

The fundamentalists of the twentieth century have parted company with the nineteenth-century policy-makers. They are separatist and schismatic and proud of it. They cooperate with each other simply on pragmatic and on quasi-military joint-defense and joint-aggression grounds. But they make no claims of spiritual union of any sort where there is not total agreement on doctrine. Virtually all fundamentalists sound like each other on this topic, and almost any of them could be taken as typical. Thus Thomas E. Baker in his manual on fundamentalism says that "new evangelicalism . . . violates the plain teaching of scripture," for example in its understanding of "the last days" or in its "departure from the truth of separation from unbelief." Thus the new evangelicalism "brought a major 'division' in the ranks of fundamentalism as well as a minor division in the philosophies of Liberalism and "Neo-Orthodoxy." Yet for Baker the difficulty the fundamentalist has with the new evangelical is found in that "he is not dealing with an unbeliever, but one who believes most of the basic fundamental truths of scripture."

Nominal agreement on these basics always has to be asserted. Baker goes on to criticize evangelicals for dealing with Pentecostals, non-Calvinists, clergy from Communist countries, but not with fundamentalists. "This . . . revealed the same attitude that prevailed in Liberalism." Fundamentalists warned evangelicals that "cooperation of belief with unbelief in Ecumenism would produce ecumenical babylon. . . . This is exactly what took place." Fundamentalists dare not allow evangelicals to share their pulpits. Such practice is unscriptural. It causes confusion. It is not necessary. There is no benefit. "The invisible line must be drawn and kept drawn at all times between fundamentalist and New Evangelical, even when the fundamentalist feels strong enough through growth spiritually, numerically or financially."

From the evangelical side, the early leader Harold Ockenga set a tone and the terms that remain consistent. "Fragmentation, segregation, separation, criticism, censoriousness, suspicion, solecism, is the order of the day for fundamentalism." Over against fundamentalism, evangelicals assert, says Millard Erickson, that "there are only two justifiable grounds for separation from an existing denomination: eviction or apostasy." Yet fundamentalists split "on the basis of personality or minor creedal items." "The new evangelicals are not separatists in the sense of seeking to withdraw from any slight taint of heterodoxy or worldiness." Bruce Shelley, speaking for evangelicals, complained of fundamentalism's " 'wowser' worship, its cultural isolationism, its sectarian separatism, its monastic ethics, its theological hair-splitting."

In the face of such sharp and consistent lines of definition and attack, the Christian observer who is not part of either movement can be forgiven if he or she is bewildered about the claims of some sort of kinship on the basis of cognitive assent to basic tenets. Thus both evangelicals and fundamentalists insist on the "inerrancy of Scripture" as being the most basic of all their fundamentals. Since they do not agree with each other or among each other on the basis of it, what does this nominal agreement on a substantive category mean? The larger world feels much more the effect of the two social behavioral patterns than it does the professed dogmatic agreements.

A second area, and one that gave rise to much of the demarcation between the two, has to do with the social and ethical realm. Here again evangelicalism would seem to have the more rightful claim on the nineteenth-century lineage, and fundamentalism would be the "modernist" deviation. It is hard to account for fundamentalism's departure from the older evangelical concern for Christianity as it relates to the whole social fabric. No doubt, premillennialism's rise in the late nineteenth century had much to do with this withdrawal into purely private and personal moral discourse on the part of fundamentalism. Premillennialism, the belief in God's forthcoming intervention to inaugurate a millennium of Christ's rule, has characteristic but not inevitable behavioral corollaries. Many evangelicals are also premillennial, but not all segregate themselves so consistently from efforts to participate positively as the church in the social sphere. (Fundamentalists are not removed from some kinds of participation, but these tend to be restricted to supporting legislation having to do with private vices—gambling, liquor, pornography—or to advocacy of the conservative status quo on the grounds of biblically based injunctions to undergird civil authority.)

Millard Erickson typically criticizes fundamentalism on this point. "During its long history orthodox, or conservative, Christianity had stressed the application of its message to social ills. . . . As the twentieth century moved on, however, fundamentalism neglected this emphasis. . . . The fundamentalist seemed to be . . . passing suffering humanity." Carl F. H. Henry, Harold Ockenga, Sherwood Eliott Wirt, and Leighton Ford among the older evangelicals have persistently concurred in this judgment. Positively, asserts Ockenga in one of the most famous passages in this literature:

> The new evangelicalism embraces the full orthodoxy of fundamentalism, but manifests a social consciousness and responsibility which was strangely absent from fundamentalism. The new evangelicalism concerns itself not only with personal salvation, doctrinal truth and an eternal point of reference, but also with the problems of race, of war, of class struggle, of liquor control, of juvenile delinquency, of immorality, and of national imperialism. . . . The new evangelicalism believes that orthodox Christians cannot abdicate their responsibility in the social scene.

The younger evangelicals, led by Richard V. Pierard, Richard Quebedeaux, Richard J. Mouw, the editors of *The Reformed Journal,* the Southern Baptist Convention's Christian Life Commission, the authors of the Chicago Declaration of Social Concern, and others have taken up this theme with a vengeance and totally part company with the fundamentalist pattern. Each side is as proud of its stand as it is rejective of the other's. Each accepts the general depiction of its own stand by the other. Meanwhile, evangelicalism distances itself somewhat from at least the position of official elites (though by no means necessarily of the majority of constituents) on the mainstream Protestant side. It remains critical of simple liberal-church-liberal-social policy syndromes, of the leadership's presumed speaking for the clienteles, of liberal Protestantism's tendency to bureaucratize social programming, of its readiness to take legislative routes reflexively. But while differences with fundamentalism are differences in kind, with the mainstream they have come more and more to be matters of degree. In the case of the prophetic criticism and occasional radicalism of the new evangelicals, it is often possible to see the main-line forces actually being eclipsed.

Once again, in the face of these obvious, profound, enduring differences concerning the *polis,* one of the most decisive spheres in theology and social life, what is the outsider to make of professed agreements between fundamentalists and evangelicals on, say, belief in Christ's Second Coming? Why should the two be seen as united in belief, when there is little agreement on other doctrines on what the vast majority of Christians—Roman Catholic, Orthodox, Lutheran, and Anglican—have always regarded as fundamental (for example, the sacraments)? Social behavior ought at least to be regarded as indicative of emerging theological flaws and faults in what was once a settled conservative Protestant landscape.

Historically of less significance but now gaining in prominence are a differing third set of behavioral responses. Fundamentalists have not been antiintellectual. The name of J. Gresham Machen is regularly invoked to show that their school was not always antiacademic and rationally roughshod. A kind of seventeenth-century scholastic philosophical approach has provided intellectual structure for much fundamentalism. Yet fundamentalists have been nervous about universities and colleges—even under their own auspices. Instead, they have cherished more focal and more easily controlled Bible schools and institutes. Not all of them shun the arts. Bob Jones University has notable art collections, and other fundamentalist organizations make much of music. But little attempt is made to integrate theologically the aesthetic vision and Christian faith.

The evangelicals want to be known as favoring both intellectuality and arts in the service of faith. In H. Richard Niebuhr's familiar typology, fundamentalism tends to represent "Christ against culture," while evangelicalism wavers between "Christ transforming culture" or "Christ and culture in paradox" but not in mutual negation. Carl F. H. Henry long ago set the terms for criticism when he accused fundamentalism of having narrowed "the whole counsel of God," becoming otherworldly in spirit, neglecting the exposition of Christian philosophy, and even being distrustful of such interests. It degenerated, to use Dr. G. B. Wurth's phrase, into "a morbid and sickly enthusiasm." It embodied "an uncritical antithesis between the heart and the head ... belittling ... the intellect." Fundamentalism "neglected the production of great exegetical and theological literature," and reprinted works from the past. Therefore, "if modernism stands discredited as a perversion of scriptural theology, certainly fundamentalism in this contemporary expression stands discredited as a perversion of the biblical spirit."

Evangelicals have supported colleges more than Bible institutes; they have reached into more and more areas of culture, though without yet having made a significant contribution to modern art or literature; they have built seminaries that allow for some internal pluralism in approach to philosophy and arts; they have made much of authors like C. S. Lewis when these embody orthodox Christianity; they have even tolerated moderate appropriations of biblical critical methods—George Ladd is usually cited as an exemplar—though the exemplars usually reply in haste that they in no way depart from their belief in complete biblical authority. The evangelicals pursue doctorates at prestigious European and American theological schools; their scholarly societies have become more and more sophisticated, even though they may require creedal assents not expected elsewhere in the American academy.

Individual fundamentalists may not find fault with all these tendencies and may occasionally pursue some of these themselves. But as a movement, fundamentalism rejects them all. The Christian who belongs to neither party has difficulty seeing why the two should be considered a single expression of Christian faith, again, for example, because of belief in both the atonement and the Resurrection of Christ, when the majority of mainstream Protestants share these beliefs and have views of intellect and culture more congruent with evangelicalism's intentions than either of them have with fundamentalism's.

A fourth area that receives perhaps the most attention in evangelical-fundamentalist polemics is the more subjective and elusive sphere of manners, mores, habits, and customs. These may be seen as adisphoral or peripheral to true dogmatists, but biblical religion and centuries of tradition count these as being extremely revelatory of the character and actual content of personal or group beliefs. The lines are clearly drawn here. The fundamentalists regard evangelicals as suave, accommodating, too genteel, too worldly. To the militants, such postures are indicative not merely of wrong manners but of wrong commitments and beliefs.

Evangelicals are just as consistent in their rejection of fundamentalism's militancy, belligerency, uncouthness, prescriptive legalism, and ad-hominem argumentation. They spend enormous amounts of energy distancing themselves from contemporary fundamentalists who manifest these traits and sorting out earlier fundamentalists who did not possess them. Virtually every commentator from the evangelical side has treated fundamentalism's moral taboos against dancing, card playing, mixed swimming, and the like as being normative and nomothetic expressions of that faith. They often believe that these taboos shroud complex problems, as in the area of sex. Daniel Stevick quotes and agrees with Carl Henry:

> The Fundamentalist catalogue of "sins" is small and specific: commercial movies, dancing, gambling, card-playing, drinking beer or wine or liquor, and smoking. No "spiritual Christian" will presumably do any of these things, and generally will have little to do with anyone who does do them. Everyone who grows up in this tradition finds that it has a vise-like grip on him. His conscience has been made sensitive to these things by the never-ending tirade against them.

The evangelicals are not exactly libertarian or antinomian, but they feel that instead of "a childish reaction into a uniformly opposite pattern of behavior," there should be a "variety of practice that indicates life, color, and the freedom for each person to be himself." Since the fundamentalist believes his or her practices to be grounded completely in the only possible scriptural interpretation of ethics, he sees such evangelical "variety" as being worldliness and apostasy.

Along with personal morals, the two clusters part company over the manner and manners of denominational fighting. Carl F. H. Henry even goes so far as to say that "the real bankruptcy of fundamentalism has resulted not so much from a reactionary spirit—

lamentable as this was—as from a harsh temperament, a spirit of lovelessness and strife contributed by much of its leadership in the recent past." "It is this character of fundamentalism as a temperament, and not primarily fundamentalism as a theology, which has brought the movement into contemporary discredit." Historically, it was a theological position. Only gradually did it become a mood and disposition as well. Yet in separating from that mood and disposition, evangelicalism takes on the risks of mainstream Protestantism. "When evangelicalism becomes respectable and even fashionable," writes Donald Bloesch, "then the temptation to accommodate to the values and goals of the world becomes almost overwhelming." Such accommodation, he says, is present and brings dangers.

One could carry these comparisons into numerous other fields; for example, differing attitudes toward the study and use of the Bible could be enlarged upon as manifesting other qualitative differences between the two conservative claimants to rightful lineage of American nineteenth-century Protestantism. These illustrations should suffice for present purposes, however. It is clear from what has been indicated that fundamentalism and evangelicalism are now at the stage where they should begin to explore at what point drastic behavioral differences reveal and represent actual substantive differences, opposing grasps of biblical and traditional Christian teaching.

The intent has not been to show that evangelicals and mainstream Protestants now will find either simple theological or social behavioral agreement or that alliances between them can easily come about. They do have more in common than they have recognized; this will become even more evident as evangelicals come increasingly to the conclusion that modernist-liberal Protestantism of the 1920s was a deviation from nineteenth-century continuities and syndromes on the Left just as the older fundamentalism was on the Right. Most important, this thesis or interpretation suggests that evangelicalism is taking on and will increasingly take on the burdens of interpretation and accommodation that have created numerous troubles for the mainstream groups. Evangelicals will have to be especially alert to the ways in which they can replenish and revitalize their theological tradition through the passing years. They cannot expect a serene life as they try to remain a "cognitive minority" while they have become a kind of social behavioral majority far beyond the borders of middle America.

Carl Henry

Carl Henry argues that the key issue of the 1980s for evangelicals will be the problem of authority and how it relates to the questions of revelation and culture. This selection is taken from his article "American Evangelicals in a Turning Time," The Christian Century, *5 November 1980, pp. 1058–62.*

W ill the world later in this century perceive Christianity as the global religion par excellence? I am now less inclined to think so than in 1970. We Christians may have to reconcile ourselves to a growing misperception that Christianity is but one among the many living religions; worse yet, we may see our commitment to it increasingly detested and persecuted. Even in the so-called free world, the educational metaview and the mass media's value ratings are already exiling Christian distinctives. Communism's vaunted world revolution, if it comes, will consign true Christians (not syncretists) to some gigantic Gulag.

Internal Weaknesses

I am even less sure of America's world leadership role. The post-Vietnam era has placed in question our nation's moral leadership, our political wisdom, our economic competence, even our military adequacy, and not least of all our national resolve and sense of fixed purpose. Leadership is God's gift to a nation, forfeiture of leadership a divine judgment upon it. While military supremacy may discourage predator powers and military weakness encourage them, national influence suspended only on military advantage is tenuous at best. Tapering all problems to politico-economic and military decisions will collapse the human spirit. America not only faces formidable foreign foes but vacillates in countering internal weaknesses that threaten to lower the flag to half-staff permanently.

I think we are now living in the very decade when God may thunder his awesome *paradidōmai* (I abandon, or I give [them] up) (Rom. 1:24 ff.) over America's professed greatness. Our massacre of a million fetuses a year; our deliberate flight from the monogamous family; our normalizing of fornication and of homosexuality and other sexual perversion; our programming of self-indulgence above social and familial concerns—all represent a quantum leap in moral deterioration, a leap more awesome than even the supposed qualitative gulf between conventional weapons and nuclear missiles. Our nation has all but tripped the worst ratings on God's Richter scale of fully deserved moral judgment.

It troubles me that some of my theological colleagues view such judgments on sexual vice as but a prudish and secondary preoccupation; they prefer, as they say, to gauge national well-being by our sensitivity to minorities and to poverty. I carry no flag for discrimination or for destitution, and readily acknowledge the importance of structural changes in society. But altered social conditions do not necessarily advance social justice. Insightful cultural concern, on the other hand, will reflect the New Testament's strong indictment of sexual infidelity and will offer a spiritual alternative to ethical emptiness.

A Strangling Humanism

When judgment falls, it will be only a matter of academic debate whether it was the disunity of professing Christians, as ecumenists think, that frustrated the emergence of "the great world church," or whether it was the doctrinal compromises of ecumenical pluralists or the shortsighted squabbling of evangelical independents that spurred the breakdown of Western technological civilization. The final denouement will reflect, no doubt, not only the spirited rebellion of an unrepentant world order and the overruling providence of God, but also both evangelical and ecumenical causal factors. In any case, Asian, African, and eastern European Christians are more prepared for suffering than are Western Christians. Will the Son of Man, when he comes, find faith in our crumbling penthouses and condominiums?

It seems to me that despite its priority for sociopolitical change, organized Protestantism shows little strength for stemming the secular tide. It ineffectively confronts the strangling humanism that permeates university learning and that shortchanges generations of young people. It powerlessly contests the mass media, particularly television, whose ideal image of humanity and portrayal of life-styles depict Christian claims as obscurantist and archaic. By defecting from revealed truths and fixed ethical principles, neo-Protestantism weakens its mediating proposals; to compensate for a lack of intellectual and moral suasion it readily aspires to political power. The conflicting claims of the Mediator and the secular media, of the Archon and of academe, seem to me to represent decisive alternatives in the battle for public perception of the right and the good throughout the eighties.

We should commend the electronic church for its venturesome outreach to parched multitudes thirsting for what activists readily overlook in their assault on social structures—namely, a personal faith. But much television religion is too experience-centered, too doctrinally thin, to provide an adequate alternative to modern religious and moral confusion. Yet critics of the charismatic movement all too easily forget that the spiritually reborn often naively accept all the marginal trappings attaching to their first discovery of the crucified and risen Redeemer. It is true, nonetheless, that charismatic religion may indeed become a catchall that shelters rival spiritual authorities and requires no specifically Christian profession whatever.

A Cognitive Vacuum

The dull theological edge of American Christianity desperately needs sharpening. No literate society can afford to postpone cognitive considerations. Why Christ and not Buddha? Why Christianity and not Hare Krishna? Why biblical theism and not process philosophy? Why the Gospel and not amphetamines? Half-generation novelties in theology, I am persuaded, offer no adequate reply.

Yo-yo theology—that is, perpetually restructured belief—is less my forte than Yahweh theology, the "faith once-for-all delivered." Neither an evening with Bultmann in a Wiesbaden *Weinhaus* nor dinner with Tillich when he gave the Gifford Lectures in Aberdeen, nor that long walk with Brunner through the streets of Zurich, nor periodic chats with Barth in his Basel home shook my conviction that scriptural theism holds a logic absent from recent modern theology. In the writings of the bright-flashing contemporary stars, including the more angry apostles of revolution theology, I find an unfilled cognitive vacuum, one that leaves the mind merely a mood ahead of those skeptical critics intent on killing the Almighty.

It was not, to be sure, the logic of Christian theism that specially spurred me to Christian decision as a young newspaper reporter and editor, although any conviction of its illogic would have turned me away. Nor had I come to Christ, as have many others, by family inheritance or by churchly absorption. What piqued my curiosity was the inviting prospect, dangled by a university graduate, of what Jesus Christ can do for one who fully trusts him. Across the years, I learned, however, that although Jesus Christ holds fast his own, one cannot confidently hold fast what Christ does unless one also embraces truth along with mercy and righteousness. The credibility of the Judeo-Christian revelation is what precludes reducing Christ to simply one option among many.

A decade ago, I thought that late twentieth century America might be on the move, however hesitantly, toward a theological renaissance. Even if Barth, Bultmann, and Tillich, beyond their notable impact on seminaries, had little influence on the temper of the universities and on the mood of the churches, might not evangelical Christianity, I wondered, break out of its evangelistic halter? Might not evangelicals who were beginning to wrestle with sociopolitical concerns also take theology more seriously?

At present, I see too little prospect of that. Instead of emphasizing the universal truth-claim exerted by the Bible upon the mind and conscience of all humankind, one spokesperson after another fulminates against evangelical "rationalism" and retreats to personal commitment. The notion of comprehensive culture-conditioning is met concessively rather than critically. The prevalent rejection of an objectively authoritative Scripture is countered by irresponsible polemic; instead of finding a Communist under every bed, it charts an enemy list within every evangelical enterprise. Where is the comprehensive sense of a mighty armory of revealed truth that calls to council the whole arena of modern learning?

Equating Justice with Socialism

Meanwhile, many ecumenically oriented seminaries, titillated by what is novel, and seemingly unable to learn from history, baptize anything revolutionary as the wave of the future. Neo-Protestant giants of the recent past, all but forgotten on much ecumenical turf, are now getting a more deferential, if belated, hearing on concessive evangelical campuses. Nonevangelicals are turning anew to the social gospel which equates biblical justice with socialism, sometimes reconstituting it as a "theology of hope" promoted by protest and pressure, and seeking allies among evangelical *Sojourners*. They project salvific universalism with new passion, emphasize ethical preaching more than theological consensus, reach for hermeneutical methods that confer biblical legitimacy on culture-oriented options; they consider doctrinal pluralism an enrichment that might foster a revival of COCU and perchance some link with Roman Catholicism.

All this adds up, as I see it, to little more than "whistling in the dark." The penetrating question that hangs over the ecumenical churches is not what form their global union might take, but whether denominations losing as many as a million members a year or making few adult converts will survive the twentieth century.

I remain unpersuaded that any theological movement can dramatically affect the course of the world while its own leaders undermine the integrity of its charter documents, or while its spokespersons domestically exhaust all their energies in internal defense of those documents. The Bible stands impressively unshaken by the fury of destructive critics, while the nonbelieving world, itself marked for destruction, urgently needs to hear its singular message of salvation.

Lost Opportunities

While 40 million evangelical Protestants in the United States have immense resources to implement this Christian world task, they too often fritter away opportunities for joint endeavor, or expect to achieve every goal through too few and too limited programs. The besetting weakness of evangelicals is their lack of a comprehensive and coordinated strategy that welds intellectual, evangelistic, and ethical resources into effective cooperation. This lack condemns them to a mainly reactionary course and a commentary role on the initiatives of nonevangelicals. The significant proportion of evangelicals within the ecumenically organized denominations has not—even if some still hope to do so—countered the drift to theological pluralism, to missionary and evangelistic retrenchment, to social-action priorities, to debatable hierarchical commitments that some aroused church members and many of the clergy resent.

What do the well-attended evangelical churches portend for the future? What will be the impact of their burgeoning colleges marked by life-changing vitality and moral earnestness? What of the vocal church memberships that now increasingly demand a voice in public affairs?

During the 1960s, I somewhat romanced the posibility that a vast evangelical alliance might arise in the United States to coordinate effectively a national impact in evangelism, education, publication, and sociopolitical action. Such an alliance is not the same thing as a new denomination. Quite apart from the question of its desirability, the remote possibility of such a national evangelical alliance was both shaped and lost, it seems to me, by evangelist Billy Graham. Penetrating the so-called main-line denominations with an evangelical rallying point, the Graham crusades reached far beyond the orbit of the National Association of Evangelicals. As the tide of enthusiasm for pluralistic ecumenism began to ebb, the prospect emerged for a mighty evangelical movement that transcended secondary denominational distinctions; it held in promise a transdenominational link involving Southern Baptists, the National Association of Evangelicals, Missouri Synod Lutherans, perhaps some associates of the American Council of Churches, and large numbers of disaffected evangelicals in ecumenically affiliated churches whom the NAE seemed unable to attract. *Christianity Today* became during my editorship (1956–68) an intellectual fulcrum for these overlapping evangelical concerns.

Graham is himself a Southern Baptist. Although he had the personal magnetism to rally and garner an umbrella alliance, he hesitated to do so. For his crusades, he sought the fullest possible ecumenical backing, even if it often came grudgingly. To call for an evangelicval countermovement that might penetrate ecumenical ranks would have eroded ecumenical support for the crusades. Graham was sitmultaneously under NAE pressures to extend that organization's paraecumenical opportunities. By the early 1970s, the prospect of a massive evangelical alliance seemed annually more remote, and by mid-decade it was gone.

Obstacles arose not simply because of denominational differences but also because of rival goals. Instead of uniting on something feasible, evangelicals too often backed away from the best opinion only to support nothing.

Prospects for a national evangelical university to be located in the suburban New York area faltered in the sixties when some conferees pushed for a new Presbyterian seminary, others for a Bible college, still others for reinforcement of Wheaton as an already existing liberal arts college. Graham's colleagues held that the evangelist should be personally rewarded with the presidency because of his unique access to necessary sources of endowment, but then opposed a university since administrative responsibilities would curtail evangelistic priorities.

New Movements to the Fore

In the seventies *Christianity Today* appealed more to lay readers and moved noticeably toward evangelical independency. The magazine gave only token support to Key '73, whose stimulus had come from an earlier editorial ("Somehow Let's Get Together"). It viewed evangelical social action with high reservation, although the editor publicly indicated support of Nixon's candidacy. Then, at the very time national newsmagazines spoke of "the year of the evangelical," *Christianity Today* turned more inward than outward by channeling all theological issues into the inerrancy debate. The present staff strives to redress these misjudgments.

Many evangelical subgroups representing special interests stepped into this vacuum of missed evangelical opportunity. Magazines like *Sojourners,* the *Other Side,* and the *Reformed Journal* took anti-Establishment positions; divergent Calvinistic and Arminian groups sought a revitalized influence; evangelical social-action groups arose with varying emphases. Additional movements came to the fore: World Vision's spectacular globe ministry of evangelical humanitarianism; the charismatic phenomenon; the flourishing electronic church; the new core of Roman Catholic evangelicals; the Fuller Theological Seminary's proecumenical stance and alignment with critical views of the Bible; ecumenical alliances by left-wing evangelicals; politically right-wing groups like Moral Majority.

Establishment evangelicalism was reinforced by the Billy Graham Center's location at Wheaton College, by *Christianity Today's* removal from Washington, D.C., to Chicago suburbs where evangelical independency has deep roots, and by formation of the International Council on Biblical Inerrancy.

Numerous crosscurrents now vex almost every effort at comprehensive evangelical liaison. At present, no single leader or agency has the respect, magnetism, or platform to summon all divergent elements to conference. Evangelical differences increasingly pose an identity crisis.

Intellectual Awakening

For all that, the strength of evangelical Christianity lies in its confident vision of the supernatural, its emphasis on revealed truths and divine commandments, its evangelistic energy and life-transforming power. That strength is all the more evident at a time when the most prestigious universities, the most influential media, and even many theologians lack any sure grip on these realities. Yet American evangelicalism is not as strong as its proponents think; it appears stronger than it is because of the disarray of ecumenical and of Catholic Christianity, as well as the ethical relativity and personal meaninglessness of secular life.

Noteworthy signs of evangelical intellectual awakening are in the wind, however. Within the American Philosophical Association, a Society of Christian Philosophers has emerged with impressive evangelical participation. Hundreds of evangelical scholars are completing specialized doctorates to prepare for teaching careers. The Institute for Advanced Christian Studies is sponsoring an important series of college textbooks on Christianity and modern intellectual concerns. Tens of thousands of university students have made evangelical commitments despite the counterthrust of radically secular humanism. From these young intellectuals will come a literate clergy and qualified academics to help realign liberal-arts learning in quest for the whole truth.

Not only has Protestant ecumenism exerted little theistic impact upon the academic and media worlds, but its insistent demand for altered social structures has achieved few decisive changes. Many Christians find both major political parties objectionably laden with humanist perspectives.

As the author of *The Uneasy Conscience of Modern Fundamentalism* (1947), I can only welcome the evangelical return to public involvement. Even if one regrets the neglect or absence of a comprehensive agenda and the pursuit, instead, of single-issue and single-candidate concerns, and regrets even more the lack of a governing political philosophy, the times and issues are such that open debate must be welcomed on as broad a platform as possible.

My mind-shifts during the past decade include a deepening conviction that justice is not self-defining and that divergent definitions of justice now plunge the modern world anew into a "struggle between the gods." I am convinced that only with great agony, and in view of the shoddy track record of recreant predatory powers, should the nation commit itself to ever more staggering military expenditures. Inflation may now be irreversible, a specter spawned by political leaders whom we entrusted to watch the storehouse. It may be also that Western middle-class affluence will soon be recognized not as the universal ideal but as a remarkable exception in human history, one bearing great stewardship opportunities and responsibilities for worldwide extension of the Gospel and for helping the underprivileged to help themselves.

Ten years ago, I put less emphasis on the requisite indictment of unjust structures. I remain less confident than social activists that any of us will achieve ideal alternatives, or even better structures. History beset by human perversity will find ideal alternatives only when the Messiah ushers in the new heaven and new earth. We must nonetheless try, guarding all the while against prejudicial and propagandistic notions of what is "better." To truncate the Christian mission simply to the changing of social structures profoundly misunderstands the biblical view of human nature and divine redemption. Yet we also truncate the Gospel if we limit or circumvent the expectation that divine deliverance will extend "far as the curse is found."

Christ's sinless life and his Resurrection as the Crucified One carry assurance of his victory over all sin's powers, including injustice and exploitation. To proclaim the criteria by which the Coming King will judge persons and nations, to exemplify those standards in the church as the new society, and to work for their recognition by the world—these are irreducible aspects of the Christian summons to the forgiveness of sins and new life, and to the lordship of the risen and returning King.

Revelation and Culture

The key intellectual issue for the eighties, as I see it, will still be the persistent problem of authority. It will concern especially the problem of hermeneutics, and centrally the question of revelation and culture. Those who argue that revelation is enculturated will be unable to exempt their own pontifications. Christianity's true immortals will insist that God addresses the truth of revelation objectively to all humans of whatever diverse cultures.

God, who has an eye on the poor, and perhaps specially on us twentieth-century theologians, in his infinite wisdom inscribed the Decalogue on tablets of stone (Dt. 4:13, 10:4) and spoke (Num. 22:28 ff.) by Balaam's ass. God's spokesmen may be confused, but the ass knows his master's manger (Is. 1:3); stones no less than scrolls will praise God's transcendent revelation (Lk. 19:40) when Christ's professing disciples are tongue-tied.

CHAPTER SIX

Roman Catholic Theology

Leslie Dewart

In the mid-1960s, Leslie Dewart proposed theological renewal through the "dehellenization of dogma" and the discernment of faith as the transcendent dimension in human experience. This selection is taken from his The Future of Belief: Theism in a World Come of Age. *New York: Herder and Herder, 1966, pp. 173–75, 180, 185–90, 191–94.*

The Being and Existence of God

The Christian theism of the future might not conceive God as *a being.* I place the stress not merely on the indeterminate article *a* but also on the substantive *being.* In Scholastic philosophy, God is not conceived as *a* being, but he is nevertheless conceived as *being (ens).* We might eventually go beyond this as well, if the methodological principle which may be operative in our future concept of God should transcend that which in Greek and, later, in Christian thought has always been at work. I refer again to the *metaphysical* method which rests on Parmenides' postulate of the convertibility of being and intelligibility. If reality is not assumed to be constituted by intelligibility—or by any (possible or actual) relation to mind—reality can no longer be identified with that-which-is (which is the usual meaning of *being, ens*). To be sure, reality will still be as a matter of fact intelligible. But its intelligibility will now be a matter of *fact,* not of *necessity.* Being is intelligible, but not *as such.* Things can be understood, and can be conceived as being, because if they in fact exist they will also have a history—and this history makes them relatable to mind. Essences, therefore, what things are, are always created, whether created by another or self-created (in the case of consciousness).

Thus, man is most truly a being, because he is present to himself as an object. Transcending the subjectivity of mere objects and the objectivity of mere subjects, he understands himself as being. His transcendence, his spirituality, consists in being conscious and thus being able to be whatever he makes himself to be.[1] On the other hand, the open background against which he becomes conscious of transcendence and which is grasped in that empirical attitude which permits faith to emerge, is precisely that which is beyond man, beyond transcendence, and therefore beyond being. In Christian language, this is called the uncreatedness of God. Well, then, the Christian must believe that God is uncreated. God cannot be created, whether by another or by himself. He should therefore not be conceived as being. . . .

The proposition that "God cannot be said to exist" can be properly and literally understood by the Christian believer in God, on the grounds that *to exist* (in the literal sense of the term, *to arise out of, to emerge*), is proper to a being, that is, to that which is created or creates itself and is, therefore, a thing (*res*), a that-which-has-essence. If God is not a *res* and if he has no essence, then he does not exist. To attribute existence to God is the most extreme form of anthropomorphism. This anthropomorphism Christian philosophy has had to indulge only because of the inability of Hellenic metaphysical thinking to discern *reality* except in *ens,* that-which-is. To be sure, the Christian experience of God *can* be cast in the concept of being. It can also be cast, however, in the concept of

1. I stipulate the latter because in the philosophy of Sartre and certain other existentialists there is a confusion between the *neutrality* of being, as it were, with relation to mind (I mean, the mere *nonmental* character of reality as such), and its supposed *absurdity*. In this confusion, we find the last refuge of the Parmenidean principle of mind-being equivalence. Sartre's transcendence of realism-idealism is less radical than he imagines. To understand reality as absurd is to understand it as intrinsically related to mind (albeit by a relation of mutual exclusion).

reality, as the presence of that which (though not itself being) manifests itself in and through being, that-which-is. That-which-exists is *as such a* manifestation of God. But it is not God himself. . . .

The Personality of God

Christian theism might in the future not conceive God as a person—or indeed as a Trinity of persons. I have already alluded to the reason why, namely, the conception of personality with intrinsic reference to the human mode of experience and existence: "Personality is not to be conceived of apart from the act by which it creates itself." Self is that which is conscious, that which can signify itself to its-self. But if a self is going to make itself into a self, if it is going to subjectify itself, it must objectify. It must objectify indeed both the world and itself. Thus, to be a subject is to be an object for oneself. Conversely, the possibility of becoming an object for oneself is what defines subjectivity, and consciousness is the process by which subjectivity comes (through objectification) into being. Now, we could hardly suppose that the ultimate reality becomes conscious and objectifies the world. This would be a regression to Hegel's evolutionary pantheism. And the substance of Hegel's doctrine, for all it owes to Scholasticism, is no more compatible with the Christian tradition than with the philosophical advances that have taken place after him.

The concept of person remains, of course, metaphorically adequate for theism. Personality has been accorded to God as long as the concept has taken its place in a philosophy for which it was "what is most perfect in all nature." In our contemporary understanding of personality, however, this is no longer true. Though it remains in a sense the principal perfection of being and existence, personality is no longer aptly predicated of God partly because, as we realize the utter transcendence of the immanent Christian God, we no longer find it fitting or truly fair to the nature of God to preoccupy ourselves with granting to God *per viam remotionis et supereminentiae* the infinite degree of the creaturely perfections. Moreover, personality is no longer apt to signify any perfection transcending man, because we no longer understand personality in relation to nature, since we do not understand being as a hierarchy of perfection and reality. It would make less sense to say that God is a superpersonal being than to say that animals are infrapersonal beings—for man has a historical-genetic relation to animals that he does not have to God. (I assume here, of course, that man has evolved from the animal, but that being, though created, has not evolved from God.) It would be rather like saying that nothingness is an infraperson. The statement is no doubt logically true; but it is scarcely significant.

Behind this is the fact that the very approach of the contemporary mind to an understanding of every reality, including personality, is at variance with the Hellenic. The ultimate reason why God was fittingly conceived as a suprarational person is the same as the reason why he was fittingly conceived as the superbeing: that for the Hellenic mind to understand any given kind of being was to find its proper place in a hierarchial scheme of being which ran from the highest to the lowest. Today we do not understand man as a rational animal—because we do not understand him as an animal to begin with. And we do not understand animals as sentient living beings for the same reason that we do not understand living beings in relation to the elementary substances totally immersed in the potency of prime matter. A person, thus, is not what is at the top of nature's organizational chart, it is just what is most immediately and directly understood. (This is why contemporary humanism asserts human values as a matter of *fact* and does not *super*impose them upon human existence as an additional requirement over and above the requirement to be.)

Moreover, personality is the proper perfection of being, consciousness, and experience at their *present* historical stage of evolution. Now, the contemporary mind does not conceive man as a body (organized and potentially having life) to which consciousness is somehow united. Consciousness is the constituent of man; it is equivalent to life and existence. It is intrinsically valuable, thus, in the same way as life and existence are valuable, that is, as an empirically verifiable matter of fact. It is, of course, what is most valuable to man: if experiential existence goes, then, as it were, all goes. And it is the highest human value in a yet deeper sense: personal conscious existence is all that we have (of ourselves) in order to *create ourselves* in time. This means that personality is the summit of man's actuality, but hardly the summit he hopes to achieve. That is evidently yet to come. For man's selfhood is what makes him transcendent. Man is the being who is sufficiently perfect to tend to transcend personality. A person is a being who knows enough to want to go beyond himself. At this point, one should be referred to Teilhard de Chardin's speculations in *The Future of Man.* But the idea is scarcely new: in the most ancient Christian tradition, too, man's ultimate achievement is not found in the circumscription of his personality. It is found, on the contrary, in its communication and expansion beyond itself into another self, indeed, into a community of selves. The ultimate hope of the Christian faith is not that man should achieve *within himself* the act of beholding God, a vision close enough to constitute an intimate union with God; it is to achieve an intimate union with every person through a union with God *in God himself;* rather, to achieve a going-out-of-one-self-into-God, an out-going that is real enough to constitute a *self*-transformation. It is an *ek-stasis* and a *theosis,* a participation in the inner self-communication of God, that is, in his "Trinity." Personality, thus, is what we start from, not what we aspire to, namely, God.

But if God is, though not himself a person, what persons (and only persons) aspire to, it follows that man's relations to God are essentially personal. Likewise, God's relations with man are personal, for *we* are persons. To say that God is not personal, but that to which persons aspire, does not reduce God to a sort of pervasive impersonal force, like gravitation. If we believe in God, we believe in the benevolence and friendship shown to persons *as such* by the openness of existence. We believe, for instance, that our own existence is a personal boon and an undeserved personal gift. Yet, the personalism of the divine-human relations might be better understood if we did not conceive the mechanics of those relations as proceeding on God's side (as they do on our own) from one—least of all from three—centers of objectification (which is the only thing that we can meaningfully and empirically call a self).

The typical experience of the disaffiliated religious person today is that "God could not possibly be a person. He must be some kind of cosmic force." This is surely a naive view to the degree that it implies that God is less than man. But this is not all that this common expression connotes. It also means that God is, rather than a center of being to which we are drawn, an expansive force which impels persons to go out from and beyond themselves. This expression represents an effort, born of understandable impatience, to transcend the primitive God-being, God-object, and God-person of absolute theism. The truth that that crude expression so mistakenly conceives may yet be redeemed in the future by Christian theism.

The Omnipotence of God

Christian theism may in the future deal with the so-called divine attributes in much the same way as with God's being, existence, essence, and personality. It is not enough to stress, as with Scholasticism, that God does not really *have* attributes (because he *is* his attributes), if we immediately proceed to conceive God as having (or, for that matter, as being) omnipotence, eternity, immateriality, infinity, immutability, omniscience, etc. In the last analysis, what matters is the attributes themselves. I cannot within the limited scope of this essay speculate on how each of these attributes might be reconceptualized by Christian theism. I will consider briefly only the two which we commonly tend to think of as principal and typical, namely, omnipotence and eternity.

The question we might ask ourselves concerning God's omnipotence is not this: What are the possibilities open to a being, God, (who, having the plenitude of being, lacks by definition all limitations), for acting *upon* other beings, that is, nature? The question is rather: What can (and what, if anything, cannot) happen, once God and man enter into personal relations. The problem is not how to explain a metaphysical property of God which would have implications for us, but how to understand the reciprocal relations between man and God and, in particular, how mutual power enters into the relationship. The problem has to do, as it were, with the politics of man and God. . . . What the Christian concept of God may perhaps stress in the future is not that, with the exception of self-contradictions, things are possible to God which are impossible to nature. It may instead foster the idea that, as the common phrase puts it, "wonders will never cease." And this, for two reasons. The first is that nature—and therefore what is naturally possible—should no longer be understood as it was by the Greek and the medieval mind. If a Christian looks at the world and understands nature through Hellenic eyes, he will find it necessary to assert the omnipotence of God *over* and *against* nature. For in this view of nature, either God is necessitated by it, or it is subject to God. But in the contemporary experience, nature is no longer understood as the principle which necessitates from within the operations of beings, and therefore makes them resist violence from without. We do not see nature as the source of independence and self-sufficiency which it was for Aristotle. Therefore, God does not have power *over* nature. The reason is that nature does not as such resist him.

The same idea might be put paradoxically: the God who is not being but who is present to being is much more powerful than if he were merely the omnipotent being. For instead of holding back a power reserve with which he could, whenever necessary, bend nature's refractory will, God communicates his power to nature, and so creates a nature that is of itself compliant with his will. But even this formula is grossly inadequate. It speaks of God's *will* and nature's *compliance,* which connote opposed finalities. Let us rather say that nature does not have its own natural finalities independently of God's. For being as such is not constituted by self-necessity, finality, or the independence of self-containment. It is essentially contingent. I mean, the contingency of nature is not merely that of its existence, but also that of its essence. And this essential and existential contingency of that-which-is is more vividly experienced today, even by the common man, than in any previous age. Nature is no longer the essentially unmiraculous, the intrinsically translucent to mind, the crystal-clear inflexible inner *nomos* of things which rules natural beings with the same blind fury with which *nemesis* rules human affairs. It is true, therefore, that "no word shall be impossible with God." What may not be true is that the impossible is that which nature forbids.

The second reason why the idea of God's omnipotence may be transcended in the future is that the Christian conception of God might stress a point the moral and practical implications of which have been somewhat neglected: that the reality of God, implying the real possibility of a world totally open to God, implies therefore a world totally open to *future creation by man.* The case is not that God can do the impossible (that is, that God has power to do that which nature cannot do), but that for God all things are possible— and that therefore with God all things are possible to man. In God, nature can do *anything*. Instead of God's omnipotence, the power to overrule nature, it might be more adequate to think of the radical openness of history—an openness which not even man's freedom can annihilate—as manifesting the true extent of the Word that is possible with God. The moral implication of this is that once it no longer has "God's omnipotence" to fall back on, our Christian conscience may be awakened to feel its adult responsibilities for taking the full initiative in "restoring all things in Christ" and for exercising its creative ingenuity in order to determine how this should be done. For we will then no longer expect miracles to happen (least of all the miracle of the glorious return of the Christ upon a cloud), and we will instead believe that, unless we make it be, the Kingdom of God shall never come.

Gregory Baum

In the late 1960s, Gregory Baum articulated a concept of faith rooted in his phenomenological approach to theology which entailed an examination of religious elements in ordinary experience and a conscious rejection of the unexperiencable "extrinsicist" forms of theology. God is the more than human in human life. This selection is taken from his Man Becoming. God in Secular Experience. *New York: The Seabury Press, 1970, pp. 170-73, 181-82, 184-86, 190-97, 282-85.*

First Principle of Reinterpretation

Let us now formulate the first principle for reinterpreting the doctrine of God. The focus of the Gospel, we have said, proclaims that God is redemptively present in human life. From this it follows that there is no human standpoint from which God is simply man's over-against. God is involved in man's coming-to-be. It is impossible to think of myself and other men over here, and then of God, the supreme being, as over against us. This is impossible because I and these others have come to be who we are through a process of dialogue and sharing in which God is redemptively involved. Since God's Word is constitutive of who we are as men, it is impossible to conceptualize God as a being, even as a supreme being, facing us. In other words, since God has entered into the definition of man, it would be an error to think of God as a being apart from man and superior to him. We formulate, therefore, as the first principle of reinterpretation that there is no human standpoint from which God is simply man's over-against.

This principle is obviously influenced by a particular view of man. But so is the new focus of the Gospel. What has taken place in the present culture is the transition from a static to a more dynamic understanding of man. If man is a finished substance, if his nature is fully determined at birth, then it does not make sense to speak of God's redemptive presence in man's becoming man. If man is such a substance, then God must be conceived of as extrinsic to him, then there *is* a human standpoint from which God is simply man's over-against. But if man is not a finished substance, if man comes to be in a complex process of dialogue and sharing in which the whole human community is involved, then it is not necessary to think of God as extrinsic to man. Again, if man is a finished reality, it is vague and indeterminate to speak of God's presence to him. Once man is defined simply in terms of his own powers and resources, God becomes an outsider and it is impossible ever to get him back in again. But if man comes to be in a process of dialogue and sharing, then he is an historical, open-ended being in which, by definition, more than he himself is involved. If man comes to be in a process of listening and responding, in which his own freedom is creatively engaged, then it is possible to see how God, summoning and freeing man, enters into the very constitution of who man is and will be.... This dynamic understanding of human life is implicit in the new Spirit-created experience of the Gospel and hence in the doctrinal development of refocusing the Gospel. It is equally implicit in the first principle of reinterpreting the doctrine of God.

There is no hint of pantheism in this first principle. To say that God has entered the definition of man is not to deny the human reality and to suggest that God is everything and man and his world are nothing. Again, if man were conceived statically as a substance whose growth is an unfolding according to laws implicit in his nature, then to deny that God is man's over-against would imply that the substance of man itself is divine. In this context, the denial that God may be conceived of as a being extrinsic to man would have pantheistic overtones. In this context, the assertion that God is constitutive of human life would be a denial of the human reality altogether. But if man is not a closed substance but comes to be in a process of dialogue and sharing, then it is possible to affirm at one and the same time that man is truly man and that God is constitutive of his personal being.

This first principle, we note, is not altogether untraditional. Theologians have always insisted that God is both transcendent and immanent to his creatures. They have always realized that any statement made about God as perfect being different from man or as supreme being superior to man has to be qualified by a corresponding statement indicating that in some way this God also engulfs or includes man. After affirming the being of God over against man, theologians always admitted that this being of God in some way pervades man and his world. By insisting that God is infinite, theologians suggested that in a certain sense there can be no being over against him. God is all in all. To say that I am here and that over against me there is the supreme being called God implies a contradiction. Why? Because if I am here and God is conceived of simply as facing me, then he is limited by me, then he is finite and by definition not God at all. There is no limit to God's presence. For this reason, any statement affirming God as man's spiritual over-against must be corrected by a statement indicating that in some sense this God is *not* man's over-against but is present in man and includes him in his own mystery. While theologians have always taught God's immanence and even admitted the special way in which man is "a part of God," they have usually done so in peripheral observations without permitting this teaching to modify their entire doctrine of God. Only too often were theologians willing to speak of God as a reality extrinsic to man and his world. Our first principle, then, gives central importance to a traditional insight that has played only a marginal role in theological reflection. . . .

The Second Principle of Reinterpretation

The preceding remarks lead us to the second principle of reinterpretation. We propose that every sentence about God can be translated into a declaration about human life.

This principle sounds startling at first. To some readers it may seem that we seek to reduce the divine to the human. They may be reminded of Feuerbach and the philosophers after him who regarded religion as the projection of man's highest ideals and loftiest sentiments into religious symbolism. According to these philosophers, religion is the symbolic celebration of what is marvelous, healing, and elevating in human life. But religion is not divine. Religion may be useful and even important, for man is in need of projecting his deepest aspirations into symbols and of being transformed by celebrating these symbols in community, but—according to these philosophers—religion is not the living contact with a reality transcending man: there is no reality transcending man. This, obviously, is not our position.

We propose, nonetheless, that every sentence about God can be translated into a declaration about human life. Since God is present in human life not through a message sent across a distance nor by gifts offered from afar but by his own Word and his own Spirit, his presence to human life is he as he is in himself. The Word of God to man is God himself. The gift of God to man is God himself. This is the Good News proclaimed by Jesus Christ. For this reason, we may not suppose that behind God's presence in history there is a God existing in himself. No, the Good News tells us that God's presence to human life *is* God as he is in himself. From this it follows that as we speak about human life in all its dimensions, we are in fact also speaking about God. Since present in human history are not simply some effects of God but God as he is in himself, it should be possible to speak about this God by clarifying certain dimensions of human history. We insist, therefore, that every sentence about God as he is in himself is equivalent to a declaration about human life. . . . Let me apply this principle immediately to the statement that God exists. This sentence is about God as he is in himself. According to the first principle of reinterpretation, we may not understand this sentence as referring to a being different from man and superior to him. In the light of the new focus of the Gospel, the question "Does God exist?" or the statement "There is a God" does not deal with a being having a supposed existence independently of man. Man may question the being of a planet or make a statement that a star exists. But since God had entered the definition of man, man cannot entertain a question or utter a statement that makes him a spectator in regard to God. According to our second principle, the statement "God exists" must be translated into a declaration about human life. "God exists" means that man is always more than man. It means that wherever people are, something new happens. *It means that man is alive by a principle that transcends him, over which he has no power, which summons him to surpass himself and frees him to be creative.* The sentence "God exists" is here translated into a declaration about human life. Man's tomorrow will be a new day. "God exists" means that man's future will not simply be determined by causes in the present, nor is his future wholly vulnerable to the malice and the blindness that mark his actions today: the new will be created. "God exists" means that tomorrow will be different from today.

This example illustrates why we have said that every sentence about God can be translated into a *declaration* about human life. The doctrine of God proclaims a mystery at work in human history, and hence acknowledging it implies an option and occurs in faith. The doctrine of God is not a description of a supreme being called God. Man can have no observer knowledge of God. The doctrine of God is Good News. It illuminates the human situation. It declares unto man the meaning and destiny of his life. . . .

God Is Personal

Let us now apply our principles of reinterpretation to the doctrine that God is personal. It is obvious, after the preceding pages, that God may not be thought of as a person or even as three persons over against men. We cannot look at the people in the room and say "Here we are" and then add "There is also God," for the true God is so present to the community of men and its coming-to-be that there is no standpoint from which he is simply their over-against. What, then, do we mean when we call God personal or insist against those who wish to make God some kind of life-force that he is a person?

Before applying our principles of reinterpretation, we must reflect for a moment on what the word *person* has come to mean today. By person, we usually understand a historical being, that is, a being that not only comes to be in history but that comes to be through a process in which his own freedom is involved. A person is not a determined being, defined as it were by its nature. A person comes to be, in part at least, through his own responses to reality. If this is the meaning of person today, it is obvious that we cannot predicate it of God. For to suggest that God comes to be or that God is historical in the sense that he creates himself in a historical process goes counter to the entire biblical witness.

It is important, therefore, that we reinterpret the doctrine of God as person. That God is person means that man's relationship to the deepest dimension of his life is personal. Man is related to God not impersonally as the effect is to the cause or the waves to the stream, but personally as a listener to the one who speaks and as the recipient of gifts to the giver. Man's relationship to God cannot be reified, it cannot be reduced to categories that apply to the relationship of things. We have shown more than once that God is present in human life as summons evoking man's response and as gift freeing man to create his future. The deepest dimension of human life is not a blind life-force or a necessary, ever-expanding dynamism but a mystery of freely chosen self-disclosure which can only be spoken of in personal terms.

We sometimes meet people who say that they no longer believe in a personal God. They tell us that they still believe in a God, in a divine principle of life present everywhere yet never identical with history, but they deny that this principle is a person. The words they haltingly use to describe this principle are *force* or *power,* "something" rather than "someone." And yet as they speak it often becomes clear that they have no intention of claiming some kind of mechanical, quasi-physical relationship between men and the divine principle of life. They simply wish to deny the existence of God, the heavenly person distinct from history, looking at man from a distance and helping him occasionally. They use impersonal words such as *force* to deny that God is person in this sense, but they do not mean to suggest that man's relationship to God can be reified. I have repeatedly found that the university students who say that they believe in God as life-force are not rejecting the God of revelation, but rather seek to purify the language about God which suggests that he is a heavenly superperson.

To say that God is person, we repeat, is not a statement about a being, a supreme being called God, who has certain properties which according to some analogy resemble the personal structure of man. Calling God person does not communicate any kind of observer knowledge of God nor does it enable us to speak about his intellect and will as if these were categories describing a heavenly supernatural being. Even if at one time Christians liked to speak and think of God in this manner, we have seen throughout this study that to a growing number of Christians this conceptualization of the divine is becoming increasingly foreign and unassimilable. That God is person, according to our interpretation, means that man's relationship to the transcendent mystery present in his life is personal and can never be reified. Man's relationship to God is dialogical. Man listens and responds to him. To clarify this personal relationship further, we turn to the church's traditional doctrine of the Trinity.

That man's relationship to God is personal is revealed in the doctrine, testified in Scripture and defined by the church, that God is Father, Word, and Spirit. Let us interpret the traditional teaching according to the principles we have adopted. It should be possible to translate the doctrine of the Trinity into declarations about human life and show how, by believing the doctrine, man is initiated into a new self-awareness. In my study *Faith and Doctrine*, I have given a detailed description of the new consciousness which the divine self-communication as Father, Word, and Spirit creates in man. I shall summarize this description in the following pages.

Man finds himself facing the world. There are other people with their needs, there are the demands made on him by society, there is his body which sometimes bothers him as a faulty and painful vehicle of communication, there is his past which upsets him and will not let him go, and there is his future, as yet unknown to him, in which his dreams and aspirations may be realized or, more likely, frustrated. In this situation, man is called upon to decide his present. Often he is frightened; reality scares him. Can he really face it and deal with it courageously? In this human predicament, the Gospel proclaims that the reality which he is and which he faces, is, in its totality, not against him but for him. The ultimate ground of reality is love. The principle of the total reality man faces in himself and in the world is not hostile to him but on his side. It is Father. Since evil is such a powerful factor in human history and deeply affects our own life, is it very difficult to believe the Christian message that God is good? For many people, it is only because

Jesus has said so and has gone through so much suffering himself that they are able to trust this message. Despite the awful things that happen, man need not be afraid of life for—according to the Good News—the reality he encounters in himself and in others is, in its totality, grounded in a principle that is personal, that is love, that is Father.

What is this principle of reality? Does it refer to the origin of man or the genesis of the universe? When man had a static view of reality, to speak of its principle made him think of what happened at the beginning. ... Today, when man has adopted a dynamic view of reality and regards the world as still coming to be, the principle of reality makes him think of the end of the world-creating process. Since the world is still being constituted, the principle of reality is its destiny. To declare, therefore, that the principle of reality is for man, is love, is Father refers not so much to the origin of man and his world as it does to his marvelous destiny. We need not be afraid of the human reality because it is involved, gratuitously and beyond historical fulfillment or despair, in the never-ending and ever-to-be renewed process of divine humanization. To say that God is Father means, therefore, that the destiny of man, which is constitutive of his self-making, is a mystery of love.

"God is Father" declares that man is a being with a destiny, defined in terms of growth and communion. To believe that God is Father is to become aware of oneself not as stranger, not as an outsider or an alienated person, but as a son who belongs or a person appointed to a marvelous destiny, which he shares with the whole community. To believe that God is Father means to be able to say "we" in regard to all men.

According to the Good News, God is not only man's gracious destiny; he is also the call addressing man in his life. Wherever a man is, he is summoned to come to self-knowledge, to recognize the destructiveness in himself and his environment, to leave the paralyzing past behind and enter creatively into his destiny. Man need not fear that he will be surrounded by total silence. God is always Word. There is no trap, no prison, no predicament into which a man might fall where the call to new life would not be available to him. This declaration about human life translates the statement that God is Word. To believe that God is Word is to become aware of oneself or experience oneself, as a listener, as open-ended, as essentially unfinished, as still in the process of coming to be.

This Word, Christians believe, has become flesh in Christ. This Word, in dialogue with which every man comes to be, was wholly present in Christ. The divine summons, which in a provisional and conditional manner addresses all men and in response to which they come to be, was present in a definitive and unconditional manner in Jesus and constituted his being in an altogether unique fashion. While God discloses himself in people in a partial manner, he discloses himself totally and exhaustively in Jesus. Jesus is the Word of God.

According to the Good News, the deepest dimension of reality not only faces man as his gracious destiny (Father) and addresses man as the call to pass beyond himself (Word) but is also alive in the hearts of men as source of creativity and new life (Holy Spirit). The Gospel assures us that alive in man is a precious gift which is power unto new life, yet over which he has no power, which transcends him, and which gratuitously continues to create life out of death. To believe that God is Holy Spirit is to become aware of oneself, and to look upon others as open to the radically new that emerges out of one's inner life yet forever transcends one's own resources.

We have here restated the doctrine of the Trinity, the church's summary of the Christian message, as the Good News regarding human life. The doctrine of God is truth about human life. The doctrine that God is person brings out the personal character of man's relationship to him. God is not a superperson, not even three superpersons; he is in no way a being, however supreme, of which man can aspire to have a spectator knowledge. That God is person reveals that man is related to the deepest dimension of his life in a personal and never-to-be reified way, by listening, trusting, hoping, receiving gifts, being grateful, and worshiping. But God is not a person objectified as man's over-against.

Even though throughout this book we refer to God as "he," we acknowledge the ambiguity of this language. To be sure, God is not an "it." God is a "he" only in the sense that man's relationship to him is personal. We even have hesitations in regard to the beautiful expression of Martin Buber and Gabriel Marcel that God is man's eternal Thou present in the human thou's he encounters. While it is true that man often turns to God as a thou, or listens and responds to him as a thou, we hesitate to objectify this relationship by calling God a thou or the eternal Thou, unless we are willing to submit this expression to the same reinterpretation as the statement that God is person. The principles adopted in this chapter enable us to proclaim God as the Good News for human life without objectifying him in any way. . . .

Conclusion

The God immanent in human history radically transcends it. We have shown . . . that the reinterpretation of the doctrine of God does not involve us in a theological reductionism. We have not reduced the divine to a factor immanent in history and determined by it. God is not caught in the human dynamics. God is the more than human in human life. This "more than human" is his transcendence situated at the heart of his immanence. While God is wholly immanent to history—and there is no standpoint from which he is simply man's over-against—he can never be identified with any aspect of history. God is always different. God's presence in history is not dominated or exhausted by it. God rules history from within. God is always transcendent to human life as critique, as newness, as orientation.

The reinterpretation of the doctrine of God has enabled us to speak about the divine mystery in words drawn from ordinary day-to-day speech and in concepts taken from man's experience of his own history. The Blondelian shift, by rejecting extrinsicism, conceives of God as the transcendent mystery present in history. Without in any way abandoning or weakening divine transcendence, we have avoided any objectification of God. God is not a supreme being or a supreme person. The divine mystery revealed in the New Testament is a dimension of human life: God is present to human life as its orientation and its source of newness and expansion. The traditional doctrine of the Trinity has enabled us to discern an empirical basis for speaking of God's presence to man: God is present, as summons and gift, in the conversation and communion by which men enter into their humanity.

The principles of reinterpretation that we have adopted enable us to translate the Christian creed into ordinary secular language without mentioning the word *God.* As Karl Rahner has reminded us more than once, it was possible at one time to compose a Christian creed by beginning with God. At one time, everyone knew what this word refers to. Christians could express their faith to others by speaking about the divinity. But today, Rahner says, to begin the creed with a reference to God makes it impossible to communicate the church's faith to men of the present culture. People do not know any more what the word *God* refers to. Should it not be possible for the church to compose a creed which proclaims the Gospel of Christ and declares the divine redemption present in human life in ordinary secular language—and only then, on the basis of the preceding, explain what Christians mean by the word *God?* Since our principles of reinterpretation have enabled us to translate the traditional titles of God into declarations about human life, they could become the basis for writing a creed in modern language expressing the traditional Gospel once for all delivered to the apostles.

It is possible to proclaim the Gospel without mentioning God by name. The church's silence about God would enable Christians to overcome the objectification of God to which they have become accustomed and thus to remove the great obstacle for the Christian faith in the modern world. At the same time, the silence about God must be broken occasionally. Truth is always threatened in this life. It is possible for people to forget that the mystery at work in their history radically transcends it. It is possible for them to identify the success of their culture with the promised Kingdom or to assume that certain cultural values are the unqualified embodiment of the divine. Then the need arises to utter the divine name. Even though the divine reality revealed in Christ can be expressed in anthropological terms, this translation must never be exclusive. There will always be times when we can only speak about God by mentioning his name.

Divine revelation can be translated into anthropological terms. Karl Rahner, as we mentioned above, has brilliantly demonstrated that this assertion is not a theological reductionism but, rather, the clarification of the heart of the Gospel. God has revealed in Jesus Christ—the doctrine of the Incarnation—that his gift to man is himself. The Triune God has revealed himself in Jesus as present, as he is in himself, in the humanization of man. Human destiny is truly filled with the divine. God's presence of man is God himself. To call this a theological reductionism would be to deny the divinity of the man Jesus and the divinity of man's link with him. God has revealed himself as the destiny and the source of human life.

In our study, we have limited the translation of doctrine to human terms to what we have called salvational knowledge. The doctrine of God, we have said, is Good News. It creates faith in man and thus transforms his consciousness. The anthropological interpretations of the doctrine of God are, therefore, not factual statements about human life; they are, rather, declarations about the marvelous things that happen wherever people are. The doctrine of God can be translated into anthropological terms only to the extent that it is Good News.

We do not claim that this is the only approach to the problem of God. For beyond the salvational knowledge of faith there is the more exclusively intellectual knowledge of theology. It should be possible to approach the insider God with the methods and tools of philosophical reasoning. The more restrictive approach that we have adopted, however, has many advantages. It has enabled us to speak about God and his revelation in ordinary, largely nontechnical terms, to bypass many philosophical issues which, in our age, seem to divide rather than unite people, and to create a language about the divine that can be used in preaching and teaching to men with no special academic background. In our approach, the doctrine of God remains, strictly speaking, Good News. In Schillebeeckx's happy phrase, God is the Good News that humanity is possible.

Avery Dulles

Avery Dulles has contended that several basic models of the church have emerged in history depending on the cultural setting. This selection is taken from his Models of the Church. *Garden City, New York: Doubleday, 1974, pp. 179–92.*

The Evaluation of Models

In all the previous chapters we have been engaged in what Bernard Lonergan might call dialectic as distinct from doctrinal theology. We have been exploring the basic models of the church that have arisen in history as a result of the differing points of view or horizons of believers and theologians of different ages and cultures. Each of the models, self-evidently, has its own uses and limitations. We must now face the problem, to what extent are the models compatible or incompatible? Are the differences of horizon mutually exclusive or mutually complementary? Are all the models equally good, or are some superior to others? Are they an opaque screen that shuts off the reality of the church, or a transparent screen that permits us to grasp the church as it really is? If the latter, what really is the church? What is the best model?

The critique and choice of models depends, or should depend, on criteria. But here lies the rub. On reflection, it becomes apparent that most of the criteria presuppose or imply a choice of values. The values, in turn, presuppose a certain understanding of the realities of faith. If one stands committed to a given model, it is relatively easy to establish criteria by which that model is to be preferred to others. Each theologian's criteria therefore tend to buttress his own preferred models. Communication is impeded by the fact that the arguments in favor of one's own preferred model are generally circular: They presuppose the very point at issue.

Some examples will make this clearer. Persons drawn to the institutional model will show a particularly high regard for values such as conceptual clarity, respect for constituted authority, law and order. They reject other models, and perhaps especially the second, as being too vague, mystical, and subjective. Partisans of the communion model, on the other hand, find the institutional outlook too rationalistic, ecclesiocentric, and rigid. They label it triumphalist, juridicist, and clericalist. An analogous dispute arises between champions of the third and fourth models. Adherents of the sacramental ecclesiology, appealing to the principle of Incarnation, find the kerygmatic theologies too exclusively centered on the Word; whereas kerygmatic theologians find the sacramental model too complacent and insufficiently prophetic. Promoters of the servant model, in turn, denounce the other four as being too introspective and churchy.

In passing, one may note that the tensions here referred to are similar to those long recognized in comparative ecclesiology under rubrics such as priestly vs. prophetic, Catholic vs. Protestant, sacred vs. secular. But these dichotomies are too crude to do justice to the full spectrum of positions.

In any effort at evaluation, we must beware of the tendency of each contestant to polemicize from a standpoint within his own preferred position. To make any real progress, we must seek criteria that are acceptable to adherents of a number of different models. Seven such criteria (not all of them equally appealing to all members of all theological schools) come to mind:

1. *Basis in Scripture.* Nearly all Christians feel more comfortable if they can find a secure biblical basis for a doctrine they wish to defend—the clearer and more explicit the better.

2. *Basis in Christian tradition.* Not all Christians set the same value on tradition, but nearly all would agree that the testimony of Christian believers in the past in favor of a given doctrine is evidence in its favor. The more universal and constant the tradition, the more convincing it is.

3. *Capacity to give church members a sense of their corporate identity and mission.* Christian believers generally are convinced that they do have a special calling as Christians, and they turn to theology to clarify this. Theology has a practical function of supporting the church in its faith and mission.

4. *Tendency to foster the virtues and values generally admired by Christians.* By their total upbringing, Christians are inclined to prize faith, hope, disinterested love of God, sacrificial love of fellow men, honesty, humility, sorrow for sin, and the like. If they find that a doctrine or theological system sustains these values, they will be favorably inclined toward it; if it negates these values, they will suspect that the idea is erroneous.

5. *Correspondence with the religious experience of men today.* In recent years there has been a revolt against making either the Bible or tradition a decisive norm apart from the experience of believers themselves. Granted the tremendous cultural shifts that have been taking place, it is to be expected that men today will approach the Christian message from a new point of view. Some models, much honored in the past, may prove to be excessively bound up with the concerns and dominant images of a culture not our own.

6. *Theological fruitfulness*. As noted in our first chapter, theological revolutions, like scientific revolutions, occur when the paradigms previously in use are found to be inadequate for the solution of present problems, and when better paradigms come into view. One criterion for the selection of new paradigms is their ability to solve problems that proved intractable by appeal to the older models, or to synthesize doctrines that previously appeared to be unrelated.

7. *Fruitfulness in enabling church members to relate successfully to those outside their own group*—for example, to Christians of other traditions, to adherents of non-Christian religions, and to dedicated secular humanists.

To measure each of our five basic models by all seven of these criteria would at this point be wearisome. . . . In a summary way, it may be proposed that the first criterion gives good support to the community and kerygmatic models; the second criterion, to the community model (though modern Roman Catholic tradition favors the institutional as well); the third criterion, to the institutional and kerygmatic models; the fourth criterion, to the sacramental and servant models; the fifth criterion, to the community and servant models; the sixth criterion, to the sacramental model; and the seventh criterion, to the community and servant models.

This variety of results makes it apparent that certain types of persons will be spontaneously drawn to certain models. Church officials have a tendency to prefer the institutional model; ecumenists, the community model; speculative theologians, the sacramental model; preachers and biblical scholars, the kerygmatic model; and secular activists, the servant model.

Are we then to conclude with an agreement to disagree—with a sterile repetition of the maxim, *"chacun à son goût"*? This author's total life-experience prompts him to reject any such conclusion. He is convinced that to immure oneself behind a fixed theological position is humanly and spiritually disastrous. It is important at all costs to keep open the lines of communication between different theological schools and traditions.

Two general working principles may be invoked to support a reconciling approach. Neither of these principles is strictly demonstrable, but both of them seem to be favored by the accumulated experience of many good and wise persons. The first is that what any large group of Christian believers have confidently held over a considerable period of time should be accepted unless one has serious reasons for questioning it. Even if one comes to the conclusion that the tenet was false, one should at least make the effort to unveil the positive reason that made people accept error and thus to disclose the truth at the heart of the heresy.

The second working principle is the view of John Stuart Mill, which commended itself to F. D. Maurice and H. Richard Niebuhr, to the effect that men are more apt to be correct in what they affirm than in what they deny. "What we deny is generally something that lies outside our experience, and about which we can therefore say nothing."

On the basis of these two principles, we must presume that the basic assertions implied in each of our five ecclesiological types are valid. Each of them in my opinion brings out certain important and necessary points. The institutional model makes it clear that the church must be a structured community and that it must remain the kind of community Christ instituted. Such a community would have to include a pastoral office equipped with authority to preside over the worship of the community as such, to prescribe the limits of tolerable dissent, and to represent the community in an official way. The community model makes it evident that the church must be united to God by grace, and that in the strength of that grace its members must be lovingly united to one another. The sacramental model brings home the idea that the church must in its visible aspects—especially in its community prayer and worship—be a sign of the continuing vitality of the grace of Christ and of hope for the redemption that he promises. The kerygmatic model accentuates the necessity for the church to continue to herald the Gospel and to move men to put their faith in Jesus as Lord and Savior. The diaconal model points up the urgency of making the church contribute to the transformation of the secular life of man, and of impregnating human society as a whole with the values of the Kingdom of God.

On the other hand, it must be recognized that we cannot without qualification accept all five models, for they to some extent come into conflict with each other. They suggest different priorities and even lead to mutually antithetical assertions. Taken in isolation, each of the ecclesiological types could lead to serious imbalances and distortions. The institutional model, by itself, tends to become rigid, doctrinaire, and conformist; it could easily substitute the official church for God, and this would be a form of idolatry. As a remedy, the structures of the church must be seen as subordinate to its communal life and mission.

The second model, that of mystical communion, can arouse an unhealthy spirit of enthusiasm; in its search for religious experiences or warm, familial relationships, it could lead to false expectations and impossible demands, considering the vastness of the church, the many goals for which it must labor, and its remoteness from its eschatological goal. As a remedy, one must call for patience, faith, and a concern for the greater and more universal good.

The third model, the sacramental, could lead to a sterile aestheticism and to an almost narcissistic self-contemplation. As a remedy, attention must be called to the values of structures, community, and mission brought out in the other models.

The fourth model, the kerygmatic, runs the risk of falling into the exaggerations of biblicist and fundamentalistic sects. It tends to oversimplify the process of salvation, to advertise "cheap grace," to be satisfied with words and professions rather than to insist on deeds, especially in the social and public arena. As a remedy, one must stress the necessity of incarnating one's faith in life and action.

The fifth model, the diaconal, could easily give the impression that man's final salvation is to be found within history, and could lure the church into an uncritical acceptance of secular values, thus muting its distinctive witness to Christ and to its own heritage. As an antidote, one must insist on the provisional character of any good or evil experienced within history, and on the importance of looking always to Christ and to his Kingdom.

Granting the distinctive values of each of the five models and the undesirability of accepting any one model to the exclusion of the others, the question arises whether we ought not to look for some supermodel that combines the virtues of each of the five without suffering their limitations. Without asserting that the five models studied in this book are the only possible ones, I would be skeptical of the possibility of finding any one model that would be truly adequate; for the church . . . is essentially a mystery. We are therefore condemned to work with models that are inadequate to the reality to which they point.

Our method must therefore be to harmonize the models in such a way that their differences become complementary rather than mutually repugnant. In order to do so, we shall have to criticize each of the models in the light of all the others. We must refrain from so affirming any one of the models as to deny, even implicitly, what the others affirm. In this way, it may be possible to gain an understanding of the church that transcends the limitations of any given model. We shall be able to qualify each of the models intrinsically in such a way as to introduce into it the values more expressly taught by the others. The models, as I understand them, are sufficiently flexible to be mutually open and compenetrable.

This being so, there is nothing to prevent a given theologian from building his own personal theology on one or another of the paradigms in the tradition. If one begins, for example, with the model of the church as servant, one may then work backward and integrate into this model the values of the other four. One may say, for instance, that the church serves mankind precisely by looking to Jesus, the Servant Lord, and by subjecting itself to the Word of the Gospel. Only by acknowledging the sovereignty of God's Word can the church avoid an uncritical and unhealthy complacency. The idea of the church as servant of the Gospel, moreover, may be said to imply that of the church as sacrament, for it is precisely in serving that the church most perfectly images forth the Son of Man, who came to serve and offer his life as a ransom for the many. A servant church can effectively herald the Gospel as a triumphal church could not. Only in becoming a faithful servant of the Servant Lord can the church effectively proclaim the Good News of the Christian revelation. Thus the three models of servant, herald, and sacrament in many respects merge to make up a composite picture.

The coalescence, moreover, does not stop at this point. It is precisely this servant church that can best claim to be the Body of Christ—the same Body that in Jesus himself has been bruised for our sakes and made whole again by God. It is this servant church, and no other, that can dare to claim that the Spirit of Christ really dwells in it. With its divine Lord, this church can say, "The Spirit of the Lord is upon me, because he has anointed me to preach good news to the poor. He has sent me to proclaim release to the captives and recovering of sight to the blind, to set at liberty those who are oppressed, to proclaim the acceptable year of the Lord" (Lk. 4:18–19). In this body, the mutual hostilities of men are brought to an end and the members are united into a holy Temple in the Lord.

Within this servant Body, anointed by the Spirit of the Lord, there will be diversities of charism and service. There will be some who will be chosen by the Spirit and approved by the communities for offices of leadership. The flock of Christ will not be without pastors, committed to a life of dedicated service. There will be order and discipline, humility and obedience. In other words, there will be church polity. Ecclesiastical office must seek to preserve the true spirit of the Gospel and at the same time to adjust the church to the needs of the times. There will be doctrine too, for the faith of the church will be constantly nourished by the better formulation of that to which all are committed in Christ. The organization of the church need not be pitted against its spirit and its life. According to the logic of the Incarnation, the church will seek always to strengthen its life by appropriate visible structures. The church will not be an invisible "Kingdom of the Spirit," but a human institution, similar in many respects to other societies.

For blending the values in the various models, the sacramental type of ecclesiology in my opinion has special merit. It preserves the value of the institutional elements because the official structures of the church give it clear and visible outlines, so that it can be a vivid sign. It preserves the community value, for if the church were not a communion of love, it could not be an authentic sign of Christ. It preserves the dimension of proclamation, because only by reliance on Christ and by bearing witness to him, whether the message is welcomed or rejected, can the church effectively point to Christ as the bearer of God's redemptive grace. This model, finally, preserves the dimension of worldly service, because without this, the church would not be a sign of Christ the servant.

One of the five models, I believe, cannot properly be taken as primary—and this is the institutional model. Of their very nature, I believe, institutions are subordinate to persons, structures are subordinate to life. "The sabbath was made for man, not man for the sabbath" (Mk. 2:27). Without calling into question the value and importance of institutions, one may feel that this value does not properly appear unless it can be seen that the structure effectively helps to make the church a community of grace, a sacrament of Christ, a herald of salvation, and a servant of mankind.

In harmonizing the models, we should not behave as if we were trying to fit together the pieces of a difficult jigsaw puzzle. In a puzzle, one has no other data than the objective elements that have to be combined. In the field of theology, the models must be seen against the horizon of the mysterious, nonobjective experience of grace from which they arose and by which they must, in turn, be revitalized. . . . Only the grace experience, or, in other terminology, the inner enlightenment of the Holy Spirit, supplies man with the necessary tact and discretion so that he can see the values and limits of different models.

One final caution may be in order. Theologians often tend to assume that the essence of the church somehow exists, like a dark continent, ready-made and awaiting only to be mapped. The church, as a sociological entity, may be more correctly viewed as a "social construct." In terms of sociological theory, one may say that the form of the church is being constantly modified by the way in which the members of the church externalize their own experience and in so doing transform the church to which they already belong. Within the myriad possibilities left open by Scripture and tradition, the church in every generation has to exercise options. It becomes what its leaders and its people choose to make of it. The fact that the church of a certain century may have been primarily an institution does not prevent the church in another generation from being more conspicuously a community of grace, a herald, a sacrament, or a servant.

The future forms of the church lie beyond our power to foresee, except that we may be sure that they will be different from the forms of yesterday and today. The church will not necessarily mirror the secular society of tomorrow, for it must avoid the kind of conformity with the world condemned by the apostle (Rom. 12:2). On the other hand, the church will have to make adjustments in order to survive in the society of the future and to confront the members of that society with the challenge of the Gospel.

In view of the long-range changes going on in secular society and the impact they have been having on the church in recent decades, it seems prudent to predict that the following five trends, already observable in recent church history, will continue:

1. *Modernization of structures.* The current structures of the church, especially in Roman Catholicism, bear a very strong im-

print of the past social structures of Western European society. In particular, the idea of an "unequal" society, in which certain members are set on a higher plane and made invulnerable to criticism and pressure from below, savors too much of earlier oligarchic regimes to be at home in the contemporary world. In its stead, modern society is adopting a more functional approach to authority. The task of Christianity will be to harmonize the right kind of functionalism and accountability with the evangelical idea of pastoral office as a representation of Christ's own authority. Here the church, in my opinion, has an important contribution to make to the modern world. The traditional Christian conception of authority as an exigent service remains valid and potentially fruitful.

2. *Ecumenical interplay.* The present denominational divisions among the churches, in great part, no longer correspond with the real issues that respectively unite and divide Christians of our day. The debates that separated the churches in 1054 and 1520, while they may be revived in contemporary controversy, are no longer the really burning issues. Some method must be found to overcome these inherited divisions so that committed Christians in different denominational traditions may find each other once again in the same community of faith, dialogue, and worship. Short of full reunion, there may be many possibilities of mutual recognition, doctrinal accord, joint worship, and practical cooperation.

3. *Internal pluralism.* Pluralism is already very great, perhaps too great, in some of the Protestant churches, but it has been slow to assert itself in Roman Catholicism. The strong centralization in modern Catholicism is due to historical accidents. It has been shaped in part by the homogeneous culture of medieval Europe and by the dominance of Rome, with its rich heritage of classical culture and legal organization. In the Counter-Reformation, this uniformity was increased by an almost military posture of resistance to the inroads of alien systems of thought such as Protestantism and deistic rationalism. The decentralization of the future will involve a certain measure of de-Romanization. There is little reason today why Roman law, the Roman language, Roman conceptual schemes, and Roman liturgical forms should continue to be normative for the worldwide church. With increasing decentralization, the Catholic Church in various regions will be able to enter more vitally into the life of different peoples and to relate itself more positively to the traditions of other Christian denominations.

4. *Provisionality.* In a world of increasing "rapidation" and "future shock," the church must continue to provide a zone of relative stability and to enable the faithful to relate meaningfully to their religious past. But the church must not allow itself to become a mere relic or museum piece. It must prove capable of responding creatively to the demands of new situations and to the needs of generations yet to come. Church decisions will increasingly take on the form not of immutable decrees but of tentative measures taken in view of passing needs and temporary opportunities.

5. *Voluntariness.* In the "post-Constantinian" or "diaspora" situation of our day, the church will not be able to rely to the same extent as formerly on canonical penalties and sociological pressures in order to keep its members in line. Anyone at any time will be able to opt out of the church without fearing legal or social sanctions. Furthermore, the internal pluralism of the church itself will be such that directives from on high will be variously applied in different regions, so that the top officers will not be able to control in detail what goes on at the local level.

In this situation, the church will have to rule more by persuasion and less by force. The officers will have to obtain a good measure of consensus behind their decisions, and this in turn will require increased dialogue. To some extent, this development may seem a humiliation for the church, but in another sense, it may appear as progress. The church will be better able to appear as a home of freedom and as "a sign and a safeguard of the transcendence of the human person."

All these predictions seem to be solidly based on the major social trends of recent centuries. If the church is to carry out its mission effectively, it must take cognizance of these social movements. But will it in fact enter vigorously into dialogue with the new world that is being born before our eyes, or will it on the contrary become more than ever a vestige of the past? In principle, it would be possible for the church to refuse to adapt itself as the times require, and thus to become an ossified remnant of its former self. Such a church would no doubt continue to exist thanks to the richness of its heritage, but it would no longer be the home of living faith and prophetic commitment.

Because the church carries with it so large a heritage from the past, there is a constant temptation for its members to cling to the ways of their ancestors and to resist the call to confront the world of today. In the wake of Vatican II, with its large promises of renewal and reform, we are presently witnessing a new surge of legalism and reaction. The staying power of the conservatives, and their determination to adhere to ancient forms, have surpassed the expectations of starry-eyed reformers who expected to have an easy time of it after the last council. Will static traditionalism have the last word? Or will churchmen of prophetic vision arise to lead the People of God resolutely into the future?

What the church is to become depends to a great degree on the responsiveness of men, but even more importantly, it depends on the free initiatives of the Holy Spirit. If man is free and dynamic, the Spirit of God is even more so. To carry out their mission in the church, Christians must therefore open their ears and hear "what the Spirit says to the churches" (Apoc. 2:17). It is not enough for them to listen to the church unless the church, through its responsible leaders, is listening to the Spirit. The Spirit alone can give the necessary judgment and discretion. "The spiritual man judges all things, but is himself judged by no one" (1 Cor. 2:15).

Like the Israelites of old, many Christians today are saying, "Our bones are dried up, our hope is lost; we are clean cut off" (Ezek. 37:11). The Lord must say to us, as he did to Ezekiel, "Behold, I will open your graves, and raise you from your graves, O my people" (Ezek. 37:13). If life is to be breathed into those dead bones of doctrinal, ritual, and hierarchical organization that, in the eyes of many viewers, now constitute the church, the Spirit of the Lord must send prophets to his people. The charismatic movement of the past few years gives signs, not wholly unambiguous, that the Holy Spirit may be answering the longings of men's hearts.

Under the leading of the Holy Spirit, the images and forms of Christian life will continue to change, as they have in previous centuries. In a healthy community of faith, the production of new myths and symbols goes on apace. The ecclesiologists of the future will no doubt devise new models for thinking about the church. But what is new in Christianity always grows out of the past and has its roots in Scripture and tradition. On the basis of the relative continuity of the past two thousand years, it seems safe to predict that the analogues and paradigms discussed in this book will retain their significance for ecclesiology through many generations yet to come.

David Tracy

*David Tracy has argued for a revisionist model for thelogy to grapple
with the dilemmas of the modern believer. This selection is taken
from his* Blessed Rage for Order: The New Pluralism in Theology.
New York: The Seabury Press, 1975, pp. 43–56.

A Revisionist Model
for Contemporary Theology

In its briefest expression, the revisionist model holds that a contemporary fundamental Christian theology can best be described
as philosophical reflection upon the meanings present in common
human experience and language, and upon the meanings present in
the Christian fact. To explain and to defend this model for the task
of theology, five theses will be proposed which are intended to
explicate the principal meanings involved in this model for the task
of theology. The structure of the present argument is best grasped
by an understanding of the interrelationships of the theses themselves. The first thesis defends the proposition that there are two
sources for theology, common human experience and language,
and Christian texts. The second thesis argues for the necessity of
correlating the results of the investigations of these two sources.
The third and fourth theses attempt to specify the most helpful
methods of investigation employed for studying these two sources.
The fifth and final thesis further specifies the final mode of critical
correlation of these investigations as an explicitly metaphysical or
transcendental one. At the time of the discussion of this final thesis,
one should be able to provide a summary of the meaning and truth
value of the present model proposed for theology, viz., philosophical reflection upon common human experience and language, and
upon Christian texts. There are, of course, thorny problems and
several alternative views possible not only for the model as a whole,
but for each "thesis" in the model. . . .

First Thesis: *The Two Principal Sources for Theology
Are Christian Texts and Common Human Experience
and Language.*

This thesis seems the least problematic of the five proposed. For it seems obvious that any enterprise called Christian theology will attempt to show the appropriateness of its chosen categories to the meanings of the major expressions and texts of the Christian tradition. This source of the theological task is variously labeled: "the message," as with Paul Tillich; the "kerygma," as with Rudolf Bultmann; the "Christian witness of faith," as with Schubert Ogden; the "tradition," as with most contemporary Catholic theologians. Whatever title is chosen, the recognition of the need for the Christian theologian to show just how and why his conclusions are appropriate to the Christian tradition remains as obvious in its demand as it proves to be difficult in its execution. A subsidiary but not unimportant corollary of this demand is that the Scriptures remain the fundamental although not exclusive expression of that Christian faith. Hence a principal task of the theologian will be to find appropriate interpretations of the major motifs of the Scriptures and of the relationship of those interpretations to the confessional, doctrinal, symbolic, theological, and *praxis* expressions of the various Christian traditions. Except for those few theologians who would maintain that theology is without remainder a philosophical reflection upon our contemporary experience and language, this commitment to determining the ability of contemporary formulations to state the meanings of Christian texts remains an obvious, albeit difficult task.

Even from the limited perspective of this understanding of the nature of a theologian's responsibility to the tradition, it would also seem that the task of theology involves an attempt to show the adequacy of the major Christian theological categories for all human experience. In fact, insofar as the Scriptures claim that the Christian self-understanding does, in fact, express an understanding of authentic human existence as such, the Christian theologian is impelled to test precisely that universalist claim. He will ordinarily do so by developing criteria that generically can be labeled "criteria of adequacy" to common human experience. Whether this source of theological reflection be called the "situation," as with Paul Tillich; the "contemporary scientific world view," as with Rudolf Bultmann; the contemporary phenomenon of a full-fledged "historical consciousness," as with Bernard Lonergan; or "common human experience," as here, again the task seems a fully necessary one. However, this demand is not forced upon the Christian theologian only by his commitment to the authentic aspects of modernity, much less by a search for contemporary relevance. Rather, that task is primarily demanded for inner theological reasons. Rudolf Bultmann, for one, clarifies these reasons by his firm insistence that demythologizing is demanded not only by the contemporary world view but also by the universalist, existential assumptions of the New Testament self-understanding itself.

This commitment to determine methods and criteria which can show the adequacy of Christian self-understanding for all human experience is a task demanded by the very logic of the Christian affirmations; more precisely, by the Christian claim to provide the authentic way to understand our common human existence. This insight *theologically* disallows any attempt to force a strictly traditional inner-theological understanding of the sources of theological reflection. Whether that inner theological self-understanding be explicated through any of the forms of theological orthodoxy or through the kind of neoorthodoxy presented by Karl Barth in the *Church Dogmatics* is a relatively minor matter. The major insight remains the insistence present in theological reflection at least since Schleiermacher: The task of a Christian theology intrinsically involves a commitment to investigate critically both the Christian faith in its several expressions and contemporary experience in its several cultural expressions. In this important sense, one may continue to find Schleiermacher's slogan for the task of theology still accurate: "The theses of faith must become the hypotheses of the theologian."

Second Thesis: *The Theological Task Will Involve a Critical Correlation of the Results of the Investigations of the Two Sources of Theology.*

Given the fact of two sources needing investigation, some way of correlating the results of these investigations must be developed. The full dimensions of this task of correlation cannot, of course, be developed until the methods of investigation analyzed in the next two theses are clarified. For the moment, however, it is sufficient to clarify the need for some method of correlation. Perhaps the clearest way to clarify the meaning of this thesis will be to compare the method of correlation proposed here with the best-known method of correlation in contemporary theology, Paul Tillich's. This "clarification through contrast" procedure is here a useful one since so many contemporary theologians are justly indebted to Tillich for formulating the task of theology in terms of the general model of a method of correlation.

There are, it is true, some significant differences between the Tillichian notions of "situation" and "message" and the present articulation of the two sources of theology as "common human experience" and "Christian texts." Still, the twofold nature of the theologian's commitment implied by these expressions, as well as the recognition that such a commitment logically involves the need for some kind of correlation, is a shared position. Moreover, one may continue to find Tillich's articulation of the ideal for contemporary theology to be fundamentally sound. As Tillich expresses it in volume one of the *Systematics,* the ideal contemporary theological position would provide an *Aufhebung* of both liberalism and neoorthodoxy. As Tillich expresses the same ideal in his introduction to volume two, the theologian must attempt to move beyond both classical "supernaturalism" and secular "naturalism" by developing some form of "self-transcending naturalism."

In sum, Paul Tillich's position continues to seem peculiarly helpful: for his expression of the proper ideal of contemporary theology; for his insistence that only an investigation of both "situation" and "message" can hope to fulfill this ideal; and for his articulation of the need for some general model of correlation as the proper response to this need.

However, many critics find Tillich's own formulation of how the method of correlation actually functions neither intrinsically convincing nor consistent with the task of theology which he himself articulates. The fact is that Tillich's method does not call for a critical correlation of the results of one's investigations of the "situation" and the "message." Rather, his method affirms the need for a correlation of the "questions" expressed in the "situation" with the "answers" provided by the Christian "message." Such a correlation, in fact, is one between "questions" from one source and "answers" from the other. Even on the limited basis of the position defended in the first thesis, one cannot but find unacceptable this formulation of the theological task of correlation. For if the "situation" is to be taken with full seriousness, then its answers to its own questions must also be investigated critically. Tillich's method cannot really allow this. A classic example of this difficulty can be found in Tillich's famous dictum, "Existentialism is the good luck of Christian theology." We are all indebted to Tillich's brilliant reinterpretation pointing out the heavy debt which existentialist analyses of man's estranged situation owe to classical Christian anthropology. Yet no one (not even a Christian theologian!) can decide that only *the questions* articulated by a particular form of contemporary thought are of real theological interest.

Correlatively, from the viewpoint of the Christian message itself, the very claim to have an answer applicable to any human situation demands logically that a critical comparison of the Christian "answer" with all other "answers" be initiated. To return to the existentialist example, why do we not find in Tillich a critical investigation of the claims that either Jean-Paul Sartre's or Karl Jaspers's philosophies of existence provide a better "answer" to the question of human estrangement than the Christian "answer" does?

In summary, a commitment to two sources for theology does imply the need to formulate a method capable of correlating the principal questions and answers of each source. Yet Tillich's method of correlation is crucially inadequate. Tillich's implicit commitment to two sources and his explicit insistence upon a theological ideal which transcends both naturalism and supernaturalism could be successfully executed only by a method which develops critical criteria for correlating the questions and the answers found in both the "situation" and the "message." Any method which attempts less than that cannot really be called a method of correlation. Tillich's method does not actually correlate; it juxtaposes questions from the "situation" with answers from the "message." Insofar as this critique is true, the contemporary theologian can accept Tillich's articulation of the need for a method of correlation, but he cannot accept Tillich's own model for theology as one which actually correlates.

Third Thesis: *The Principal Method of Investigation
of the Source "Common Human Experience and Language"
Can Be Described as a Phenomenology of the
"Religious Dimension" Present in Everyday and
Scientific Experience and Language.*

The principal intention of this thesis is to clarify the method
needed to investigate the first source of theology. It should be
emphasized at once, however, that the present thesis does not
involve a determination of the truth value of the meanings uncovered. Rather, this thesis merely attempts to analyze what method
will best allow those meanings to be explicated as accurately as
possible.

A widely accepted dictum of contemporary theological thought
holds that all theological statements involve an existential dimension, indeed, a dimension which includes a claim to universal
existential relevance. On that basis, it seems fair to conclude that
the theologian is obliged to explicate how and why the existential
meanings proper to Christian self-understanding are present in
common human experience. As long as one's understanding of the
concept experience is not confined to Humean sense-data but involves a recognition of the prereflective, preconceptual, prethematic
realm of the everyday, then the task of theology in this moment of
its enterprise seems clear. That task is the need to explicate a
preconceptual dimension to our common shared experience that
can legitimately be described as religious. Historically, that task is
best represented by the liberal theological tradition's search for a
method capable of explicating an ultimate or final horizon of meaning to our common everyday life and language, and to our scientific
and ethical reflection which can properly be described as both
ultimate and religious.

One way of formulating this task is to suggest that contemporary
phenomenological method is the method best suited for it. The
reasons for the choice of the title "phenomenology" at this point
are basically twofold. First, several major figures in the phenomenological tradition from Max Scheler through the recent work of
Langdon Gilkey have demonstrated the effectiveness of phenomenological reflection in explicating that final or ultimate horizon
precisely *as a religious one.* Second, the history of phenomenologi-

cal reflection on the nature of the method itself has developed ever more sophisticated ways to formulate the full dimensions of any phenomenological investigation. Indeed, phenomenological method has undergone several important transformations from the earlier "eidetic" formulations of Husserl and the Göttingen circle through the existential phenomenology of Sartre, Merleau-Ponty, Scheler, and the early Heidegger to the hermeneutic phenomenology of Gadamer, the later Heidegger, and Paul Ricoeur. Each of these redefinitions of the nature of phenomenology has been impelled by the inability of an earlier method to explicate the full dimensions of the phenomena uncovered by earlier reflection. If the most recent formulations of phenomenology's task (the hermeneutic) be sound, then it seems reasonable to suggest that theologians might employ such a method to analyze those symbols and gestures present to our everyday life and language that may legitimately manifest a religious dimension to our lives.

To be sure, the present position does not argue that only phenomenological method can succeed in this analysis. It does argue that a recognition of the real possibilities of that method promises a new surety to the several attempts to explicate the religious dimension of our common experience and language. As one example of phenomenology's relative adequacy for theology's task, consider the crucial question of the linguistic and symbolic character of our experience. On that question, it seems clear that so-called hermeneutic phenomenology is far better prepared than either the "reformed subjectivist principle" of the Whiteheadians or the earlier "critical phenomenology" of Paul Tillich to explicate the linguistic (usually symbolic) character of everyday experience; this holds as well for the properly linguistic and symbolic dimensions of the final and ultimate horizon of that world as religious. Not a plea for exclusive rights, the argument for phenomenology takes the form of suggesting its relative adequacy for uncovering the full dimensions of the common task.

Thus far in this third thesis the emphasis has been upon the kind of method needed for this common theological task. Hopefully, such an emphasis does not obscure the nature of the task itself: the continued search in most contemporary theology for an adequate expression of the religious dimension of our common experience and language. To repeat, that task seems demanded both by the universalist claim of Christian self-understanding and by the otherwise inexplicable character of our shared experience itself.

In fact, so complex does this aspect of theology's contemporary task become that only a phenomenology in continued conversation with those human sciences which investigate the religious dimension in human existence, and in conversation with other philosophical methods can really hope to succeed. As an example of such collaboration, it may prove helpful to close this thesis with mention of a few conversation partners available at the moment. The work of Paul Tillich on this question (viz., his analysis of the religious "ultimate concern" involved in the human "situation") has, in fact, been continued and refined by the work of such diverse interpreters of Tillich as Langdon Gilkey, Tom Driver, Nathan Scott, and David Kelsey. The work of Bernard Lonergan on the religious dimension in human cognition and action is presently being advanced both by Lonergan himself, in his more recent work, and by Lonergan interpreters such as John Dunne, David Burrell, and Michael Novak. Enterprises like these are, I believe, central to any serious contemporary attempt at fundamental theology.

Fourth Thesis: *The Principal Method of Investigation of the Source "The Christian Tradition" Can Be Described as an Historical and Hermeneutical Investigation of Classical Christian Texts.*

This thesis begins with a truism: if the Christian theologian must articulate the meanings of the phenomenon variously called the "Christian fact," "witness," "message," or "tradition," then he is obliged to enter into the discussion of the nature of the disciplines of history and hermeneutics. This thesis does not pretend to resolve the many problems encompassed by historical and hermeneutical knowledge. Rather, it attempts only to outline the particular understandings of the historical and hermeneutical methods that may prove helpful for this aspect of the theological task.

The theological *need* for history and hermeneutics concerns us first. If the phenomenon labeled the "Christian fact" includes the significant gestures, symbols, and actions of the various Christian traditions, then the theologian must learn those historical methods capable of determining exactly what facts can be affirmed as probable. For the present investigation of texts, he must also learn historical methods in order to allow for the historical reconstruction of the basic texts of Christian self-understanding. On that historical basis of reconstruction, the theologian must then find a hermeneutic method capable of discerning *at least* the central meanings of the principal textual expressions of Christianity (viz., the scriptural). The general need for historical method articulated here is a modest one. It does not imply that the theologian employ a specific category like "salvation-history" as a useful theological one. The call for historical method does imply that the theologian as historian pay heed to those historical reconstructions of Christian events and texts which modern historical scholarship has made available. The argument for historical method implied by the first three theses, then, is a limited but important aspect of the theologian's larger task. If one were to define Christian theology as simply a philosophy of religion, then historical method need not be employed. But if Christian theology is adequately defined only as a philosophical reflection upon both common human experience and language and upon Christian texts, then a historical reconstruction of the central texts of that tradition is imperative.

Perhaps the exact nature of the historical task of the theologian might best be understood by recalling a familiar instance of its exercise. That instance is the common Christian affirmation "Jesus of Nazareth is the Christ." That exercise is the attempt to determine what historical and hermeneutical methods can best aid the contemporary theologian to understand what Christians have actually meant by this familiar affirmation. Rather than spelling out at length an understanding of historical and hermeneutic methods, in the remainder of this thesis I shall risk the belief that these crucial theological tasks are best grasped by examining their emergence in a specific theological problem. That problem is the primary existential meanings of Christological texts.

The first questions to be addressed to the affirmation that "Jesus is the Christ" are ordinarily historical ones. The historian does want to know what conclusions historical inquiry can reach about the person Jesus of Nazareth and about the belief of the Christian community that Jesus was the Christ. On these historical questions, it seems fair to state that, short of a position like J. M.

Allegro's at least, the accumulation of historical evidence on the existence of Jesus of Nazareth seems secure, even if the range of interpretations of his significance is wide indeed. Yet whatever interpretation of the "historical Jesus" is accepted as most probable by various historians through old and new "quests," the principal factor demanding *theological* clarification is the religious existential meanings expressed in the New Testament Christological texts as those texts are reconstructed by contemporary historical scholarship.

If the historian can reconstruct the texts in question, then the next problem becomes the need to discover what discipline will allow one to determine the meanings of those metaphors, symbols, and "images" used in the New Testament texts to express the religious significance of the proclamation that Jesus of Nazareth is the Christ. Much of the language of the New Testament texts is metaphorical, symbolic, and parabolic as distinct from conceptual; the principal meaning expressed by the texts is one which manifests or represents what can be properly labeled a religious meaning, a religious way of being-in-the-world. These two factors can be discerned by various combinations of historical and linguistic methods. Yet to determine with greater exactness the full meaning of the "images" demands a more explicit formulation of the hermeneutic as distinct from the historical task. The present discussion of that hermeneutical task does not pretend to provide an exhaustive analysis. Indeed, the history of reflection on the nature of that notoriously complex discipline makes one justifiably wary of any exhaustive claims. For the moment, I will simply advance certain contemporary refinements of the hermeneutic tradition which seem applicable to the problem of discerning the meanings embedded in any written text—and only such developments in recent hermeneutic theory which seem particularly apt for illustrating the nature of the theologian's hermeneutic commitment.

The first development with which we are concerned is the process of linguistic "distanciation" expressed, for example, in the character of written as distinct from spoken language. Summarily stated, this recent development in contemporary linguistic and hermeneutic theory allows the prospective interpreter to understand that a written text, precisely as written, is distanced both from the original intention of the author and from its original reception by its first addresses. If this be correct, the hermeneutic circle as it is ordinarily formulated by theologians needs reformulation. For the task of interpretation is not best understood in terms of the interpreter's own subjectivity attempting to grasp the subjectivity either of the author's intentions or of the original addressee's reception of its meaning. Neither should the interpreter, as his principal concern, attempt to uncover the subjectivity of the historical person (here, Jesus of Nazareth) described in certain images and symbols (e.g., "Son of Man," "the Christ," "Prophet") which seemed especially germane for representing the existential significance of this person. If this be the case, it does not seem to be of major theological import to engage in old and new quests for the historical Jesus as something distinct from finding a hermeneutic method capable of explicating the meanings of those Christological texts referring both to Jesus and to a certain Christian mode-of-being-in-the-world.

A second major development in contemporary hermeneutic and linguistic theory should allow one to approach that latter task with greater surety. That development is the insistence that the contemporary interpreter must distinguish clearly between the "sense" and the "referents" of the text and hence between the methods needed to explicate each. The "sense" of the text means the internal structure and meaning of the text as that structure can be determined through the ordinary methods of semantic and literary-critical inquiries. The "referents" of the text do not pertain to the meaning "behind" the text (e.g., the author's *real* intention or the social-cultural situation of the text). Rather, to shift metaphors, "referent" basically manifests the meaning "in front of" the text, i.e., that way of perceiving reality, that mode of being-in-the-world which the text opens up for the intelligent reader.

Although this understanding of "referent" is not divorced from either prior historical or semantic investigations, still "referent" here is clearly distinct from those prior factors. Further, the referents of the text, on this understanding, are *the* factors demanding a properly hermeneutical as distinct from either a historical or a semantic exercise. To show why this understanding of the hermeneutic task of the theologian seems sound, one can concretize the discussion by applying it to the task of understanding the existential referent of the New Testament affirmation that "Jesus is the Christ." At least four related methods are needed for this task: the historical method, semantics, literary-critical methods, and, finally, the explicitly hermeneutical.

First, the historian, by a full application of his methods of historical inquiry, can reconstruct the Christological texts, i.e., both those texts of Jesus and about Jesus. Semantics can then help the interpreter to determine the linguistic structure of the images and symbols involved in the text; with literary-critical methods, the interpreter can determine the particular character of the literary genres by means of which the images, metaphors, and symbols are structured, codified, and transformed. Still, the meaning of major import *to the theologian* remains a concern that can be formulated by a question like the following: What is the mode-of-being-in-the-world *referred to* by the text? That question is not really answered until an explicitly hermeneutic enterprise is advanced. On this understanding, hermeneutics is the discipline capable of explicating *the referent* as distinct from either the sense of the text or the historical reconstruction of the text.

To continue this reflection upon the Christological example, let us suppose that a prospective interpreter of the New Testament Christological texts found a degree of high probability in Herbert Braun's dictum that in the New Testament the Christologies are the variable while a theological anthropology (the understanding of humanity as existing in the presence of a gracious God) is the constant. In one's search for the theological anthropology referred to by the Christological texts, one would be engaged in the explicitly hermeneutical (as distinct from historical, semantic, or literary-critical) task of explicating that mode-of-being-in-the-world, that way of looking at reality which the texts express (a religious, Christian way of being-in-the-world). It seems fair to state that this understanding of hermeneutics could then show that the referent of the Christological texts is properly described as a theological anthropology. In short, that referent is the specifically religious mode of being-in-the-world characterized by Braun in the statement that the existential meaning of the Christological texts is that one can now live as though in the presence of a gracious God.

Such a determination of a religious referent would, in fact, complete the explicitly hermeneutic task of the theologian. The further question of the truth status of the referent explicated by hermeneutics remains. For that question, a distinct mode of reflection is needed. Even if his hermeneutic enterprise were successful, the theologian must still face the further task of correlating the results of his hermeneutic reflections with the results of his reflections upon contemporary experience and language. To achieve this correlation, he must ask what further reflective discipline will allow him to determine whether his earlier conclusions can legitimately be described not only as accurate meanings but also as true. It will be the purpose of the fifth and final thesis to articulate one understanding of what discipline can undertake this.

Fifth Thesis: *To Determine the Truth Status of the Results of One's Investigations into the Meaning of Both Common Human Experience and Christian Texts the Theologian Should Employ an Explicitly Transcendental or Metaphysical Mode of Reflection.*

This final thesis on the task of fundamental theology is probably the least commonly accepted position of those argued for thus far. For that reason, I will concern myself here with the attempt to show only the need for and the basic nature of the metaphysical reflection involved in the task of theology.

The word *need* is used advisedly, since the proposed argument for metaphysical inquiry is not posed as one alternative way of doing theology. Rather, the present claim is that, if the argument of the first four theses is sound, then one cannot but recognize an exigence for metaphysical or transcendental reflection. Indeed, by recalling the conclusions of these earlier theses, we should also be able to show the need for the metaphysical reflection suggested here. Summarily stated, the argument has had the following structure: There are two sources for theology (common human experience and language, and Christian texts); those two sources are to be investigated by a hermeneutic phenomenology of the religious dimension in common human experience and language and by historical and hermeneutical investigations of the meanings referred to by Christian texts; the results of these investigations should be correlated to determine their significant similarities and differences and their truth value. The kind of correlation needed depends, of course, primarily upon the nature of the phenomena manifested in the prior investigation of the two sources. Thus far, the argument has been principally for the formal methods of investigation needed as distinct from the material conclusions reached by such methods. Yet in order to show the need for metaphysical inquiry, it will be necessary to advance the earlier discussion by suggesting what conclusions may be reached by contemporary investigations of the type outlined above.

In the case of a phenomenology of ordinary experience and language, several contemporary thinkers have tried to show how a religious dimension is present in our cognitive, moral, and everyday experience and language. . . . At the moment, it will be possible only to mention rather than to demonstrate a few widely known examples of such reflection. As a first example, let us recall the existentialist analysis of the manifestation of No-thing (i.e., no object in the world alongside other objects) in an analysis of the phenomenon of anxiety as distinct from the phenomenon of fear. That analysis has provided an occasion not only to show the meaning and possibility of metaphysics (as for Heidegger), but also to show the meaning and possibility of a "negative" entry point to a final, ultimate, and properly religious horizon to our everyday lives. As a second example, the process philosopher's analysis of the phenomenon of that fundamental confidence or trust in existence continually re-presented in the self-conscious faith of our everyday, our scientific, and our moral activities has also provided a way of rendering meaningful the basic "faith" operative in our secular lives. As a third example, Paul Tillich's analysis of the inevitable presence of an ultimate (as distinct from a finite) concern in all human activity (however "demonic" the forms of such ultimacy may become) has rendered intelligible the ontological status of an authentically religious dimension. As a final example, Bernard Lonergan's analysis of the "formally unconditioned" factor presupposed by scientific and moral inquiry as well as his more recent analysis of explicitly religious experience as "a being-in-love-*without-qualification*" manifests a similar explication of the kinds of meanings present in either the implicitly religious dimensions of our secular lives or the explicitly religious language of the Christian tradition.

Moreover, in an intellectual context where a religious dimension to everyday experience and language has been rendered intelligible, the question of God can be formulated anew as the question of the necessary referent (or object) of such a religious or "basic faith" dimension. This theistic question, to be sure, involves further and extensive reflection insofar as it is the case that even some explicitly religious persons (e.g., some Buddhist and lately some Christian theologians) are also nontheistic. However, the theistic question itself seems both logically unavoidable and . . . capable of receiving a positive answer once an authentically religious dimension is admitted and explicated.

Correlatively, if one accepts the notion of "referent" articulated in the previous thesis, then religious and theistic meanings can also emerge from properly hermeneutical investigations of Christian texts. From the viewpoint of historical investigation, a secure conclusion would seem to be that whatever else Christianity has been, it has also been (and ordinarily understood itself to be) a theistic religion. From the viewpoint of the kind of hermeneutic enterprise suggested above, *the* referent of the classical texts of the Christian tradition can be described as a religious way of being-in-the-world which understands itself in explicitly theistic terms. It is true, of course, that the further specifications of that Christian way of being-in-the-world can be and will continue to be variously described. An interpreter might hold, for example, that Herbert Braun's description of that specification as "humanity living before a gracious God" is the primary Christian self-understanding. Yet whether one accepts Braun's description or some other religious and theistic anthropology as the principal existential referent of Christian texts, any further specifications will not really call into question the basic religious and theistic referents which the theologian seeks.

If the interpretation of both contemporary experience and language and of Christian texts could legitimately reach such similar conclusions, then the first moment of critical correlation—the comparative moment—would be accomplished. For the results of one's investigations into both major sources of theology would conclude to an identical insight: the fundamentally religious and theistic self-understanding presupposed by common human experience and language and explicitly referred to in representative Christian texts. But even this moment of correlation does not complete the theological task. Comparative analysis may allow one to know the basic religious referents of Christian texts and the fundamental meaningfulness of religious and theistic categories for common experience and language. Such analysis does not of and by itself resolve the question of the truth status of such meanings.

For that we must ask what reflective discipline can adequately investigate the truth claims of the religious and theistic meanings manifested by the prior investigations. The exact nature of that discipline is admittedly difficult to determine. However, certain characteristics of the discipline needed seem clear. First, the discipline will have to be a reflective one capable of articulating *conceptual* and not merely *symbolic* categories. Otherwise, the theologian can never be sure that he has avoided either incoherence or vagueness in determining the cognitive character of religious and theistic claims. Second, the discipline must be able to explicate its criteria for precisely those cognitive claims. It seems fair to affirm that such criteria will involve at least such widely accepted criteria as the following: There must be a necessary and a sufficient ground in our common experience for such claims; any such claims must have a coherence both internally and with other essential categories of our knowledge and belief.

If such criteria are in fact the criteria widely accepted for any cognitive claims, it becomes imperative for the theologian to specify how such criteria might function in theology, since theology too makes cognitive claims about the nature of experience. Yet the dimension of meaning in question for theology (the religious) is not simply a meaning coordinate with other meanings like the scientific, the aesthetic, or the ethical. Rather, the religious dimension precisely as such can be phenomenologically described as an ultimate or grounding dimension or horizon to all meaningful human activities. The reflective discipline needed to decide upon the cognitive claims of religion and theism will itself have to be able to account not merely for some particular dimension of experience but for *all experience* as such. Indeed, precisely this latter insight is required to show why the theologian cannot resolve the religious and theistic cognitive claims of theology by any ordinary criteria of verification or falsification. Rather, the very nature of the cognitive claim involved in religious and theistic statements demands a metaphysical or transcendental mediation. As Antony Flew quite properly insists, an investigation of the cognitive claims of religion and theism demands that one seek to answer two fundamental questions: (1)

the ground in our common experience for having any notions of religion and God at all; (2) how these notions may be conceptually explicated to avoid both vagueness and incoherence. But as it has been argued that Antony Flew fails to see, only a reflective discipline capable of explicating criteria for the "conditions of the possibility" of all experience could really resolve the question of the meaning and truth of authentically religious and theistic claims.

One clear way of articulating the nature of the reflective discipline capable of such inquiry is to describe it as "transcendental" in its modern formulation or "metaphysical" in its more traditional expression. As transcendental, such reflection attempts the explicit mediation of the basic presuppositions (or "beliefs") that are the conditions of the possibility of our existing or understanding at all. Metaphysical reflection means essentially the same thing: the philosophical validation of the concepts "religion" and "God" as necessarily affirmed or necessarily denied by all our basic beliefs and understanding. We seem to be unavoidably led to the conclusion that the task of fundamental theology can only be successfully resolved when the theologian fully and frankly develops an explicitly metaphysical study of the cognitive claims of religion and theism as an integral moment in his larger task.

For a variety of reasons, such a position is unacceptable to many, probably even most contemporary theologians. However, one hopes that the argument of the fifth thesis may be critically investigated in the context of its relationship to the first four theses. If it is correct to state that the task of theology demands that the theologian first uncover the religious and theistic meanings in both our common human experience and language and in explicitly Christian texts, then I find it impossible not to affirm the need for metaphysical or transcendental reflection to investigate the cognitive claims of those religious and theistic meanings.

In outline form, I have tried to present the principal elements in the revisionist model of a contemporary fundamental theology. Whether that model can be successfully employed is, of course, another and more difficult question. However, one may continue to take heart from the fact that others who have a similar understanding of the basic elements involved in the task of theology will continue to advance these collaborative efforts which may lead to its resolution. . . .

Raimundo Panikkar

Raimundo Panikkar has been unusually creative in promoting a positive relationship between Christianity and the religions of the East, particularly Hinduism and Buddhism. This selection is taken from his The Intra-Religious Dialogue. *New York: Paulist Press, 1978, pp. 26–37.*

The meeting of religions is an inescapable fact today. I would like to formulate one principle that should govern the meeting of religions, and draw from it a few corollary consequences.

The principle is this: *The religious encounter must be a truly religious one.* Anything short of this simply will not do.

Some consequences are the following:

1. It Must be Free from Particular Apologetics

If the Christian or Buddhist or believer in whatever religion approaches another religious person with the *a priori* idea of defending his own religion by all (obviously honest) means, we shall have perhaps a valuable defense of that religion and undoubtedly exciting discussions, but no religious dialogue, no encounter, much less a mutual enrichment and fecundation. One need not give up one's beliefs and convictions—surely not, but we must eliminate any apologetics if we really want to meet a person from another religious tradition. By apologetics, I understand that part of the science of a particular religion that tends to prove the truth and value of that religion. Apologetics has its function and its proper place, but not here in the meeting of religions.

2. It Must Be Free from General Apologetics

I understand very well the anguish of the modern religious person seeing the wave of "unreligion" and even "irreligion" in our times, and yet I would consider it misguided to fall prey to such a fear by founding a kind of religious league—not to say crusade—of the "pious" of religious people of all confessions, defenders of the "sacred rights" of religion.

If to forget the first corollary would indicate a lack of confidence in our partner and imply that he is wrong and that I must "convert" him, to neglect this second point would betray a lack of confidence in the truth of religion itself and represent an indiscriminate accusation against "modern" man. The attitude proposing a common front for religion or against unbelief may be understandable, but it is not a religious attitude—not according to the present degree of religious consciousness.

3. One Must Face the Challenge of Conversion

If the encounter is to be an authentically religious one, it must be totally loyal to truth and open to reality. The genuinely religious spirit is not loyal only to the past, it also keeps faith with the present. A religious man is neither a fanatic nor someone who already has all the answers. He also is a seeker, a pilgrim making his own uncharted way; the track ahead is yet virgin, inviolate. The religious man finds each moment new and is but the more pleased to see in this both the beauty of a personal discovery and the depth of a perennial treasure that his ancestors in the faith have handed down.

And yet, to enter the new field of the religious encounter is a challenge and a risk. The religious person enters this arena without prejudices and preconceived solutions, knowing full well he may in fact have to lose a particular belief or particular religion altogether. He trusts in truth. He enters unarmed and ready to be converted himself. He may lose his life—he may also be born again.

4. The Historical Dimension Is Necessary but Not Sufficient

Religion is not just *Privatsache,* nor just a vertical "link" with the Absolute, but it is also a connection with mankind; it has a tradition, a historical dimension. The religious encounter is not merely the meeting of two or more people in their capacity as strictly private individuals, severed from their respective religious traditions. A truly religious man bears at once the burden of tradition and the riches of his ancestors. But he is not an official representative, as it were, speaking only on behalf of others or from sheer hearsay: He is a living member of a community, a believer in a living religious tradition.

The religious encounter must deal with the historical dimension, not stop with it. It is not an encounter of historians, still less of archeologists; but a living dialogue, a place for creative thinking and imaginative new ways that do not break with the past but continue and extend it.

This is hardly to disparage historical considerations; quite the contrary, I would insist on an understanding of the traditions in question that is at once deep and broad. The first implies not only that we be familiar with the age-old tradition, but also with the present state of that particular religion. Taking as our example that bundle of religions which goes under the name of "Hinduism," I would contend that a profound understanding of this tradition cannot ignore its evolution up to the present day, unless we are ready to accept an arbitrary and skewed interpretation. A scholar may indeed limit himself to Vedic studies, for example, but someone engaged in a truly religious encounter can scarcely justify basing his understandings of Hinduism solely on Sāyana's interpretation of the Vedas while completely ignoring that of, say, Dayānānda or Aurobindo (the relative merits of various interpretations is not our concern here). Similarly, no modern Christian can be satisfied with Jerome's interpretation of the Bible, or with the medieval understanding of it.

Our point is that no study of an idea, cultural pattern, or religious tradition is adequate unless we consider all its possibilities, just as no botanist can claim to know a seed until he knows the plant that grows up from that seed. Moreover, in this case, the movement of understanding is dynamic and reciprocal. Thus I would contend not only that any study of the nature of *dharma,* for instance, is incomplete if it does not consider the present-day understanding of that concept, but also that the ancient notion is likely to be only partially understood if its development up to modern times is left aside. This also implies that someone who tries to understand the notion of *dharma,* whether in ancient or modern India, cannot do so *in vacuo*: the very words he uses are already culturally charged with meanings and values.

Further, the traditions must also be understood in a broader perspective, one that oversteps the provincial boundaries of geography and culture. To understand the Hindu tradition—staying with our example—we cannot limit ourselves to the Indian subcontinent: The impact of Buddhism on eastern and central Asia is so well known that I need only mention it; the Rāmāyāna and the Mahābhārata have been shaping forces in many countries south of Burma; Śiva is worshiped in Indonesia. Pursuing these avenues of research is not a mere academic tangent, but serves to complete the picture we begin to see through indigenous sources. Even more, we cannot limit our attention to past crosscultural contacts, and ignore the multitude of contemporary instances. Many an Indian value asserts itself today on the shores of California and in universities throughout Europe. Whether the change in climate distorts or enhances the original values is a separate question; the influence is unmistakable. In return, Western values have, for better or for worse, deeply penetrated not only the great cities, but also the most remote villages of India. Given such developments, can our understanding of Indian religions remain imprisoned in a scholarly ivory tower whose drawbridge was raised when the Muslims arrived? The phenomenon of feedback does not refer only to the diffusion of gadgets and other technological paraphernalia throughout the world; popularized ideas from every continent now travel literally at the speed of light to the farthest corners of the planet and the deepest recesses of the human psyche.

The importance of the historical dimension notwithstanding, what is at stake in the religious encounter is not "History of Religions" or even "Comparative Religion," but a living and demanding faith. Faith is life and life cannot be reduced to imitating the past or merely reinterpreting it. The religious encounter is a religious event.

5. It Is Not Just a Congress of Philosophy

Needless to say, without a certain degree of philosophy no encounter is possible, and yet the religious dialogue is not just a meeting of philosophers to discuss intellectual problems. Religions are much more than doctrines. Within one religion there may even be a pluralism of doctrines. To pin down a religion to a certain definite doctrinal set is to kill that religion. No particular doctrine *as such* can be considered the unique and irreplaceable expression of a religion. Indeed, *denying* a particular doctrine without over-coming it or substituting another for it may be heresy, but no religion is satisfied to be *only* orthodoxy, ignoring orthopraxis. To be sure, creation, God, *nirvāṇa* and the like are important concepts, but the real religious issue lies elsewhere: in the real "thing" meant by these and other notions. I may share with my Muslim colleague the same idea of the transcendence of God and he may be of the same opinion as his Buddhist partner regarding the law of *karma* and yet none of us may feel compelled to change his religion.

Clearly, I need to understand what the other is saying, that is, what he means to say, and this involves a new understanding of interpretation itself. Now, the golden rule of any hermeneutic is that the interpreted thing can recognize itself in the interpretation. In other words, any interpretation from outside a tradition has to coincide, at least phenomenologically, with an interpretation from within, i.e., with the believer's viewpoint. To label a *mūrtipūjaka* an idol worshiper, for instance, using idol as it is commonly understood in the Judeo-Christian-Muslim context rather than beginning with what the worshiper affirms of himself, is to transgress this rule. An entire philosophical and religious context underpins the notion of *mūrti*; we cannot simply impose alien categories on it. Although the problem remains formidable, one of the most positive achievements of our times is that we have come to realize that there are no immutable categories that can serve as absolute criteria for judging everything under the sun.

Briefly then, I would like to consider two principles that govern any sound hermeneutical method and the way in which they may be critically coordinated.

The *principle of homogeneity*: An ancient conviction, held in both East and West, has it that only like can know like. In other words, a concept can be properly understood and evaluated only from within a homogeneous context. Every cultural value has a definite sphere where it is valid and meaningful; any unwarranted extrapolation can only lead to confusion and misunderstanding. Nothing is more harmful than hurried syntheses or superficial par-allelisms. Here is the place and the great value of traditional theology, which provides the internal understanding of a religion, the self-understanding of that religion as it is lived. Without this previous work, fruitful interreligious encounters would not be possible.

The *dialogical principle*: Applying the principle of homogeneity with strict rigor or exclusivity would paralyze a critical approach and halt any progress toward mutual understanding. I may understand the world view that underlies the religious practice of another—human sacrifice, for instance—yet I may still consider it immature, wrong, even barbaric. Why is this? It may be that I have developed another form of awareness or discovered another principle of understanding that leads me to see the inadequacy of a certain notion (here that which upholds human sacrifice). I may have acquired a perspective under which I am able to criticize another point of view; perhaps I can now detect incongruencies or assumptions that are no longer tenable. In this sort of activity, the dialogical principle is at work. Only through an internal or external dialogue can we become aware of uncritical or unwarranted assumptions. This dialogue does not merely look for new sources of information, but leads to a deeper understanding of the other and of oneself. We are all learning to welcome light and criticism, even when it comes from foreign shores.

Coordination: By themselves, each these principles is barren and unsatisfying; together they provide a means of crosscultural understanding that is both valid and critical. Those concerned with Indian traditions, whatever their background, are convinced that they cannot disregard the methodological principles of modern critical scholarship. At the same time, they are quite aware that neither science nor Western categories constitute an absolute standard, nor do they have universal applicability. These two insights give rise to the coordination of the two principles. Here we cannot elaborate the guidelines for such a coordination. It is enough to say that the effort must be truly interdisciplinary and interpersonal, involving not only the traditional fields of "academia," but also the people whose religions we are considering. No statement is valid and meaningful if it cannot be heard, understood, and, in a way, verified by all those concerned, and not merely bandied about by the *literati*.

Indeed, philosophical clarification is today extremely important, since by and large religions have lived in restricted areas and closed circles, and have tended to identify a particular set of philosophical doctrines—because they were useful to convey the religious message—with the core of the religion. The mutual enrichment of real encounter and the consequent liberation may be enormous.

6. It Is Not Only a Theological Symposium

As an authentic venture, the true religious encounter is filled with a sort of prophetic charisma; it is not just an effort to make the outsider understand my point. Indeed, at least according to more than one school, true theology also claims to be a charismatic deepening in meaning of a particular revelation or religion. Generally, however, theologians are more concerned with explaining given data than with exploring tasks ahead. Obviously, hermeneutics is indispensable; but still more important is to *grasp* what is to be interpreted prior to any (more or less plausible) explanation. Theology may furnish the tools for mutual understanding but must remember that the religious encounter imperative today is a new problem, and that the tools furnished by the theologies are not fit to master the new task unless purified, chiseled, and perhaps forged anew in the very encounter.

As an example of what is needed, we may use the notion of homology, which does not connote a mere comparison of concepts from one tradition with those of another. I want to suggest this notion as the correlation between points of two different systems so that a point in one system corresponds to a point in the other. The method does not imply that one system is better (logically, morally, or whatever) than the other, nor that the two points are interchangeable: You cannot, as it were, transplant a point from one system to the other. The method only discovers homologous correlations.

Now, a homology is not identical to an analogy, although they are related. Homology does not mean that two notions are analogous, i.e., partially the same and partially different, since this implies that both share in a "tertium quid" that provides the basis for the analogy. Homology means rather that the notions play equivalent roles, that they occupy homologous places within their respective systems. Homology is perhaps a kind of existential-functional analogy.

An example may clarify what I mean.

It is quite clearly false, for instance, to equate the upanisadic concept of *Brahman* with the biblical notion of *Yahweh*. Nevertheless, it is equally unsatisfactory to say that these concepts have nothing whatever in common. True, their context and contents are utterly different, they are not mutually translatable, nor do they have a direct relationship. But they are homologous, each plays a similar role, albeit in different cultural settings. They both refer to a highest value and an absolute term. On the other hand, we cannot say that *Brahman* is provident and even transcendent, or that *Yahweh* is all-pervading, without attributes, etc. Nevertheless, we can assert that both function homologously within their own cultures.

Or, to give another example, an examination of the traditional Indian notion of *karma* and the modern Western understanding of historicity under the aegis of this principle could reveal a common homologous role: Each one stands for that temporal ingredient of the human being which transcends individuality. Even more intriguing, perhaps, would be a consideration that homologizes the Indian notion of Iśvara (Lord) and the Western idea of Christ.

Whatever shape it will take, whatever contents it will carry, I am convinced that a new theology (though this very name means nothing to a Buddhist) will emerge precisely out of these encounters between sincere and enlightened believers of the various religious traditions.

Yet the religious encounter is not a mere theological reflection. Theologies—in the widest sense of the word—have a given basis: They are efforts at intelligibility of a given religious tradition and generally within that tradition itself (*fides quaerens intellectum*). But here we do not have such a belief or such a basis. There is neither a common given nor an accepted basis, revelation, event, or even tradition. Both the very subject matter and the method are to be determined in the encounter itself. There is no common language at the outset. Short of this radical understanding, the encounter of religions becomes a mere cultural entertainment.

7. It Is Not Merely an Ecclesiastical Endeavor

To be sure, the dialogue among religions may take place at different levels, and on each level it has its peculiarities. Official encounter among representatives of the world's organized religious groups is today an inescapable duty. Yet the issues in such meetings are not the same as those in a dialogue that tries to reach the deepest possible level. Ecclesiastical dignitaries are bound to preserve tradition; they must consider the multitude of believers who follow that religion, for and to whom they are responsible. They are faced with practical and immediate problems, they must discover ways to tolerate, to collaborate, to understand. But in general they cannot risk new solutions. They have to approve and put into practice already proven fruitful ways. But where are those proofs to come from? The religious encounter we have in mind will certainly pave the way for ecclesiastical meetings and vice versa, but must be differentiated and separated from them.

8. It Is a Religious Encounter in Faith, Hope, and Love

I apologize for the Christian overtones of this terminology and yet I think its meaning is universal.

By *faith* I mean an attitude that transcends the simple data, and the dogmatic formulations of the different confessions as well; that attitude which reaches an understanding even when words and concepts differ, because it pierces them, as it were, goes deep down to that realm which is the religious realm par excellence. We do not discuss systems but realities, and the way in which these realities manifest themselves so that they also make sense for our partner.

By *hope* I understand that attitude which, hoping against all hope, is able to leap over not only the initial human obstacles, our weakness and unconscious adherences, but also over all kinds of purely profane views and into the heart of the dialogue, as if urged from above to perform a sacred duty.

By *love*, finally, I mean that impulse, that force impelling us to our fellow beings and leading us to discover in them what is lacking in us. To be sure, real love does not aim for victory in the encounter. It longs for common recognition of the truth, without blotting out the differences or muting the various melodies in the single polyphonic symphony.

9. Appendix

a. Some Practical Lessons

What do these rules mean in practice? The chief lessons gleaned from my experience could be summarized as follows:

There must be *equal preparation* for the encounter on both sides, and this means cultural as well as theological preparation. Any dialogue—including the religious one—depends on the cultural settings of the partners. To overlook the cultural differences that give rise to different religious beliefs is to court unavoidable misunderstandings. The first function of the dialogue is to discover the ground where the dialogue may properly take place.

There must be real *mutual trust* between those involved in the encounter, something that is possible only when all the cards are on the table, i.e., when neither partner "brackets" his personal beliefs.

The *different issues* (theological, practical, institutional, etc.) have to be carefully distinguished; otherwise there is going to be confusion.

b. A Christian Example

Christ is the Lord, but the Lord is neither only Jesus nor does my understanding exhaust the meaning of the word.

Church, as the sociological dimension of religion, is the organism of salvation (by definition); but the church is not coextensive with the visible Christian Church.

Christendeom is the socioreligious structure of Christianity and as such is a religion like any other. It must be judged on its own merits without any special privileges.

God wills that all men should reach salvation. Here salvation is that which is considered to be the end, goal, destination, or destiny of man, however this may be conceived.

There is no salvation without faith, but this is not the privilege of Christians, nor of any special group.

The means of salvation are to be found in any authentic religion (old or new), since a man follows a particular religion because in it he believes he finds the ultimate fulfillment of his life.

Christ is the only mediator, but he is not the monopoly of Christians and, in fact, he is present and effective in any authentic religion, whatever the form or the name. Christ is the symbol, which Christians call by this name, of the ever-transcending but equally ever-humanly immanent Mystery. Now these principles should be confronted with parallel humanist, Buddhist, and other principles, and then one should be able to detect points of convergence and of discrepancy with all the required qualifications. Further, the Christian principles have no *a priori* paradigmatic value, so that is not a question of just searching for possible equivalents elsewhere. The fair procedure is to start from all possible starting points and witness to the actual encounters taking place along the way.

c. *Summing Up*

The religious encounter is a religious, and hence sacred, act through which are taken up by the truth and by loyalty to the "three worlds" with no further aim or intention. In this creative religious act, the very vitality of religion manifests itself.

H. Richard McBrien

Richard McBrien believes that the Catholic Church can transcend the present crisis primarily through a reform of the process by which church leaders are chosen. This selection is taken from his article "The Roman Catholic Church: Can It Transcend the Crisis?" in The Christian Century, *17 January 1979, pp. 42–45.*

Not since 1605 had the papacy changed hands twice in the same year. The fact that this statistic was repeated in 1978 may not mean very much in itself (after all, neither Paul VI nor John Paul I was killed in battle, murdered, or deposed), but surely it dramatizes the special character of the times in which we live.

The Catholic Church is by no realistic standard enjoying a period of normalcy, much less one of spiritual and institutional prosperity. On the contrary, there have been sharp declines in mass attendance, in the number and quality of vocations to the priesthood and religious life, and in the level of obedience to papal and episcopal teachings and directives.

Authority, Tradition, Priesthood

These trends are only symptomatic of problems lurking much deeper below the surface. One can better formulate them as questions: (1) How can the faith, spirituality, and missionary impulse of large numbers of Catholics be reignited, or ignited for the first time in the case of the church's younger members? (2) How can the church more effectively proclaim the Gospel of Jesus Christ in word, in sacrament, and in its corporate witness? (3) How can highly qualified and intensely motivated Catholics, especially among the young, be attracted once again to the official service of the church as priests, as members of religious congregations, and as lay ministers in a wide variety of apostolates? (4) How can all of these ministries become more compelling, and therefore more effective, signs and instruments of the church's mission for the Kingdom of God? (5) How can the church's pastoral leaders construct and communicate teachings on complex and controversial issues of faith and morality in such a way that those teachings elicit respect, if not always agreement? (6) Indeed, how can the credibility of Catholic authority in general be restored, whether that authority be vested in particular offices, in the Bible, in traditions, in teachers, in parents, or in other embodiments and carriers of the Christian message and spirit?

The emphasis here is on authority, tradition, and priesthood because these are part of the constellation of signs and values which have characterized Catholicism, if not also distinguished it from other corporate expressions of Christian faith. If the Catholic Church is successfully to transcend its present historical crisis, it will do so through recovery and reappropriation of its special ecclesial and theological identity.

No emphasis has been more characteristic of Catholicism over the centuries than the sacramental. Paul Tillich in his *Protestant Era* and, more recently, Langdon Gilkey in his *Catholicism Confronts Modernity* are among those outside observers who have not failed to note this point. Catholicism is committed to the principle of mediation: The created world mediates the presence of God (what was once called "natural revelation"); Jesus of Nazareth mediates the redemptive activity of God (Catholic theologian Edward Schillebeeckx refers to Christ as the "sacrament of encounter with God"); the church mediates Christ. The seven sacraments mediate the saving work of Christ in and through the church; priests and other ministers continue—even supervise and direct— the mediating action of God in Christ. The Word of God is mediated through the preaching and doctrines of the church; and their reliability, in turn, is ensured by those who have been set apart (*cleros*) to oversee (*episcopos*) the whole Spirit-directed process. The love, mercy, and justice of God and Christ are mediated through the love, mercy, and justice of the church in mission.

Signs of Life

Contemporary Catholicism is marked by vitality, growth, and even excitement at those points where it reaffirms its abiding commitment to the sacramental principle. Indeed, Catholicism since the Second Vatican Council has emphasized anew its conviction that the church is first and foremost the people of God and, as such, the sacrament of the Lord's presence among us (*Dogmatic Constitution on the Church,* n. 1). The church is, before all else, a mystery— that is, "a reality imbued with the hidden presence of God" (Pope Paul VI).

1. Because the Catholic Church perceives itself primarily as a people rather than as a hierarchical organization (and the issue was sharply drawn at Vatican II in the debate over the ordering of chapters 2 and 3 of the *Dogmatic Constitution on the Church*; i.e., whether the chapter on the hierarchy would come before or after the chapter on the people of God), coresponsibility is now in process of becoming fully operative at every level of the church's ecclesiastical life and government. And the new pope, John Paul II, was already a champion of the collegial principle at the Second Vatican Council and in subsequent international synods of bishops. He remains so today.

2. The liturgical renewal, under way from the earliest decades of this century, has advanced at a truly extraordinary pace, so much so that Catholics take for granted that worship (the Eucharist, the new rites of baptism and of reconciliation, etc.) must be intelligible, meaningful, joyous, and spiritually enriching—and at the same time engage the active participation of all for whom and by whom it is celebrated.

3. Ministry is seen less and less as a clerical preserve and increasingly as a service open in principle to every qualified member of the church, without regard for sex, marital status, or ordination. The emergence of pastoral-ministry-degree programs in Catholic colleges and universities is only one indication of this important trend. The prominence of laypersons in the religious education field, often as parish directors (DREs), is another.

Involvement in the Sociopolitical Order

4. The church's commitment to social justice, already mandated so forcefully in the great papal encyclicals from Pope Leo XIII to Pope Paul VI and in Vatican II's *Pastoral Constitution on the Church in the Modern World,* moves constantly into higher gear—whether through the lobbying activities of the United States Catholic Conference, the broadly based "Call to Action" conference in Detroit, the U.S. Bishops' Campaign for Human Development, or any number of others, less heralded social-action ventures at the diocesan and parish levels. Nor are the recent popularity and influence of liberation theology to be discounted, its several deficiencies notwithstanding.

Correlative with this renewed involvement in the sociopolitical order is the church's increasing sensitivity to the public impact of its style of life. A bishop's purchase of an expensive residence evokes strong protest. Congregations of religious women commit themselves to live simply, as a way of identifying with the poor. The urge to travel first class when economy or even standby will do is noticeably on the wane. Where it is not, such journalistic outlets as the *National Catholic Reporter* will see to it that excesses are properly reported and skewered in public view.

5. Theological renewal also reflects Catholicism's persistent effort to exploit its own best traditions. Scholars like Avery Dulles, David Tracy, Richard McCormick, and Charles Curran continue to stand out in the United States, as Karl Rahner, Edward Schillebeeckx, Yves Congar, and Hans Küng do on the European front. The sacramentality of Jesus Christ is underscored in recent efforts to construct a Christology "from below," focusing on the humanity of Christ ("man for others") as the mediating principle of divine grace. Revelation is understood no longer as simply a "deposit" of

truths given once and for all and then given over to the proprietary care of the magisterium, but as a continuing process of divine self-disclosure and self-communication through the "signs of the times."

6. Because of the widening of its theological and educational horizons, Catholicism today is more deliberately and intentionally ecumenical in its ecclesial practice than ever before in its history. Dialogue has replaced polemics (the bilateral consultations are, of course, a principal case in point); ecumenical collaboration in seminary training is the rule rather than the exception (the Boston Theological Institute is a good example); common prayer and sometimes intercommunion set a new tone for joint retreats, study days, workshops, and social-action projects.

7. Whereas holiness and spirituality were once regarded as the private pursuits of priests and nuns, an increasing number of laity are engaged in the quest for a personal relationship with Jesus Christ, the nourishment offered by God's biblical Word, and a life transformed and enriched by the Holy Spirit. And even priests and sisters have come to acknowledge a certain aridity in their own spiritual formation and routine. The Catholic Charismatic Renewal has provided an alternative style of Christian experience for many thousands of U.S. Catholics. Books once condescendingly categorized as "spiritual reading" shoot to the top of the religious best-seller lists. Interest in retreats and spiritual direction is heightened among the young as well as the middle-aged.

Playing by the Old Rules

But our report is necessarily mixed; otherwise, how explain the facts with which we began? For every impulse toward growth in U.S. Catholicism there seems to be a corresponding pull in the opposite direction:

1. Where parish councils exist, they are often without decision-making authority, are distracted by relatively trivial issues, and do not attract the most gifted and involved members of a local community. Few dioceses even have a pastoral council, and almost none of these works at or near its potential. Vatican bureaucracies try to play by the "old rules," whether in attempting to put over the revised Code of Canon Law or in correcting "abuses" or "distor-

tions" in American Catholic pastoral practice. And no one needs to be told that autocratic styles of leadership still obtain in more dioceses, parishes, and religious communities than many would care to dwell on. Bishops, meanwhile, are still selected by a process that is at once secret and restricted. Those who are appointed to the large, prestigious archdioceses are, for the most part, theologically "safe" and pastorally "prudent"—which means that they are often either firmly conservative or personally colorless.

2. The liturgy of the church is too often corrupted by theological ignorance and aesthetic clumsiness. Some planners and celebrants haven't learned the difference between therapy or play on the one hand, and the worship of God refined and structured by the objective spirit of Roman liturgy on the other. On the other side, even such modest breakthroughs as the use of altar girls at Mass are still stubbornly resisted.

3. Ministry, newly broadened to appeal to lay as well as clerical and religious candidates, frequently attracts the hurt, the alienated, the naive, and the intellectually weak. And in the case of the ordained ministry of priesthood, one senses a bull market in rigidity, fascination with clerical prerogatives, and psychic and intellectual flaccidity. Women, meanwhile, are still excluded from ordination, and so, too, are the married and those who would like the option to marry. The new pope, on this score at least, gives little promise of change.

Lost in a Fogbank of Denunciations

4. The commitment to social justice is sometimes embarrassing in its simplicity and romanticism, and offensive in its appalling selectivity of targets. South Africa is always a sure bet to bring out the marchers or elicit a convention resolution, but never the bloodbath drawn by the Khymer Rouge "liberators" of Cambodia. Catholicism's historic care for the clarification of moral principles and the responsible application thereof is lost in a fogbank of pop-Marxist, hate-America-first "prophetic" denunciations and exhortations. On the other side, conservative opposition to Catholic social activism is as vehement as ever, and occasionally the bishops yield to the pressure where it counts; i.e., in the writing of their budgets.

Meanwhile, the right-to-life zealotry escalates without a word of reproach or even the mildest of public criticisms from the church's leadership. How can any Catholic, committed to his or her church's rich social doctrine, be less than outraged by the senseless defeats of Senator Dick Clark in Iowa and Congressman Donald Fraser in Minnesota because they failed to pass this one-issue test?

5. There is such stress at times on the humanity of Jesus that his Lordship is all but lost. He becomes a model or an exemplar, but no more. And revelation is so "ongoing," so much in "process," that we risk losing all meaningful contact with our roots and our principal points of passage. At the other end of the spectrum, small groups continue to agitate for suppression of "heresy," generating a chilling effect on the invitation of competent theologians to lecture in certain dioceses or to serve as consultants to the body of bishops.

6. Ecumenism, if the truth be told, is almost dead in the water, at least at the officially approved levels. U.S. bishops regularly receive reports on the progress of bilateral consultations (most recently at their November, 1978 meeting), and just as regularly ignore them in practice. We are no closer to intercommunion, even under canonically controlled circumstances, nor to the mutual recognition of ordained ministries, recommended by the most sophisticated of the dialogues—the Roman Catholic-Lutheran consultation.

7. The new surge of Catholic spirituality is not unmixed with biblical fundamentalism, authoritarianism, and political conservatism. What began as an essentially progressive movement has developed too often into an antiintellectual, Jesus-the-Spirit-and-I pietism. The charismatic movement might just as possibly be a sign of the sickness of contemporary Catholicism as of its vitality. Complete returns are not yet in.

Needed Reforms

How, then, are we to get from here to there? For the Roman Catholic, as for any Christian of a high-church tradition, the course requires renewed fidelity to one's own theological and pastoral identity and to the principle of quality in official leadership. The papacy, the episcopacy, and the ordained priesthood are not simply ecclesiological problems to be explained away under the hot lights of ecumenical exchange. They are gifts to the church, without which the church lacks something constitutive to its being as the Body of Christ and to its mission as God's holy people.

There is no single formula for Catholic progress, to be sure. But if any human instrument stands above the rest, it is a reform of the process by which pastoral leaders are formed, selected, and evaluated. Pope John XXIII showed the world what the papacy can be like and what it can accomplish in the name of Christ and for the sake of the Kingdom of God when the right person occupies the chair of Peter—just as Gregory XVI in the nineteenth century showed us how disastrous such a pontificate can be when the bark of Peter has an unintelligent naysayer at the helm.

Closer to home, the same can be said of the Catholic Church's present episcopal, institutional, and intellectual leadership. Place Notre Dame's Father Theodore Hesburgh as the cardinal-archbishop of a major U.S. diocese like New York or Chicago and then as president of the National Conference of Catholic Bishops, and see what new life the Spirit can breathe into the church. Adopt the Canadian model where bishops of smaller dioceses are effectively eligible for positions of national leadership, and a new course can be plotted for U.S. Catholic policies. Among the more promising of such U.S. bishops are James Malone (Youngstown, Ohio), Cletus O'Donnell (Madison, Wisconsin), John Cummins (Oakland), Frank Hurley (Anchorage, Alaska), Walter Sullivan (Richmond, Virginia), Rembert Weakland (Milwaukee), and Frank Rodimer (Paterson, New Jersey).

And then let these be joined by the extraordinary leadership talent among the religious communities of women: Nadine Foley, Margaret Brennan, Kathleen Keating, and the like. For the Catholic Church is going to go nowhere from here without the active participation and support of its most capable and committed women. Indeed, it is almost an axiom of recent U.S. Catholic history that the sisters have been the one group consistently out front in exploring new styles of Christian existence, new kinds of apostolates, new modes of decision making, new ways of educating. It may be the success of the women's movement within the church and the emergence of leadership from that movement which will determine the forward course of Catholicism for the next several decades.

Pope John Paul II has the power to free that creative energy if he chooses. It is still too early to tell which ecclesiological and pastoral instincts will eventually dominate his pontificate: his theological commitment to collegiality or his culturally conditioned concerns about nuns' habits and priestly celibacy. Which of two predecessors will guide his ministry—John XXIII or Paul VI? If John, the renewal of the Catholic Church will be advanced; if Paul, the tensions and conflicts of the past fifteen years will intensify, and Catholicism will have to wait at least another generation (and another papacy) to emerge from its present trauma.

In the end, it is the new pope's sheer power of intellect and apparent depth of character which give one hope.

77489